An Unexpected Life

An Unexpected Life

JOSEPH BLOTNER

Louisiana State University Press

Baton Rouge

Published with the assistance of the
V. Ray Cardozier Fund

Designer: Laura Roubique Gleason
Typeface: Whitman text with Ribbon display
Typesetter: G & S Typesetters, Inc.
Printer and binder: Thomson-Shore, Inc.

Frontispiece: Joseph Blotner, Copenhagen, 1958

Library of Congress Cataloging-in-Publication Data
Blotner, Joseph Leo, 1923–
    An unexpected life / Joseph Blotner.
        p.   cm.
    ISBN 0-8071-3039-7 (hardcover : alk. paper)
1. Blotner, Joseph Leo, 1923–   2. Literary historians—United
States—Biography.   3. English teachers—United States—
Biography.   4. Biographers—United States—Biography.
5. Critics—United States—Biography.   I. Title.
PS29.B58A3 2005
810.9—dc22
                                             2004019016

AGAIN, FOR *Marnie*

Contents

Illustrations follow page 82

Preface

At first my children would ask me to read them a story. Then later they would ask me to tell them one of *my* stories—about when I was a little boy, or when I was in the army. And later still they urged me to write these stories down. At last, past the three-quarter-century mark, I decided it was time to redeem that long-ago pledge.

I began examining old letters—not to certify the reality of experience, not with the need of the myriad graffitists, the Kilroys who left their legends on the world's walls to say, I was here. It was just that life speeds by so fast, and so much of memory fades or vanishes. I can remember my seventh birthday vividly, and I hope I'll continue to be able to remember my eightieth. There are many slides I can retrieve for my imaginary stereopticon, like one of the bright June morning when I skipped home to summer vacation holding my report card and promotion to third grade. And there are others I intend to leave unviewed, like that stifling July morning when the phone shocked me awake with the news that my father had died. But many streams of days fade as they merge, like riffling calendar pages in an old movie.

It is spring now, and the Blue Ridge is daubed with forsythia, the golden daffodils unfolding. Soon it will be enriched with early redbud and dogwood, and then flame out with the gallant azaleas bursting up into the sunshine. In a few weeks Marnie will turn the clock ahead. Never nostalgic for the snows of yesteryear, I suppose I want to recapture something of the springs and early summers, ever gorgeous to me, especially June, my natal month. Those seasons stood for the beginnings of my world. But I'm peering backward; I'm seeking more than just snapshots of those times.

Once, in England, I stood at the end of a mess hall line. There where squares of cake should have been were only crumbs and a hand-lettered sign, "You've Had It." It was a phrase we heard often, usually announcing sardonically that we had missed out on something. But I think of it too in the sense of what I've had: plenty of life's desserts in addition to the good things I missed and the bad ones I caught. I do want to experience something of them again.

So this is a look backward at the crucial acts, the role of chance, and the events that have befallen me. I don't think anyone has ever put the great variables better than Herman Melville. As Ishmael and Queequeg weave a mat in *Moby-Dick*, pushing the wooden "sword" carrying the yarn down securely between the warp and woof, Ishmael reflects, "This easy, indifferent sword must be chance—aye, chance, free will, and necessity—no wise incompatible—all interweavingly working together." But I want to link choice with chance and what Mark Twain calls foreordination. In *The Mysterious Stranger* Satan explains how the consequences of altering one link in the chain of life can be disastrous. "That is human life," he says. "A child's first act knocks over the initial brick, and the rest will follow inexorably." I am not so much interested in Twain's domino effect as I am in focusing on the cruxes that lead to all that will follow.

I did not think it would be hard to find a voice to tell my story. I had written literary lives, and I thought that the experience had prepared me to look at my own life and tell its story. I never thought of my new undertaking as an autobiography, because that sounded pompous, and besides, I intended to concentrate on highlights rather than give a full account. It was not until the second draft that friends helped me to see that I had told much about what I had done and said, but not a great deal about what I had felt. So I'll warn the reader of two things. One is the persistence of the personal pronoun's limited focus. The other is the shifting of consciousness and memory. I have tried for a kind of double vision, to reproduce my sense of the thing as it was happening, but also to supply the hindsight that only time and reflection can provide.

So I came to think of this as a memoir but never realized how American my story was until I began to set it down—a familiar kind of story, no Horatio Alger tale of hardship and heroism, but an account of wanting things and being blessed with luck along the way. It has been an adventure, too. There has been some excitement and danger; in one period I began to keep a mental account of what I called Times I Almost Got Killed. There has been the adventure of places far-off and exotic. There has been the adventure of the mind, covering distances from my beginnings I could not have anticipated. There have been rewards I could not have anticipated. And if I'm as typical as I think

I am in many ways, parts of this chronicle should resonate with other lives, and whenever this happens, I hope the reader will say, "Yes, that's right! That's how it was."

For help and encouragement I thank old friends who read this book more than once with the scrutiny of artists and professionals: George Garrett and George Core, and Carl Brandt, patient and loyal agent for many years. And I thank my children—Tracy, Pamela, and Nancy—archivists of memories as well as photographs. The dedication acknowledges my largest debt, the one to my wife.

An Unexpected Life

ONE

The Real Thing

THIS WAS WHERE IT HAD ALL BEEN POINTING, EVER since we had received our wings and bars that bright first day of June 1944 on the Kirtland Field parade ground in Albuquerque. Now we were an ocean away, assigned to the First Division, Fortieth Combat Wing, of the Eighth Air Force.

Our first month in the 368th Squadron of the 306th Heavy Bombardment Group had gone quickly. Before September was out we had logged four practice flights. On the first one we were aloft for seven hours. The English farms and fields below were the gold and tan of early autumn as we climbed and turned to seek our place in a three-plane element beneath a sky that seemed full of B-17s. We would have the next day off, then we would fly on three straight days. The last flight, nearly nine hours long, was to prepare us for missions that would take us far into Germany. At squadron strength, now more than ever we had to be alert to the other airplanes in our formations. Bill and George had the exhausting job of maintaining position, constantly adjusting the wheel, rudder pedals, and throttles, with Corbin behind them carefully monitoring the instrument panel's gauges. "Keep it tight! Keep it tight!" the group commander's voice crackled on the intercom.

We hit the sack early these nights because we didn't know when we would draw our first mission. It was 0300 hours one October morning when the sergeant thrust open the barracks door. Playing his flashlight beam over us, he strode between the cots. "Alert, gentlemen!" he called. "Briefing at four." One of the veterans asked, "How many gallons?" We knew that the Flying Fortress could hold 2,780, and there was a groan when the sergeant replied, "Twenty-five hundred." That could keep us in the air for ten hours, taking us northeast toward the Baltic or southeast toward the Tyrol or due east into the heart of Germany. This was it—the first of our regulation thirty missions. If we survived them, we would go home.

We slept in our olive drab long johns, and so it was only a matter of minutes for us to pull on pants, shirt, and flight jacket for the walk in the darkness to the latrine and then the quick shave so that the tight oxygen mask wouldn't produce maddening irritation during the hours of flying above ten thousand feet. Under the bright lights of the mess hall we ate the rubbery bacon and tasteless powdered eggs. But the steaming coffee and heavy English bread were welcome. It would be a long time before we ate again.

The loud hum of the briefing room was cut short as the adjutant climbed the platform and shouted, "Tench-hut!" Rapid steps sounded behind us as the group commander strode to the lectern. "At ease," he said. This tall, beefy, beribboned man was Lieutenant Colonel Salada. The adjutant stepped to his side and removed a cloth from an easel. "Gentlemen," said the colonel, "the target for today is Nuremberg." The response was a chorus of muted curses and groans. On the easel a wide red ribbon stretched from our base across the North Sea beyond Belgium and almost to Czechoslovakia. The colonel told us that Nuremberg was responsible for half of Germany's production of airplane, tank, and submarine engines. Wielding his pointer like a conductor over a score, he indicated the expected resistance and the predicted but often unpredictable weather. Then the adjutant dismissed us for our specialized briefings. The lead bombardier told us the numbers for altitude and airspeed he was putting into the bombsight, the estimated time of arrival at the IP, the initial point to begin the bomb run, and the secondary target if the primary was obscured.

With mixed feelings I walked toward the flight line under the dark sky. I knew that after 1933, Hitler had turned Nuremberg into a national shrine where Nazi party congresses soon enacted laws depriving Jews of civic rights and much else. In those years I had been captivated by Richard Wagner. Now I thought of *Die Meistersinger von Nürnberg*. I was not worried about the moral implications of the actions I was about to perform. The rationale was clear: I was going to bomb what the colonel had told us, not people but things, the materials that had permitted the Wehrmacht, the SS, and the Luftwaffe to carry out their atrocities against enormous numbers of innocent people. I simply didn't think about the possibility that some of our bombs would hit people and homes. And there was a remoteness about what we were doing. By the time the bombs detonated, we would be miles away.

The reality of the mission became increasingly immediate as we drew our gear in the equipment hut. We lugged it to the flight line locker room and piled it on a bench—the parachute and harness, the oxygen mask and big yellow goggles, the large tureen-shaped helmet and the heavy canvas flak jacket with its stitched-in sheets of armor. I had rushed to get a bombardier's model, one with a crotch piece like that on a catcher's body protector, "to protect the family jewels." Like players girding for kickoff, we pulled on the heated suit coveralls that would plug into the plane's electrical system, the gloves and cloth helmets that would plug into the suits, for the cabin temperature at thirty thousand feet would be forty below zero. We stamped into fleece-lined boots bigger than the arctics of childhood. Like bears we clambered onto the truck waiting to take us along the narrow roads that curved among the sheltering revetments to our plane.

Seeing her on the hardstand was a letdown. She was not the shining beauty we had brought to the European Theater of Operations. Innocent of sexy nose art or even a name, she sat, faded green in the paling dawn, her yellow tailband outlining in black the big block G that identified her squadron, an amazon veteran of the wars, patiently awaiting her newest crew. But even immobile with her nose pointed skyward, she looked poised on those delicate nether limbs to run, spread her wings, and soar.

It was time for us to climb aboard, the ten men of 7–39, assembled three months before at Drew Field in Tampa to learn to become B-17 aircrew members, to fly formation and navigate long distances. Burly figures in the half-light, they were my latest air force unit, but I was still getting to know most of the other three officers and six enlisted men. William Moroz was our first pilot. He pronounced it "morose," and that was how he appeared to me. He said his people came from Georgia in Russia. When I met some of them later, they looked Mediterranean, with sallow complexions, dark hair, and black eyes that could seem almost lustrous. Bill was a second lieutenant too long in rank. Our navigator, Seymour Feinstein, was a curly-haired New Yorker, like me a reservist called up out of college. George Coward, the second pilot, was a pale-faced, nervous, slightly inept man who seemed always to need a shave. Standing near them was Robert Corbin, our engineer, his sturdy frame well padded, his hair thinning, and his tanned face creased with smile lines. He knew more about our airplane than any of us. He was the senior noncom and, I would later conclude, probably the best man in the plane.

During the night, Supply and Ordnance had pumped the 2,500 gallons into the tanks and hung the ten 500-pound bombs on the racks. Our ground crew had labored through the night to check all the systems. At the nose hatch Sy and I slung our equipment up into our compartment. We grasped the edge of the hatch, swung our feet up and into the cabin, hooked them there, and twisted our legs to one side and swung our bodies up after them. While Sy spread his gear out on the navigator's table, I put on my whole outfit behind him—the Mae West, the flak suit and helmet and goggles. Last was the heavy .45 automatic in its holster tied around my thigh with a thong as though for a shootout at the old corral. Rising on my toes, arms high and hands looming menacingly like Frankenstein's monster, I nudged his back with my knee. A good audience, he did a double take and threw up his arms in mock horror. I took off the flak suit I wouldn't need for a while yet, and the goggles and leather helmet that reminded me of my childhood Lucky Lindy helmet with its earflaps.

As I surveyed my station from the bombardier's seat, there was the familiar incongruity: no bombsight. Twelve bombardiers, each at a bombsight guiding his aircraft in a tightly patterned squadron, could have produced not just an uncoordinated bombing pattern but also unacceptable risk of collision. So we would drop our bombs when we saw the lead bombardier drop his. If we lived long enough we might become lead bombardiers, but for now we were what some might have called not bombardiers but togglers. I went over my brief checklist. Most of my pockets seemed full. There was a bulge on my right thigh from the plastic escape kit. It held a cloth map, a small compass, cubes of food concentrate, and German marks. One object didn't show in the other thigh pocket. It was my rosary, the string of blessed black beads given me at confirmation. I hadn't used it very often, but either Mother or I must have put it in my overnight bag when I left Scotch Plains, New Jersey. Others carried various talismans—a sixpence, a St. Christopher's medal, a small doll, or a poppy plucked from the edge of the meadow.

There was enough to do at this stage to prevent moody brooding. At each station, men ran through their checklists, the pilot and copilot like priests in their antiphonal statement and repetition, the flight engineer behind them like a deacon observing to prevent any omission in the liturgy. With the rechecking done, the time began to drag. A red flare would mean the mission was scrubbed. A green one would mean it was on. But it might be an hour before Weather gave final clearance.

At last the green flare soared from the Very pistol into the clearing sky. Bill and George ran through a last check, and after the order "Energize. . . . Mesh!" the propellers began to spin. The primed engines caught one after another with blasts of blue smoke, and the four merged into one roaring crescendo that shook the ship. Taxiing out to the runway, the big birds formed into two lines at angles to each other, and for a few minutes more like ducks than eagles these creatures in transition decorously deferred to each other as in some minuet, each on the tail of its predecessor.

Now the first dangerous moment loomed. Feet on the brakes, our pilots pushed the throttles to the panel while the plane shuddered, frantic to get its seventy thousand pounds aloft. They released the brakes, and we lunged down the runway as Corbin called out the speed. At 90 miles an hour we could no longer stop safely. With full flaps extended we hit 105 miles an hour, stalling speed, and we had to exceed that to stay airborne. From my catbird seat I saw it suddenly looming closer, a farmer's wagon parked broadside in the rough at the end of the runway. It seemed to be rushing at us like a runaway locomotive in the Saturday afternoon movies.

"A hundred and twenty!" Corbin called, and Bill hauled back on the controls. "Wheels up!" he shouted, and we cleared the last obstacles seeming to clutch upward for us. We were climbing as we would do for the next hours. Bill called for a crew check, and we reported from each position. Intercom discipline was now in force. I was surprised to hear staccato voices. They must be coming from such as the idiots who had mindlessly shouted "Hubba, hubba!" in preflight PT classes. "Fightin' bitin'!" called out one, then off the air in a flash. "Eager beavers!" responded another instantly. These were cheerleaders from two other squadrons in our group. I didn't know it yet, but Bomber Command calculated that if a crew got through its first five missions, its chances of survival were almost doubled. God help us with gunners like these to protect us from enemy fighters.

"Test-fire your guns," came Bill's metallic intercom voice. The aircraft shook with the hammering of four sets of twin .50s and one more from each of the waist gunners. I liked the feel of my guns smoothly tracking and their jolt when I pressed the firing buttons. There was no target sleeve for practice out there now, just an empty vastness that might change at any moment.

Flocking together in steady accretion, the squadrons displayed another spectacle of beauty in this time of danger: hundreds of great deadly birds ascending and weaving in a graceful ballet. At nearly 200 miles an hour, they seemed to slide across the sky. I watched one Fort gliding below us toward a place up ahead. It was close to us for a few seconds, almost too close, and then it was gone from my view. This mission was a major effort, and now we were part of a group of three dozen airplanes. We crossed the dark North Sea to a greeting of small black puffs from coastal flak batteries, and we knew that soon we would meet a major barrage. Thanks to our escorting P-51s with their wing tanks, it was not German fighters but primarily the massed *Fliegerabwehrkannonen* with their long-barreled radar-aimed guns that were the bomber killers. Several hundred of them were deployed around Merseburg to the northeast. They could be shifted south rapidly, and the gunners at Schweinfurt would be on full alert.

There below was the Belgian coast and to the north the coastal islands of the Netherlands. We were on oxygen, and when Bill asked for a check I pressed the buttons on my throat mike and answered, "Bombardier, OK." Already the rubber of the tight mask was feeling clammy. I was grateful for the heated suit as we climbed above twenty thousand feet and headed for the German border.

The lead squadron had left its traces ahead of us. Condensation vapor pouring back from the heated exhausts of each ship's four engines produced streaming white contrails like enormous ski tracks on a photo negative. Ahead materialized their opposite, distant black bursts like a forbidding fence. Gunners could track a specific target or set fuses to fire at the attackers' altitude. What I was seeing under the sun-bathed thirty-thousand-foot clouds was a vast box barrage of flak. As many as sixteen gunners were firing 88-millimeter guns to fill a rectangle of sky with 25-pound shells that broke into half-inch red-hot fragments. We had passed the initial point, and now, unable to take evasive action on the bomb run, we had to fly a straight line through the barrage. As the puffs came closer, it felt like driving a car through mounting flurries of a snowstorm. Now came another sound like hail on a tin roof or gravel flung against a house. Though we couldn't see any damage and the gauges registered no trouble, I felt the trickle of sweat. It was not fear so much as a heightened consciousness of danger. These combat conditions were new, and I was feeling almost an overload of sight and sound.

Then, two groups ahead, I saw the Fort on the leader's left wing rise out of formation. Instead of correcting the climb, it faded to the left and headed down. We waited to see it pull out of that deadly descent but instead saw the belly and wings as the dive steepened. I squinted to see the letter and numbers on the tail. I pressed my mike button and called, "Look out for 'chutes!" But none appeared, and then the bomber was gone from sight.

We were nearing the target, and the barrier of black bursts dirtying the air began to show orange centers. I felt my feet bracing against the Plexiglas nose frame as if to jam on the brakes and hold us back from that hedge and thicket of shrapnel. The organism was reacting as if to protect itself. The blasts of the bursts bounced us as I got set to perform the act the air force had been training me to do for over a year and a half.

I had set the intervalometer to salvo the bombs. There were two switches, one to open the bomb-bay doors and the other to toggle all the bombs. I had adjusted the flak jacket carefully under me and tightened the straps at my waist. My helmet jammed down, I watched and armed the bombs with another switch. I flipped the safety bracket off the bombing switch and waited to drop our ten 500-pound bombs. Up ahead I saw the lead ship's svelte belly split as her bomb-bay doors swung open. I hit my switch and called out, "Bomb-bay doors open!"

Suddenly Sy was at my shoulder. "Let me drop them," he mouthed. I was almost indignant. I understood how he could feel an agent of retribution here above Nuremberg, where so much had been fomented against his people. But this was *my* job. So I shouted, "Put your hand on mine." An instant later, when the group lead dropped his stream of high explosives through the tortured air, we dropped ours. "Bombs away!" I shouted and instantly felt the lift of our lightened ship. "Bomb-bay doors closed," I called. We turned off the target behind us, tightened our formation, and regrouped to head for home. I kept scanning the ships of several groups and saw no one in trouble. When we heard of no bandits in the target area or bogies searching for stragglers, we felt relief. The flak thinned, and we moved faster now, with less fuel and the bombs gone.

As we descended we piled our flak suits and helmets in the corner on top of our parachutes. I disconnected my headset, plugged my oxygen tube into a bottle, and hooked it onto my belt. By the door back in the waist hung a funnel whose tube went through the ship's skin and emptied outside. I worked my way through my four layers of clothing to respond to the delayed call of nature. The relief tube was well named.

Homecoming was wonderful. Groups began peeling off as we left the North Sea behind. The English countryside looked mellow in the afternoon sun, and soon we saw cyclists spinning along lanes making their way home or off to the pubs for a pint. Our runways at Thurleigh were welcome mats as we descended onto the final approaches, soon to touch down with puffs of smoke and the squeak of tires. Slowly we floated down until Bill stalled her out, and with a thump we were creatures of land again. I liked being in the nose now much better than I had four hours ago. As the tail touched down, I sat highest in the airplane, bouncing along like a lord in a chariot, seeing crews walking to debriefing and Red Cross girls, all of them suddenly pretty, handing out coffee and doughnuts to famished crews. I felt exultation mixed with fatigue and relief. I was a veteran—of only one mission, but still a veteran. In the eight hours past my stomach had tightened time and again. I had felt anxiety but not fear, perhaps because I had not felt in danger of death or wounds or disfigurement, though I had been. It was not just that I was young. I was naive, too. I had seen the empty cots, but that was something that happened to somebody else, or so my psyche seemed to assume.

In a large hut each crew sat at a table while the intelligence officer debriefed them, businesslike and unemotional. Bill, George, and Corbin filled out forms and answered questions. Our debriefer asked, Did we see any planes go down or any 'chutes open up, theirs or ours? I tried to describe as accurately as I could what I had seen of the Fort falling away. There was a kind of delayed reaction now. Here we were, back at the base, and God knows where those poor devils were. We took the dangers of flying for granted, but to fall from the sky like Icarus! The idea had not been real to me, and now I thrust it from my consciousness. I had twenty-nine more missions to go before I could feel safe from what I had seen this day.

Now the crews made their way to a table where a corporal was handing out two-ounce shots of bourbon. I had not yet developed a taste for whiskey, and I started to hand it back. Bill didn't miss a beat. "Can I have yours?" he asked. He knocked it back and then did the same with his. He was entitled to it.

Now the missions came quickly and close together. Some of the targets had names I knew from history. Others—Stralsund on the Baltic, Stargard beyond the Oder—were strange, a mix of places with ball-bearing factories, rocket-launching bases, marshaling yards, and complexes where scientists were working on the V-1 and V-2 "reprisal weapons," flights of screaming pilotless craft that rained down on London and other cities.

Our missions were long hauls, far more so than our raids on Nuremberg and Schweinfurt, and we were thankful again for the P-51 Mustangs' wing tanks. The days blended into each other with the sergeant's summons cutting through the deep levels of sleep: "Alert, gentlemen!" But now he added, "Briefing at three." We were ten hours in the air one day and nine hours and a half the next. We had a day off but not a whole day, for we hit the sack early, feeling the sleep deficit and awaiting the next mission. The drill was familiar now: the preparations in the hours of darkness, the ritual in the crowded room with the charts, a sinister parody of sessions behind ivied walls a year and a half earlier. My feet would still stamp down on the nonexistent brakes to slow the devil's sleigh ride through the tortured air until I would put my gauntleted hand on the bright red switch.

After the brief respite from combat, we were thrust back again, not just to heavily defended targets but into Flak Alley itself. There was no more fiercely guarded area in the whole of the Reich. Our fifth target was Coblenz, an eight-hour round trip—not nearly as far as Nuremberg or Stralsund, but more heavily defended by flak and fighters. Now we were eligible for the Air Medal, but I didn't know anyone who thought about medals. Survival was the name of the game, but I don't remember anyone's talking about that, either. More important to us than medals was our first leave, a weekend away from the murderous routine.

London beckoned. Waiting on the station platform, we felt smart in our trim green blouses and neatly pressed gabardine pinks. We carried wallets lined with crisp new five-pound notes. The express was on time, and it produced an excitement I had felt before only on the Jersey Central on my first trip to Manhattan. But this was a different kind of excitement, to be riding in the first-class compartment, lounging against the green cushions and watching the English landscape flee by. It was a fine green countryside. I had seen it through the eyes of long-dead writers, and this was my chance to see it through my own. I had seen it too in the pageantry of Noel Coward's *Cavalcade* and the romantic mist of *Waterloo Bridge* as Robert Taylor sought his lost love, Vivien Leigh, there by the long span over the river's dark waters.

With a hissing of steam and grinding of brakes we descended into Victoria Station, crowded with soldiers and civilians of many different colors and uniforms, the babel of language punctuated by train whistles and the hoots and cries of porters and conductors. We took a boxy black English taxi, gawking at the Jaguars and Humbers and Morrises, at the old-fashioned yet exotic shops on the way to the hotel, a staid respectable old one taken over for officers. I was feeling sensory overload again in the aura of the past, there even in something as mundane as the water closet's wooden tank and chain high against our bathroom wall.

We bought good seats for Noel Coward's *Blithe Spirit,* surprised at prices cheap by New York standards and admiring the actors' precise diction. Emerging into the pale afternoon sunlight, we meant to cram in everything we could. A large hotel advertised a tea dance, and we sat at a small table to hear a six-piece orchestra play sedate foxtrots from the 1930s. We consumed dainty watercress sandwiches. I didn't know how naive I was. The poor, gallant English, I thought, they're making do with clover. Too shy to try to pick up any of the chattering smartly dressed girls or cut in on the dancers, we watched and admired. We ate dinner in Willow Run, the huge U.S. Army officers' mess in Grosvenor Square, trying to look unimpressed by the sprinkling of gold and silver leaves on the shoulders around us. We ate better than we had since the cadet mess at bombardier school in Albuquerque.

Even in the blackout the great city was teeming with myriad identities. I saw men with shoulder patches of the RAF Polish Squadron, soldiers wearing the caps of the Royal Marines, trim Wrens in their navy blue, and husky khaki-clad girls of the Army Territorial Service. Many of the civilians caught my eye too, especially a few Picadilly commandos. One was a dark-eyed number in a dress slashed to the waist, her Pekingese trotting behind her on a rhinestone-decorated leash. There was an excitement and glamour in the night, undisturbed by the shriek of sirens or the roar of buzz bombs. We went to the Windmill Theatre, famous for its boast, "We Never Closed." From the time before the blitz, peaches-and-cream British beauties had posed there topless in exotic *tableaux vivants.* They were most striking as naked Grecian goddesses parading seductively in stale skits before their audiences of oyster-eyed old men and satyr-eyed young ones. I had read that most of the voluptuous girls in the Folies Bergère were English, and, gazing at these diaphanous-gowned strutters, I could well believe it. We returned to the hotel determined to enjoy less passive pleasures the next night, our last one in London—our last only for this leave, we hoped.

The next morning we walked abroad—to Westminster Abbey, to St. Paul's and beyond—until matinee time and another West End comedy. We had made our gestures toward culture, and so nightfall found us in a crowded after-hours club. The price of admission was high, but we still had plenty of pound notes, and there seemed to be a promising female-to-male ratio in this smoky room with the crowded bar where the ivory-handled beer pulls shone. Two shapely girls passing our table promptly accepted our invitation to join us for a drink. Their names were Mavis and Elspeth, they told us. Fresh-cheeked brunettes, they gazed at us amiably and offered a stream of lively conversation in blithe rapid accents. Feeling suave and sophisticated, we chatted them up and soon ordered another round of drinks. Time passed quickly, and we ordered another round, a plan already in mind.

Before we could propose it, Mavis, the livelier of the two, asked, "Where's the party tonight, boys?"

Inspired, Sy replied, "We know just the place." At the bar I paid an exorbitant price for a bottle of scotch and four glasses to go.

We hailed a taxi, and I held the door while Sy pulled down the two jump seats and handed the girls into the cab. I leaned into the stubbled driver's front-seat compartment and asked if he could take us to a nice place for rooms for the night.

"Know just the place, guv," he said, with what could have been a wink. We drove for what seemed quite a while, past Regent's Park, Lord's Cricket Ground, and then Paddington Station. At last our driver turned into a residential street and pulled up at the curb.

"You're sure they have rooms here?" I asked him.

"Sure thing, guv," he said. I paid him, adding a generous tip, and he sped off.

To my relief the door opened when I turned the knob, and there in the foyer a sleepy-looking man sat at a desk. With what I thought was complete aplomb I asked for two rooms for the night.

"I'll have to look, sir," he said. He opened a large ledger and paused, frowning.

"We're just about full up," he said, "but I do have a room with two beds I could let you have." I looked at Sy, and he nodded.

"It's number four on the next floor up," the man said, handing me a large brass key, "last room on the right, end of the hall next to the loo."

Holding Mavis's hand, I led the way up the carpeted stairs and along the decorous, dimly lighted Victorian hall. These were hardly the romantic trappings of *Waterloo Bridge*, but we were four young adventurers, and the next morning Sy and I would have to return to the base. Mavis giggled when I inserted the key into the large brass plate of the lock and turned it noisily. "Dark, i'nit?" she whispered. The table lamp revealed wallpaper of faded roses and two ornately framed pastoral scenes. We talked quietly as we sipped our nightcaps. The sound of occasional cars diminished and then ceased.

Sy and I had wakened as the first light began seeping under the tasseled curtains. We dressed silently, and there was no creak of the door or stairs as we descended. I paid the drowsy clerk, and we stepped out into the brightening dawn. The city was stirring, and by the time our taxi got us to the station, the streets were pulsating again with the sound and energy that had excited me with my first breath of it. Four uniformed men were already seated in our compartment, two of them asleep. As I leaned back against the green plush, I thought back on the last two days. It had been a fine leave, all we could have hoped for. I didn't think myself a sophisticate, but I didn't think badly of myself either, now a combat veteran feeling at ease in one of the world's great cities. I had been lucky five times already, and maybe my luck would hold. I was already looking forward to our next leave.

TWO

The Sixth Mission

THE SQUEAK OF THE OPENING DOOR AND THE BRIGHT shaft of the sergeant's flashlight cut through the darkness and rumbling snores of the barracks.

"Alert, gentlemen," he called. "Briefing at four."

"Oh, shit," Bill grumbled, groping for a cigarette. "How many gallons?"

"Twenty-five hundred," the sergeant said. Enough for ten hours in the air. I tried to slide back into sleep again even though I knew I couldn't stay there. I abandoned the effort and rolled out of my cot.

Soon we knew where we would go on this day. It was Flak Alley again: the marshaling yards of Cologne that sent metals, chemicals, and machinery all over the Reich. In the brightening morning we climbed out over the sea and ascended, the lowlands of Holland and Belgium unrolling beneath us. Skirting the guns of Düsseldorf, we turned south. Not as far east as our earlier target of Coblenz but farther north, Cologne was another thousand-year-old settlement where Claudius had sent his legions to subdue the warlike Teutons. No stranger to warfare, the city nonetheless had become a focal point of German culture as part of the Holy Roman Empire and the Hanseatic League. I was vaguely aware of this, but not of Cologne's position as center of north German Catholicism or of its Gothic cathedral enshrining relics of the Wise Men of the East. And now here we were, bringing our five tons of bombs on the Ides of October.

It was a maximum effort. Armadas of B-17s and -24s stretched across the heavens, silvery fighters weaving above them. Highest flew the slim and muscular P-51 Mustangs, their wings flashing in the sun. Below them came the P-38 Lightnings, like strange stinging insects with their slim twin tails. Beneath them swarmed the blunt-nosed P-47 Thunderbolts, destroyers of tanks and protectors of bombers. No enemy fighters appeared, but on the command frequency sounded the hackle-raising "Bandits in the target area!" I swiveled my guns over their 180-degree arc, peering through the orange electric ring sight but seeing only our own groups moving inexorably forward. The vast, now cloudy carpet was striped with the contrails and stained with the black bursts that bumped closer as the gunners manning the 88s found the range. We had been briefed that new ME-262 jets were now operational, and even though they flew faster than a turret could track them, we had to stay alert. We had turned onto the IP and were minutes from the target. My feet did it again, jamming down on invisible brakes to slow our precipitate entry into the thickening black curtain. The turbulence jostled us, and then we felt the momentary drag as I followed the lead ship and opened the bomb-bay doors.

At last I hit the red switch and felt the roller coaster lift as I called out, "Bombs away!" But then as I closed the doors I felt another bump and heard a sound like hail on a tin roof. I had already started thinking ahead to our home field and letting down to hear the shriek of tires hitting the concrete. Then we would taxi down the runway, I bouncing high in my grandstand seat, surveying the bee-busy field, passing the Red Cross girls with the steaming urns and cups. No longer an abstainer from straight shots, I was anticipating the tang of the debriefing whiskey with the draining of tension and the exhilaration of being alive after another mission. I heard the prop pitch changing as we tried to reform into our element, but we were not catching up. I couldn't tell how much trouble we were in, but I was using body english to urge the plane into swifter effort as if she were a runner dragging her feet.

Bill's voice pulled me up straight. "Number four! Number four!" he shouted to Corbin. The oil pressure was dropping, and the engine temperature was rising as Bill jockeyed the throttles. Time was a continuum without minutes, a stream broken by staccato phrases from the cockpit. Number four was now a source of danger. They prepared to feather it as the prop blades slowed, to turn them perpendicular to the airstream to avoid resistance or vibration. Bill called the squadron leader for permission to leave the formation. No doubt sorry to lose her but probably glad to be free of this wounded bird, he radioed it back. "Good luck!" he added.

We could fly on three engines, but how fast? And how long? Number four's shining circle slowly disappeared, resolving itself into the three static propeller blades. For us there was nothing to do but keep scanning the skies. We were drifting down from the formation, dependent only on our own dozen .50 calibers. Suddenly the sky was larger, and I felt lonely and exposed. As

Corbin called out our decreasing altitude, I remembered the earlier warning of bandits in the target area. Soon we dropped under twenty thousand feet, and Bill called for fighter cover. I looked ahead beyond the glowing ring sight. We would soon see fighters, but until nearly the last minute we wouldn't be sure whose. At last we heard a wonderfully assured voice: "Hello, big friend! Hello, big friend!" Involuntarily I mouthed the response along with Bill: "Hello, little friend! Hello, little friend!"

Then there they were. The voice had come from the leader of three gorgeous Mustangs. He banked to show us his silhouette, that slim shape more beautiful than any woman's. He was probably following procedure, though there was slight chance that any of us would have fired a nervous burst. They throttled back to stay with us, but they couldn't stay long. Now number three was heating up. Had the barrage hit oil lines that ran to all four engines? We didn't know, but Bill and Corbin feared that we were going to lose three. They feathered it, its three blades spinning slowly to a stop. The Mustang leader dipped his wings and led his wingmen away, disappearing swiftly into the distance. The feeling of loneliness grew.

It was like a dream scene slowly sliding by, details of the ground clearly emerging. "Jettison everything!" Bill shouted. The waist gunners threw out all the ammunition and shoveled out cartridge casings. They dismounted the guns and heaved them after the ammunition. Sy and I tossed our flak jackets and helmets out the nose hatch and looked for more to jettison. Now we were totally vulnerable, and in a strange aberration I found myself humming as I hurled objects like a fireman stoking a boiler. "I'm gonna settle down and never more roam, and make the San Fernando Valley my home"—through the chaos the refrain repeated itself like irrelevant radio background music, adding to the strangeness of the descent.

I felt not so much afraid as like a spectator at some unfamiliar event waiting to see what would happen next. We didn't know how close the battle lines were, and we were desperate to stay airborne. We threw out the Mae Wests and parachutes and harnesses. Before long we would be too low to jump anyway. A sheet of armor plate came tumbling down from the pilots' compartment, and I thrust it out the hatch. We threw out Sy's instruments and books along with our oxygen masks. Then as we drifted inexorably lower, there was nothing more to throw. Three jagged black puffs exploded fifty yards in front of my Plexiglas, and I regretted the jettisoned flak suit. They looked to be 40-millimeter shells, but they could still kill you. If they had been the 88s that had knocked us down, we would have been splattered over the wooded landscape. Another cluster exploded off to starboard. All air force terminology forgotten, I shrieked, "Turn left into that cloud, Bill!" We left the flak behind.

"Where the hell are we?" he shouted as Sy scrabbled in the chaos of his charts. I saw gun flashes close below, and phrases from the pulp fiction of *Daredevil Aces* surged up from memory.

"We're over No-Man's Land!" I called back.

"Where the hell is that?" Bill shouted furiously.

Sy struggled to give him a fix, but our course changes and evasive action made that impossible. Coming off the target we had been heading west, but now we were heading south. Sy gave Bill a heading due west, but the battle lines were fluid, and all we could hope was to stay aloft until we made Allied-held territory. At one thousand feet, only number one was still pulling us. Wrestling the controls with George's help, Bill began to line up on a stretch of cleared fields that had miraculously appeared.

"Dinghy, dinghy!" he cried. "Prepare for ditching!"

We scrambled up the steps between the pilots' seats and into the radio compartment. I pushed the door shut with my back, dropped to the floor, and braced Sy's head with my hands. The wind shrieked along the fuselage as our treacherous power-off glide prolonged itself. Then into a strange near-silence came the first outraged scream of tearing metal. It was like a monstrous belly-whopper, the sound of a gargantuan sled raking a concrete pavement. The frames shuddered under us and scraped onward. With jaw clenched and eyes squeezed tight shut I waited for some all-smashing impact. Then at last there was no motion, only silence. We stood and looked down to see neither bomb-bay nor cartridge cases nor debris, only churned reddish earth faintly smoking in the violated belly of our airplane. We had survived our crash landing.

Galvanized into motion by fear of a fiery explosion, we clumped in our clumsy boots down the ruined belly and out the waist door into the air. But then we stopped as we heard shouting behind us. It was George. Inept as ever, he was struggling desperately with his jammed window. Bill and Corbin rushed back toward the steaming fuselage and up the canted wing. They wrenched him out and dragged him stumbling to a safe distance. Still our airplane didn't blow, her last service to her deserted children.

After evasive action in the air, it was time for evasive action on the ground. Running across the beet field we had re-plowed, we pulled up puffing inside its border of trees. We shucked off our heated suits and hid them under some brush. I was surprised to find that at the last minute I had grabbed my GI shoes. Now I replaced the boots. We split up, Bill and Corbin and I heading west where artillery rumbled. We had to find some patch of No Man's Land we could cross. It had been raining, but now the sun shone in myriad sparkles of light on the evergreens. It was incredible. What was I doing here in this forest at 11:30 in the morning? The bright spangling in the trees came from tangled clusters of what looked like Christmas tree icicles, but they were not festive. They were what we called chaff and the British called window: aluminum strips that showed up as aircraft on the enemy's radar. We might be on the wrong side of the lines. We were collecting our wits to strike out to the west when we heard the rifle shots and barking dogs. It was bright daylight, no time to play hare and hounds. We went to ground, achingly hungry and Bill mad for a cigarette. We brushed the dirt from the kohlrabi bulbs we had dug from the farmer's field, anything to appease the growling stomach. The pitiful supply of iron rations in our escape kits had provided little sustenance. Without hope, I searched my other pockets and realized that one thing was missing: my rosary. I couldn't think where it could be. I hadn't taken it to London.

Awake for more than twelve hours now, we found a gully and rolled our jackets into pillows. The mission had made one more addition to the list of Times I Almost Got Killed, and so had its conclusion in the farmer's field. I hadn't had to hit the silk to fling myself into the troubled air, hauling on shroud lines, at risk of landing spread-eagled in a tree with a farmer's pitchfork menacing me and his dogs snapping at my vitals. My bones felt intact, and I could walk. That was what we would have to do, but first we would sleep, like animals gone to earth.

We woke to darkness and misty rain. Spreading out the escape kit's linen map under the flicker of Bill's Zippo, we aligned the tiny blue compass needle with north. We could still hear the sullen mutter and grumble of the guns, knowing we must head west toward them. We plodded along a narrow trail threading through the trees. I hunched my shoulders against the drizzle and peered under the visor of my sodden cap. Suddenly a figure loomed ahead. He did not break stride nor did I as we passed each other. Expelling breath, I thought of our flight jackets and U.S. officers' cap badges. He would have had to be blind to miss them. How soon would he alert pursuers? We trudged on until the light began to reveal thinning glades of trees. We would have to take cover soon.

Then I saw it, off to the left at the edge of a clearing: a long, low building, perhaps a potter's shed. Cautiously approaching, we were frozen by the hoarse shout: *"Halt!"* Four helmeted figures materialized out of the gloom. I stopped abruptly, my .45 flapping heavily against my thigh. We didn't speak as four long rifles swung down on us.

Should I pull the pistol as I had seen Gary Cooper and John Wayne do? I stood motionless in the lifting mist. I saw behind the four figures the long, low building—not a building at all, a second look told me, but our own battered airplane. We had performed the classic maneuver of the tenderfoot: a 360-degree circle that led back to the starting point. In that instant I had a chance with one motion to add another entry to the growing list of Times I Almost Got Killed. But I didn't do it, and neither did Bill or Corbin. We had been loose for twelve hours.

"*Handen Hoch!*" came the guttural voice again. We raised them, and this act of our drama was over. Later we would learn that, miles away, John Holzermer, our tail gunner, had waved his escape kit as a white flag at a group of civilians, and one of them shot him. We had gone down near Trier in Luxembourg, on the wrong side of the lines. Aloft a few more minutes, we might have landed safely and been back in Thurleigh on alert to fly another mission in a few days. Given a choice, we would have taken our chances on flying combat again. That situation we knew, but now we were coping with the unknown. The patrol relieved us of our pistols and the contents of our pockets, my wallet containing fifty pounds earmarked for London. The guards prodded us onto a truck that took us to Wetzlar, further east, not far from the great hub of Frankfurt am Main. Bill begged a cigarette for relief from his longest nicotine deprival in years.

We slumped in chairs in a burgomaster's office, stupid from lack of sleep. A bespectacled old man with a ragged toothbrush mustache, he began to question us about our electronic equipment—the "Identification Friend or Foe" that transmitted our credentials for safe landing, and the "Gee Box" radar that gave our position. Bill and Corbin were snoring, and the burgomaster turned to me.

"*Sprechen sie Deutsch?*" he asked. I knew a smattering, but I wasn't going to let on to him.

"*Nein,*" I said, and he gave me a skeptical look.

"*Wo ist die. . .?*" He groped for terms and moved his fingers as if on a keyboard. When I remained silent he tried another charade. It may have been silliness of fatigue that prompted me.

"*Ich weiss nicht,*" I said.

"*Aha!*" he said and repeated his question. Just then one of the listeners asked him a question, and I fell asleep.

How long I slept before we were prodded awake I didn't know. The same guards were there, in the harsh light from the unshaded bulb, heavyset and probably too old for the eastern front. They rose, and the burgomaster motioned us outside into the darkness. They marched us down a small road into the woods. I had not been afraid before, but now I was. This would be a good place to dispose of unwanted captives. A half-formed shout to Bill and Corbin fluttered through my mind: "You hit 'em high, and I'll hit 'em low." But three against four armed with rifles? Reason won without argument, and I kept silent. There might not have been any danger with soldiers apparently under military discipline, but the crash landing had not disabled my imagination. The road led to a garage where they ordered us into a gray canvas-topped truck and sat on the side opposite us, mumbling to each other from time to time. Again we slept.

It was light when we were ordered out, stiff and hungry. By now I was feeling disoriented, and the whole sequence of events had taken on a kind of unreality. They had parked in front of a structure of white bricks bordered by gravel paths. We were back in the army—their army. After supervised visits to the latrine we were led to a mess hall for our first real food in twenty-four hours. We would come to know it well: black bread spread with a thin film of jam. Like the mug of thin coffee, it was ersatz. The Germans had learned to do without, and so would we.

Another hour's ride took us south to a larger complex. Led into a small room, we sat in turn before a camera. An assistant chalked my name on a slate, under it 5280. That was my *Kriegsgefangennummer,* my POW number. I had now received my third military serial number—as a German prisoner of war. Much later I would see the pink card with my photo pasted on it: unshaven, dirty, tired, and depressed—a faithful representation. I was a "Kriegie."

We were now in Oberursel, in Dulag Luft, the main interrogation center for captured airmen. I was led to a long hall lined with closed doors. The guard opened one and motioned me inside. It was a small whitewashed-brick room lit by one high, narrow window. It was bare but for narrow wooden planks fixed to the wall for a bed with one worn blanket. All was silence. Bill must have been nearby, but I would never see Corbin again. He was a non-commissioned officer, and he would go to a separate camp. I had no idea then of the provisions of the Geneva Convention formulated eighty years earlier.

The silence intensified. This was the low point so far. Depressed and lachrymose, I folded the thin blanket under my head and lay there gazing at the unlit bulb in the ceiling—and thinking. I grieved for my parents, imagining them receiving the terse missing-in-action telegram, not knowing if their only son was alive or dead, only that he was missing. Maybe they could take comfort from the old "No news is good news." I could only hope they had been told about the delay for information to pass to the Red Cross and to America. I could imagine my mother telling her beads, my father trying to comfort her in his inarticulate way. I sorrowed for them, undeniably sorry for myself, too. I should have been offering thanksgiving, but the blank, unknowable future induced instead only a kind of numbness.

I slept intermittently on the hard boards of the heatless cell. Grateful for my flight jacket, I was awake before gray light filtered in to make a pale square on the bare wall. After a series of distant muffled sounds I heard steps coming nearer and then a key turning in the lock. The door opened to admit a tall, dour-looking guard in an ill-fitting uniform. He led me to the *Abort,* stood outside the locked door of the creosote-smelling toilet, and then led me back to my cell. In this way would my small German vocabulary grow. Why hadn't I had the sense to take German in college? At last came the bread and ersatz jam and coffee. It tasted delicious. The hours of silence resumed, broken only once by footsteps in the corridor.

I didn't know what to expect of interrogation. My movie memories were no help. The last I had seen was *Purple Heart,* where the Japanese tortured Dane Clark and his crew until one of them broke ignominiously. I knew I was supposed to give only name, rank, and serial number. Two of those were on the dog tags around my neck and the other was on my Adjutant General's Office card in my confiscated wallet. What could I know that would be of any value to them? They were not going to ask about the missing bombsight. They probably had the same instructional manuals we had used at Kirtland Field. They hadn't even taken my old square-faced Bulova, which told me I had been fully awake for two near-silent hours.

The silence was broken again by footsteps and then a defiant American voice. "Time!" it shouted. "That's all I've got plenty of—time!" The voice trailed away and the footfalls ceased. Soon the tall guard reappeared and led me down the corridor to a room where an officer bent over a slim folder. He was trim in his tight uniform with its choker-style collar showing his rank. He straightened and indicated the chair placed before his uncluttered desk so that the light fell directly on my face. He was a lieutenant in his thirties, his thin face a series of planes and angles that reminded me of Helmut Dantine, often featured in movies as a Nazi officer.

"Would you care for a cigarette?" he asked in clear, clipped English, sliding the pack across the desk to me. The brand name, I noticed, was West Point.

"No, thank you," I said. They weren't going to soften me up. I knew about that game.

"Your name is Blotner," he said. Trying to keep my face impassive, I supplied my name, rank, and serial number. Let him be under no illusions, I thought. That's all the information he'll get from me. Looking down at the folder, he read off the numbers and location of my squadron and group. "Your commanding officer is Lieutenant Colonel Salada," he added.

This was embarrassing. I waited for the next question but none came. He

knew as much as I did and probably more. I was just another second lieutenant. This had been a formality. I wasn't exactly disappointed, but I saw just
what my status was in this war. At least I had made no slip to reproach myself
for, and I had undergone another ritual of initiation. The worst of it had been
the time in solitary, where I had learned the unpleasant truth that I had fewer
inner resources than I had thought. The best thing about the interrogation
was that it got me out of solitary.

Dulag Luft held a largely transient population, with some hard cases like
the officer who had shouted his defiance. He must have been fairly high ranking, and the Germans might have been hoping to sweat some information out
of him: American losses, new bombing and defense tactics, or perhaps new
aircraft and weaponry. But most of the aircrew prisoners were in Oberursel
for two weeks or less. We slept in large tents on tarpaulins, two blankets per
man. I saw little of Bill. We were both second lieutenants, but as the pilot he
had been my superior. Now there was nothing to make us seek out each
other's company. In my time as a Kriegie I would exchange a few words on occasion with him, but that was all. Sy almost immediately met two men from
navigator school. The only other man I recognized was Ernie Price. A tall,
thin blond I had not seen since the train trip to Savannah to pick up our airplane, he now looked even thinner. "I'll see you after chow," Ernie said.

Our prisoner's mess was a spartan affair, but we were ravenous and ate
the first meal with relish even though it was only mashed potatoes with shreds
of salmon, probably from Red Cross parcels. When we finished, a youngish
major spoke to us. He and others like him had difficult jobs, working under
German authority with their only appeal being to the Swiss representatives of
the Geneva Convention. Part of his responsibility was morale. He explained
our status under the Convention and gave a brief pep talk. "If there are any
people here from that Institute of Correction for Young Men on the Hudson,"
he concluded, "I'd like to see them in my quarters."

Afterward Ernie explained: "He meant West Point. He gave us each a shot
of brandy in his tent."

Ernie's combat career had been even shorter than mine. On his second
mission he had gone to Dresden and encountered flak so intense that they had
been hit when they turned off the target and he had ordered his crew to bail
out. He saw his bombardier and copilot out the hatch and waited while his
navigator poised to jump, then froze. Pat Patillo was a good navigator, but
he could not propel himself into empty space. "Jump, Pat!" Ernie shouted.
But Pat was transfixed, his white-knuckled hands gripping the hatch. Ernie
waited another second and then planted his foot on the seat of Pat's coveralls

and pushed. Then he followed him, the last man out of the burning plane. A round-faced, normally jolly man, Pat told me with a grimace, "Ernie saved my life."

I had forgotten that Ernie was a West Pointer, and if captivity was demoralizing to us, it was even more so to Academy graduates. Building a record as a combat pilot, a West Point man might be assigned to squadron or group staff. With skill and luck, he might end up with his own squadron. So war was not just part of the army's trade. It was a boon that produced bright young stars. Many were pilots whose kills had made them aces. Some were fair game for satirists, like the playwright who wrote a fresh-faced young general into a postwar comedy, a stripling who would come bounding in at intervals, champagne glass lifted, shouting, "To the Blue Lady of the clouds!"

It was inevitable that Ernie and Donald Dargue should talk about their classmates—how they would be promoted while they themselves would be stuck in rank. Don's father was a West Pointer who had risen to the rank of general, and when Don graduated from the Point, he had given him his own inscribed pistol, now doubtless reposing in some German holster. In Stalag Luft III, where we were headed, there would be an escape committee. I learned that it was the duty of West Pointers to attempt to escape. To me that seemed an easy way to add to the Times I Almost Got Killed. But I had no doubt that Ernie and Don would report to the committee as soon as we arrived.

The Red Cross would pass our names from the Luftwaffe to our next of kin, but it would be some time before we could send messages of our own, much less receive mail. Time dragged. The wounded had been treated, and we saw disfigured faces and hands when they rejoined us. Now we traded stories and rumors. Our move further east would depend on many things, rail transport not the least of them. Would we be held in some alpine redoubt as bargaining chips in negotiations? Our numbers put a strain on the German economy, and especially the transportation system we were bombing almost every day. The Germans would presumably live up to their obligations to American POWs and would probably transport us with careful scheduling to preserve as much of their rolling stock as they could under the relentless aerial pounding. As the cloudy November days grew shorter, we waited.

When the day arrived that brought the order to prepare for movement, we had little to do other than devise some way to pack our few spare garments and the toilet articles that had been conveyed to us by the Red Cross. That proved to be easy. A simply secured blanket took the place of the heavy barracks bags we had grumbled about in the States. Our own ranking officers formed us into lines under German supervision. We were not yet quite used to the clumping guards in their long dark overcoats, their heavy Mausers slung over their shoulders. They wore the villainous-looking steel coal-scuttle helmets we knew from movies about the First World War. As I observed them, I couldn't help concluding that these helmets must have given better protection than any others we had seen, including the streamlined models we had worn. Their officers' uniforms were far different from ours, with their grommeted high-peaked caps, choker collars, whipcord breeches, and leather boots. Their short tunics stuck up in the back so that they looked like a species of fowl. But the belts that cinched them in place also bore cartridge boxes and holsters carrying their Luger automatics. There was nothing comic about them. Being "under the gun" was now more than just a metaphor.

Our next transportation was in old railroad cars, high and narrow with four strange-looking connectors at each end that served as shock absorbers, thick metal rods ending in horizontal plates that clanked against each other. We climbed aboard to be crowded in, six to a compartment with seats and backs saturated with dust and cinders. Suspended a few feet below the ceiling was coarse netting for baggage. These cars had obviously been designed years before for nineteenth-century bodily proportions. One of our six, a bombardier who must have fitted very comfortably in the lower ball turret, sized things up immediately. "I'll take an upper," he volunteered and vaulted into the netting.

Ernie looked up at him from his six-foot height and smiled wryly. "Nothing but the best for the Kriegies," he said.

"Hurry up and wait" was even truer for German movements than it had been for our army. We might be halted unexpectedly at any moment. We pulled onto a siding to allow a series of flatcars holding tarpaulin-covered tanks to rumble past. We had cracked a window and sat there to the sound of steam hissing. Then there was something else. "Is that artillery?" Pat Patillo asked as muffled explosions sounded intermittently.

"It sounds like a stick of hundred-pounders to me," Ernie said.

"I hope that's not 47s shooting up trains," I said.

"Wish we had a POW sign on the roof," Pat said.

"It wouldn't do any good tonight when the RAF comes over," Ernie told him.

At any moment we might suddenly be on the receiving end of high explosives. They might be meant for marshaling yards, but if they hit a train, that would simply be an error. "*C'est la guerre,*" was gradually becoming part of our vocabulary. As the night closed down we pulled onto another siding, farther away from the main line this time. Guards came through to check the blackout curtains.

We were traveling northeast across Germany, Frankfurt am Main behind us, Frankfurt an der Oder ahead. By fits and starts we passed places the Eighth had bombed, or near them—Schweinfurt once more for me, then Merseburg and Leipzig. By now we were a little more than a hundred miles south of Berlin. After another night we crossed a repaired bridge over the Oder into Silesia. Some of it was farmland and some of it forest, land that had been Prussian and Polish, German and Czechoslovakian, and one day would be Polish again. On the third day we turned southeast from the Oder to follow a smaller river for fifty miles to a town called Sagan, and then along a spur line into heavily forested land.

Off the cars at last, we formed up again to march along gravel roads. In a large clearing a mile or so away lay Stalag Luft III, literally Camp Air Three, clearly visible though there wasn't much to see. One very tall brick smokestack reared up from among a number of long, low buildings. I would not later recall hearing anything that made it seem ominous. I would remember just a few ironically joking remarks about the scene. Later we would learn about other camps whose main gates greeted prisoners with the sign reading *Arbeit Macht Frei*. Because we were officers, we wouldn't be forced to work, and we wouldn't be free behind all that barbed wire.

"Here we are, boys," Ernie said. "Home sweet home."

THREE

Kriegsgefangen

UNDER THE LOWERING SKIES WE MARCHED TO THE main gate. In a dark forest of thin and scraggly pine stood weathered barracks, the surrounding earth pounded flat by myriad footsteps, the withered garden patches dead in the sandy soil. At the camp perimeter, we stood before two parallel barbed-wire fences that rose nine feet high. In the seven-foot space between the two fences stood a guard tower, a partially enclosed shack set on thick stilts. Surveying us from that thirty-foot height were two impassive-looking guards in bulky winter overcoats and cloth garrison caps. No need for the steel helmets here where a machine-gun muzzle poked out. Just below it was an enormous searchlight. Guards swung the gate open, and we entered Stalag Luft III. Crossing thirty feet of open space, they led us through an opening in another perimeter formed by an inner guardrail of single planks that circled the camp. That, we would learn, was the Deadline.

We passed between wire fences lined with prisoners, and some of them shouted questions. Had comrades made it back to the base? Had Allied forces crossed the Rhine? A few called out the old army greeting to new arrivals: "You'll be sor-r-r-y!" A soon-to-be familiar line was delivered in an execrable accent by some would-be comedian: "For you, der var iss over!"

Reunions had to wait for quarantine, and we were led to the *Vorlager,* a separate area that housed supply buildings and the Cooler, a block of un-heated disciplinary cells. We were not vermin-infested, and so we were spared the Germans' rudimentary delousing. We slipped out of our improvised packs, wolfed down the meager rations handed out, and prepared for a night in blan-kets on hard floors. Tomorrow's quarters have to be better, we thought. The guards turned out the bare ceiling lights.

"Tell me a story, Daddy," said Pat.

"Tomorrow," said Ernie.

We were glad to leave the Cooler in the gray light of morning. After we passed through yet another gate we saw more buildings and wire. To our right was a cleared space of a hundred feet before the woods began. That left a large field of fire for the guard towers. To our left were walls of wire that separated our compound from what looked to be two others with identical rows of barracks. Ernie and I were assigned to 167. With us was Ray Tag, a B-26 pilot. As tall as Ernie but at least thirty pounds heavier, he looked like a jolly Charles Laughton. Tag was in remarkably good spirits, having escaped uninjured from a crash landing into a row of flats.

We were welcomed by a short man wearing oak leaves on the shoulders of his chamois-colored fleece-lined coat. "I'm Major Saunders," he said, speaking rapidly. As the highest-ranking Kriegie in the barracks, he was its commander. His blue eyes were pale under the pale lids and cropped reddish hair that receded above a lined forehead. "You'll be in room 12," he told us. "The men will help you get settled. There's not much you'll have to do except follow orders—the goons' and mine. Be on time for *Appell*. If you screw up the count, they'll keep everybody out in the cold standing at attention while they start searching the whole goddam barracks. That's all." He started off but then whipped around, fixing us with his intense, deep-set blue eyes. "Remember that they mean business about the Deadline. If you hit a ball in there, signal the guard in the tower and get permission to go after it. If you don't, they'll shoot your ass off." He turned to go again but stopped and gestured to a man in a leather pilot's jacket. "This is Merg," he said. "He'll clue you in." And then he was gone.

"Mergenthal," the man said and extended his hand. "Come on and I'll help you with your bunk." Just under six feet tall, perhaps approaching thirty, he looked remarkably robust for someone who had apparently been in Stalag Luft III for months. He was a good-looking man with wavy brown hair and an aquiline nose. He led us down a narrow hall.

"Is Major Saunders always like that?" I asked him.

"Pretty much. He's a little strange sometimes, but he's OK. He's been here two years. He was shot down in North Africa, but he hasn't gone round the bend yet."

"Does he always wear that hat and sling those mittens around his neck?" It was a fine thick hat of blond fur with earflaps and two other pieces fore and aft. Large mittens dangling at his sleeves were connected by a strip of rawhide that ran up inside.

"He's proud of them," Merg said, "and they're great in cold weather. His folks sent the whole outfit from the States. It took a year for the parcel to get here. They sent his oak leaves too when he got promoted. He's forty-three, and he'd be a bird colonel now if he hadn't gone down. That's probably why he's a little strange."

We turned into the third room on the left. It was empty. "The guys will start drifting in before long," Merg said. Under the window opposite the door was what looked like a clothing cabinet lying on its side. Distributed along the walls were four triple-decker bunk beds. "You can flip for bunks," he said.

"Looks like there's not much difference," I said. All three empty ones were on the bottom. Merg smiled. Our roommates obviously had priority and seniority that we didn't begrudge them.

"That's right," he said. "The ones near the ceiling are the warmest. Except for those." He gestured toward the bunks next to a pot-bellied stove near one corner.

"Do you cook on that?" I asked.

"The kitchen is across the hall," Merg said. "We toast bread on the lid here for breakfast." He reached over to one of the bunks for a heap of burlap. "We might as well do your Beauty Rest." He handed the three of us large sacks and pulled over a box of coarse wood shavings. He began stuffing a sack and handed it over to me to finish. "Each bunk has exactly nine slats. If the goons find any missing, they assume they've been pinched for an escape tunnel, and they begin a general search. They make surprise searches all the time."

"The goons?" I asked.

"The guards," he said. "That's what we call them. They're touchy about it. One day one heard me and said, 'I am not a goon! I am a German soldier!' He was really pissed."

"Who are the ones in the coveralls?"

"They're ferrets. They crawl under the barracks and search there and any other place where somebody might start a tunnel or hide something."

I filled the sack and tried to pat it smooth. "You'll be surprised," Merg told Ernie and Tag. "It's pretty comfortable once you get used to it." He reached to another bunk and handed us blankets. One was a U.S. Army issue, and the other two were thin German ones. These won't be a lot of help when the stove goes out at night, I thought. "A lot of guys sleep in their clothes," Merg said.

"That'll be me," I said.

"Not me," Tag said. "I've got enough blubber for insulation."

"You'll lose it here," Merg assured him.

This was a compact barracks of sixteen rooms. "When the cookhouse issues rations," Merg continued, "the guys on the cookhouse detail bring them here until the two guys on KP from each room come to get their share. Besides water for morning coffee, there's not much to keep hot except soup—pea soup and barley soup, pretty thin but better than the other one the goons make out of dehydrated vegetables. We call it the Green Death."

"Sounds pretty appetizing," Tag said.

"Wait until you taste the *Blutwurst*."

"I've eaten bloodwurst at home."

"It's not quite the same here. They say somebody in the South Compound found a Russian belt buckle in it."

"Can we see the rest of the barracks now?" I said, swallowing.

Merg led us to the washroom next door and then to the night latrine at the end of the building. "There's nothing to see in there but the buckets. They're emptied every morning, but at night it's pretty intense when the barracks is locked and the shutters are closed for the blackout."

This time there was activity in the kitchen as we passed it, and Merg stopped. "Here's the most important man in the barracks," he said, "Bill Fagan. He's our cook."

"Democratically elected," Bill said with a smile. Curly-headed and pink-cheeked, he looked twenty-three or -four at most. "I hope Merg told you about the high-class chow here."

"He told us about the soup," Tag said.

"That's none of my work," Bill said. "Wait until Sunday. I'm going to do my baked Virginia Spam."

"It's good," Merg said. "No kidding."

"You'll draw KP next week," Bill said. "But you can get a head start now." He gestured toward a stack of oblong parcels in the corner stamped with red crosses. "Uncle Sam pays for them, but the Red Cross gets them to us. Here's what we get from the Krauts." He opened one of the doors of the cabinet and with both hands extracted a large oblong dark brown object. When he dropped it on the table, it made a loud thud. "Finest German army ration," he said. "Five pounds, one loaf per man per week. They issue flour and salt and jam when they feel like it." He pointed to a small pile of knobby potatoes on the bottom shelf. "We have to wait until we accumulate enough of them to go around."

"Here's the good stuff," he said, opening another door. "We can add the new parcels to it." We opened the heavy cardboard boxes and stacked the items inside the cabinet, sixteen different kinds of items to a box. The largest were sixteen-ounce packages of margarine and cans of powdered "Klim"—milk spelled backwards. "You'll see the cook pans the guys make out of them," Bill said, "even miniature blowers that boost the heat for outside cookfires."

We stacked the cans, salivating at the pictures of Spam, corned beef, liver paste, salmon, and processed cheese. There were cans of Nescafé powdered coffee and eight-ounce boxes of sugar. "Here comes the dessert," Bill said, and we stacked the cans of prunes and orange preserves. Beside them we put packages of K ration biscuits. "You'll like them as a pie crust," Bill told us. "But this is the Big Casino." He was holding packages of D bars, four-ounce pieces of unsweetened army baking chocolate. "They'll taste better than anything you ever ate. I'm not kidding."

"We can pass out the soap later," he continued. "There's always enough of that to go around. It's different with these," he said, pointing to the two packs of cigarettes each parcel yielded: Chesterfields, Camels, Lucky Strikes, and Old Golds, with an occasional pack of Wings. "For a real nicotine fiend, two packs a week isn't much. The guys who don't smoke use them for barter, for D bars or other stuff. Or to play poker with. There's a guy in 167 who's a good artist, Bob Neary. For four packs he'll draw an enlargement of a photo of your girlfriend or your wife." He handed each of us two packs of Lucky Strikes, the red bull's-eye gleaming against the white background. Ernie and Tag opened packs and lit up. I put mine in my pocket to think about the choices later. I had smoked briefly in high school but then quit after having proved to myself that I could inhale and blow smoke rings like the other guys.

We finished unpacking the parcels. "The British and Canadian parcels are about the same," Bill said. "The Brits get ground coffee instead of Nescafé and bacon instead of liver paste. I'd like that for a change. But once we got one of their parcels that had lentils from India. I nearly broke a tooth because they had harvested gravel along with the lentils." He paused. "That supply there looks like we're better off than we really are," he told us. "The docs say we need about three thousand calories a day. We get about half of that from the Krauts. These parcels add a thousand—I mean they did. Just about the time you got here, they cut the ration in half—half a parcel per man per week. We don't know why. They've probably got them stacked up out in the *Vorlager*. Oh, and here's some advice about the bottom bunks. After you tie your shoelaces, don't stand up too fast. You may black out."

I sat down on my bunk and looked at my two packs of Luckies. Should I use them for barter or poker? I considered the arguments for smoking them. They said tobacco cut your appetite. That certainly would be a plus here. And I remembered that smoking gave some mild pleasure, no matter that some people called them gaspers or coffin nails and said they cut your wind. Well, I thought, there's not much foreseeable pleasure here, and I'm not going to do too much running. I broke the cellophane and tore out the square inner wrap

beside the tax stamp. I inhaled the pungent odor and remembered the cigarettes Dad kept in the humidor. I knocked the pack against my index finger
and extracted a cigarette. I tapped it on one end, then lit it and took a deep
drag. A second later I was back in the junior-class play, feeling clever for lighting up on stage. Again I nearly passed out and just sat there until my head
cleared. I had just performed the first action in a new pattern, one I would
later recognize as Dumb Things I Have Done.

Outside, the sky had swiftly darkened. Bill Fagan came in and tucked a
rag in his belt for an apron. "The cook's work is never done," he sighed.

"You love it," Merg said.

Bill took two double handfuls of the knobby potatoes out of the cupboard and peeled them carefully, so as to lose no fragment. Bill's helper, a guy
named Larry, made up some milk from the Klim can. He mixed it in with the
corned beef and potatoes and then spread the result evenly over a flat metal
sheet. I thought of Mother's corned-beef hash, with the savory ground brisket
and diced potatoes and onion that would brown so beautifully.

"That's not all there is for supper," Larry told me. "There's a slice of bread
too, and at ten o'clock we get a piece of cake and coffee or cocoa."

"What time is breakfast?" Tag asked Larry.

"Nine A.M. You're going to be hungry all the time, so we try to space the
food out."

Others began drifting in, and Merg introduced us. "This is Luke, Dick Lu-
cas. He used to fly a P-47. And this one is Cokey. He's not really cokey, but
sometimes he talks that way. He was a navigator." Ed Stern blinked his blue
eyes and shook his head. "These guys have very limited vocabularies," he said.
"I'm from Washington, and they just haven't had my advantages."

Two short men wearing pilot's wings appeared. "These guys," Merg said,
"are the two shortest first pilots in the Eighth." The curly-haired one smiled
and held out his hand. "Tall enough to fly fifteen missions," he said, his eyes
crinkling. "Jake Glantz, and this is Willie Hirsch. Five more, and he would
have gone home. Wouldn't you, Willie?"

Willie wore a pleasant expression, but he seemed to leave the talking
to Jake. He was clean-shaven, but with the shadow of a beard visible beneath
the skin of his pale cheeks. "Are you going to eat with us tonight, Willie?" Jake
asked.

"Maybe," he said. He picked up a knitted cap from his bunk and turned
to the door, as if the conversation had wearied him.

"Don't stay out until the last minute, Willie," Jake said as he left. "I keep
his supper warm on the stove," Jake told us. "He likes to take it to his bunk

and eat there after the rest of us are finished. That's him. The army is not his style. He was going to be a CPA. I think he likes numbers better than people."

"He should have gotten a defense job and a deferment," Tag said.

"No," Jake said, "he wanted to be in the war. He hates Hitler. He was always quiet, but not the way he is now. I think it's what happened when he went down. A bunch of civilians were going to lynch him. They had the rope ready when some troops got there."

"Hell," Tag said, "he wasn't the only one had a rough time. We went down in Düsseldorf right after we bombed it. The place was still smoking. The 26 is a hot airplane to land, and when we couldn't make it beyond the city, I thought we were dead. We wound up in the wreckage. Sam, my copilot, almost didn't make it. A crowd of civilians had him down. One old bastard was trying to get his shotgun to work, and this old woman was slicing at him with a carving knife."

"What did Sam do?"

"Nothing," Tag said with a laugh. "He was groggy. I cold-cocked the old bastard with a timber and kicked that bitch ass over teacup. Just then some troops came up and got us out of there. But Sam's OK, and so am I."

"Willie's OK," Jake said, "he's just quiet. He's not as bad off as the major."

"The major's not going to go round the bend," Merg said. "He's too mean. But Willie's too quiet."

"He'll be OK," Jake said. "Don't worry about Willie. He just likes to walk."

"Where do these guys go?" Tag asked.

"Anywhere they want. As long as they stay clear of the Deadline, they can walk all day if they have the energy. Or they can shoot baskets. Or they can go to the library. It's the education program, reference books in 157 and the lending library in 158. Major says it's probably the greatest morale factor in the camp next to the Red Army."

"Yeah," Cokey said, "hot from Radio Breslau. Courtesy of the *Oberkommando von der Wehrmacht.* You can hear how the goons have 'moved to previously prepared positions.' Not 'retreated.' *Das ist verboten.*"

"It's better to hear something than nothing," Merg said.

"I'd rather wait and get my news from Sammy," Cokey said.

"Who's Sammy?" I asked him.

"You'll find out," he said.

"Try the library," Merg said. "A lot of the books are pretty beat up, but there are Westerns and mysteries, lots of stuff. The reference library is full ten hours a day, and it's warm."

"Some guys do a lot of studying there," Larry said.

"Studying what?" Tag asked.

"Whatever they want. Somebody said there's a dozen guys studying law and the ministry. I guess the Luftwaffe scared the hell out of them."

"Scared hell out of who?" asked another voice.

"Ernie," I said, "where've you been?"

"I met a couple of guys from the Point," he said, "a year ahead of me."

"Going to form a USMA alumni chapter?"

"They've already done it," he said.

"You were almost late for chow," Larry said, bearing in the tray of hash with two rags for potholders. "That's one formation most guys don't miss around here."

Bill meticulously cut the hash into equal squares and served them onto crockery plates while Larry sliced the bread and spread it lightly with margarine. Then he poured the coffee. As we were about to sit down, Jake said, "Let me put Willie's dinner on the stovetop." We fell to. There was little conversation, and the hash was gone quickly. It had tasted even better than I had expected. The men lingered over the coffee and bread, trying to make it last, I thought, as I was doing.

Everybody at the table but Jake lit up. This time I savored the cigarette. I had read somewhere that they gave oral gratification, and now I knew what that meant. It was like another dinner course. You put it in your mouth and drew from it into your body. I was hooked. Some men drifted out. Others sat there, smoking and talking desultorily.

I've got to go to the library, I told myself. I put my hands behind my head and thought back over the day, trying to assimilate some of the experience. I'd gotten past the bugaboo of the unknown. The quarters were cramped but not impossible. Our new roommates seemed a decent enough cross-section of the Army Air Corps as I knew it. A few of them might turn into friends, and none of them seemed obnoxious. I could live with them. And I didn't think I would go round the bend. I would keep busy. There was the compound newspaper, hand lettered and tacked onto the wall in the newsroom. And Bill Fagan had told me they did drama in the compound theater. Staying busy would not be the problem. The problem was the uncertainty. There had always been the rhythm of school or training to tell me what lay ahead. But now I didn't know what form the future would take. The Allies would win—I believed that. But would we live to see it? When the Red Army rolled in from the east and the Wehrmacht tanks and artillery opened up, would we be caught in the middle? Would the Germans move us before that could happen? Would they ship us somewhere for use as a bargaining chip when Hitler was convinced his

Götterdämmerung was approaching? What could we do, anyway? Try to escape? Dig tunnels as the British had been doing, unsuccessfully, for two years? Find the escape committee and ask to join it? The uncertainty created inroads fear could follow.

Bill had told us that tomorrow we might receive aerograms, thin blue sheets on which to write home. You wrote the address and then *Mit Luft Post nach Nord Amerika.* Nobody was sure how long it would take for them to reach home. And how long would it take for a reply to reach us? Nothing showed so clearly how cut off we were. But I would have to write as often as I could to Mother and Dad, sitting there in Scotch Plains, wondering exactly where I was—and how I was. Surely they must know by now that I was alive. But did they? And I would have to write to Moira, the girl I had met in Tampa who had transformed in the subtropical summer the small part of my life left to me by the air force while we were being formed into an aircrew. During our brief time together we had lived in the here and now, and the distance of that experience gave me once more a sense of how time was out of joint. Maybe in writing to her I could momentarily recapture something of that lost time.

The clatter of thrown-back blackout shutters woke me with a start. Still groggy, I pulled pants and a shirt on over my long johns and got into my flight jacket and new army overcoat, courtesy of the Red Cross. I walked first into the crowded latrine and then fell in with the rest of 167 for *Appell.* Cold under a dull gray sky, I wondered how many more *Appellen* I would have to stand.

Back in the barracks I held the hot coffee cup in both hands. It didn't take long to absorb its heat and consume the two slices of black bread. I wondered how to spend the day. Keep busy, the major had told us. I had no intention of going round the bend in this desolate reach of Silesia.

Ernie and I walked to the library. As we walked, he showed me snapshots of his family. One showed Winnie, a striking brunette who came barely to his shoulder. He had married her right after graduating from the Military Academy. The other showed a small blonde child who had been born not long before Ernie was ordered to Tampa to begin training with his crew. He missed both his girls, but his optimistic disposition was beginning to reassert itself. We scanned the bookshelves. He borrowed a Civil War history and said he'd see me at lunch. Now he was going to meet friends from the Point.

I borrowed a paperback, *Eight Great Tragedies* by William Shakespeare. I had been away from English classes for a year and a half, and I could try to make up for lost time. I wandered over to the newsroom and looked at the six pages of the carefully hand-lettered *Kriege Klarion* tacked on the wall. There was no military news of any account on the front page. An issue of the *Gefan-genen Gazette* on the opposite wall bore a collection of Dear John letters. "You were posted missing a month ago," ran one, "so I got married." Another former fiancée wrote, "Darling, I have just married your father. Love, Mother." These letters were presented as being authentic. The phenomenon of jilted sweethearts was common enough to elicit sympathy along with sardonic amusement.

Becoming an observer of Kriegie life, I walked every day under the gray skies. One day a man stopped me for a light, and it was Bill Moroz. We stood there in the cold as he drew on his cigarette. I asked how he was doing. He told me he had gotten in a fight with a man in his barracks. We stood there for a few minutes, but we had nothing to say to one another, and it was a relief when we set out in opposite directions.

The next request for a light was more memorable. This stroller made the usual gesture with his cigarette, and I blew on mine to give him a good light even though it cost my cigarette a fraction of an inch. Then I noticed his hand. The texture of the skin was very fine, and the color was deep red, like that of a sunburned baby. Then I realized this was the hand of a burn case. He might have been a fighter pilot who had been unable to free his jammed canopy quickly enough to bail out of his burning cockpit in time. I avoided looking at his face, partly covered by the bill of his cap as he bent to puff at the cigarette. He gestured his thanks with a jerk of his head and walked on past me.

And there were the goons. Bill Fagan had told me that the captain who took down the number of prisoners present each morning at *Appell* was *Haupt-mann* Eisenmann. *Feldwebel* Eiler, who never relaxed from his position of attention as he consulted his clipboard, supplied the number of men present to him. He was shorter than the *Hauptmann* and followed two paces behind him, his stiff gait almost a parody, the *Hauptmann* in his blue uniform, his collar tabs and shining boots, the sergeant a drab figure behind him. They both appeared to be in their fifties, red-cheeked from the weather. Their jobs looked like dull routine, though their superiors doubtless harped on the need to be alert for anything suspicious, like fresh dirt from an escape tunnel. But these two might have consoled themselves that theirs was better duty than the infantryman's lot in a line company near the Rhine or a freezing dugout on the eastern front. The ferrets in their lumpy coveralls looked interchangeable, plodding around the compound, hands behind them, stopping occasionally to peer on all fours past the foundation under the barracks.

Walking back to the barracks I saw a familiar figure ahead of me in oversized hat and gloves. It was Major Saunders. When I spoke to him he simply returned my greeting. On an impulse I spoke again. "Sir," I said, "I couldn't help noticing the black armband some of the men in the North Compound are wearing. Could you tell me what they're for?"

"You're damn right I can," he said, staring straight ahead, his gait unchanging. I waited. "It was seven months ago. The Brits had finished a new tunnel thirty feet below the surface. One night they broke out, eighty of them."

"Did they escape?"

"Seventy-six of them cleared the camp area."

"Did they get far?"

"Not far enough. The sonsabitches shot fifty of them. Hitler's orders." Major Saunders turned and walked rapidly away.

Merg told me the rest of the story. It was Tunnel Harry, the best of the three they had going—Tom, Dick, and Harry. Shored up with wooden partitions, lighted, and ventilated, they were the work of thousands of hours, a marvel of planning, patient engineering, and construction. After the foiled escape, the goons collapsed Harry. Nobody knew why the men crawling out of the mouth of the tunnel found themselves looking into the barrels of Mausers. Perhaps one of the ferrets had seen telltale signs of fresh earth or heard strange sounds, or perhaps an electrician had noticed a change in power consumption. In these close quarters any imposter would have been eventually detected. So there was no final answer. The ranking officers who survived were held under arrest. Three of the seventy-six made it back to England.

Did Ernie know this history and these odds? Probably. Not long before our arrival the English had decreed that escape was no longer a duty, and the Americans had followed suit. I didn't think that made any difference to Ernie. If he could join in an attempted break, he would do it. I would sweat it out behind the wire. My life had been divided into periods of waiting and work with gradual ascents from one level to another. That pattern had been broken by the reserve call-up. It resumed with basic training and preflight. Then I had made it through gunnery and bombardier school. After the next ascent, to combat status, had come the dramatic descent that had lodged me here. Now I thought of another ascent. For our high school graduation ceremony, I had been assigned one of the inspirational speeches Miss Higgins had provided, beginning "We shall climb the hill and look for tomorrow." I would have to try to think of the future in those terms. I would walk the perimeter with the others. Let those who would be heroes. I wanted to get home alive. I just prayed that deliverance would come soon, before I lost as much of my lifetime as the major had.

As the end of 1944 approached, the population of the Stalag's six compounds was approaching ten thousand. The West Compound had a drama group that met in the camp theater. The leader was Red Baird, a New Yorker who looked about the age of a high school senior but conducted himself with assurance. He welcomed me and showed me around. Canadian Red Cross boxes had supplied the wood the prisoners used to build a three-hundred-seat theater in each compound. German blankets provided material for stage curtains. The same ingenuity created costumes and paper stage sets. The YMCA supplied enough instruments to support an orchestra in each compound. Ours was the Flying Syncopators.

"We're doing radio drama right now," Red told me, "and next week we'll start rehearsing for the Christmas variety show."

"Radio?" I said.

"Yeah, we have a YMCA public address system. We put mikes behind the curtain and the audience sits out front. We are the Mercury Theater of Stalag Luft III, and I am its Orson Welles. You have any radio experience?"

"Yes," I said.

"Great," Red said. "Do you know *The Front Page?*" I nodded, remembering that it was a comedy about profane and hard-drinking Chicago newspapermen.

"Here's the script. Come back for a run-through tomorrow afternoon."

By the next day I thought I had mastered every nuance. The five of us grouped around the microphones seemed to me to be doing beautifully, delivering our lines with gusto, especially the vulgar ones about the peccadilloes of Chicago politicians, but I realized that I had lost the attention of the others. They were looking at a tall figure in British battle dress who was now striding toward the exit with a face like a thundercloud.

"What's his problem?" I asked.

"That's Father McVey," Red said. "He's the Catholic chaplain. He was captured in that balls-up at Arnhem, and he doesn't have much of a sense of humor left."

"He's got a tough job," said one of the others, "saying masses every day and hearing confessions and talking to head cases. He went to the sick quarters in the *Vorlager* last week to see a guy the medics said had gone round the bend."

"Had he?"

"Well, McVey talked with him for a half-hour and decided he was as sane as the next guy."

"Will he get him out?"

"McVey promised that he would talk to the medics for him, and the guy thanked him. But then just before McVey got to the gate, he felt a hell of a wallop in the small of his back that knocked him on his face. It was a rock. McVey looked back, and the head case was smiling at him. 'I didn't want you to forget,' he said."

Red said we could have one more script run-through and do the show on Saturday. So the next day we were reading without a hitch when a voice broke in.

"Tench-hut!" We came to attention and turned to see an American major leading a group of four Germans. "Colonel-General Mannheim is inspecting the camp," the major said. Red took over, explaining how we created a make-believe world to divert our fellow Kriegies. The general followed attentively and asked a few interested questions. Red answered smoothly as we all listened. We were fascinated by the general in his long shining leather greatcoat. He was a portly pink-faced man who made me think of Hermann Goering, the creator of the Luftwaffe. But this general was not only at ease but jovial.

His explanations completed, Red continued his conversational gambit. "Was the general ever in New York?" he asked our visitor.

The general squared his shoulders and regarded him with a smile. "Vas I ever in New York?" he said. "Vas I ever in New York?" And he began to laugh, his face reddening and his jowls swelling over the tabs of his uniform collar. "Vy, in nineteen twenty-tree I vas a bartender in Hans Jaeger's in Yorkville!" His staff of three joined in his own explosive laughter. He thanked us, and they departed with a great clumping of the shiny black boots. Maybe our drama group, I thought, had struck a blow for better German-American relations.

The Front Page was a success with our entertainment-starved audience, and Red plunged into preparations for the variety show. The Flying Syncopators would of course be the mainstay, but he would need all the performers he could get. The first volunteer, a navigator, told Red that he was an experienced hypnotist, and he was accepted without an audition. The next day Red was there with two others. One was a scrawny bombardier from Kentucky. "This is Homer," Red said. "He plays the harmonica, and he can imitate other instruments on it. He had it in his coveralls when he went down, and the Germans let him keep it."

Homer smiled amiably. "Mah specialty is the musical saw," he drawled. "But even if we could find one, I don't reckon they would let me have it."

"Right," said Red, who now looked as though his spirits were beginning to sag. "I think we may have the material for another number," he said briskly, gesturing at the man next to Homer. "This is Zip Zapinski. He's from Cleveland. He'll need a partner." Thin-faced, sallow, and heavy-lidded, Zip looked to me as though he came from Transylvania. He seemed to be regarding me with suspicion.

"Can you sing?" he asked in a nasal voice. I was taken aback, regarding myself here as an assistant impresario rather than a performer.

"Sure," I replied on an impulse, confident that I could keep up with this entertainer whose principal venues, I gathered, had been lodge entertainments and small nightclubs.

"Can you dance?" he asked me. I had gotten in too far to get out without losing face with Red, so I nodded.

"Come on over to my barracks, and we can start."

Fortunately none of Zip's roommates were there. I was already beginning to feel apprehensive as he showed me the steps. He demonstrated the way we would twirl our canes and then lean on them while we did our patter. To my dismay I saw that this would require a kind of light-footedness I had never possessed. Zip rapidly ran through the ten-minute routine, gesturing with an invisible cane and straw hat. He was no Fred Astaire, but plainly he had the routine down pat. Then suddenly I recognized it from *The Road to Zanzibar,* a comedy with Bob Hope and Bing Crosby. And then I realized what kind of dancer Zip was. Lanky and almost gangling, he was what was called an eccentric dancer. He ran through the steps once more.

"Let's do it again," he said grimly. I thought I was beginning to get it, but he only muttered, "We'll have to work on this." Back in my barracks I went over the steps, holding the pages of our routine. I had to learn to be a hoofer.

Remembering the advice to guard against barbed-wire psychosis by staying busy, I thought of a notice in the *Klarion.* Father McVey was conducting the First Fridays, a devotional observance of receiving the Eucharist on the first Friday of nine consecutive months. According to Blessed Margaret Mary Alacoque, Christ had appeared to her and promised that anyone who kept the First Fridays would not die in sin. McVey was also conducting the First Saturdays, devotions performed on the first Saturday of five consecutive months. The reward was not specified as precisely as that for the First Fridays. I had gone to mass every Sunday, but an honest examination of conscience revealed that my devotions had consisted principally of prayers for delivery from Stalag Luft III and intercession for my loved ones. As I pondered, it seemed to me that the First Saturdays offered a better deal than the First Fridays—only five months rather than nine, by which time I hoped to have been home for quite a while.

I went to the first service with a dozen of so from our barracks. We had barely made it, because it was one of those mornings when the count at *Appell* was off, probably due to a mistake by one of the goons, because a real escape would have alerted the whole camp. So we stood outside in the cold for an hour until they got it right. When we got back to the barracks I was able to see why my hands and feet had started to bother me. In spite of mittens, two fingers on my left hand were numb and had turned the color of wax. Two toes on my right foot were the same.

"It's only frostbite. Just rub them gently," Merg said. After half an hour they looked normal. Father McVey's homily was far from inspirational, but I thought that any observer could hardly have failed to detect my piety. I've started the First Saturdays just in time, I thought.

There were other currents above and below the surface. Ernie was close-mouthed about escape activity, but soon we had evidence of stirrings. After lunch one day, Bill Fagan handed out some extras: raisins and D bars. Simmered together in water, then dried hard and cut into pieces the size of a candy bar, they would become "iron rations"—a high-energy food we could take on any forced march. Ernie and I paired up and took our turn in the kitchen. Ernie stirred the pot, and then I stirred. "Taste it," he said. I did and stopped after half a teaspoonful, knowing that my deprived stomach could not have tolerated more.

There was another reason for my caution. One evening some weeks earlier as I bit down on a morsel of Spam, I had heard a crunch. It was a filling from a molar. As our nutritional level dropped, we became subject to various ailments. One day, walking through Red's barracks, I passed a man lying on his stomach in his bunk while another massaged his scalp. He woke each morning to find tufts on what passed for his pillow and widening patches of his scalp emerging from the hair he had left. His barracks mates now called him "Haid." Was this the medical problem called alopecia? The result of a vitamin deficiency? Or a manifestation of uncertainty and mental anguish? There was remarkably little disease in Stalag Luft III, so far as we knew. Maybe it was owing to the relatively stable population, with only occasional influxes of new Kriegies bringing new germs.

One night a week later Cokey became the focus of attention when he walked in with a man I didn't recognize. Conversation stopped as Cokey cleared his throat and paused for three beats. "Sammy says," he announced distinctly.

"Good!" said Bill. He had told me about "Sammy." Two years earlier, NCOs transferred from Stalag Luft I in Poland had smuggled into the East Compound a radio receiver they had put together by means of bribery and blackmail. Parts were obtained from a guard in exchange for cigarettes, chocolate, and other currency. If the source of supply threatened to stop co-operating, he could be threatened with exposure. It was well known that the German penalty for treason was beheading. Eventually each compound had its own receiver, concealed variously in a hollow table leg or a playable accordion. Monitors listened to the BBC newscasts through earphones and produced summaries on flimsy pages that could be swallowed in an emergency. "Stooges" were posted to ensure that the coast was clear as the courier was escorted from one barracks to the next.

Cokey enjoyed this nerve-wracking assignment, and he led off with the big news. "Russian armies are advancing rapidly from the east," he read. There were murmurs from the listeners, swiftly silenced by Cokey's escort. We already knew that the Third Army, under General George S. Patton, Jr., was fighting its way forward from the west. As Cokey finished, he was overcome by a surge of optimism. He closed out with the standard "Sammy says" and then added, "Bash your iron rations." We would have been glad of an excuse to eat them. Maybe we could simply stay where we were and wait for liberation.

"Hot damn!" Merg said.

I nudged Ernie in the ribs and winked. "Maybe they'll just come to you," I said. He only grinned.

There was one unlooked-for consequence of Cokey's remark about the iron rations. The breach of security cost him his job as one of the voices of Sammy.

FOUR

The Turn of the Year

THE VARIETY SHOW USHERED IN THE HOLIDAY SEASON.
The Syncopators sounded fine in their warmup. When the curtains parted on
a full house, Red rattled off a series of jokes about ferrets, Dear John letters,
and the deprivations of Kriegie life. Then, under his vigorous arm waving, the
singers launched into a song about a troopship:

> There'll be no promotions this side of the ocean, so cheer up my lads,
> Bless 'em all!

"That was great!" Red shouted and led them into a slower tempo:

> Darling I remember how you used to wait . . .
> My Lily of the lamplight, my own Lily Marlene.

It didn't matter that it was a German song, and Red didn't have to tell them
to sing it with feeling, for the simple refrain captured shared longing and
nostalgia.

"Now we have a different treat for you music lovers," he announced
and introduced Captain Harry Osborne as "a celebrated hypnotist who has
displayed his powers both in America and abroad." The intense gaze and black
mustache made me think of the comic strips' Mandrake the Magician. When
he asked for a volunteer, a man from room 12 rose. It was Dudley Digges, a
lanky, rough-hewn Texan who stood there grinning.

"What I am going to do," said the captain, "is use the power of suggestion.
He will do things that will surprise you and might even surprise him."

Digges chortled and sat down in the chair and swept back the black hair
from his forehead. He would have looked almost Lincolnesque but for a grin

that was just this side of a sneer. "Lieutenant Digges is going to show us some of his skills," the captain told the audience.

"You are now ready for takeoff," he said and read off the checklist. Digges followed it obediently, setting invisible dials and pushing switches, advancing throttles and releasing brakes, and at last pulling back on the wheel. When the captain told him, "We're approaching the IP," Digges's arms and hands tensed. "That flak is driving us off course! Correct before we start the bomb run!" Now Digges was being jostled as he struggled with the wheel and rudder pedals. "Give her some more throttle and hold her steady," the captain said. Digges grew more intense. At last his body lurched upward. Then as he turned off the target he seemed to relax, and I thought I could see sweat on his face.

"Now you're going to bring her in for a nice smooth landing," the captain told him. "But as soon as you get her parked and cut the engines, you're going to have to pee worse than you ever did before."

Digges brought his airplane in and went through the motions of taxiing and parking. The minute he cut the throttles, a look crossed his face as from some imperative summons. Staring ahead of him, he rushed off the stage to thunderous laughter and applause. With a nonchalant salute, the captain made his exit, too.

Then came the moment I had been dreading. "For a real change of pace," Red announced, "here are Zip Zapinski and friend!" The costume department had dyed two pairs of long johns gray, then starched and pressed them to look like tight Edwardian trousers. Our jackets were blue-and-white-striped seersucker. We tipped our imitation straw hats and swung our imitation rattan sticks as the pianist vamped to the opening line. "We're goin' south," we sang in a recital of the things we would do. Then I missed a step and hurried to catch up. By the last chorus Zip's expression was darker than Father McVey's at our radio rehearsal. The applause was generous, but Zip didn't even look at me as we tipped our skimmers and shuffled off, still out of step.

"Great!" Red said to me. "Just great."

"Thanks," I said, "but I'm retiring from show business."

It was Christmas, and Bill Fagan was busy with the help of Cokey and Luke. For his Christmas menu he planned an omelet and pancakes for breakfast, macaroni and cheese for lunch, and molded dishes of salmon and corned beef for the feast itself. He was going to bash all of our prune and sugar rations to create a plum pudding. Frank Grabowski and Larry were making table decorations, and Red had scheduled Christmas Eve carols.

But on Saturday, Bill was thrown into consternation. Our barracks was scheduled for delousing in the *Vorlager* cooler all day Sunday. "I won't be able to get anything done," he said, "and the schedule is tight from Friday on!" He protested to Major Saunders, who told him that the Germans were inflexible. "Goddamit," Bill fumed. "Goddam atheists!" We had seen no signs of parasites, but Sunday morning still found us wrapped in our blankets, freezing on bare benches during the long day it took for fumigation.

"Merry Christmas," Ernie said.

"Happy New Year," I replied.

When we returned after dark, Bill and Cokey and Luke resumed their mixing and patting. It was too late for carols at the theater, but at snack time Ernie and Don Dargue struck up "God Rest Ye, Merry Gentlemen." Thinking of home, we ushered in Christmas with coffee and toasted black bread and kitchen scraps saved for our delayed celebration.

It seemed as though more men than usual were out walking around the next day, as if trying to make up for the calls they might have made this day at home. Even Willie was there in time for the late-afternoon dinner. At last, after extra helpings of mashed potatoes with the savory gravy Bill had somehow created, there appeared a rich plum pudding. Afterward all the diners declared themselves unable to eat a bite more. Some had managed to trade for cigars, and now aromatic blue clouds rose in the overheated room.

"That was wonderful," Merg said.

"I think I even ate too much," said the man we all called the Swede. Thoughts of nausea began to circulate.

"We can walk around inside," Don said and began to circle the table. Soon four others joined him.

The insidious thought of nausea was so threatening that I decided to try some distraction, as much for myself as for the others. I began to imitate the racetrack announcer Clem McCarthy at the microphone: "The track is fast, and it's a great field! They're off! Glantz is on the inside rail, moving easily. Mergenthal is moving up steadily on the outside." After a few minutes, some of the contestants began to lag, and two sat down. At the finish I said, "It's a dead heat!" I hadn't realized that Don had left the room until he slowly reentered, ashen-faced. "What a shame," he said mournfully. "What a waste. All that good food."

Two weeks earlier we had learned from "Sammy" that von Runstedt had broken the American front in the Ardennes. In this desperate attack, an outnumbered American force held out in a strong point at Bastogne. In the days after Christmas we learned of the counterattack by Patton's Third Army that had ended the Battle of the Bulge with the destruction of the attacking force.

On January 23 Ernie burst into the room. "Come on," he said, "there's some kind of a notice in the library." Pushing up behind the group that had gathered, we read the short page: "ATTENTION ALL ARMY AIR FORCE OFFICERS: Starting tomorrow all prisoners will begin walking ten laps daily around the camp perimeter." It could mean only one thing: evacuation.

The air was charged with a sense of expectation that needled the nerves like the icy snowflakes steadily falling. We followed the regimen each day, circling the whole inner perimeter and then beginning a second lap. As we walked, we speculated about the route if the Germans decided to evacuate.

"Three hundred miles south would put us in Berchtesgaden," Ray Tag said. "They could put us in the Elite Guard's barracks."

"The truth, probably, is that right now they don't know what the hell to do," Ernie said. "But I'll tell you what some of the transport will be. It'll be shanks' mare."

"Goddamit," Tag said. "I joined the air corps to stay out of the infantry." He jerked his collar up further around his neck. "I hope you're wrong. If you're right, we'll have our stuff to carry."

"You've marched with a pack before," Ernie said. "You can do it again."

By Friday, January 25, there was a half-foot of snow. The sky was still threatening, and the wind chill ate at the men doggedly marching their circuit. Tag had converted his scarf into a hood that tucked into his collar. Ernie had fashioned a backpack out of a buttoned-up wool shirt with the shirttails doubled up and pinned to form a closed bottom. He tied the sleeve ends together around his neck. Then he tied the lower ends together with a rope that secured it in front. He hoped it would travel.

At 8:30 on Saturday night we heard rapid steps in the hallway and loud knocking. We looked to see Major Saunders with a captain we didn't recognize. His name, we later learned, was Campbell. The major's reedy voice was high-pitched and strident. "Men," he said, "a half-hour ago Colonel von Lindeiner's adjutant called a meeting. A Russian spearhead is pushing in from the northeast. It sounds as though it may be about thirty miles away. We're on notice to be ready to evacuate in an hour." The response was an angry murmur. "Take only what you absolutely need." The repressed babble of voices swelled.

"At ease! At ease!" shouted the captain.

"I want you men to remember," Major Saunders shrilled, "that you are American officers under military discipline. The Germans will give their orders to us, and we'll relay them to you. And I want you to remember this:

Don't do anything stupid. This will be tough enough even if everybody uses his head." He nodded to the captain. "Dismissed!"

"Get your stuff ready," Bill Fagan called, "and we'll share out the rations." With Larry's help he emptied the cupboards of the last Red Cross parcels. From under bunks everybody brought out clothing and toiletries. I stuck my paperback Shakespeare into a sack made of my second spare shirt. Ernie put our iron rations into his pack, and I carried corned beef and sardines.

Just past midnight, with snow coming down heavily, the order came to fall in. It was a bizarre-looking group. One man had stuffed his possessions into a suit of long johns and tied the legs around his waist. "If it ain't five below," said the Swede, "I never lived in Wisconsin. This is a goddam blizzard!" From somewhere Tag had scrounged a sled and some rope to run through the wooden runners. He began arranging clothing in a box atop the platform between the runners. Pink-cheeked, he puffed clouds of steam.

The Swede stood there laughing. "Hey, Santa," he said. "Gimme a ride!"

"Kiss my ass," Tag said.

"All right, men," called the major, "let's get the lead out. We've got a long way to go."

The ragged column moved in single file with occasional stops for repairs on flimsy contraptions. At the theater in the center of the West Compound there was a sudden blaze of light as four men pushed steaming drums out of the cookhouse. They ladled out coffee—hot and rich and sweet, the best I had ever tasted. Stores would be left for the Russians, and our officers had concluded that we might as well use up what we couldn't carry. The cold was creeping into my toes in spite of two pairs of socks under my loosely tied shoes. We stamped our feet. "Goddamit, let's *go*," Grabowski said. "We're freezing our tails off."

I was grateful once again for the GI overcoats the Red Cross had transported. Mine made a tight fit over my flight jacket, but I needed every thread, and I wished I had a scarf like Tag's around my head.

Captain Campbell looked down the column. "Let's move it!" he shouted as we plodded into the West Compound *Vorlager*. The scene turned eerie bluewhite as searchlights from three towers crisscrossed, lighting up the Deadline and playing over the guards. They were wearing their coal scuttles now over knitted balaclavas. Just inside the fence the major stood with Colonel Spivey, the second-ranking American officer. Beyond them were *Hauptmann* Eisenmann and *Feldwebel* Eiler in their long greatcoats and the leather boots I now envied. They surrounded a tall man with braid in his cap and a fur collar— Colonel von Lindeiner, I thought, overseeing the evacuation of Stalag Luft III. Again the German forces were "moving to previously prepared positions."

We marched through the main gate onto the trail that had brought us to Stalag Luft III. Forlorn-looking goons stood there, the snow forming white capes on their coats and casques on their helmets. "Watch out for the Russkis!" a voice called to them.

My shoulders were aching, and my knitted gloves gave slight protection. I jammed my hands into my pockets, but this turned my progress into a shambling walk. At last came the cry of "Halt!" We dropped our parcels and painfully slipped off our lumpy packs.

"Wow!" Ernie said, massaging his shoulders. "We've got to lighten the load." We decided to keep the Spam, corned beef, liver paste, salmon, and cheese. We would ditch the powdered milk and margarine. We lit cigarettes and chewed small handfuls of raisins. The temperature must have dropped nearly to zero, and through the black air came the unmistakable thudding of artillery from the northeast.

"Come on, you red bastards," somebody shouted. "Get your asses in gear! We're your goddam *comrades* freezing out here!"

We were moving more slowly now, and talking less. I saw two figures passing us. I could tell that one was Major Saunders, his fur hat huge with snow. On either side of our column I saw discarded objects: fragments of Grabowski's suitcase, and here and there even a can of Spam or salmon. Clothing became covered with snow almost as I watched, squinting into the driving wind. "God," Ernie said, "it's the Retreat from Moscow."

We were passing small isolated houses, then fences and barns, some shapeless and monstrous under the masses of white. Up ahead I could see the column turning at a crossroads. There I made out a road sign. Someone brushed off the snow to reveal the German script: "Halbau 3 KM."

"Christ! Fourteen kilometers is all the further we've gone from Sagan?" said the Swede.

Halbau was shrouded in snow and darkness. "Take ten!" Captain Campbell called out, and I slumped down in the snow. When the ten minutes had elapsed and we roused slowly, we saw another signpost. Tag read it out: "Freiwaldau 11 KM."

We walked on through the night, shifting our packs, lighting tasteless cigarettes. Plodding, I kept waiting for some sign of dawn. Then we were galvanized by a sudden sound. It was a rapid burst of fire, the whine of high-velocity bullets over our heads. Ernie and I leaped into a snow bank. "Jesus Christ!" he shouted.

The snow was sifting under my collar and down my neck. I thought about John Holzermer and his attempt to surrender. These shots had come from the rear of the column. The high scream sounded as if they had been aimed at me personally. We waited while the echoes faded into the whine of the wind. After several long minutes we rose laboriously and brushed off more snow. Slowly the column straggled back onto the road. Later we would learn that some men had been hit as they dived for cover.

Freiwaldau offered shelter—no barracks, no beds, just a place to flop. These were outbuildings, we learned later, of a concentration camp. Sprawled on the hard floor, I descended into depths so deep that when the grumbling of the men next to me wakened me, it was all I could do to sit up and wait for commands. Not even an hour had passed, but others just in from the cold needed our places. Groggily we smoked cigarettes and ate the last of the raisins.

It was four o'clock on the morning of January 29. We were marching northwest now, traveling toward Muskau, another new name. Men were falling asleep on their feet, stumbling in the ruts. Small groups had struck out for barns. Tag called to us from a clump of trees and shadows twenty yards away. He had found an inn whose owner was willing to open his door for a dozen of us to throw ourselves down on his barroom floor. We sat on the cold tile by the heatless fireplace. My feet were aching, my toes chafed inside the wet socks and shoes. I put on dry socks, then fell onto the bedroll to drift down into consecutive hours of sleep for the first time in forty-eight.

That afternoon, the landscape beyond the white-etched windowpanes was still obscured. The snow was still falling. Ernie and I ate half of our cheese and crackers and drank from the water tap behind the bar. As we were called to form up, a horse-drawn wagon creaked past. The guard had a scarf around his head that made him look like a man with a toothache. In the wagon six men lay huddled, the lame and the halt. We continued tramping northwestward as the early-winter dark descended. It felt like the wrong way, but we would have to continue until we reached Muskau. We had no clear idea how our journey was going, and we weren't sure the Germans did, either. A break came on a small exposed bridge over an ice-covered stream. Ernie and Tag and I sheltered against the wall near one end of the bridge and held fluttering flames to our cigarettes. The merciless wind was keen. I thought to myself, This is the coldest I have ever been in my whole life. It was too cold even to shiver. We were absorbed into night and stasis, and I had the feeling we might never move from that bridge.

When the command finally started us up again, we found that the last ten kilometers had brought us to Muskau, scarcely distinguishable from Halbau or Freiwaldau. Someone had found shelter for us in a small pottery plant. By now I had almost come to expect the incongruous, and we flopped down between the treadles the potters pumped to shape the clay. Then, blessedly, there came an issue of bread. Dipping into our salmon and orange preserves, we made a meal.

We couldn't know two days later as we struck out for Graustein, sixteen kilometers away, that the worst of this phase was over. The snow continued though the temperature began to rise, and we had an enforced respite because of treacherous ice on the roads. In a barn we received bread and a potato and a half apiece. "Hey, fellas," Tag said, seated in the haymow, a chunk of each in either hand, "this is a regular picnic."

Our Silesian tour included one more stop, at Spremberg, eight more kilometers to the west. "What do you think they make in *Sperm*berg," Tag asked, "condoms?"

"The only thing you have to know about Spremberg," Ernie told him, "is that it's on the railroad. Cross your fingers."

At nightfall in a Wehrmacht garrison we were issued a ration of soup. Ernie said, "See what I mean?" Not only was it not the Green Death, it was hot with fragments of meat and potatoes. The grainy floor was made of timbers cut crosswise and packed together vertically. I smelled gasoline and wondered if this *Lager* had housed a panzer division's Tiger tanks, now perhaps snowbound on some Siberian steppe. God help their crews, I thought.

As we put on our further lightened packs the next day, we walked out into strangely springlike February weather. The green branches dropping their fluffy pads of snow were bright. After the soup and the sunshine, there seemed something celebratory about the scene, as if nature was momentarily in tune with the lift we felt. I thought about the English class I had taken at Drew University shortly before being called up. What was it that our teacher, Dr. Aldrich, had said about poets—that sometimes they attributed their own emotions to nature? The pathetic fallacy, that was it. No, I thought, don't harbor any stupid feelings. Yet even as we clumped painfully alongside the track into the freight yards, I still felt the lift of the spirit. Four kilometers further on somebody calculated that we had covered one hundred kilometers, sixty-two miles, in four days.

Up ahead I could see American medics. I joined the line, and an efficient sergeant swabbed my feet. "That's a nice case of frostbite you have there," he told me. "And with those shoes, it's no wonder you have open wounds." He sprinkled powder on them. "This is all we've got, but it's sulfa. Another day and you would have had a promising case of blood-poisoning."

I looked up to see two familiar figures. Major Saunders led the way over the rails past the battered rolling stock and flatcars of armored personnel carriers. He halted and pointed ahead. "There we are," said Captain Campbell. "The Twentieth Century Limited."

"Goddam," said Tag. "I don't believe it."

From history books I recognized the "forty-and-eight" boxcars of the First World War, designed to carry forty men or eight horses. They were long and narrow with a sliding door on each side. The captain began walking down the line counting off men into groups. The Swede followed him. "Captain," he said, "that's over fifty men! Is that for a single car?"

"Yeah," he replied, "and a guard with a rifle."

"My God," I said.

"Ve haf our orders," said Tag.

"Somebody said it's a little over two hundred miles to go," Fagan told us, "outside of Nuremberg."

"There's not going to be enough room for us," the Swede protested, "even without all this stuff and the guard."

This time the captain just looked at him. "There's a big camp for civilians a hundred miles further down the line near Munich. Maybe we could send you there. It's called Dachau."

"No, thank you—*sir*," the Swede answered.

With surprising agility Jake hoisted himself up and leaned out. "Give me your stuff, Willie," he said reaching down. Slowly Willie complied. He looked no worse than the rest of us, but his gaze created his own zone of privacy.

"How ya doin', Willie?" Fagan asked.

"He's OK," Jake said, "just pooped like the rest of us."

As the boxcar filled there were grunts and curses. When it seemed that there was no more room, they jammed more men inside. Two guards boosted another aboard and then handed him his helmet, coat, and Mauser. "Don't hit me with that goddam thing!" somebody said. The guard looked to be in his fifties, his gray hair cropped and his face pasty. Finally they slid the doors nearly closed, leaving a three-foot opening on each side. "What do we do for air!" the Swede yelled as the creaking car lurched.

"We're like a bunch of goddam sardines," Grabowski declared. The men by the walls could lean against them, but the rest sat jammed randomly, their arms encircling their knees, with nothing to do but twist and turn for brief relief.

I thought of William Blake's drawings but realized that they showed nothing like this. No, this wasn't Blake, I decided. Was it Breughel? I remembered images of men with funnels for skulls and bodies with toads' faces. Then I found the name I was seeking: Hieronymus Bosch. Our boxcar showed nothing like his *Last Judgment,* and it was not in the same class with the preacher's picture of hell that sickened Stephen Dedalus. It would do, though, I thought, until the real thing came along.

Hemingway had once written derisively of "the comfortable stench of comrades." Unwashed for three months, we were an odoriferous group—not really stinking yet, though we soon would be if only from the atmosphere we breathed, fetid with our own gases. I slept fitfully to the sound of snores and clanking wheels. The stops seemed longer than the stretches of chugging movement. At last, with daylight, the doors were slid open for bread and coffee. The guard signaled us to exit. When Tag started to don his pack, the guard waved his arm in a gesture meaning no. "Just a comfort stop, men," Tag said. He and Ernie stamped and stretched. Ernie grunted as he rotated his upper body. "I'm not six feet two anymore," he groaned.

We walked into the fields. Toilet paper was nonexistent, and one cigarette pack would yield four wipes, not soft but usable. The meadow was transformed into a vast toilet. Fortunately, the wind that swept down from the ridge above was fragrant with winter grasses. The day was cold, but after the boxcar, probably smelling worse than from any intended cargo of eight horses, I dragged the keen wind avidly into my lungs.

Another day and night passed with increasing wretchedness. Twice the car was rocked as a train rocketed past us. From the fact that the Germans moved us only in darkness we could take comfort in the knowledge that the war was going badly for them. Forty-eight hours after we had boarded the cars, we climbed out in Nuremberg's marshaling yards, a complex I had first seen from an altitude of thirty thousand feet. We had come 250 kilometers as the crow flies, but our tortuous march from Sagan and our rail journey had covered much more. We had passed close to Bayreuth, where Wagner's Festspielhaus presented his *Ring des Nibelungen.*

Stalag XIII-D looked drably familiar with its double outer fences, huge rolls of wire, Deadline, and towers. But everything was larger than at Sagan, and there were slit trenches around the barracks. When darkness fell, we saw that there were more troops here, some of the guards holding leashed German shepherds. I wondered if Ernie would find an escape committee. He had never said what he found in Sagan.

It was clear that our standard of living would decline in every way. The dingy barracks were divided into six large bays, twenty-four bunks stacked in each of them. Each bay held a brick stove fitted with bits of tin to provide a chimney stack. Bill Fagan stood with his hands on his hips, shaking his head. Tag kicked the table. "What a dump," he said. "What a dump!"

The Four Horsemen of the Apocalypse had not bypassed Stalag XIII. War and Death we had already seen, with B-17s spiraling down in smoke and none of the ten parachutes billowing out. Now we could hear the hoofbeats of the other pale riders. Famine was not yet among us, just hunger, but we had reason to fear that Pestilence might not be far behind. We were not the first occupants of these barracks. We didn't know when Brown Shirts or Black Shirts had first jammed prisoners into them, but we blamed them for the residents left behind.

Tag's voice woke me from the bunk below. "Good Christ!" he said. Standing by the window, he pulled up his undershirt to reveal a belly speckled with red dots. "Bedbugs!" he said with a grimace.

Turning back the mattresses, we found their colonies under boards and in cracks in the wood. "Maybe I can drown some of the bastards," Tag said. Soon the inner fences along the main road were festooned with laundry. But he had failed to take one thing into account. By nightfall his long johns were far from dry, and in the morning he found that pants and shirt and socks had afforded no protection. Seated by the table, he looked at his leg, bemused.

"What did you find, Tag?" Ernie asked him.

"Eighty bites on my left leg," he said, "and that's not counting fleas."

I had always been susceptible to sunburn, poison ivy, and rashes, and now I found the vermin a torture. I didn't find as many red spots as Tag had. I just scratched and complained along with the others.

The next day, with what seemed to me a combination of German meticulousness and *Alice in Wonderland* logic, the goons marched us through one of the *Vorlager* buildings to check us against the cards with our photos and Kriegie numbers. We queued up at a table bearing file boxes of records. Seated behind it were *Hauptmann* Eisenmann and *Feldwebel* Eiler, looking a bit worn and a little haggard. I watched as they checked to be sure that Heinz Seltzman, the man in front of me, was the same second lieutenant who had been photographed months before. As I took his place, I saw no flash of recognition in the two men scrutinizing my card. Waved on, I moved ahead and waited as *Feldwebel* Eiler drew Tag's card from the file and handed it to Eisenmann. He studied it and then glanced at Tag.

"*Ja,*" he said and handed it back to Eiler, who passed his hand wearily over his forehead.

"*Ach,*" he said. "Seltzman, Blotner, und now Tag. Good German names."

Tag turned back toward him. "Hell, *Hauptmann,*" he said, "that's nothing. The whole air force is German!" Anything the *Hauptmann* said in reply was lost in the laughter.

The sun had come out, so we sat outside our barracks. I took off my socks and saw that the sulfa had done its work. Where there had been blood and swelling there were now the cicatrices of healing tissue. And the fingers that had been frostbitten looked and felt normal. But when I took out the pocket Shakespeare, I felt a new itch, in my armpit. Turning my shirt inside out, I checked the inseams. There they were, like tiny decorations along the stitches, myriad minuscule white lice. My God, I thought, like doughboys searching for cooties in France.

As our outsides suffered from too much, our insides suffered from too little. The bread and potato rations had been cut, and the Green Death was to most of us inedible. I kept my vow to bypass the *Blutwurst* no matter how ravenous I felt. The ersatz coffee was so bad that we began to believe the rumor that it was made from acorns. Some preferred shavings of black bread charred on the stove and then immersed in water to brew. We heard that one prisoner had steeled himself not to eat his share of pie one week and cake the next and then sold the four pieces for $135 each. How he protected his merchandise and then arranged the sale we didn't know.

In spite of stepped-up Allied air warfare, a small convoy of trucks made it through Nuremberg to Stalag XIII-D with a small supply of Red Cross parcels. But after a few more shipments, they stopped. We were surprised that any of them had gotten through. February 20 and 21 had brought daylight saturation raids. For about an hour and a half we watched B-17s flying majestically across the sky, group after group, their high white contrails pocked by the great bursts of black flak. I did not see fighters swarming down on them, and I never saw one dive or slide out of formation. Leaning on the windowsill at my side, Ernie said, "In three hours they'll be home."

Wistfully the Swede added, "Lucky bastards."

Ten days later there was a night show just as the camp lights were being extinguished. We heard the engines and then distant bomb blasts. A few minutes later somebody in the next bay with extraordinary night vision shouted, "They're Mosquitoes!" They came in one after another at low level, black-painted two-engine British bombers made largely of wood, fast and light. A few of them must have carried only a single bomb, but one big enough to produce a sequence of blasts that sucked the air out of the barracks and broke windows. "Willie!" said a voice behind me. "Down here!" It was Jake, from under a bunk where he crouched with several others. "Come on! Come on!" Willie stood gazing out the window at the searchlight beams seeking the low-flying Mosquitoes. Another of the big bombs, called "cookies" by the veterans, fell and brought down a shower of plaster. I could have sworn that one side of the barracks bulged. I made a dive to join Jake. "Willie!" he called again, but then there was only the drone of the departing swarm and the diminishing racket of the flak batteries.

The next day, men in the bay opposite us went to work, carefully loosening the shutters outside their windows so that they could carry them to the slit trenches for cover. Merg said, "That's a hell of a good idea." Prisoners were not permitted to leave the barracks during air raids, but Tag said, "The goons ain't gonna be out there playing games with us during a raid just to keep some idiot from killing himself trying to escape. Come on, I'll help you."

They had just started loosening the shutter hinges when they stopped, transfixed. "It's 51s," Tag shouted. Two Mustangs were drifting over the camp at three thousand feet, banking from side to side as if thumbing their sleek noses at the frantic flak gunners ineffectually pumping shells at them that exploded well behind the blast of their slipstreams. Tag shook his fist at the flak and shouted like a man whose team had just made a touchdown. "Where are your MEs?" he screamed. "Where are your fuckin' Focke-Wulfs?"

We were prepared to hear sirens every night. Between the noise and the attentions of the insects, I slept fitfully. By mid-March we began to wonder if other targets had received priority, but the night of the sixteenth showed that Nuremberg was still high on the list of RAF Bomber Command. An hour after our meager supper, we heard a stream of German from the loudspeaker. Tag cocked his head, cupping his ear. "It's the position and direction of the planes," he told us.

As we flung open the blackout shutters we could see the unfolding combat. At the edge of the city Pathfinders in the lead squadron were dropping two parallel rows of yellow flares that advanced toward us from the west. Following them came other Pathfinders dropping clusters of green flares within the yellow swath the first Pathfinders had outlined. "That gives them the Go!" shouted Grabowski.

From bomb-bay doors streams of explosives were falling. The yellow beams of crisscrossing searchlights knifed into the dark skies as bright splashes of flak shells sought the range of the rumbling bombers. Then enormous reverberations began to shake the camp as the first salvos pushed waves of sound toward us. Plaster fell as crockery smashed on the floor.

"Oh, Christ!" Fagan screamed. One window down from us the distant sky blazed with an unmistakable fireball. A Lancaster or a Halifax had disintegrated in flame. A minute later another exploded as the waves of aircraft kept coming, and now the blazes aloft were matched by massive fires soaring up from the targets below. The sirens were a thin scream in the cacophony. We were whelmed with sensory overload as the flak batteries fired as fast as they could reload and track another target.

"Hey, look!" Jake shouted to Fagan. "The flares!"

"It's the wind," Fagan told him. "It's shifted!"

I realized that the green flares were drifting toward us. I saw from the flak bursts that the bombers had shifted their course only slightly, but enough so that they would be dropping bombs on us if the raid lasted much longer, and there was no sign of its diminishing as new waves came in. We could hear a medley of shouts from the slit trenches. They were calling us to get out there where it would take a direct hit to kill us.

"Come on, Willie," Jake called out. "Let's go!"

"Wait!" Merg shouted. "Look!"

Then for the first time I heard Willie's voice, barely audible in the din. "What's happening?"

Looking out, I saw a cluster of red flares exploding from a new wave of bombers. "They're canceling it!" Merg said. "They won't start again until they see some more green when they're beyond us."

"Thank God!" Fagan said.

So now we continued to stare at the consuming pyrotechnics of the flaming blocks beyond the camp, at the searchlights and flak bursts in the golden corridor in the dark sky above. And still we saw the horrifying flame-edged silhouettes of bombers alight across their whole wingspans, fluttering down like falling leaves.

"Poor devils," Merg breathed.

"May God have mercy on their souls," Fagan said.

It wasn't until morning that I realized that this Walpurgis Night constituted another entry in my list of Times I Almost Got Killed. Then I saw the symmetry of it. My first mission to Nuremberg had been my introduction, and this one could have been my conclusion.

The early breeze wafted the smoke from burning buildings and last night's cordite stench. The goons skipped *Appell,* and volunteers began to work on walls of the slit trenches. "Let's go," Merg said.

"Wait," Larry said, pointing out the window. There, north of the camp, were gleaming spots of light. As they came closer we counted a flight of four P-38s, then three more. Suddenly they dove in a long swoop climaxed by bursts from the guns in the leading edges of their wings. One flight after another, they strafed the ground.

"What are they strafing?" Willie asked.

"Communications," Jake told him. "Anything that moves."

Three days later they were back, probably photographing the results of the recent strikes. A week after that, nine P-47s appeared. Even at about seven thousand feet we could see the bombs under the wings of the bullet-shaped fighters. Shock waves of bomb blasts reached us in their wake. Pillars of smoke rose from where they had been. Luke put his hands in his pockets and strutted away from the window. "*My* airplane," he said. Cokey gave him a raspberry.

On April 1 a carload of supplies from Switzerland was unloaded. There were cans of insect powder, khaki pants, barracks bags, and toilet articles.

"Christ," the Swede said, "safety pins."

"April Fool!" Merg said, picking up a can of the insect powder. "Slap this stuff on and quit yer bitchin'."

Two mornings later, as we were eating the toasted black bread and jam and drinking our rapidly diminishing powdered coffee, there was a knock at the door. Larry opened it to hear a voice down the hall. "Get your asses in gear," Captain Campbell shouted. "We hit the road again tomorrow morning!"

FIVE

The End of the Road

WE COULDN'T JUST SIT STILL AND WAIT TO BE LIB-
erated. We could try to escape, but the fluid conditions would make any attempt more difficult and dangerous than it would have been in Sagan. We
were undernourished and generally below par. Haid was almost totally bald
now. I still had to be careful to rise slowly after bending over so as not to pass
out, and I had lost another filling. As the food supply had dwindled, so had the
fuel supply. Some of the wash houses were now only skeletal, their roofs supported by vertical timbers, the boards on the sides removed in the night by
skillful thieves.

When we formed up in rows of three at 11:30 on the morning of April 4,
the snow had stopped and the temperature seemed right for early April. In
the pale spring sunshine we were heading southeast into Bavaria's first green-
ing. Two hours after passing through a town called Feucht we sat on a slight
rise and ate a skimpy lunch as we watched distant P-47 Thunderbolts dive-
bomb and strafe it. "That's exactly what we are," Tag said. "Feucht."

As I stretched and put my pack on, I looked ahead. Curving along the
road, our column stretched until it threaded through copses of faintly bud-
ding oak. I turned to look back and saw a mirror image of the one ahead.

"This is one big column," I said to Ernie. "How long do you think it is?"

"I'll guess five miles anyway," he said.

"What I want to know is," said the Swede, "where are we going to sleep
tonight?"

"Probably in some deluxe barn," Merg told him. "You'll like it, just like
this country air. It's good for you."

"I've had enough of this hike already," the Swede said, "and it's not even
dark yet."

By the time we did stop, at a small town with a sign labeled Polling, it was full dark. In spite of the long day on the road, there was not a great deal of griping. The barn was roomy, and the hay almost fragrant.

"See? What did I tell you?" Merg said.

"I know one thing," Larry said. "I think the bugs are gone."

By the time we were back on the road in the bright morning sun of April 5, groups from the rear had begun to overtake us, men we hadn't seen since Sagan. When we stopped for a break at Neumarkt, I saw Red Baird.

"Have you got the other guys with you?" I asked him.

"Hell, no," he said. "They decided to see what they could scrounge."

"Good for them, but the major gave strict orders that we're supposed to stay with the column."

"Yeah. You know why?" Red asked. "Some of our guys got strafed at Feucht along with whatever the target was. Troops are moving faster than intelligence can keep up with them."

"Guys killed?"

"That's what they say."

Just then, sounds we had been hearing materialized into aircraft, not 47s or 38s but more distant B-17s. About fifteen miles southeast of Nuremberg we had seen their work. The freight yards were pocked with bomb craters. Railroad ties had been blasted into kindling. One length of track surmounted a peaked roof as if a mischievous child tired of his train set had thrown it there. A dozen men had taken what miscellaneous scraps of white cloth they could find to a small cleared field to fashion into the letters POW. A mile away the group lead had dropped his bombs and the smoke markers that told the others where their five-ton loads should fall. A moment later the group's lead squadron swept toward us with open bomb-bay doors. The P-47s and P-51s ranged all around them. I saw civilians from Neumarkt fleeing into the woods. Soon the 17s were gone again, even before the contrails had begun to dissipate like veils blown by the spring breeze. The fighters had seen our sign, and after circling above us they cut away for another target.

We camped in the woods until nightfall and began getting organized to resume the march. Ernie's watch said eight o'clock. By the time the column was on the road, the rain had begun.

"Damn," Fagan said. "I wish I had a slicker instead of this coat. If this keeps up it's going to weigh a ton."

"Get used to it," Tag said.

Six hours later, long since wet to the skin, the column stopped for one of the ten-minute breaks. "Seven and a half miles of drowned rats," Red said.

"I'll tell you one thing," Tag said, wringing out his improvised headgear. "This column ain't going to be that long tomorrow."

"What do you mean?" Larry asked.

"Didn't you see those guys slipping away during the night?"

"I didn't hear any shots from the guards," Larry said.

"Those poor bastards have enough trouble staying on their feet without unlimbering their rifles." Ernie told him. "They're twice as old as you are."

"I feel like they look," Larry said.

By two in the morning the rain had stopped. Twelve hours later and thirteen miles from Neumarkt, we halted at Berching, another small Bavarian town. Again most of us were billeted in barns. Fagan and some dozens of others found space in the pews and aisles of the Catholic church, but it was so crowded that they were glad to move out into the cemetery as soon as the sun came out. Red and Tag and I found them there.

"Listen," Fagan said, "I've got an idea. Why don't we go to confession?"

Tag laughed. "What'll I say? 'Bless me, Father, for I have sinned. It has been a year and an half since my last confession'?"

"Why not?" Fagan said.

Together we found the weary-looking priest and tried to explain our visit. He shook his head and began to speak labored English. Then he gave it up, pointed at us, and tapped his chest with his fist. *"Mea culpa, mea culpa,"* he said, then clasped his hands as if in prayer. We thanked him and left with a dumb show of understanding.

We had better luck with other efforts. The word had come down that we were free to trade, so we knocked on doors to barter and beg. Our stock was cigarettes and chocolate, coffee and tea, which we traded for eggs and potatoes we could fry over campfires in our Klim-can utensils. Red's German was more effective than Tag's or mine, and his *"Dankeschön, Grossmutter"* seemed to combine gratitude and affection. The housewives appeared to warm to him immediately, and I was unprepared for some of the emotional responses in these encounters. Other marchers had been to some of these doors before us, and when the lady had nothing left to trade she might explain apologetically, *"Zu viele Kameraden."*

On our last try we were just about to leave when the door opened. She must have been sixty, another stout *Grossmutter*, her white hair pulled into a small bun. She had only two eggs left to trade, and she said she was sorry she had no more. Then she paused and told us to sit down at her kitchen table. From the back of her black wood stove she brought thick white soup plates. As we watched, salivating, she filled them with dark steaming sauerkraut and broth. I had never tasted better. From her cupboard she drew a thick round loaf of dark *Bauernbrot*. Holding it under her arm against her ample waist, she cut for each of us an eight-inch slice, thin on one end and thick on the other. It was more than delicious. As Red gave her elaborate thanks, I looked at black-framed photographs over the fireplace. There were two handsome boys, smart in their black uniforms. Below each was the hard-to-read German gothic script. I made out one as *"Gefallen im Westen."* The other read *"Gefallen im Osten."* Were they sons? I wondered. Grandsons? Brothers? As I turned quickly to leave, I impulsively kissed her on the cheek.

We plodded dispiritedly through small farm hamlets, sodden again, through the deepening dusk. It was becoming harder to spot the puddles and sloughs of ankle-deep mud before we sloshed into them. It was almost midnight when we saw barns again, on the outskirts of Barnsdorf. We had covered fifteen miles in ten hours, and we collapsed in the hay. All the next day we stayed there. We improvised clotheslines and rested. Every part of me ached.

The sun came out the next morning, Sunday, April 8, and we set out again. Moving slowly along our route was an incongruous figure, a German nurse on a bicycle patrolling the line. When we passed her, she was treating angry red sores on a prisoner's feet. We continued southeast all day and crossed a small river. Ernie checked the rough map he had made.

"It doesn't look very damn blue to me," he said.

"Why should it?" Larry asked him.

"Well, it ought to," Ernie said. "Didn't you see that sign back there? It's the Danube." Looking at that muddy stream and remembering the way my teacher Miss Lissenden had drilled me on that waltz, I felt somehow cheated.

We continued south into Neustadt, feeling keenly the hostile stares of the people lining the main street. "A hell of a lot different from Berching," I said to Red.

"I'll tell you something," Red said. "You still think we're going to Berchtesgaden, don't you?"

"I never bought that scenario."

"Good, because I'll tell you where we *are* going. We would have turned east from Nuremberg to get there. We're heading south, to a Stalag near Munich."

"How the hell did you learn all this?"

"I listened, buddy, I listened."

"To what? We haven't had any Sammy since Sagan." The transmissions from our jerry-built secret radio didn't bring in much, but when the barracks blackout curtains were drawn and the courier began his recital with "Sammy says," we knew we would get more than we did from the canned bulletins of the *Oberkommado der Wehrmacht*.

"No. But the staff had been getting McGuffy—just as much BBC as Sammy. And McGuffy says Patton's Third Army is northeast of Munich."

"Wow! OK, then. Where the bloody hell are we going?"

"To Stalag VII-A."

"Where's that?"

"In Moosburg, twenty-five miles north of Munich. Now, it's not just a Stalag Luft, and all the goddam POWs in the ETO will be there."

I still felt more than ever that our lives were governed by some uncertainty principle, that we never knew what lay beyond the next hill. We saw the principle in operation after we marched through the outskirts of the city. In the distance were flights of 47s and 51s. We could see them diving and heard the sound of strafing and frag bombs. Then as we spilled into a large field, I smelled something wonderful. It was goulash. A three-man German detail was pouring a modest ladleful for each man, and at that moment I was back in my bedroom at our old Remington Standard typing out Dad's menu: "Hungarian Goulash . . .35¢." Another food detail appeared, cutting off an eighth of a loaf of black bread and ladling out three boiled potatoes per man. At almost the same moment I saw a detail of Americans rushing out toward the center of the field and spreading the makeshift POW sign. Just as the last letter was formed, the fighters zoomed overhead, but no one dropped his goulash to flee. We looked up, spoons suspended.

"At least they know where we are now," Jake said.

"Don't be too sure," Tag said as he resumed eating. "Don't you remember what the Eighth and Ninth did before the breakout in Normandy?"

"What?"

"They flew close support of the infantry—killed a thousand and wounded five hundred more."

"Way to go!"

"The ones they got were *ours*, you dumb bastard!"

The fighters circled back, then disappeared quickly. "Whew!" Jake said.

In the meadow behind our barn ran a stream from the flower-covered hill. The clear water was too cold for immersion, but it did for our skins what the goulash had done for our stomachs. It said, "For this moment, your life is normal again—no dirt and no lice." It was my first bath in six months, and I was glad we hadn't used all of our soap for barter.

The next day we passed the tall poles of the hop fields, and I thought of the Bavarian beer Dad and I used to drink at the kitchen table. We saw not just the churches in the towns but also the wayside shrines with figures that looked as though they had been carved by peasant artists. I remembered D. H. Lawrence's distaste at the sight of the crucified Christ. The bunches of wildflowers placed there by the devout somehow emphasized the contrast between the rebirth of the burgeoning spring and the agony of the dead god. I tried to feel the appropriate devotional response, to utter prayers along these peasant Stations of the Cross. I think one thing that underlay my emotions was actually cautious joy that I was still alive in this precarious springtime.

By nightfall on April 11, we had the sense that the pace of events was accelerating. A sign with an arrow pointing south read, "Moosburg 10.5 KM."

"That's it," Red said, "Stalag VII-A."

In the absence of immediate orders to march, we pitched another makeshift camp, and foragers headed out into the surrounding countryside. We saw bombers and smoke markers as far away as the horizon in five separate attacks. In the late afternoon Red and Luke returned with their proceeds: bread, eggs, and matches.

"Some of it I can't show you," Red said. "The ladies were sisters, and one's husband is a POW in Russia. Before we left she asked me if I would like a drink. She poured something out of a stone jug."

"How was it?" Tag asked him.

"I was glad I was sitting down when I was drinking it. I don't care what it was. I've had a bath and now a drink, and I'm beginning to feel human again," Red said.

I woke to fragrant woodsmoke. We had made camp between a friendly farmer's house and his barn, Ernie had a fire going, and we sat on logs and watched Fagan fry potatoes and eggs while we toasted bread on sharpened sticks. Red had even thought to trade for salt. He produced sugar, and Larry boiled water for coffee.

"Where's the cream?" Tag asked.

"How ya fixed for spit?" Larry replied.

For a few minutes there was silence except for crunching on the black bread and the scraping of our German army utensils on the Klim-can plates. We leaned back against the logs and lit up. Tag exhaled a long plume of smoke. "Not bad," he said, "not bad."

"Amen," Ernie said.

We would be moving again soon, and as I got up to check my pack, Merg walked into our circle.

"Did you hear the news?" he asked.

"What news?" Ernie asked.

"Roosevelt died, and Truman's been sworn in." A few others joined us as he gave us the details that had come in via McGuffy.

"Who's Truman?" Grabowski asked.

"The vice president," Red said.

"I know that! I mean, what's he done?"

Ernie told him about Truman's Senate career and the Truman Committee, but the rest of us had little to add. There was a sense of surprise but not shock among us. Although much of Roosevelt's physical condition had been concealed from the public, we knew that he was old and that he had been under great strain for years. I had meant to vote for him, but I hadn't received my absentee ballot. I felt no personal sense of loss. He had been elected when I was nine and had been a kind of fixed pole in my sense of the American political universe. The most intense responses to him that I could remember came from the animus of well-to-do fathers of my high school friends. His death now was a distant event, far overshadowed by our own immediate situation.

Our muted conversation was interrupted by Cokey. "Come on, you guys," he said. "We're hitting the road for Moosburg." So my memory of the death of our thirty-second president would be only a scene like a tableau—men sitting on the hay of a German farmyard in the aroma of woodsmoke, a bit meditative but preparing to march again.

It was Friday the thirteenth, but I felt nothing ominous about this ninth day on the road. Moosburg was ninety miles south of Nuremberg. If there hadn't been the occasional guards with their rifles, it would have seemed a lark, under blue Bavarian skies with white apple blossoms dotting the road and robins' calls rippling from the branches. The column had been growing, and in a curious way I found myself resenting this addition of men who hadn't been with us all the way, though many of them had probably been behind the wire longer than I had.

"Where did all these guys come from?" Tag asked.

"They're from other camps," Red said. "McGuffy says that because the Allies are coming in from both directions, the Krauts are evacuating some camps before they're overrun."

"This morning I even saw a guy with an infantry shoulder patch," Fagan said.

"There goes the neighborhood," Tag said.

We had ascended a long hill, and when we crested it we saw a vast stalag in a cleared space beyond a cordon of firs. There were the familiar barbed wire and guard towers, and there were blocks of tents as well as barracks. Here were more men than I had seen in one place since the Saturday-morning parades at preflight school in Santa Ana. It made me think of an enormous anthill. There were slit trenches like those at Nuremberg, reinforced with logs at intervals at the side and the top. Near some of the barracks were the signs of cooking combines ranging from spits over ashes to elaborate Klim-can stoves and jiffy blowers with hand-cranked propellers that blew into a firebox.

"I'm going to case the barracks," Ernie said. He ducked into one and re-turned quickly. "They haven't got enough bunks," he reported. Making our way through the center of the camp, we saw the same conditions repeated.

"What a dump," Tag said.

Now we were moving toward the northern corner of the camp where large tents took the place of barracks.

"There must be three hundred men in that one," Tag said.

"Come on over here," Ernie said and led us off to a smaller tent close to the Deadline. "Throw down your stuff," he told us. When we did, a dozen of us had our own space near the rear opening. "It'll be a breezy hike to the la-trine," he said, "but we'll be able to breathe something besides our own smell."

Red found us, and we made room for him. "Don't worry about rations," he said. "Moosburg is the supply center for Red Cross parcels in southern Germany. They've been handing out a parcel per man per week." We would receive our parcels in a day or two, and late that afternoon one German detail supplied bread, potatoes, and soup. Another followed them with wurst, cheese, and margarine.

"Maybe a Swiss inspection team is due," Merg said.

"If that's it, I certainly admire the Krauts' respect for the Geneva Con-vention," Larry said.

"Like I told you," Tag said, "they're looking ahead to the end of this war."

Walking in the twilight, we saw an international mix. There were Brits from the RAF, Americans from ground force units, and uniforms we didn't recognize. "Who the hell are those jokers?" Luke asked, looking at a slope in a cordoned-off area where half a dozen men stood smoking. Some looked to be in their sixties, and their long unbuttoned overcoats revealed red linings.

"It's the Palace Guard of Ruritania," Cokey said.

"What?" said Fagan.

"Yes," Cokey said, "the court of King Rudolf Friml the First."

Red smiled. "He's not so far wrong. It's the general staff of the Yugosla-vian army."

"Where the hell do you get this stuff?" Fagan asked him.

"I ask questions, my boy," said Red.

The guard towers were manned, but we saw no leashed dogs near the Deadline. Not far from one of the towers stood a cluster of prisoners. We got close enough to see a Luftwaffe lieutenant at its center. He was not giving orders but talking casually in colloquial English. When he walked away, Tag asked a man what the lieutenant had said. "He told us how he got here," the man said. "He lived in the States for a while and then decided to come back here, but he picked the wrong time, and they drafted him before he could return home."

"That's real T.S.," Tag said. "He'll be OK. This is not bad duty. He's not in the ranks, and he should be able to talk himself into some sort of deal if our army gets here first."

Walking back through the tents, we sensed a general loosening of discipline. The ratio of prisoners to guards had increased, and though much of the activity followed familiar patterns such as drawing water from the spigots by the latrines, there were new ones such as going outside the gate under guard to gather firewood. Much of the activity was social, looking for friends from Sagan and Nuremberg and trying to find out about men who had been flying combat when we last saw them. In a way these last months had recapitulated that familiar army experience. When you shipped out from one place heading for another, you inevitably left behind people you knew well, but you soon formed new associations. This was simply what happened in the army, and it made me think of my freshman sociology text.

More powerful in memory, though, was *The Grapes of Wrath* for the way Steinbeck's Joad family embodied processes of fusion and then dissolution. I thought of their exodus from drought-ravaged Oklahoma for the road that led to California, with new microsocieties formed each night at the roadside camps and forming again each morning into smaller units. As the Joads dwindled from their original thirteen, so our Sagan group changed and shrank. Somewhere in this last move we had lost track of Grabowski and the Swede. Willie and Jake had become an even closer unit of two. Jake had proved an expert at bartering and scrounging on the road. Here in Moosburg they had wound up in another tent. Merg had found fellow Californians from the past, just as Luke had found fellow Chicagoans. We were glad that Fagan and Larry still ran our cooking combine. Tag still showed the resilience that had carried him through being shot down and attacked by civilians in the rubble of his bomb drop. He looked as if he had actually put on weight on the march from Nuremberg. Growing round-faced again, he was almost an embodiment of the spirit of survival. And Ernie and I had found that we had more in common than our diverse backgrounds would have made likely.

The promising early spring had turned into a cold April, and Ernie proved to be a good buddy in a familiar army way. For mattresses we had wood shavings on the tent's dirt floor. We each put one of our two blankets on the shavings and the other on top of us. Fully dressed in OD shirt and pants, flight jacket, and overcoat, I was still cold in our now crowded tent.

"Damn this weather!" I said.

"You said it," Ernie grumbled. "But wait a minute. Let's sleep spoon fashion." I had never slept in the same bed with another man, let alone in spoon fashion, but the increased warmth dispelled the sense of oddness. It became comic when I turned over and saw that there were six of us in a row like horizontal toy soldiers. The last one on the left, I began to laugh.

"What's so funny?" Ernie said.

"I wonder who's Lucky Pierre?" I said, but Ernie was already asleep.

The process of accretion continued too. Steve Middlebrook, an infantryman blown out of a personnel carrier and miraculously suffering only a concussion, knew the same parts of New Jersey I did. Henry Greenberg, inevitably called Hank, was the son of a Brooklyn druggist. His dark hair and neatly trimmed moustache made him look like a gigolo rather than a veteran bombardier. A reader like me, he introduced me to the world of Yiddish words and phrases. He loaned me a paperback edition of Arthur Kober's *My Dear Bella*, and I loaned him my paperback Shakespeare.

We hadn't seen Major Saunders or Captain Campbell since our arrival in Moosburg. There was no daily *Appell* for us in Stalag VII-A, and I wondered without regret what those two were doing now. I never wondered what became of *Hauptmann* Eisenmann or *Feldwebel* Eiler. By now they might have traveled west too if they were lucky or been transferred into a combat unit if they weren't. The Germans were scraping the bottom of the barrel now, pressing into battle the teenagers of the Hitler *Jugend* and the grandfathers of the *Landsturm*.

On another walk near our tent around the perimeter where the Deadline still exacted its sinister respect, Tag and Red and I encountered another group like the one we had seen a few days before. At its center was a German officer, and it was not hard to see him from the outer fringe of the Americans encircling him. We sidled closer and listened.

"He's bigger than I am," Tag said, and he was—burly in his shiny leather greatcoat. His jowls bulged out over his jacket collar with its major's tabs, and below his high-peaked blue Luftwaffe cap his cropped black hair emerged above a shaven neck. His cheeks were red with laughter.

"He looks like Oliver Hardy," Red said.

"What's he laughing about?" I wondered.

"He said he's not worried about the end of the war."

"Ask him why," I said.

The officer fixed Red in his genial gaze. "I vill tell you," he said. "Ten minutes after the end, I vill be an American prisoner." He joined in his audience's laughter.

"What'll you do after that?" Tag asked him.

"I haf a cousin in the leather business. I vill move to Zin-zinn-ati and become an American!" Shaking with laughter, he waved and moved off.

A day later, as we sat on wood shavings outside the tent flap in the warming sun, Red said, "I think the major knew what he was talking about."

"Why?"

"Listen to that." A distant hum grew louder and closer. As I was about to sprint for a slit trench, two ME-109s came hedge-hopping over the fir trees beyond the wire. There wasn't time to run. Instinctively, I rolled over and shielded my head from the enormous roar. These fighters were almost as close as the Marine Corsairs that had buzzed us during that Saturday-morning review at Santa Ana.

"Goddam!" Ernie said. "They're gonna kill somebody that way."

"Yeah, us!" Tag said.

"They're flying low so those high 38s won't spot them," Red said.

"That makes three days in a row," Larry said. "MEs or Focke-Wulfs."

Ernie stood up and brushed shavings off his pants. "I'll tell you something," he said. "You may not have noticed, but there aren't as many goons around now as last week."

"Are you going to make a break for it?" I asked him.

He laughed. "We talked about it, but we never got the chance in Sagan," he said, "and now we don't need to."

"Yeah," Tag agreed, "all you'll have to do is keep from getting your ass shot off when they have the shootout at high noon."

That night we heard a rumble in the northwest. "That's artillery," Ernie said.

We heard it again the next night. As we stood outside the tent for a last cigarette we could see flashes. Ernie timed the interval. "That's not much more than five miles away," he said.

During the day we could look up and see the groups of heavies to the south going over in strength. McGuffy told us that they were hitting Munich, thirty miles away, and B-26 groups were plastering smaller cities to the south and west.

"That's my airplane!" Tag said, raising a clenched fist.

"You wish you were up there in the wild blue with them again, don't you," Larry said, smiling.

"My ass I do," Tag answered. "Fifteen missions were enough for me. I wouldn't want to press my luck."

I had trouble falling asleep. From time to time I would hear the scratch of a match. I saw a figure at the tent opening as the flare lit up his profile against the darkness. I settled down to try to go back to sleep. When I woke later that night from an uneasy dream, the distant murmur was muted but almost continuous.

After a hasty breakfast of coffee and bread, Red and I made our way to the latrine. The man ahead of him in line took a last drag that left barely enough of the cigarette to hold. "Whaddya think, Red?" he asked him.

"I think that if that artillery keeps on like it's doing, I'm gonna be lucky to make it to the latrine next time."

Ernie was standing there when we came outside. "Let's walk," he said. We joined the pacers making their way along, just inside the Deadline. Almost all the uniforms in the line seemed to be OD, with only a few figures in the Luftwaffe blue. They walked in twos, their rifles slung on their shoulders. We hadn't seen them with guard dogs since we left Nuremberg.

"Where are all the goons?" I asked.

"Don't jump to conclusions," Ernie said. "They're still up there." He gestured toward the guard tower ahead, where two steel-helmeted figures, their heads close together, looked to be deep in conversation.

"Where do you think their lieutenant is?" I asked. "What is he doing this morning?"

"Telling his troubles to Jesus," Red said.

The day dragged on. We walked again, but after a while I'd had enough of that. There was nothing to do to damp down the tension of the waiting. I picked up my tattered Shakespeare, its covers gone now, and tried to get into *Henry V,* but I couldn't concentrate. Tag and the others took a blanket outside and sat around it playing cards and smoking.

Just then we heard the sound of single-engine aircraft, but we knew we didn't have to duck. Tag spotted them.

"LC-5s," he shouted, pointing at two olive drab–painted monoplanes with white stars on their wings. They descended, buzzing the camp and rolling from side to side as they passed over us. We stood up and waved.

"Go get 'em, you guys!" Tag shouted. For an instant time raced backward, and I was a child standing on our lawn again, looking up and shouting, "Hey, Lindy! Gimme a ride!" This is where that foolishness got you, said a voice inside my head. We cheered and waved and waited for them to come back.

"They're artillery spotters," Tag said. "They're sending Kraut positions back to the batteries."

"I hope to hell they get them right," Ernie said.

Now when we walked near the perimeter, there were no blue Luftwaffe uniforms among the ODs.

On April 27 we heard more firing, but not close enough to prompt the impulse to dash for the slit trench. During the afternoon there were sporadic bursts. When Red came back to the tent at noon, he had checked with his sources.

"What the hell's going on?" Fagan asked, handing him a slice of toasted bread and cheese.

"Our guys are already closing in on Moosburg," Red said. "The Luftwaffe guards want to get out of here, but there are SS troops trying to hold the line. So they've got quite a firefight going on—with each other."

"Stupid bastards," Tag said. "They'll just get themselves killed all the sooner."

"That's the SS," Ernie said, "but we'll see who's still here in the morning."

In the light of day it was neither the black-clad SS nor the blue-clad Luftwaffe. "They've taken off!" Larry shouted from the tent opening.

When Red came back later, he said he thought the Luftwaffe guards were managing to withdraw. In the center of the camp were goons who looked to be cleaning out records and stores. "Those sonsabitches," Red said. "There go our Red Cross parcels they kept for themselves!"

It was Sunday morning, April 29, and we could hear the artillery, just north-northwest of us over the hill, laying down fire, probably to soften up remaining SS strong points. It was a temptation to move from the tent toward the main gate of the camp. I looked up to see Fagan and beside him Larry striding out.

"Where are you going?" I asked.

"To mass," Fagan said. "Want to come?"

I realized that my piety had diminished in direct proportion to my sense of potential danger. Later I learned the name for my pusillanimous state. I was a foxhole Catholic.

"I'll pass," I said. They went on while the rest of us lay low there by the tent, and once again we heard not only the chattering machine guns but rifle fire too, and once more the whine like those of the bullets that had flung me into the snowdrift on our midnight march from Stalag Luft III.

They were back in less than an hour. "It got pretty hairy," Fagan explained. "Just before the end of mass there were bullets whistling through the recreation field. When the priest said, '*Ite, missa est,*' I thought to myself, what he's really saying is, 'Go, *you* are finished'!"

Just then Red was back again, pushing aside the tent flap, red-faced and puffing. "Come on," he said, "they're here!"

"Who?" I asked.

"The whole fucking Fourteenth Armored Division, that's who!"

As if leading the van, an LC-5 appeared from the west at about three hundred feet. He had barely completed his circuit of the camp when the chugging sound of his small engine was drowned out by the roar of two P-51s. Not content with merely buzzing the camp, they zoomed off, then returned, pulled up, and did victory rolls over the main barracks. Now another sound entered the medley, the rumble and clanking of tanks. We headed for the main gate but saw that we wouldn't be able to get near it. We stopped where we were, five hundred yards away in the shadow of a guard tower built on a slight rise. We watched the mass of men extending from inside the wire back to the main road, swelling as others streamed there from all over the camp. Instead of parting to make way, the mob grew as the first jeeps drove past the wire and into the camp. After them came the Shermans, but on each armored monster we could see only the cannon barrel poking out of the turret and the machine gun beside it. All the rest was covered with shouting, waving, cheering Kriegies. Two more jeeps came through and after them a command car with flags fluttering on the bumpers. Standing in the front, grasping the windshield, was a familiar figure. Even at our distance I could see the stars on his helmet and the ivory-handled pistols at his waist—General George S. Patton, leading the spearhead of his Third Army. The cheering of the massed soldiers swelled until it drowned the tanks' rumble.

The whole immense column moved forward slowly along the road and away to our right toward the center of Stalag VII-A. Now we noticed activity down to our left around the main building inside the wire just beyond the Deadline. Out of the crowd at the base of the large flagpole emerged a single figure. It was a skinny American who grasped the pole with arms and legs and started shinnying upward, one lunge after another. When his painful progress ended at the top, he fumbled to extract something from his jacket. He reached out and grasped the halyard line and drew it to him. He detached the hateful red and black flag with its swastika and dropped it into the crowd below.

From his belt he pulled the flag we would learn he had carried since Sagan. He attached it to the halyard, and a second later the Stars and Stripes soared to flutter in the breeze. My throat was tight. Around me I was conscious of men cheering with tears running down their cheeks. I realized that mine were wet, too.

At last and finally, we were liberated. Within limits, we were free.

SIX

Return and Reentry

For the rest of that sunny sunday afternoon of April 29, Hank and Red and Tag and I roamed over Stalag VII-A. The whole scene reminded me of an open-air market or a county fair, with the same hum of voices, the same air of possibility and excitement and intoxication. It was the freedom that was intoxicating. Kriegie Brew had been attempted in the stalags without much success. There was neither grain for mash nor enough potatoes to try for vodka. It may have been just as well for this undernourished clientele. It would take time for us to adjust even to normal eating. Among the field rations the Fourteenth Armored Division had left after they roared off to liberate other camps was white bread that tasted like cake. Even the air seemed to feed appetites starved for change and diversion—not just the smells of the warm Bavarian spring but also the scents of cooking fires made different from our own by foreign food parcels.

As we walked, we could tell when we were among the Brits, their uniforms only slightly different from ours. There were troops out of *Lives of a Bengal Lancer,* though, with shorts and rolled-up sleeves and neat turbans above elaborate beards. From up ahead came a high-pitched skirling at the upper edge of human hearing. It was generated by two men whose cheeks puffed out as they fingered dark pipes depending from an inflated bag. Others in tartans danced on an improvised platform. They struck stylized poses, juxtaposed arms aloft. Their feet executed careful movements with a finicky precision in the spaces between crossed weapons. It was a sword dance with bayonets rather than dirks and claymores. Men were passing us, bent on "liberating" the spoils of battle. Hank had been behind the wire longer than I, and he set off with Red and Tag to take advantage of this opportunity as well.

Back at the tent, Larry was tending to the fire and Fagan to the food. He had saved black bread from the daily ration and mixed broken-up slices of it with water and our remaining raisins. We waited impatiently for the others to return for supper. When they did, Tag showed us a ceremonial sword with an engraved eagle and braided cord at the hilt. "I may wear it to American Legion meetings," he said.

Red had found the POW records in the main building. "Here," he said, handing me a card with a photo on it. It was the mug shot the goons had taken, my *Kriegsgefangennummer* neatly lettered beneath it. In my wrinkled shirt and dirty flight jacket I looked as I remembered feeling: tired, dirty, and sorry for myself.

"*Achtung!*" came a voice from outside the tent. "*Ich habe zurück kommen!* I have returned!"

"Who the hell is that?" asked Tag.

Outside the tent by the open flap stood a man in a rakishly tilted German helmet, leaning on a stick with a cigarette dangling from his lips. "*Oberst* von Stroheim, at your service," he said, clicking his heels. "At ease," he added. "No need to salute." It was Hank. "All the good stuff was gone," he said, "but I thought this would remind you of old times." It was a flat metal case holding the compasses and protractors of a German aerial navigation set.

The next morning, some of us still having difficulty digesting the hearty U.S. Army fare, we boarded trucks to an airfield. There the propellers of two transports were already turning over. It was fine to feel the old vibration as we prepared to taxi out to the runway. The plane stopped for the final runup and then began moving again.

"We're airborne!" Tag shouted. It was exhilarating, like the delight of an unexpected day off from school. We wore no oxygen masks or headsets, no flak jackets or Mae Wests, just what we had left from the marches, looking like shabby tourists. Our course was a straight flight to the great embarkation port at Le Havre. Some of these passengers had not been aloft in months or even years, so the stench of vomit permeated that bumpy low-altitude flight from Germany to France. The countryside presented a postcard vista with the poplar-bordered roads running beside carefully tended vineyards. Applause broke out at the screech of the tires on the runway. The air was fresh and clear, and I breathed it in deeply. Aboard the open trucks again, we lit up as we headed for Camp Lucky Strike.

Hank and Ernie and I made our way up behind the cab and stood there where the glorious spring breeze fanned our uncut hair. Passing through the villages, we were greeted like heroes by cheering shopkeepers and waving children. Hank struck poses as he waved, a mixture of General de Gaulle and the Queen Mother. Suddenly I heard a grunt beside me and saw him staggering back just as we passed a flower-laden group of young schoolgirls. He was brushing at his face and chest.

"Goddamit!" he growled. "Somebody ought to make them take the blossoms off the branches before they throw them!"

Lucky Strike looked more like a city than an army camp. As part of Project R (for repatriation), we were first thoroughly deloused. Then there were medical checkups and gloriously hot showers. We were issued new clothing and barracks bags. In a week we were at the embarkation docks that still bore the scars of fighting. Ten days later we were walking up the wide gangway of the USS *Michigan Victory*, the American flag rippling at her stern.

We lugged our barracks bags along the gray decks and down the narrow ladders, filing into a narrow space filled with skeletal four-bed bunks. "Hey!" Tag said. "There's been a mistake. Where's our stateroom?"

"Room 12 was better than this," Fagan said.

"Well," I said, looking out into the passageway, "at least we're close to the latrine."

"They call it the head," Fagan said.

"Have you ever been at sea in rough weather?" Ernie asked. "You may be glad to be this close to the head."

Back on deck we watched the crews unloading lighters and operating cranes to raise cargo from the dock and deposit it near the gaping holds for storage.

"You think there's any chance of getting into town?" Hank asked.

"I guess he wants to look for the USO," Red said.

"Man, you don't know how long I've been away from feminine society," Hank told him.

"You're not going to find any here, soldier," Ernie said.

The roll of the ship got us out of our bunks before chow on Wednesday morning, May 15. There were ships as far as I could see, old Liberty ships that had carried Lend-Lease cargo to Britain since 1941, a few survivors of the deadly Murmansk run, and Victory ships replacing those sent to the bottom by U-boats.

At sea we would occasionally glimpse a camouflaged destroyer or a converted flattop carrying patrol aircraft to spot submarines. Sometimes we saw corvettes throwing up white bow waves as they sliced through the slow formations, depth charges poised on their decks to be flung overboard if the pinging of sonar raised the threat of U-boats.

"I'm glad they don't hunt in packs anymore," Pat Patillo said.

"All it takes is one," Ernie said.

After breakfast we would go on deck, a fine opportunity for poker games, with scores to be settled after we reached the USA and drew our back pay. The play of light on the water was brilliant, with the colors changing hourly and the deep blue of the skies reflected around us. When the sea turned to a steel gray, I had a memory of Herman Melville's description of the myriad shapes that moved in the ocean's depths. We would shout to one another not to miss the cavorting porpoises gleaming blackly in racing arabesques of power and grace like a corps de ballet.

On afternoons when the sun was strong we would strip down to shorts and lie there at ease on the deck. And we read. I finished working my way through my paperback Shakespeare and scanned the grab bag of Armed Forces paperbacks, where I found an unmarked copy of *Death in Venice*. In college I had felt adventurous reading Joyce, and now, in the company of Mann's Gustave von Aschenbach, I knew that I was moving into another realm.

By the end of the third week of May the ocean had begun to show its power. The ship was pitching and rolling, and the traffic to the head had increased steadily. The flow of fresh air remained constant but was increasingly tainted. The simple act of walking became a challenge. One day, as the convoy made its way through heavy swells and thickening fog, there was a sudden cacophony. The lead ships had collided with icebergs in a chaos of foghorns. Sixteen of them were damaged by the lurking white masses or by other ships changing course abruptly to avoid them.

At last the sea birds were joined by land birds. The fringe of ships on the horizon thickened with coastal vessels. Then, in the last days of May, the continent began to emerge, a thin pale line in the distant haze. There was nothing romantic in the sight of Brooklyn and Staten Island, but a sight gradually materialized to move even the most hardened. Up between the Narrows and into the Upper Bay we glided to the medley of a spring thunderstorm and piping toots from skippers saluting homecoming troopships. The storm gave way to haze, and from it emerged a mythic form, a queenly woman with an upraised arm. My throat contracted again as it had done that day when the American flag rose over Moosburg. In this instant the Statue of Liberty was not just a monument but also a great emblematic presence.

The docks and wharves of Bayonne and Elizabeth, the oil tanks and factories with their iridescent smears on the water, reminded me that there was no prettifying Newark Bay, even under the bright sun that had followed the rain. I was almost back in my native state, a few miles from the factories where summer jobs had provided money for college. My face must have reflected my reactions to this change from the majesty of our initial arrival. Hank drew deeply on his cigarette. "Look up there," he said, gesturing toward the northeast where the gleaming shafts of the Empire State Building and the Chrysler Building pierced the clouds. "It ain't so bad, Joe," he said with a smile.

Men were waving at the dock as the engines were revved in reverse. Braided hawsers were tossed out and wrapped around the stubby stanchions to warp us fast to the dock. Over the rattle of the gangway rose the shouts of men calling out to wives and sweethearts and friends. Ernie waved furiously at a short, pretty woman holding a small child. "Winnie!" he shouted. "Winnie!" Crying, she waved the child's small arm up at her father. Ernie cried too, shouting their names.

Our convoy of trucks gradually picked up speed as we passed buildings that hadn't been there before. Then at last we pulled into Fort Kilmer. I wouldn't have had to be an English major to recognize the name of Joyce Kilmer. No high school student could have escaped "Trees," with its mawkish but memorable "Poems are made by fools like me, / But only God can make a tree." I felt some distant kinship, in these surroundings, with the Morristown schoolteacher who had written those lines and then died in France in the last year of the First World War. For us now returning—at least for me—the world seemed full of promise.

The permanent party that ran this expanse of clapboard barracks, offices, and warehouses accomplished a lot in these hours when we were impatient to be returning home. Then two days later, on May 29, we got our orders. We were to report for processing and reassignment to Army Air Force Redistribution Station No. 1 in Atlantic City. These orders seemed like a gift, and my childhood memories of digging with a shovel and pail on the broad reaches of the sand reinforced my sense of holiday to come. But there was also another gift. We would first receive ordinary leave time and then "a delay en route in the interest of public service" by way of our homes. We had no idea how this would constitute public service, but it was a welcome bonanza.

A short ride on a post bus took me to the station, where I peeled off newly issued dollars for the familiar bus that would take me to Scotch Plains. Now the reentry syndrome bloomed into full culture shock. This was the route I had taken to Plainfield for movies at the Strand and the Paramount. Stores thickened into the business district past Rosenbaum's and Tepper's, where I had bought my tux and black shoes for the senior prom. As twilight deepened into evening, I had no sense of an easy knitting up of past and present. I was carrying two years of faraway experiences back with me into this town where

I had walked to school on Front Street and skated on Hoppel's Pond. I was home on Memorial Day.

As the bus jounced into Westfield Road, I got out of my seat, timed my steps like a sailor on a bumpy sea, and asked the driver to let me off at Union Avenue. With my barracks bag increasingly heavy, I walked through the shadows of maple leaves under the streetlights. The night air was mild and fragrant, and lights glowed dimly on a few porches. Near the end of the block I ascended the steps I had descended thirty months before. I eased the front door open and set the barracks bag down gently. As I straightened up, there was Mother, emerging from the hall bedroom in her robe. She had done up her hair for the night, and in the light from the shaded lamp her expression was more wan than any I remembered.

"Mother," I said, and put my arms around her.

"Son," she said, and drew me into the kitchen. Her kiss was soft, on the cheek as always, never on the lips. She put on her glasses and looked at me carefully. She didn't weep, but I almost did.

"Are you all right?" she asked. "Are you hungry?"

"I'm fine," I said. "Where's Dad?"

She went to the bedroom, and a moment later he appeared in that faded bathrobe I remembered. I put my arms around him and kissed him awkwardly on the cheek.

"Sit down," Mother said. There at the kitchen table were two slices of apple pie.

"Son," Dad said, "how did they treat you?" And I began to tell them my story of the last year—but not all of it.

At first, being home was wonderful, with all the comforts of the familiar: my room, my bed, the overstuffed chair in the living room where I had sat to read so many books under the lamp with the fringed shade. In these sunny days of early June the screened front porch was fine too for sitting on the glider, swinging gently as I used to do when I moved from simple swashbuckling to historical fiction, from *Captain Blood* to *The Three Musketeers*.

"Son, would you like me to put up the hammock?" Dad asked. That had been one of my favorite spots, the hammock where I swung in the shade, but now, though I had enjoyed sleeping late and lounging, I was growing restless. It was culture shock again, being back in the familiar small town with no diversion save what I created myself. My school friends had lived in nearby Fanwood rather than Scotch Plains, and there was absolutely nothing in this pleasant, stultifying town to divert me.

I might simply have spent time with Mother and Dad. I had received none of the letters Mother had sent to Germany, and they had received only one of my aerograms sent *mit Luft Post nach Nord Amerika.* I had a qualm thinking again how they must have felt when all they had received for weeks was the formulaic telegram that reported me missing in action.

Mother showed me a glossy photo taken at a meeting of POW families, she in her best dress and flowered hat, Dad alongside in his Sunday suit. She also showed me a form from the Decorations and Awards Branch, dated 18 October 1944. It had accompanied a leather box containing the Air Medal. The citation read, "For meritorious achievement while participating in sustained bomber combat operations over Germany and German occupied countries. The courage, coolness and skill displayed by these Officers and Enlisted Men upon these occasions reflect great credit upon themselves and the Armed Forces of the United States." I could imagine something of what her mixed feelings must have been when she first read it. Looking at a photo of me in my summer dress uniform, she had shaken her head and said, "They dressed you boys up so nice." I understood the irony and felt it myself as I read about my "courage, coolness and skill." I did not feel that I had displayed any exceptional coolness or skill in opening and closing bomb-bay doors and dropping bombs. As for courage, I had been moved along in the air corps pipeline, and it would have been unthinkable to do anything to get myself out of it. I had wanted my wings and my commission, and I had wanted to keep the respect and friendship of my comrades. Each time we took off on combat operations, there was enough excitement to keep me busy and my mind occupied. Like a rodeo rider, I was in the chute, and the only way out was forward.

Born to them in their forties, I had been increasingly distanced from my parents by radically different experience. They were loving but undemonstrative, and almost everything I knew about their lives had come from my own superficial questioning. Reticence was a family trait that persisted. And one day, when Mother asked me about Moira, I said only that she was a good friend who had been hospitable to me in Florida.

"She sent me a beautiful expensive purse," Mother said, and "she felt as though she should be calling me Mother."

I tried to conceal the impact of that comment, which took me back to the steamy summer of 1944 in Tampa. We were stationed there at Drew Field to learn how to fly formation with other B-17s, to cover long distances and to replace crews that had survived their thirty missions or been written off as killed or missing in action. By late July we were in the air nearly every day, usually in six-hour flights. One night over the Everglades we were slowly climbing the black air when blinking lights ahead were suddenly closing with us at nightmare speed. This fatal Doppelgänger might have been the last image my retinas would ever hold if Bill Moroz had not hit the throttles with a scream and yanked the wheel back in a climb that flooded my mouth with the taste of copper.

When we were briefly free from the long exercises of simulated bombing runs, gunnery practice, and cross-country flights, we explored what we could of Tampa and the resort cities of St. Petersburg and Clearwater. Strolling near the boats tied up at the wharves along Old Tampa Bay, we experienced exotic sights and smells: the salt breeze from the Gulf, the scent of savory pompano baked in paper bags wafting out to the street from cafés. The management winked at the liquor laws, and the slight middle-aged waitress who let me try my Spanish on her would bring us scotch in coffee cups.

One sunny Saturday of high wispy cirrus clouds, I took a bus across the bay to Clearwater with Eric Anderson, a classmate from bombardier school. We found a large, crowded pool, and after baking for a half-hour in the sun we slipped into the cool water. Then we made friends with two of the other bathers. Hanging onto the edge, half-floating, we paired off, Eric with the taller girl, as blonde as he. Perhaps it was some sort of genetic imprinting that attracted me to her friend. Born outside Vienna, my father had emigrated at age one with his large family to grow up in Massachusetts. Leaving them to work as the chef in Bonnie Burn Sanatorium in New Jersey, he had married Josephine Slattery and been absorbed into her large Irish-American Catholic family. With her Celtic mix of green eyes, black hair, and pale skin glistening under the suntan oil, Moira might have been a Slattery.

I brought four Cokes to a cluster of chairs. With the sort of light and easy conversation we had been missing in our world of men and machines, the afternoon passed quickly. Flush after our $250 monthly payday, we took the girls to dinner at an expensive restaurant. We spent the rest of the evening deep in two separate conversations in Moira's comfortable bungalow, with soft radio music for background. At last Eric and I got a taxi back to the base for a few hours of sleep before going out to the flight line again.

Much later he would say, "We could have had a good time in Tampa if you hadn't gotten involved." But I cared more about being involved than about the calibration of instruments and the cross-countries that took us droning out over the Caribbean and the Everglades. Moira helped me to live intensely those parts of the days that were my own. The hours stolen from the great organism that owned me—stolen not under the chill English sky of the film *Brief Encounter* but under balmy Florida heavens—were to be lived as fully as possible, even in their uncertainty. This time in late summer that seemed to me somehow like fall was swiftly streaming away toward its end. Our new orders, covering forty-six ten-man B-17 crews, would take us to Savannah.

There at Hunter Field we were assigned the shiny new craft we would test and then fly to England. We would not be confined to the base, and so Moira rode the train north to spend the final hours with me. The memories of the lush live oaks and tropical piazzas and sultry coastal skies would overlay those of humid Tampa. And now there was something of the ambience of another film, *Waterloo Bridge,* that permeated those brief days near the river flowing steadily away into the ocean. Soon it was time for goodbyes and last-minute pledges made with no foreknowledge of the future.

We had never talked about marriage in those days of uncertainty, when emotions could be expressed sincerely in songs such as "I'll Be Seeing You" and "I'll Walk Alone." Being with Moira had been precious to me then, because I knew that the here and now might be all I would ever have. I had not performed any examination of conscience about this part of my life, the kind you were meant to do before you went to confession, nor had I gone to confession. If I had tried to verbalize my feelings, I might have said that I still had only the here and now. The future would remain uncertain until the air force revealed its plans for me. This temporary vacuum made possible a comfortable kind of avoidance. I had written to Moira from Germany, but no reply ever reached me, and I did not write to her now.

"Here's the car keys," Dad said. I had never fully realized how fortunate I had been. Almost anything I had wanted that was within my parents' power to give me had been mine. This was our family car, used very little beyond Sunday outings or a trip to the Jersey Shore. A 1932 Dodge, it was a sturdy blue four-door sedan equipped with running boards and bumpers. There were also two small glass vases attached inside between the doors. I was glad Mother had never decided to put flowers in them.

It was through the car that I made an unpremeditated gesture that may have been prompted by feelings of guilt or inadequacy. Not long after my return home, Mother said one day, "You certainly were religious in Germany." With unspoken reluctance I had continued going with her to early mass on Sundays. Dad went only on Holy Days of Obligation and slept late on his one free morning of the week. But I conceived the idea of his going with me to the eleven o'clock Sunday mass in nearby Westfield. I knew that this would please Mother, and it would be something he and I could share.

One Sunday as we drove back home I pulled over to the side of the quiet road and turned off the ignition. Hesitantly I began, telling him I wanted him to know that I thought he had been a fine father and that I knew how difficult it must have been, living all these years with a woman as sure of being right as Mother was. It came out haltingly, the kind of spoken sentiment foreign to both of us. I paused and then turned to him and said I was sorry that I had not been more of an emotional support to him. For a moment he said nothing. Then he looked at me and said, "Son, you're the best kid ever was."

This was a time for expressions of emotion. Mr. Adams, my tall, lanky high school math teacher, had asked me to be his guest speaker at the Rotary Club. He presided, and the congenial hum stopped when he rose to say grace. After the ceremonial American lunch of chicken à la king on toast, he asked me to talk about my experiences and introduced me as "one of our own boys." I decided to take them through a mission step by step, and they were a good audience, listening avidly and asking intelligent questions. I didn't mind talking about being a prisoner of war, but even after this brief time back home I was beginning to tire of these recitals. Soon they would become almost formulaic. I minded least when pretty girls were present. At a party I might even find myself imitating the dialect war stories of a brilliant young comedian named Sid Caesar. But most of us had had enough of the army, and now talking about it was boring.

I was glad when Mr. Adams rose at last but was surprised when he reached over and grasped my hand. "Sing along with us, Joe," he said.

"R-O-T-A-R-Y," we sang, "that spells Rotary!" I did my best to harmonize, and it was strangely warming to see these elders joined in this jolly but earnest declaration of belief and affection. And it was not a little strange to be holding hands with them. So the occasion turned out to be neither a burden nor a bore but a good introduction to gatherings to come.

But my social life was uneventful, for most of the men sent overseas from this area had not returned yet. Any desire to see my extended family had been satisfied by one trip to our East Orange relatives and by their return visit. I felt no impulse to revisit Drew, my former college, where most of the men were preministerial students and seminarians. My leave time was becoming devoted chiefly to reading, and I was bored.

Driving to AAF Redistribution Station No. 1 reminded me of childhood trips to Atlantic City in the same old 1932 Dodge. The roadside gradually faded to become pale and sandy until we smelled at last the keen tang of salt air. At the Chalfont-Haddon Hall I picked up my air force packet. It contained orders for three dozen officers, "for training or schooling purposes," all but a few of them members of Project R. I would be going to the Central School for Bombing at Midland, Texas. I told Mother and Dad, glossing lightly over the "training or schooling." I didn't quite know what that meant. Having been a POW in Germany, would I now have to face the risk, if I survived combat again, of becoming a POW of the Japanese? In any case, this was a better parting from my parents than the one nearly three years earlier at the Newark train station.

The twelfth-floor windows looked out on the ubiquitous Atlantic. I hung up my clothes and unpacked my B-4 bag. I put a pint of Jack Daniel's in a dresser drawer and sat on the bed, feeling at loose ends. I was trying, not very successfully, to read a magazine when the phone rang.

"Lieutenant Blotner," said a male voice, "there's a long-distance call for you. You'll have to come down here to take it."

The clerk at the desk pointed to a telephone booth. Without knowing why, I was nervous as I closed the isolating door.

"Joe," came the attenuated voice over the long-distance hum. "It's me. It's Moira!"

"Moira! Where are you?" It was a call I hadn't expected this day, though I had known it was bound to come.

"I just learned where you were from the Air Force. Why haven't you called me? When are you coming down?"

"We just got here," I lied. "After we were liberated they moved us around until we got on the ship for home."

"Are you all right? Can you come down?"

I wanted a cigarette but had left my pack in the room. "We haven't had all of our physicals yet, but I'm OK."

"I can't wait to see you. I've been so worried. Can't you get leave?"

"We've just received our orders transferring us to Texas."

"Where? For how long?"

"To Midland, but we don't know yet for how long. There'll be examinations and maybe some retraining and then reassignment, I guess."

"We need to spend some time together." There was a note of urgency in her voice. "When the war ended I quit my job. I thought you'd be back soon. We've got to make plans."

"I'm afraid the air force will be making all the plans." My mouth was dry, and again I wished for a cigarette.

"But they won't need all of you boys now, will they? And they should let the POWs out first, shouldn't they?"

"Moira, nobody knows anything, and there's still the war in the Pacific."

"But we ought to be able to make some plans. I've put my whole life on hold for you. We can take up where we left off, even if we can't be together all the time."

I wanted to make explanations, but for a moment nothing came. "I've got to decide what I'm going to do after I get out, whenever that will be."

"Well, whatever you decide, we can be together, can't we?"

I paused and swallowed while the line hummed. "Moira," I said, "after everything that's happened, I'm not quite the same person I was. I've changed."

"What do you mean?" she asked, the note of urgency strong in her voice. "I'll change you back!"

"After we get to Texas I'll write you," I said quickly. I tried to strike a reassuring note. "I'll call you and tell you what's happening."

She was silent. Then we both spoke at once in hurried, inarticulate phrases that gave way to pauses and halts, and a moment later we said goodbye. I hung up the phone, pulled the door open, and sat there, looking at the people passing in the lobby without seeing them. I felt a mixture of emotions I would have to try to sort out.

Back in the room, I extracted the Jack Daniel's from the dresser drawer and sat looking out at the beach, where a few bathers clung to the ropes and leaped up with each long rolling wave. In the bathroom I poured two fingers into a glass and added water. Loosening my tie and unbuttoning my collar, I returned to the window and sat on the windowsill. I lit a cigarette and watched the plume of smoke drift up toward the vent in the wall.

What did I feel? Watching the green rollers spend themselves on the sand in the paling sun, I realized that it was a mixture of regret and relief. The tone of Moira's questions echoed in my mind. I thought of Stephen Dedalus in *Ulysses* with his *agenbite of inwit,* his nagging remorse of conscience, but I checked the thought. I wanted no examination of conscience now. I reflected that I had been caught up in a train of circumstances I hadn't planned. Our love affair had been conditioned more than most, I saw now, by time and place. I remembered telling her, in one of our evening talks in her bungalow, that I had a feeling I might not come back from Europe, and she had responded to that feeling. If I survived the rest of this war, I would soon be back in my interrupted life. With college yet to complete, how could I move to Tampa, where I had been a soldier on an air base who knew the city only through fleeting hours snatched from grim military necessity? The idea of introducing Moira to Scotch Plains, I realized, had never entered my mind.

There was no action I *had* to take now, and none I wanted to take. I was in the chute again, and the army was still ringmaster. I was reaching for the bottle again when a peremptory knock sounded. I opened the door, and there in the hall, with his back to me, was an officer in suntans. He turned as he spoke.

"You're out of uniform, Lieutenant," he said. It was Hank Greenberg, as trim as ever, his mustache neatly clipped and his brass polished. With that familiar look of a smiling buccaneer, he laughed as he grasped my hand and shook my shoulder.

"What the hell are you doing up here all by yourself?" he asked. "Let's go down to the bar and check out the action."

Mother and Dad, Rocky Hill, N.J., 1917.

Joseph Blotner, Albuquerque, New Mexico, 1944.

Martha Marjorie Cortelyou, Oberlin, Ohio, 1945.

Tracy Wright Blotner, Nancy Wright Blotner, and Pamela Wright Blotner, Hellerup, Denmark, 1959.

Yvonne Wright Blotner, Bellagio, Italy, 1980.

Tracy, Nancy, and Pamela, Ann Arbor, Michigan, 1990.

With William Faulkner, Charlottesville, Virginia, 1962 (photograph by Dean Cadle).

At the home of Nikolai Anastasyev, Moscow, 1984.

With Cleanth Brooks and Eleanor Clark Warren, Bowling Green, Kentucky, 1998.

With Richard Ford, at a conference in Rennes, France, 1994.

Ann Arbor, Michigan, 2000 (photograph by
Dr. Barry Siegel).

SEVEN

Getting on with Life

"IT'S WORSE THAN I THOUGHT," HANK SAID, GAZING out the window as he sprawled on one elbow in his bunk in the BOQ. "If you go out to the highway and turn right, in seven miles you're in Midland, population four thousand. Turn left, and in fifteen miles you're in Odessa, population three thousand. There's tumbleweed on the highway. I thought it grew just out on the lone prairie. You can't even see a deer or an antelope, just telegraph poles or a coyote or a prairie dog—or a tarantula, for variety. Of course, you can drive west five hours and then you're in El Paso, if you want to be in El Paso."

We had been through the eye tests, where I learned that my depth perception wasn't as good as it had been during classification in Nashville, but I was still on flying status. The scars on my feet from the frostbite and infection had long since healed, and the air force dentists had replaced my lost fillings. "You want to use your new dental work?" Hank asked.

"Let's go catch a ride to town," I said.

The plain exterior of the Midland Arms hadn't prepared me for the lobby. High on the wall at each end of the room was a set of enormous horns. A good six feet wide, they were obviously from Texas longhorns. They dominated the room. The Old Corral Bar and dining room were off to the right. To the left a sign reading KMID pointed down a corridor, and I made a mental note to check it out after we had eaten. The genial waitress fluffed her yellow hair while we looked at the menu. "You can't miss with the T-bone," she said.

The corridor led to a smaller lobby where a door marked "Office" faced a large glass window that provided a good view of a radio station's broadcasting booths. The man at the microphone removed a twelve-inch vinyl disc from the turntable on his left, replaced it with another, and cued it up. Then he started the turntable on his right. The whining strains of a string band filled the small lobby:

> Ridin' down the canyon, just to see the sun go down,
> A picture that no artist dares to paint. . . .

The man took off his headphones and made a welcoming gesture. With his high shock of brown hair he looked six and a half feet tall. He opened the door and walked to the Teletype in three steps.

"I'll just turn this damn bell off," he said. "It's the eleven o'clock five-minute summary."

A moment later he turned to me. "Howdy," he said. "I'm Slim Lindsey. That's my engineer there next door, Clem Russell. He ain't very bright, but he knows how to ride the gain on that board and keep us on the air." He scanned the sheets of copy paper and folded them. "You interested in the radio business?" he asked me.

"Yes," I said.

"Come on into the booth," Slim said. "I'll do the newscast, and then we can talk for a spell. I'm tired of hearing my own voice." The nasal insistence of the music followed us.

Slim was good at his job. His patter was easy and well paced. He was hoping for a career that would take him to larger stations in the network. He turned back to his console. "Come back and see me," he said. "You want to sit in for me some night? Just to keep your hand in? I can't pay you, but you don't want to get stale."

"Right," I said. "Maybe I could do some newscasts for you."

"Fine, pardner," he said. "I'll be lookin' for you. Any night but Saturday." He waved as I left, the strains from the disc on the spinning turntable following me out of the small lobby.

"Deep within my heart lies a memory, a song of old San Antone. . . ." I was still singing it as I entered the quiet BOQ. Hank's bunk was empty. I sat on mine, poured a little Jack Daniel's, and added a splash of water. I crawled between the harshly starched sheets, still holding residual warmth from the day. I read for a while before falling asleep—to dream of sitting before a live microphone, preparing to read the eleven o'clock news.

When I woke it was nine and already hot. As we emerged from our PX breakfast Hank said, "Let's go by the Squadron Orderly Room and see if we can find out anything."

The officer of the day was a tired-looking captain, not a flying officer but a ground-gripper who looked as though he had been in rank too long. He had one bit of information for us. "You're definitely on flying status, so you should get flight pay." Walking back to the BOQ, we were still assimilating recent history. The Japanese had surrendered on August 14, and people were being discharged on an elaborate point system. All we could do was wait. But I congratulated myself on now having one option—not exactly an ace in the hole, but a resource to avoid that old bugbear of going round the bend.

It was KMID. I had been stopping by the station during the week to do newscasts for Slim and an occasional record show. I liked the work, and the station manager was glad to have another announcer, especially one who worked for nothing. One day after I finished a five-minute newscast, Gloria, the office secretary, called me. "There's somebody here who wants to talk to you," she said, pointing to the lobby.

It was a well-dressed man who looked to be in his fifties. When we sat down he handed me his card. It gave his name and listed his address as WALA, in Mobile, Alabama. I knew it was a 50,000-watt clear-channel station and a major NBC affiliate.

"What are you going to do after you get out of the army?" he asked. I told him I would probably go back to college.

"Well," he said, "if you ever want a job, come and see me."

But the Air Force prevented me from making a choice I might have regretted. A week later we received Special Order No. 230, dated September 27, 1945. Six Project R bombardiers were to proceed to their homes with a delay en route to a separation center for processing—relief from active duty, with a Certificate of Service and Terminal Leave. Hank and I had a celebratory drink at the Old Corral.

There was a lot of paperwork at the separation base in Newark. Most of the forms were routine, but one gave us the opportunity to join the air force reserve. It could be the *inactive* reserve, with no monthly meetings or other responsibilities unless we were called up for active duty, which seemed like a remote possibility in all the flurry of demobilization. But I had worked hard and long to earn my commission, and in spite of the ceremonies of American-Soviet comradeship on the Elbe after VE Day, who could be sure that we might not be liable for military service again? If I had to go again, I wanted to be an officer. So without further thought I signed up for a reserve commission. It seemed the sensible thing to do. Besides, I would be back in Scotch Plains in a day, and I would soon take up my real life again. If there was muted laughter offstage, I failed to hear it.

On October 5 I was back home. Like most returning veterans, I wanted to make up for lost time. Drew University would give me credit for courses I had taken in preflight. I registered for a full five-course load, and the registrar said he would help me work out some reading courses. This would bring me to six courses each semester and at least one in the summer—enough to complete my B.A. It was not just a ploy for credit hours. Russian literature in translation and German literature in translation would also help to fill some of the wide gaps in my reading. I would take more of Dr. Aldrich's English courses, and for pleasure I would take psychology.

One thing, however, I did feel strongly: I wasn't going back to dormitory living. I had planned it so that I had classes on only four days of the week, and the old Dodge was still in good shape. The answer was to commute, as many of my cohort would be doing.

Back at Drew, I found few changes in my work apart from new books in the course syllabi. Dr. Aldrich still clung to the method he had learned at Harvard: to point out specific passages and define individual phrases or explore figures of speech. There was little class participation or explication. He might point to one passage as "exquisite" or another as "detestable." I had signed up for the only upper-level course he was giving that semester, Victorian prose and poetry. This was his favorite area, and I feared that it would be deadly. I did find Thomas Carlyle and Walter Pater heavy going, but to my surprise I was taken with some of the great stylists, especially Matthew Arnold and John Henry Newman.

When we got to the poetry, some of the old warhorses such as "The Charge of the Light Brigade" were missing from our anthology. But many of those that appeared had something appealing about them: the old man's heroism in Tennyson's "Ulysses," the sadist's self-revealing cruelty in Browning's "My Last Duchess." And there was material new to me: Gerard Manley Hopkins's "The Windhover" and Hardy's "Hap," both of them challenging. Skipping ahead, I saw that I was going to like reading Swinburne, watching how "The ivy falls with the Bacchanal's hair . . . / Her bright breast shortening into sighs." And it summoned up memories of the recent past to hear the stirring notes of Housman's reveille, "Clay lies still, but blood's a rover; / Breath's a ware that will not keep."

Most of what I was studying I liked, especially the psychology courses. But I had learned that increasing laboratory work would involve a new kind of study and writing involving probability theory. I would learn that it wasn't as forbidding as I thought, but I would go on with the requirements for the English major and the Bachelor of Arts degree.

When I entered the army, Dad finally sold the restaurant and found a supervisor's job at Mack Motors in South Plainfield, where I had worked one summer. So now he could put in an eight-hour day and come home for supper. And now I was there too, and the three of us would have the kind of family life Mother had longed for over the years. This was an orderly and comfortable life for me, a regression to childhood, some might have said, with food, lodging, laundry, and transportation provided.

By mid-fall 1946 the weather was frosty, and the fragrance from burning leaves saturated the autumn air. When I drove up the mountain road, the Watchung forest was shaped into waves of yellow and bronze. The town of Madison was the same as I remembered it, but not the Drew campus. Signs of change were everywhere. We had not been there to see the midshipmen of the V-12 program marching in their formations incongruously past the Methodist Seminary buildings. But now we witnessed a far finer transformation, for during our absence, Brothers College had begun admitting women as commuters. Girls strolling in their cashmere cardigans and pleated skirts, slim shapely legs and white bobby sox above shiny leather loafers—like the fall colors, they not only brightened the scene but changed its very sound and ambience.

One day after my last class I went down the hall toward the lounge on the main floor, where students relaxed between classes on the comfortable leather couches and easy chairs. Some tried to study while others read papers or gossiped or played bridge. Music floated from the upright piano in the corner. The man closest to the piano I recognized as a commuter. He was about my height and looked to be about my age. He was round-faced, his dark hair a crew cut. He stubbed out a cigarette and sat down at the keyboard. Standing beside him was a man I knew. Jim Eagen was a good six feet tall, and his dark thinning hair, sallow complexion, and ample waistline set him apart from the other undergraduates. He was more comfortable in the lounge than in Asbury Hall, where he had a room. He had been at Drew for three years before joining the navy, and now he was using the GI Bill to complete his degree in chemistry. He saw me and waved me over.

"Joe," he said, "this is Karl Marx. That's right—I'm not kidding, Karl Marx with a *K* and an *X*."

Karl smiled. "It's really Karl Nils Marx," he said, shaking my hand, "but nobody knows me by it, and the short form gets a laugh every time." He struck a chord and ran off an arpeggio in the bass and then the treble.

"Play that one you did last night," Jim said, "that tricky one."

Karl rested his short fingers on the keys, and after a few preliminary chords, he flooded the room with syncopation. I had gone through a phase when I was taken by boogie-woogie, but what I was hearing now was electrifying—full of melody, rapid but graceful, a profusion of notes that seemed to rise in clouds from Karl's nimble fingers. The slow parts held a kind of sentimental appeal for me, and the alternation with strong syncopation created a wonderful effect. I knew what I was hearing: it was ragtime, the kind of music I had always wanted to learn.

"Karl, what *is* that one?" I asked.

"You never heard that? It's 'The Maple Leaf Rag.' Scott Joplin."

He launched into it again gracefully, and it was even catchier this time. "If you want to come over to the gym tomorrow night, I'll play you some more. We're doing a variety show. We've got a band, and we've got a chorus with some pretty good-looking girls."

"What time?" I asked.

EIGHT

Resetting the Compass

THE NOTES OF THE STRIDENT TRUMPET AND MELLOW sax bounced off the backboards of the small, ancient gymnasium. They stopped, and I heard Karl's voice. "Let's go back and take it from A." I sat on one of the chairs to listen and watch. He had been right when he told me they were not bad.

"What kind of show is this?" I asked him.

"It's the All-College Capers," he told me. "It's sort of a variety show, I guess you'd call it. We're putting it together as we go. Want to work on it?"

"Doing what?"

"You sing, don't you? Maybe we could work up a routine." I repressed memories of my debut with Zip Zapinski. What Karl suggested might be fun.

The chorus had materialized, six or seven girls in white blouses, black vests, brief red shorts, and net stockings. Karl struck a chord and led them in a comedy number. He took them through it again. This time there was applause and an ear-piercing whistle. It came from Jim Eagen.

"How do you like 'em?" he asked me. "The little blonde on the left end is Alicia Laird," he told me. "She lives in Rogers House."

"Who's the one in the middle?" I asked.

"The one with the dark hair?"

"Yes, and the nice legs. Do you know her?"

"Yes, I do. That's Yvonne Wright. She's a junior, a religion major."

"A what?"

"A religion major. She wants to be a foreign missionary."

"Great," I said.

"Don't jump to any conclusions," he told me.

Karl approached the chorus. "Yvonne," he said, "let's do your number."

"I don't have it down very well yet," she said, clearly nervous. Something over medium height, she had green eyes and a strong nose in an oval face, with a figure Hank Greenberg would have called *zaftig*.

"Here's your note," Karl said. He hit it three times, and she began "In Room Two Hundred and Two," in a small voice that wavered.

I thought I could detect a minstrel ancestry in this comic number. She gained confidence and got through a second chorus. Jim whistled at his shrillest pitch, then brought her over and introduced me. When I added my encouragement, she bloomed. I liked her immediately. I reminded Karl that he had promised to play more ragtime for me.

"Come on over to Rogers House," Yvonne said. "It's almost five, so we can use the piano in the lounge."

In the comfortable room Karl adjusted the bench and did a quick run. "Here's some Jelly Roll Morton for you," he said. It was a kind of ragtime new to me, with plenty of bass reinforced by strong, heel-tapping chords ornamented by trills and syncopation. "What *is* that?" I asked him.

"It's 'The Wolverine Blues.' Jelly Roll was one of the great characters of ragtime—and jazz, too. He played all over, from New Orleans to Lansing and from whorehouses to Harlem theaters."

Karl looked up as three girls came down into the lounge.

"Don't stop now," Yvonne said.

Karl fingered a chord progression in a slow tempo, the melody moving down an octave past middle C into the bass. He moved into the treble and began to sing, "Thought I heard Buddy Bolden say. . . ." He stopped again and turned to us. "I'll try to learn it all for next time." Then he launched into "The Maple Leaf Rag."

He had library work to do, and instead of our going home for supper he suggested that we go to the nearby Goumas's Diner. I had liked him immediately too, and I wanted to tell him about an idea for the Capers variety show. We were both only children who had received piano lessons with differing results. Mine had ended after two years by mutual agreement, but I sang well enough, and my idea was to do Stories in Song. We began laughing as we improvised story lines.

We had our generation's shared experience of the war. Karl and I felt it with Jim Eagen, who had been a certain kind of casualty. During his three years in the Pacific, his pay allotment had flowed home regularly, but when he returned at last, his money was gone, as was his wife. He was deeply cynical for a man of twenty-eight, a quality that gave a certain edge to his wartime slang. Few of us could have duplicated his sardonic smile as he delivered his favorite dismissal: "Shove off, coxswain, your boat's loaded."

Karl and I had a lot in common, and he was a good storyteller. One of his stories concerned his war injury. By the time we reached the Eighth Air Force, the days of the cross-channel and coastal milk runs were long past. Apart from the dangers of combat were the discomforts of missions that could last eleven hours and more. For smokers like Bill Moroz, my pilot, tobacco deprivation had been a painful hardship, but there was another and potentially greater one that all of us knew. You always made a last latrine stop before climbing aboard, but inevitably the call would come again later, and that meant disconnecting the safety belt and the three equipment tethers and clipping on the walk-around oxygen bottle. Then you could make the expedition back to the relief tube in the waist.

Flying as engineer gunner in the group lead to Frankfurt, Karl hadn't felt the internal pressure building until they turned onto the IP to begin the bomb run. It got worse during eleven minutes of intense flak. Even after they dropped their bombs, he had to stay at his crew position. When he was able to go to the rear to the relief tube, he had the obstacles of long johns, pants, heated suit, and coveralls. Removing his gloves as briefly as possible in the fifty-below-zero degrees of the fuselage, he was back at his station in time to hear the pilot ask for a check on battle damage and injuries. It was then that he saw the blood on his coveralls. The frigid temperature had at first prevented him from feeling the pain that was now starting to throb. In his haste to return to his position, he had somehow caught his member in the zipper. His report on the intercom was received with a chorus of laughter.

When finally they were circling the field, the radio operator fired the red flare that meant "injured on board." Waiting were an ambulance and the chaplain. Karl sensed something like disappointment in the medics because the patient was ambulatory, but they gave him a ride to the infirmary anyway. The surgeon inserted four stitches to repair the damage. Struggling down from the table and standing up, Karl found that the dressing forced him into a bow-legged gait. The surgeon gave him pain pills and tried to suppress a smile. "You might as well know now, Sergeant," he said. "You won't get a Purple Heart."

The next day the crew was scheduled for flak leave. The leave was too precious to waste, and Karl decided to go in spite of his wound. The rest of the crew were going to London, but Karl concluded that this was not the destination for him. Instead of risking buzz bombs for the amusements of London, he spent a rainy leave at Granville Court at the seaside. The great benefit of this decision was that there he met a pretty Scottish member of the Army Territorial Service who would become his bride two years later.

Though Karl and I shared the bond of our generation's great adventure, music soon became our main bond. We were fond of the songs of the 1920s and '30s, and between us we remembered most of the lyrics. Before long we had a sizable repertoire. We thought the upcoming All-College Capers could be our trial performance. I devised a routine I called "The Story of a Graduate Student." Like all our routines to come, the plot had a simple structure: falling in love, encountering romantic and academic difficulties, and surmounting them. We ranged from vintage plaints like "I Wonder Who's Kissing Her Now" to amorous show tunes in the style of "Thou Swell." And we gave the routine some schmaltz with "Those Wedding Bells Are Breaking up That Old Gang of Mine." Our responsive audience seemed to like it.

Yvonne and I continued to see each other, and I noticed that she seemed never to be alone—in the refectory, in classrooms, or simply strolling the campus. She sometimes invited me to join a group going to lunch or a musical performance. I usually declined, and once when she asked me why, I said, "I'm not going to be one of your squadron." And indeed she was often followed or surrounded by several male friends. She loved this kind of attention and, I would later suspect, needed it on some deep level. She had an outgoing personality and a lively sense of humor, but one day as we lingered after lunch she seemed uncharacteristically subdued. Finally she confided that she was worried about her grades and afraid of losing her scholarship.

"If I lost it," she said, "Gramma would kill me, or it would kill her."

"Who?"

"My grandmother. She and my uncle are putting up most of the money for me to come here, and if I lose my scholarship I don't know what they'll do, or what I'll do." She seemed near tears.

"Look," I said, "I've got a deal for you. Go back and hit the books, and I won't take any of your time between now and Saturday. Then we'll go out Saturday night." She looked at me doubtfully for a moment and then smiled.

"Great!" she said, and looked at her watch. "Oh, God, I've gotta go." She squeezed my hand, raced down the steps, and sprinted for Rogers House.

That Saturday night, as we walked to the car, I remembered the lyrics of the number Karl had been practicing:

> I know that you know
> That I'll go where you go. . . .

The night air was crisp and chill, and we walked rapidly. In the car, Yvonne snuggled against me, and I didn't turn on the heater. We didn't talk, and I hoped she was feeling the same glow that I felt. I parked in front of Rogers House, and as we stood outside the door my watch showed ten minutes before eleven. I pulled her to me and kissed her quickly. She ducked into the foyer blowing a kiss as the door closed behind her.

A month later the refectory was filled for yet another version of the All-College Capers. I had written a thirty-minute routine of songs and patter, but the plot was essentially the same one—our own version of soap opera. Some of the songs must have been familiar to the older faculty whose tastes had extended beyond the Methodist Hymnal. We interlarded comic numbers with vintage laments and the mildly risqué such as Cole Porter's "Let's Do It," and if there were many blue noses in the audience, you couldn't tell from the applause.

When we got back to Rogers House, Yvonne and I lingered on the porch, close together against the cold. "I forgot to tell you," she said. "Gramma told me I could invite you home for Sunday dinner next week. They want to meet you. Can you come?"

It wasn't a long trip, and I couldn't have wanted a warmer welcome. In the comfortable living room of their two-story white clapboard home, they might have been models for a Norman Rockwell magazine cover. Yvonne's grandmother, born Carrie Jane Magee, was a stout woman, her gray hair neatly pulled back from an apple-cheeked face. Yvonne's uncle, Lamont Wright, was tall and slim. Friends in his hometown had called him Francis, after Francis X. Bushman, a star of silent films. Yvonne had carefully explained to me some of the family's relationships. Her mother, Marion Rought, the daughter of Carrie Jane Magee, had married Galusha Grow Wright, a younger brother of Lamont Wright. When I tried to repeat these relationships back to her, Yvonne told me not even to try.

Yvonne's sister Nancy, four years her junior at sixteen, helped serve the dinner: chicken and dressing with four kinds of vegetables. Yvonne's grandmother—Gramma—chaired the Women's Society for Christian Service of the Princeton Methodist Church, and I saw that if I contemplated a continuing relationship, there were two facts I needn't emphasize: that I drank and that I was, at least nominally, a Roman Catholic.

During the Christmas break I met Yvonne's mother, Marion, and began to learn about this family and its dynamics. Marion—or Nonnie, as everyone called her—had a pert face James Montgomery Flagg might have drawn for a Scott Fitzgerald story, but her body was almost grotesque from the rheumatoid arthritis that had begun to appear after Yvonne's birth. Other misfortunes had befallen her. Nearly twenty years older and a decorated sergeant in the First World War, her husband, Galusha, worked with his brothers as the mechanic of their three-man Ford agency in Factoryville, Pennsylvania, just north of Scranton. His National Guard pay was especially welcome in the summer of 1932. In August he went to the annual encampment. It was a summer of ferocious heat, and that afternoon when the phone rang in Factoryville, it was the captain. Galusha had died of a heart attack. His daughters were just seven and four. Lamont moved them to New Jersey, where his big break came with a firm of builders. It was the family's big break, too. Carrie's energy and determination fueled her ambition. She insisted that they rent a big house in Rocky Hill, not far from the Princeton University campus. She took in boarders, and in a few years they bought the house and started remodeling it.

The return to Madison after Christmas break brought the present back sharply into focus. In the fall of 1946 I would begin my last semester at Drew, but I still had no idea what I would do with a B.A. The prospect of WALA in Mobile was more remote now than ever. It looked as though I would graduate *cum laude,* and now with the GI Bill paying my way, I wished I had done better enough to earn high honors.

One day I received a note asking me to see the dean. There was nothing of the stiff administrator about Frank Glenn Lankard. He swung around in his chair and crossed his legs. With the ceiling light glinting on the shiny dome of his ruddy face, he opened a manila folder. "It looks as though you've just had your best semester," he said. "Have you thought about graduate school? With your record and the recommendations you would get, you could apply to a good graduate school for a career in English."

I had never seriously considered that option. He asked me about specific interests in English, and I mentioned the Victorians without thinking how incongruous that might sound in the light of some of our material in the All-College Capers.

"Splendid," he said. I mentioned having thought that radio journalism might lead to other things. He listened carefully, but I began to perceive that he felt I was meant for finer things, whatever they might be. "Look at some of the graduate school catalogues and then come back and see me," he said briskly.

I had been thinking of completing the requirements and piling up the necessary credits in the most agreeable way, but had I experienced any intellectual excitement? Could I make any claim to any kind of intellectual development? I must have mentioned the Victorians because my sense of the discipline of English had been formed by chronological periods. The offerings at Drew were limited, with no courses in areas such as literary criticism. The idea of reading magazines—the *Sewanee Review,* the *Hudson Review,* the *Virginia Quarterly Review*—simply wasn't there in my frame of reference. I continued to read Hemingway's short stories as they appeared, but my reading among the moderns as a whole was eclectic and unsystematic. I kept on taking class notes and writing term papers, building up a sense of exploration in the way a coral reef enlarges itself through steady accretion.

By March I hadn't done much more than look at catalogues, though there had been considerable other activity. I had driven to Rocky Hill often, and Yvonne had made her feelings clear. One night when we had gone to a dance on the campus, she had said, "Let's leave in plenty of time so that we can park before you have to take me back to the dorm and drive home." I found myself swabbing condensation from the windows of the Dodge before I could crank up for the ride home.

One morning Yvonne and I had taken a drive from the Wrights' Rocky Hill home to visit my high school classmate Jesse Jackson, who had recently married after long service in the Pacific. Now he and his wife were remodeling a small house in New Providence, models of happy domesticity. As we started back to Rocky Hill, Yvonne was quiet. We drove along the Passaic River toward Somerville where the Watchungs rose up on either side. As we turned south, Yvonne opened a new subject without preamble.

"If we were to get married this summer," she said, "when would we do it? August?"

The question surprised me and abruptly brought others along in train. Biology had asserted its imperative again. Prudence would have counseled delay, but this was not what we wanted to hear. We were romantics, though soon we would encounter reality, and we tried to map out our strategy. It was not very complex. I would complete the semester and plan for graduate school. The immediate problem would be finding an M.A. program I could enter in January.

"What will we do about your school work?" I asked Yvonne. "You've still got two semesters to go after this one." The subsistence checks from the GI Bill hadn't started coming in, and there was no indication when they would start. "We're going to have to figure on supporting ourselves next year. I've still got some of the back pay in the bank, but it won't last forever."

"That's OK," she said. "I'll get a job. After we get on our feet I can go back to school."

"I guess you'll want to get married in Princeton," I said, and she nodded.

"That means the Methodist Church. Can you imagine how that will go over with Mother? Dad won't care, but nobody in Mother's family has ever been married outside the Catholic Church." We were silent.

"Maybe we could have two ceremonies," Yvonne said hesitantly, "a Methodist one in Princeton and a Catholic one in Scotch Plains."

When we arrived at the rectory of the church of St. John the Apostle, I felt a chill. We sat silently until a tall nun in a black habit gestured us into an office. "Father Haig will see you now," she said.

From behind a massive desk a man in his early forties rose energetically with his hand outstretched. "Haig is the name," he said, smiling warmly, "H–A–I–G, like Haig Pinch Bottle."

I took a deep breath, encouraged by his geniality. "We're Drew students," I said, "and we want to get married in August. What we want to do, Father," I added, "is to have two weddings."

"Why won't one do?"

"Well, Yvonne is Protestant and I'm Catholic, and we want to keep both of our families happy."

Father Haig turned to her. "Tell me about yourself, Yvonne," he said. When she said she was majoring in religion and drama, he smiled.

"I was thinking about the Foreign Mission field," she said.

"That's very fine," he said, "but I think you might be able to do some missionary work right here at home. First, though, I'll tell you that the Church believes that one marriage is enough. Have you thought about becoming a Catholic?" Somewhere down the hall I heard a clock ticking.

"No, I haven't. My parents are very strong Methodists."

"You'd still be a Christian, Yvonne," he said with a reassuring smile. "We get converts here all the time, and some of them are Methodists." He was amiable but inflexible. Finally he said, "Why don't you two think it over and come back and see me? Give me a call," he said, smiling, "and remember-Father Haig, just like the scotch!"

In the car we were silent. We spent an hour over coffee at Goumas's, going over the same ground. I did not want to leave the Church, but I did not want to lose Yvonne. And she did not want to become a Catholic. Dependent on her family financially and tied strongly to them emotionally, she could not contemplate a break.

At home, I waited until after dinner to bring up the subject. Dad said little and so did Mother, at first. Then she spoke. "Son," she said, "mixed marriages never work." She used the term with the kind of fatality that suggested a dread disease. I could have said that I knew of some unmixed marriages in our own family that hadn't worked either, but I refrained.

"I wonder if you know your own mind," she said. "I told you about what Moira told me when she sent that purse. And now it's Yvonne. How will you feel when another girl comes along?"

"I'll feel the same way about Yvonne that I do now."

"That's what you say now. What about children?"

"We've talked about that. We'll take them to more than one church, and when they get older they can pick the church they want."

"And they'll be nothing," Mother said, with a bitterness I hadn't heard in her voice before. With her white hair and deep blue eyes, her compressed lips and set jaw, she had never looked more Irish.

Dad sat there looking miserable, staring down at the rug as if he were studying it for some pattern or meaning. Only later would I wonder what resonance these bitter words would have for him, when the woman he loved had agreed to marry him—in the Rectory—only after he became a Catholic convert.

The next morning I waited outside Yvonne's class. "Uh-oh," she said when she saw my face. "Bad?"

"Yes," I said.

"I just couldn't quit being a Methodist and become a Catholic," she said. "My family, my friends, most of the people I've been close to all my life have been Methodists. It would be changing one whole world for another. I wouldn't be me anymore."

"Let's call Rocky Hill and see if we can come today. I'd like to find out where we stand now and clear the air." I knew I was being impatient, but the adage "Marry in haste and repent at leisure" was far from my thoughts now.

At Rocky Hill, Gramma's first response was to hug us. Then she cut pieces of a newly baked layer cake. "It's good that you went to see the priest," she said. "But I want to tell you something, Joe. I've known Catholics all my life, and so has Uncle La. In Factoryville my mother's best friend was our next-door neighbor, Mary Murphy. She was a Catholic. We went to our own churches and stayed good friends."

Then Gramma began talking about her brother Bill, and I wondered where the story was going. "Mother had a hard time raising him," she said, "and when he was thirteen he came down with a high fever. Dr. Evans wasn't sure what it was until the next day when he said, 'Jane, it's gone into pneumonia.'" She went for medicine, Gramma said, and in her absence Mrs. Murphy had called, bringing Father Flynn. The next day, Bill was worse. "And I think I know why. When Mother went to give him an alcohol rub, she found that his nightshirt was wet."

"Maybe it was a night sweat," I said.

"No," she said and paused. "I think it was holy water. By the next morning, Bill was gone. And then it was the funeral and all that. But Mother never wanted to see Father Flynn's face again, and she was never close to Mrs. Murphy again."

I looked at Yvonne. "It's hard to believe that Father Flynn killed Bill with holy water."

"I don't know," Gramma said. "But Bill died, and after that I could never forgive him and his sacraments. So you see, Joe, why I could never see my granddaughter married in the Catholic Church."

As we headed back to Madison, Yvonne and I didn't talk much. At last I said, "Do you believe that about Father Flynn and brother Bill?"

"I've heard it all my life," she said.

"But can you believe it—that they go out to the store and Mrs. Murphy hustles Father Flynn over there to douse the patient before they get back?"

"Joe, it doesn't matter what I believe. *She* believes it."

I thought about John Henry Newman lamenting the invincibility of passion and pride. For my mother, Methodism was beyond the pale, and for Gramma, Catholicism was unthinkable. Good God, I thought. What an impasse—prejudice and suspicion and bigotry. We sat parked in front of Rogers House, and I couldn't think of a promising strategy.

"Don't worry," Yvonne said. "We'll work it out somehow." She kissed me and vanished up the stairs.

Though our focus had been narrowed, other concerns were pressing—money, for one. Yvonne learned that she could have her old summer job back. She was a maid-of-all-work at Palmer Physics Lab, checking parts in as they arrived and helping to assemble delicate apparatus on the engineers' benches. As for me, radio was the only thing I could think of. I remembered listening to record shows and baseball scores over WAAT, an independent station less than twenty miles away in Newark with a powerful signal all over the metropolitan area. So one day I headed north on Highway 22 through the fens and factories of the Jersey meadows with their vapors from oil refineries and decaying vegetation.

I made my way into Newark and located the Sheraton Hotel. I found a parking space and went in cold, having feared that if I had written or telephoned I might have been turned down at the outset. When the receptionist sent me up to the tenth floor, I felt encouraged. There the thirtyish thin-faced woman at the desk handed me a two-page form. "Fill this out," she said, holding out a clipboard, "and I'll see if Mr. Laux is coming in." I didn't falsify my record, but I elaborated so that a reader might get the impression that I had done everything at KMID from adjusting the transmitting antennas to selling radio time.

Ed Laux proved to be a tall, ruddy-faced man with blue eyes and sandy hair. He welcomed me cordially in a mellifluous bass voice. "You picked a good time," he said. "We've actually got a full complement of staff announcers, but we've got to hire a summer relief man. It's mainly newscasts and record shows. We pay union scale, and there's a separate check for your commercials. Here's some copy for you to read."

He led me into the unoccupied one of the two broadcast booths. I sat down in the comfortable swivel chair and looked into the glass-enclosed engineer's booth. "That's Patsy, the engineer," Laux said.

There looking at me was a stocky, swarthy man in a wildly colored shirt wearing thick-lensed glasses and large earphones. Expressionless, he looked at me as I took up the top sheet, a spot commercial for Jack Dempsey's Restaurant in Times Square, and put it down on the copy stand behind the microphone. Patsy raised his right fist, then pointed his finger at me as a red light lit up at the base of his console.

Close to the microphone, I began describing the delicious lobster and crab and steaks and chops that drew celebrities to the celebrated restaurant of the near-mythical Manassa Mauler. Amplified by my cupped palms behind my ears, my own baritone sounded just as mellifluous to me as Laux's. I tried to damp down my nervousness enough to read slowly and clearly, just as if I were reporting the latest cattle prices in Midland County. The lead AP story described preparations for the upcoming trial of Nazi leaders in Nuremberg. As I gathered up the sheets and rose, Patsy looked at me. Still deadpan, he made a circle with his thumb and forefinger and held it up to me. I felt exhilarated.

Laux was there as I left the booth. "That was good, Joe," he said matter-of-factly. "Just wait here. We had another audition scheduled, and he just showed up."

My heart fell. A nattily dressed man in his forties entered the booth I had just left. As the minutes passed I was sure that he was getting more time than I had. At last Laux joined him, and they talked. Laux shook the man's hand vigorously and walked back toward his office. The other man was walking toward me. Holding out his hand, he said hello and told me his name, which I didn't get, but I did get the next words.

"Congratulations," he said. "Good luck with the job." My smile was not for him but for God.

Laux emerged, and he shook my hand. "We're going to hire you," he said, smiling, and led me toward his office. The walls bore professional photographs of glossy-looking people. He opened a desk drawer and pulled out a sheaf of forms. "You belong to AFRA, don't you?" When I hesitated, he took two of the forms and handed them across the desk to me. "That's the American Federation of Radio Artists. You'll get your talent checks from them. Do you use a professional name? There's nothing wrong with Blotner, but—"

I interrupted, grasping at the first one that surfaced in my mind. "Is Joe Blair OK?"

"Fine. You can start next Monday."

I had to walk up and down both sides of the block before I could find the Dodge. I was still savoring words and phrases as I drove across the Pulaski Skyway. "This is Joe Blair," I intoned, "speaking to you from Station WAAT, high atop the beautiful Sheraton Hotel in downtown Newark, New Jersey."

When I took the news to Rocky Hill, Yvonne and Gramma were in the kitchen. Yvonne stopped working on the wedding invitation list, and Gramma put down her recipe books for a brief celebration. They were happy about my job, but they soon returned to their interrupted activities. Over the next eleven weeks that kitchen would be nerve center and command post for this great American ritual of the tribe. The wedding would take place, I was informed, on Saturday, August 24.

I was glad that I could retreat to the world of WAAT. I was enjoying the work, and I liked the people. After two weeks into the job I had collected my first checks for more than a month's pay as a second lieutenant. Their arrival had coincided with my twenty-third birthday. And I had acquired a fan club of one. A woman had been writing me in ballpoint ink on lined pages from a dimestore tablet. She liked waltzes, and so on an evening program I would say, "Here is Wayne King playing 'The Waltz You Saved for Me' especially for Mrs. Godowski in Metuchen, New Jersey." At first she wrote to "Dear Joe Blair," then later to "Dear Dolly," enclosing two or three dollars "for you to buy yourself some candy."

While the summer wore on, I tried to keeping thinking of both the short-term and the long-term future. I was enjoying the undemanding work and the checks that I regularly banked. I needed less preparation for my air time now than when I had started, and so I brought along books for another reading course I had constructed, under the rubric Classic Modern Novels. On my breaks I read *War and Peace* while "Tuxedo Junction" and other pop favorites played in the background. For my air time I would try to choose long medleys and then read a paragraph or two of *Buddenbrooks* after introducing Benny Goodman and Lionel Hampton. Caught up in the multigenerational story of one of the minor merchant princes of the old Hanseatic League, I was glad I had never bombed Lübeck.

When I turned to new books that challenged me, I felt intellectually alive again. Leaving the north Germany of *Buddenbrooks* for Davos in the Swiss Alps of *The Magic Mountain,* I empathized with Mann's hero, unexpectedly confined in a tuberculosis sanatorium. I followed Hans Castorp undergoing an education that enlarged my own. The conflict between humanism and decadence embodied in exotic patients and physicians took me deeper into psychoanalysis and aestheticism than I had ever been before. This was the kind of challenge I had felt in James Joyce's transactions between the worlds of the present and the mythic past, and I didn't feel in the least schizophrenic turning from the brilliance of Harry James's "Trumpet Blues" to Thomas Mann's complex symbolism. I enjoyed the music I played, and my voice sounded no less enchanting in my cupped ears now as I relayed the disasters of the world to my listeners. But I began to suspect that if the studio were to become my livelihood, my brain might begin ossifying. Maybe Dean Lankard had been right.

It was getting late to undertake graduate study in English. I thought about Princeton, Harvard, and Yale, but I feared that my total record would give me no chance. And of course I hadn't prepared at a place like Exeter or St. Mark's or gone on to one of the elite of the Ivy League. There was another consideration. Where could I begin work in January? Consulting the catalogues carefully, I found a university where a student could earn an M.A. in three terms. It was Northwestern, where I could begin in January and complete the degree requirements by September.

I had already committed myself to one crucial act, marriage. Now I was approaching another. Ed Laux had intimated that I could try for a steady job. I knew what a career in radio could be like, but I had only a general sense of a teaching career. I did have some idea of the difference in salaries. I had never asked myself if I had done enough looking before leaping, and now it was as if all the momentum of the past half-dozen years was carrying me forward, as it was doing for so many others in their twenties like me.

NINE

Beginning the Climb

THERE WAS ALMOST NO INTERVAL, IT SEEMED, BETWEEN my last WAAT check and the first of the wedding bills. And then it was Saturday, August 24, 1946, a morning of bright sunshine and wispy cirrus streamers against a high blue sky. Already the early arrivals were mounting the steps of the massive stone Methodist church. The Wrights were getting used to the new member of their extended family, just as my family—not all of the Slatterys, though—were getting used to the notion of Protestantism. The bride's side was well populated with Wrights and Roughts and Princeton friends and neighbors. I was proud of my five groomsmen in white jackets and black trousers. Tallest was my high school classmate Bruce Todd, indispensable as my best man and provider of his almost new Mercury convertible for our honeymoon.

It was a fine occasion, all in all, though Hank Greenberg arrived two hours late owing to difficulties penetrating southerly New Jersey. Nonnie, Yvonne's mother, who had a penchant for taking umbrage on family occasions, did not act up, and the half grapefruit jammed onto the tailpipe of Bruce's car was discovered in time. Dad and Mother were at their best: Dad smiling and warm, Mother drawing on reserves of Irish charm and a magnanimity I hadn't known were there. Nothing was omitted, not the soap-scrawled graffiti on the windshield, not the clattering tin cans, not the layer of Rice Krispies sprinkled over the interior.

We were tired, and I, who had tried to stay on the alert for errors, had made the worst one of all. Our route took us through heavily traveled roads in New Jersey, New York, and Connecticut. When at last I presented myself at the Naugatuck Inn, darkness had fallen. The clerk informed me that reservations for late arrivals had to be guaranteed in advance. There was a small ho-tel down toward Danbury that might have a room. So a quarter-hour later my exhausted bride and I finally pulled up before a modest structure that could have been a roadhouse of the 1920s. The walls were of dark, heavily varnished tongue-and-groove wood, and it seemed more like a setting from an early Theodore Dreiser novel than an ideal nuptial ambience.

The next morning we continued on through the northern greenery until golden leaves began to highlight hardwood trees among the rolling tide of evergreens. Then we rounded a curve to see the glitter where white sails and color-splashed spinnakers rode. Camp Wawbeek was set near the water just beyond the secluded cabins on a hillside of silver birches. That summer Win-nipesaukee was a lake I might have dreamed, serene and uncluttered. From its shores at dawning came the trills of wood thrushes and the liquid *cheerios* of robins. When the sounds of day diminished and darkness covered all, I re-membered Yeats: "I hear lake water lapping with low sounds by the shore . . . I hear it in the deep heart's core."

If there was no serpent in our garden, there was a reminder of Frost's warning that "nothing gold can stay." We came down with strep throat. An-tibiotics soon cured us, but now the days were dwindling, and there was a chill in the air.

Back at Drew we began our strange life of cramped furnished rooms, and it was only juice and sometimes coffee that sent us out each morning. We drove to Princeton or Scotch Plains for Sunday dinner with parents who feared we weren't getting enough to eat. Yvonne had exchanged her student status for a clerkship at Lerner's, where she sold costume jewelry like golden birds with ruby eyes by Corot.

I labored to leap the final hurdles to the B.A. Yvonne gamely caught the bus each morning, and then she helped me each night when I memorized for comprehensive exams. Then finally we got the crucial word: I had been ad-mitted to the graduate school of Northwestern University. We would be liv-ing close to the line on Yvonne's salary and withdrawals from my dwindling bank account until the GI subsistence checks came through. The next Sunday in Scotch Plains for dinner, I told Mother and Dad that after Christmas we would be leaving for Evanston. Mother said nothing for a moment but then audibly cleared her throat, an unfailing sign of emotion. "Son," she said, "you just *got* a degree."

On January 4, 1947, we stepped off the Pennsylvania Limited at Union Station in Chicago carrying three suitcases and a mimeographed list of one-room rentals. We were fortunate in finding one that day in a two-story frame house on a side street fifteen minutes from the campus. There was a decent restaurant called the Blue Plate at a halfway point. It became a hospice for us as the winter days advanced and the wind from Lake Michigan seemed to cut to the bone. The wind blew so savagely that when we ventured down Orrington Avenue for one of our few extravagances, Sunday dinner at the Orrington Hotel, we would sometimes have to stop in the foyers of residential hotels to thaw our frozen faces.

Yvonne found a job and began her forty-hour workweeks at the nearby Grey-Mills Company, which made typewriter-cleaning equipment and morticians' pumps. One of the salesmen had pinned an ad to the wall of the office's large main room: "Yes, that body looks fine on top, but is it black on the bottom?"

My daytime working hours were spent in the library at Northwestern or College Hall, a structure of massive blocks that was quite possibly the ugliest building on an otherwise harmonious scene. It housed one of the best faculties in the Big Ten. With the nine courses I would take over my three quarters there, I could try to make up my deficiencies in drama, the Middle Ages, the Renaissance, and American literature.

I was both unlucky and lucky in that winter's faculty at Northwestern. I missed Richard Ellmann, biographer of William Butler Yeats, who was then just beginning his biography of James Joyce. Learned, kind, and engaging, he was a quiet and natty professor who would help shape the careers of many graduate students. Still there was Leon Howard, a tanned, freckled Alabamian with a shock of brown hair that fell over his forehead as he lectured. With his Deep South accent and ready wit, he was one of a special type of Southerner I would come to know, the brilliant scholar and engaging raconteur. His survey course took us through Cooper, Twain, Dickinson, and Melville and gave me a sense of the breadth and diversity of my own native literature. In Leon Howard's courses I didn't have to worry about staying awake as I filled up my spiral notebooks. I elected his Melville course in the spring and followed him, fascinated, as he took us through Melville's days before the mast and the prodigies of work that took shape in his novels of the South Seas, and then his great triumph in *Moby-Dick*.

A student could earn the M.A. at Northwestern by completing coursework and either writing a thesis or passing a comprehensive examination. I was determined to complete the M.A. in three terms because we were homesick and lonely and wanted to return home as soon as we could. A thesis could take much more time than preparing for an examination, and so I began studying for it.

After dinner, usually a nourishing cheeseburger and rich milkshake at the Big Dipper, I would settle in for the night at the desk and Yvonne would sit propped against the headboard. About ten o'clock we would turn to radio programs introduced by familiar organ themes—"The Shadow" or "Murder at Midnight," simple relaxation that required no concentration. If there was no class the next morning, I would work on one of the two papers that would be due before the end of the term.

One of the papers was for a course I was taking to fill gaps in my background. As it turned out, Modern Drama did more than that. Clearly I needed to know the work of George Bernard Shaw, and I enjoyed the comic iconoclasm of *Pygmalion* and even the philosophical bent of *Man and Superman*. But the most exciting and provocative playwrights for me were J. M. Synge and Sean O'Casey. I was absorbed and excited by Synge's use of the Irish peasantry in the tragic *Riders to the Sea* and his own kind of iconoclasm in the satiric comedy of *The Playboy of the Western World*. There was the same range of material in O'Casey's exploitation of Irish history and culture, tragic in *The Plough and the Stars* and tragicomic in *Juno and the Paycock*. The course showed me the breadth and influence of the Irish renaissance. I had known something of Yeats and Joyce, but here were other stars in that large and brilliant constellation.

This course also did something for me that was quite personal. From Mother's family I had absorbed a fair amount of Irish popular culture. I knew the usual sentimental songs plus a few more memorable others such as "The Londonderry Air" and "The Wearin' of the Green." And I had sat upstairs in the attic playing on the old Victrola records of traditional airs sung by the celebrated John McCormack. But reading O'Casey's depiction of revolution in Ireland was very different from listening to my Aunt Tillie's memories of how awful the English were. These plays, poems, and stories were helping me to internalize a sense of what Irishness was. I didn't believe C. G. Jung's theory of a racial memory, but perhaps there were links besides the blood that ran in my veins, an inheritance that I saw so clearly in the Slatterys and Sullivans, the Carrolls and Connollys.

Classes ended, and it was time for the comprehensives. They were given in the largest lecture room in College Hall, and on the first morning there must have been seventy-five people waiting to take them. In this morning's three-hour session, we would select three of the four topics offered. I opened my blue book to the first of the lined pages and read all four topics. Then I read them again, because something strange had happened. My mind had gone blank. I couldn't think of *anything*. I couldn't choose a topic. All four seemed impossible. Around me people were scribbling vigorously. I rested my head in my hand and looked up to see if the chief proctor was staring at me, divining my sudden panic. He was apparently immersed in a book. Time ticked on. Then suddenly a phrase popped into my mind: "Hieronimo Is Mad Agayne," the subtitle of *The Spanish Tragedy.* Immediately the plot began to unreel in my mind. One of the exam topics dealt with Renaissance drama. Thomas Kyd and his Elizabethan revenge drama had saved me. When the proctor called a halt at noon, I felt exhausted, but I had completed the three essays. I was fortified by a sandwich, a Coke, and two Clark Bars, and by the sight of proctor Leon Howard's encouraging expression as he looked out at the room. I slipped into first gear and cruised through the rest of the afternoon exam and the one the next morning.

A week later my name was on the passed list. Now all I had to do was complete my coursework. Some of the pressure had been relieved, but I now saw that I had barely started my climb up the ladder. An M.A. would not be enough for the kind of career I envisioned. I had to go on for the Ph.D. This looming act was not just cold careerism. I *liked* what I was doing. The adventures of Frank Merriwell and Scaramouch had led me to the voyagings of the Ishmaels and Emperor Joneses, farther than I had ever been before.

At the end of the term I would have not only the M.A. but probably the grades and recommendations necessary for entry into a Ph.D. program. But where? Our homesickness and rented-room life had combined irresistibly in an urge toward home. I had thought again of Princeton, Harvard, and Yale, but all three required a reading knowledge of Latin, French, and German. My heart fell. I had three years of high school Latin but no French. The German I had picked up during the war was for bartering tobacco and sugar for bread and potatoes, not for reading scholarship and criticism. I returned to my search and soon found an institution that required only French and German: the University of Pennsylvania. I knew that Penn had one of the most prominent of the Ivy League graduate schools, and now I learned that it was in fact the oldest university in the United States. The commute from Princeton to Philadelphia would be a little more than an hour. If I could acquire some proficiency in the two languages on my own, I could press on with the required coursework in a reasonable amount of time.

Not long after I had passed the comprehensive examinations, the University of Pennsylvania accepted me. In a few weeks we were ready for the East and a march on one of the prestigious eastern citadels of Academia.

Gramma had come through for us. She had found an affordable four-room apartment on Alexander Street across from the Princeton Inn within easy distance of the railroad station and Nassau Street, and Yvonne lost no time in

hunting down a job. She applied for one in the burgeoning Princeton industry of opinion research and was offered an entry-level clerical job at Dr.
George Gallup's American Institute of Public Opinion. She did the work
uncomplainingly like so many of the other young wives who said they were
working on their Ph.T.'s ("Putting Hubby Through").

Most weekday mornings I would make the five-minute walk up Alexander Street to the Pennsylvania Railroad Station. I had bought a monthly ticket
to ride the shuttle out to Princeton Junction and to travel the main line among
the army of commuters. Emerging into the humming hive of the Thirtieth
Street Station, I would board the clanging No. 9 to Chestnut Street for the
five-minute walk to tree-shaded College Hall at the University of Pennsylvania. I would be spending twelve hours a week on this journey. Quite a price to
pay, I reflected, for neglecting my Latin and not learning German.

With what was left of my Latin I thought I could acquire enough French
to pass the Ph.D. reading exam. I would try to find a tutor who could help me
put an overlay of grammar on my sketchy German. I would have to do a lot of
learning on my own to pass another set of comprehensives. To fill one gap in
my background, I elected a historical survey of literary criticism, but I found
it so excruciatingly dull that I couldn't stay awake. I decided to pursue my
interest in Victorian literature, but a traditional course in the nineteenth-
century novel proved to be heavy going. This was not a promising beginning,
but my acute problem lay elsewhere.

The degree requirements included a sequence of semester-long courses
in Old English, Middle English, and Modern English. Riding home on the
train, I examined my used textbooks. Opening *Bright's Anglo-Saxon Reader* was
a shock. It looked like a foreign language. Some words that looked familiar
were the ancestors of Modern English words, but you couldn't be sure. I
opened our text, *Beowulf,* thinking that the difficulty of this alliterative verse
saga might somehow be redeemed by the dramatic struggle between the hero
and his monstrous adversary. When I turned to the first page, I was appalled:
"*Hwaet ur Gar-Dena . . . in gear-dagum. . . .*" I knew then that Beowulf's exploits
would be as opaque to me as the demon-infested pond Grendel and his mother
inhabited. "The Seafarer" and "The Wanderer" seemed more promising, but I
knew that if there was such a thing as a knack for Old English, I didn't have it.

I found two allies. One was a classmate, the possessor of an old New England name. Tristram P. Coffin was an expert tennis player who also had a
firm grip on the fundamentals of Old English. When we had time, we would
go over assignments together. We were fortunate in our instructor. Professor
Harold Stine was a short, rotund man with a broad, placid face beneath silver
hair parted neatly in the middle. One day when the class had finished the as-

signed translation without my having been called on, I sighed with relief. Dr. Stine paused, looked up, and said, "We've still got a few minutes left. Mr. Blotner, would you like to have a go at the next two lines?" It was as if he had asked, "Would you like to leap out of that window?"

I was stuck, and I knew it, but I heard myself say, "I'll try, Dr. Stine." He smiled and sat back to give me his full attention. When I stalled at the end of the first sentence, Dr. Stine offered a phrase, which I hastily accepted. When I paused again he said, "I'm afraid our time is up. Thank you, Mr. Blotner." I leaned back. Maybe I could make it through this course after all.

I wanted to get the language requirements out of the way by the beginning of the next academic year, so I bought a used German-English dictionary and pondered my next move. One of Yvonne's high school classmates was a tall, striking brunette named Barbara Johnson. Her boyfriend turned out to be a Swiss physicist at the RCA Laboratories in nearby Penn's Neck. His name was Dietrich Jenny. His long shock of dark hair was usually tousled from riding in his white Porsche with the top down. Dietrich said, "I've got a book that's different from the usual text because it's based on the structure of the German sentence." I accepted immediately. Dietrich's book proved to be a large one with diagrams. The author emphasized the way the typical German sentence placed the subject at the beginning and the verb at the end, with everything else fitted in between. I borrowed a volume of German prose and began spending some time on the project every day, and to my surprise the method began to work. I felt like a cautious tightrope walker grasping a long pole across his midriff to keep him from plunging into the abyss.

If my plate was full, so was Yvonne's. She never missed a day at AIPO. She shopped and cooked and cleaned, and I tried to remember to help. But there was the unexpected. One Saturday when I returned home she met me at the door, tearful and out of breath. "Nonnie called me from Palmer Square," she explained. Nonnie had said, "I've got blood poisoning," and Yvonne had run the half-mile to her mother's small room. She had installed her in our spare room, her foot elevated and wrapped in hot towels. She would have to rest there until the swelling subsided. "You won't mind if she stays here for a while, will you?" Yvonne asked. So we entered into a new phase as young marrieds scraping along on two incomes that barely made ends meet, with a mother-in-law completing our ménage.

The holidays came and went, and I had a decision to make. I had passed all my first-semester courses, and the department offered me a job as an "acting assistant instructor" while I continued my work. The position sounded so provisional that it was almost funny, but it paid $75 a month for three classes a week teaching English composition to freshman engineers. Now I would also have to confront a question I had avoided: How did I feel about teaching? I had enjoyed talking about literature and analyzing it, but standing up before two dozen undergraduates was something else, and drilling them in the structure of an essay and the avoidance of sentence fragments and comma splices would be totally new.

With no formal training as teachers, we instructors had been thrown off the end of the dock to sink or swim. Albert C. Baugh, the chairman of the department, undertook the task of teaching us raw beginners how to teach English. A silver eminence who had written a standard text on literature and language, he addressed us once a week. We took notes on his observations, which were often mainly anecdotal. Without a composition textbook, we were left to make up our own lectures and devise our own writing exercises. I cut stories and essays out of the *Saturday Evening Post* and *Harper's* and pasted them on sheets with my lecture notes. I talked about narration, description, and exposition. There were several problems for me: how to fill up the fifty-minute periods, how to gain the participation of students who seemed to think that the course was a waste of time. We assigned five-hundred-word themes, and so now I had something to do on the train besides study. With my briefcase on my knees, I marked up the pages in red pencil. After I handed them back, I would hold conferences in the small room I shared with my fellow instructors.

I felt insecure, and I hated the work. The days seemed especially long when I rode the train home with a new batch of themes and walked down Alexander Street to our apartment and greeted my wife—back from a long day at AIPO with the opinions of the man in the street. With her pathetic semi-invalid mother installed in the spare room, this was a new kind of domesticity, and as the next academic year approached, I did not look forward to it, much less to the rest of the long haul toward the Ph.D.

The Old English that had made me think of throwing in the sponge was in the past—thanks, I was convinced, to blessed Harold Stine. Middle English, the next semester, had required looking up a lot of words, but in it you could recognize our own English tongue, and when I first read "Whan that Aprill with his shoures soote / The droghte of March hath perced to the roote," I could almost feel the sweet April showers and understand how it was that the folk "of Engelonde to Caunterbury they wende." I was grateful now to Geoffrey Chaucer for more than the delightful bawdiness I had sought out in "The Miller's Tale" in high school. At last I could begin to see things coming together. Modern English, the third course in the sequence, was taught by a kind and attractive middle-aged professor named Caroline Brady, who made the shifts and changes in the language understandable.

As winter came in, I began my fourth semester at Penn. I had hoped that another course in the Victorian novel would lead to a dissertation topic, but it did not. I would have to start searching again. But I realized that I was riding in a steeplechase. I had to try to approach the obstacles one at a time. If I tried to look down the whole course at once, I would take a header. So I decided to take the German exam, and to my surprise I passed it. Now I could turn to classes.

I was lucky enough to get into a class that was essential for me. Robert E. Spiller, a fifty-one-year-old Philadelphian teaching American literature, was the most prestigious scholar in the department, and his courses were always full. He and such colleagues as Sculley Bradley had made Penn one of the foremost graduate schools for a new comprehensive approach presented under the rubric of American Civilization. Choosing Penn for the wrong reasons, I had chosen better than I knew. Bob Spiller's seminar was as large as some survey courses, but his emphasis was on research. A thin man with silver-rimmed spectacles and thinning brown hair that fell over the brow of his large cranium, he would sit puffing a pipe with an extraordinarily large bowl. When a student finished a report, he would offer brief comments or questions.

I was glad when my conference with him came. He made me feel comfortable in his large office crammed with books and papers, the air redolent of his strong tobacco. He smiled, stuffed the bowl, scratched a kitchen match, and puffed blue clouds into the shafts of late afternoon sunlight. "Well," he said, "what do you think you would like to do for your paper?"

"That's the problem," I said. "I don't know. I was happy to get through Old English, but now that I can see the end of the coursework, I feel sort of becalmed."

He took out a handkerchief and began polishing his glasses. "You know Professor Quinn, don't you?" Arthur Hobson Quinn was a Poe scholar who had helped to foster the study of American literature in the United States. Spiller tamped the dottle in the large bowl and relit it. "I'll tell you something. After I finished my coursework, I kept on reading until I was desperate. Finally I went in to Professor Quinn and said, 'Please, give me a dissertation!'" The remembered desperation struck a chord in me. "And he gave me one," Spiller said, smiling. "Tell me about the books you've enjoyed."

"I've enjoyed a lot of them, but I'm afraid that some of the ones I've enjoyed most wouldn't be serious enough for a dissertation."

"Tell me about some of them," he said.

Now that I'd made that dumb comment, I hesitated, trying to find something to back it up. "Do you know the novels of Thorne Smith?"

"*Topper*," he said, "*Topper Takes a Trip.*"

"Right!" I said, delighted.

"They were amusing," he said. "I remember them."

"After thirty years the books are still selling. Thorne Smith's two daughters were in high school with me, and I was curious to see what his books were like."

"I remember that he used comedy and a kind of supernatural fantasy, and the books had risqué covers of girls in their underwear," Spiller said.

"Yes," I said, "and quite a bit of satire about the world of the twenties and thirties, and they're only mildly risqué, although they sold a lot of copies."

"Did you talk to his daughters about him?"

"Not much, because he died when they were eight or ten. He was an alcoholic and so was his wife, so there weren't a whole lot of happy memories, I gathered. But they still have all his books, and I think the older one, Marion, said something about his manuscripts once."

He poked at his pipe. "You said you thought the novels were satirical. So you saw something there besides comic fantasy and sex."

"Oh, yes. In a way you could say he was a kind of social critic."

"Why don't you talk with the daughters and ask them to let you see what they've got? Then come back and we can talk about it."

I left in a state of cautious optimism. From June Smith I got Marion's number in Berkeley Heights. "We've got most of the books," she told me, "and I'll have a look in the attic to see what else there is."

After Sunday dinner with Mother and Dad, Yvonne and I drove up the familiar winding road to Berkeley Heights and Free Acres. The rambling cottage with its large screened porch was as I remembered it. Marion hadn't changed either, a slim blue-eyed woman with her father's prominent nose and hair so blonde that her eyelashes were almost invisible. Two years younger, June was an opposite: short, quiet, and brunette. After reminiscences and catching up, I asked Marion if she had found any of the materials.

"Yes," she said, "but I didn't feel like going through it all. It would save time if you'd just see what's there." She called to her husband, who carried in a large, old-fashioned trunk. Marion undid the straps and lifted the lid. It was almost full. "There's a lot of old stuff here," she said, lifting objects out and setting them on an end table.

There appeared to be a dozen of Thorne Smith's books—probably first editions, from the look of the jackets. Underneath the books was a layer of white and yellow pages. The ones on top had been gnawed on the edges. Paper clips had imprinted the top sheets with their rusty marks. "Nobody's been in here for years," Marion said. "The yellow paper is notes and manuscripts. The white paper is typescripts." At the bottom of the trunk were a notebook, rodent-gnawed packets of letters, and a few clippings. "You might as well take it all with you," Marion said. "Keep it as long as you want."

I remembered Leon Howard telling us at Northwestern about Raymond Weaver's visiting Herman Melville's granddaughter. She had shown him a trunk of papers, among them the manuscript of a novella called *Billy Budd, Foretopman*. Melville had left it unfinished at his death in 1891, his name obscure and his reputation kept alive by a small group of admirers. The publication of Weaver's edition of *Billy Budd* in 1924 gave an essential impetus to the Melville revival that established him as one of America's literary giants. By no stretch could one put Thorne Smith in Herman Melville's company. All I hoped for was a workable dissertation topic. I knew I could do it, but would Spiller buy the idea? I was encouraged, and not just by his story of his own dissertation problems. Although he had made his reputation with studies of James Fenimore Cooper, his first book was called *The Americans in England during the First Half-Century of Independence*. It sounded off the main line of literary studies to me, and he had possessed the initiative to go ahead with it. Maybe that impulse would work in my favor, too.

As soon as we got the trunk home, we spread its contents on the living room rug. Sorting them, we found manuscripts of *Topper, The Nightlife of the Gods, Did She Fall?* and *Rain in the Doorway*. Written in pencil on yellow copy paper and marked with erasures, cancellations, and interlineations, they represented various stages of composition. There were also manuscript fragments of *Turnabout* and *The Bishop's Jaegers*. These white pages were typescripts of four of the novels, showing many deletions and additions. This would be plenty to reveal Smith's development over the prolific last eight years of his short life.

In the week before my appointment with Spiller, I had a chance to start reviewing Smith's novels and working my way through the materials from the trunk. He had certainly been a popular novelist. Since 1926 his books had sold over ten million copies in the United States, and they had been published in fourteen other countries. And as I continued to try to put him in a literary context, I saw antecedents for the kinds of novels he wrote, even in work as different as that of James Branch Cabell and Sinclair Lewis. Smith's novels came to be stereotyped by some critics as ribald stories abounding in alcohol, nudity, and Rabelaisian humor. Cosmo Topper, a repressed and unhappily married businessman, was clearly his creator's favorite, a character who had a good deal in common with Sinclair Lewis's Sam Dodsworth. The freedom and change of values Topper achieves help to reinforce Smith's social commentary and satire.

I saw how devices transcending reality drove most of his episodic plots. In *Topper,* George and Marion Kerby were not just debonair spirits but also ghosts whose ectoplasm unpredictably rendered them visible or invisible. In *Turnabout,* two complaisant but temperamental lovers found themselves inexplicably inhabiting each other's bodies. In *The Night Life of the Gods,* statues came to life and Olympians disported themselves with mortals. Smith exploited these devices imaginatively. What gave the novels a redeeming quality that transcended fantasy was the change in the mortals who inhabit Smith's pages. It was a fundamental transvaluation that freed them from their previous roles. His favorite objects of satire included big business and advertising, as well as accepted codes of sexual behavior and the bigotry and prejudice he saw around him. I wondered about the many deletions in the manuscripts and typescripts. Were they purely stylistic, or had they been made—perhaps at the behest of an editor or agent—to make the novels more acceptable in the literary marketplace?

Gradually Smith's life was coming into focus for me. He was the great-grandson of Don José Maxwell, a Brazilian coffee planter and fleet owner, and the son of James Thorne Smith, an Annapolis-trained commodore. Named for his father, the boy spent an unhappy childhood in boarding schools and relatives' homes. He entered Dartmouth only to leave after two years to write advertising copy in Manhattan. Tied there by the need to support a wife and two small children, "Jimmy" Smith worked at his own writing on the kitchen table of their small Greenwich Village apartment. A colleague sketched a description of him: "Thorne was a small pixie-like man, blond and blue-eyed, pink cheeked and very innocent looking, dressed to the teeth (derby, cane, fitted navy-blue overcoat, white muffler, and I think spats) and was the enfant terrible of the organization. He had a habit of leaving a sober piece of financial advertising copy in the middle of a sentence and disappearing for weeks. The executives all seemed to have proper respect for his ability because he was never fired, but was always received with open arms when he returned."

He worked at another agency before his writing began to sell, and he often fell victim to fits of despondency. Fervently made resolutions would dissolve in weekends that found him lying naked on a bed, quietly drinking and deaf to the entreaties of his wife, Celia, from the other side of the locked door. But Monday morning, or sometimes Tuesday, would find him back at his desk, generating what creativity he could in ads for Electrol Oil Burners or the American Tobacco Company. Another colleague described a changed Smith, no longer the dandy he had been: "He was a strange person without appearing in the least eccentric. He was inconspicuous in both looks and manner. . . . You might have to look twice to see that he was there. I suppose his very light coloring may have helped, but he could come as near to disappearing as any human being I ever saw. He was not only quiet; there was a stillness about him."

I could only speculate whether or not this rare bird in American literature would seem substantial enough to support a Ph.D. candidacy at the University of Pennsylvania. Smith was no Melville.

As I walked from the streetcar stop, I rehearsed my arguments. Spiller's office door was open, the blue haze as thick as last time. He waved me to the chair by his desk.

"Did you have any luck?" he asked.

"I think I did," I told him and handed across my one-page inventory of the old trunk's contents. He put down his pipe and leaned back in his chair.

"Here's a book you should look at," he told me. He had written out, "*Golden Multitudes: The Story of Best-Sellers in the United States,* Frank Luther Mott." He searched among the papers on his desk. "That one has just come out, and Jimmy Hart at UCLA is working on a history of popular books in this country."

"You mean that you think this will make a dissertation?" I asked.

"I think it might," he said, "if we present it on a basis other than solely literary merit. Will that bother you?"

"No," I said immediately.

"It's the kind of topic you usually find in American Civilization programs rather than conventional English departments. It won't help you compete for a job in departments looking to fill a conventional slot, but we can call your dissertation something like, 'Thorne Smith: A Study in Popular Fiction.' "

This was new, high-level stuff to me. I nodded as I would have nodded at anything he said, relieved that now I had a dissertation topic.

Spiller fired his pipe's big bowl, and as the aromatic blue cloud rose, it was as though he had performed a celebratory act.

"You've got a lot to do," he said with a smile. "After you've done some more checking and thought about your approach, come in and we'll do some paperwork and get you started."

Yvonne and I went to Lahiere's for dinner that night. What lay ahead was the French language exam and one more three-hour course that I could take on Saturdays, which would reduce the commuting to one day a week. The comprehensives would be the last of that set of requirements. Finally would come the dissertation and defense. For Yvonne, the prospect would remain the same: the routine at AIPO.

There was another problem, though: whether or not I could still draw the GI Bill check with just a partial course load. But Yvonne had been working for quite a while now, and even if I couldn't get a job that would allow her to quit, I wanted to get one for other reasons too, to move beyond my pinchpenny graduate-student circumstances and function fully as a man in the outside world again.

TEN

Is That All There Is?

IN THE SECOND SEMESTER OF 1948 I THOUGHT I COULD see something like freedom ahead. I would walk down Alexander Street only on Saturday mornings for my trains to Philadelphia for my last course. My instructorship had gone to some other graduate student. Good luck to him. My deliverance would mean saving time and money and, more important, relief from the depression I felt each time I left my wife and home.

I hadn't gotten to know any of my fellow commuters, and few of them would have attracted attention, although one day as the shuttle left Princeton, I noticed a stooped figure shuffling past me. He had caught my attention because of the pajama bottoms and carpet slippers showing beneath the raincoat. The face under the hat brim was that of Kurt Gödel, the formulator of Gödel's incompleteness theorem. A member of the Institute for Advanced Study, he might have been off to New York for a conference or a think tank.

That was Princeton for you. You never knew whom you might see. One friend told us about standing before the glass cases of the Princeton Delicatessen in Palmer Square and fishing through her purse only to find her pack of cigarettes empty. A tall, thin man beside her said, "Here," and held out his own near-empty pack.

"Oh, no, I couldn't take your last one," she told him. As he turned in profile, the bladelike nose and cropped poll made him instantly recognizable. It was J. Robert Oppenheimer, the nuclear-physicist director of atomic science at Los Alamos.

"I have many cigarettes," he said, patting his pockets and withdrawing a pack. "Take it!" he told her imperiously. That was Princeton too, like seeing

Brian Aherne, in town for *The Barretts of Wimpole Street,* buying a newspaper on Nassau Street.

My malaise was one many commuters must feel, but for me there was also a special twinge. Penn was stuck in the middle of a big city, and all I knew of it was College Hall and the library, but Princeton had been for me the archetypal university since my first glimpse of it. I hated to see the spires and towers fade as the train pulled out. I enjoyed seeing them reappear, but I couldn't help thinking of Hardy's *Jude the Obscure*—of Jude Fawley looking at the university from which he was excluded. The realist in me had dictated what seemed the proper course of action, but the romantic in me continued to react on an almost subliminal level. I was putting down roots in Princeton, a process with the potential for problems.

When classes ended, I realized that the brief promise of freedom would prove an illusion. I continued studying French. Anticipating the final comprehensive exam, I made reading lists. On one I had written, "*Must Read* more Faulkner, Hemingway, Wolfe, Conrad, Lawrence, Huxley." I didn't realize that I was apparently trying to make myself into a modernist. Other inclusive lists reminded me of one of Jay Gatsby's boyhood resolutions for self-improvement: "Study needed inventions." I continued reading and rereading Thorne Smith's novels, for theme and satire. And periodically I saw Spiller, who said I should begin with a biographical chapter. Celia Smith had died some years ago, and Marion and June thereafter had lived with relatives. The aunt closest to their parents was dead, and so was Smith's literary agent. I would have to keep on digging.

Naively, I thought I might learn something about the milieu of Smith's early life as a writer from one who lived just up the street from us. The novelist John O'Hara was a recognizable figure, driving his green MG roadster with "J O'H" in gold on the door. I wrote to him cold, asking if he could spare a little time to give me some sense of what it was like in the twenties and thirties for a young writer to make his way in the New York publishing world. I had no great hopes for my appeal to an industrious and sometimes irascible novelist. Just when I had concluded that there would be no reply, a letter arrived. It contained a single line: "Does the University of Pennsylvania give Ph.D.'s on Thorne Smith?" It was signed, "Faithfully, John O'Hara."

I had better luck with a memory from Marion Smith. Someone had mentioned Roland Young, a British character actor successful in various whimsical roles. Short and balding, he wore a brushlike moustache that complemented a very British accent. It was produced, said one of his friends, by a delivery that made his upper lip appear to have been injected with Novocain. He had played the title role in the film version of *Topper* in 1937, and again two years later in *Topper Takes a Trip*. "I remember him," Marion said. "He used to come to our apartment on Bank Street to see Daddy, and they would sit at the kitchen table drinking beer and eating cheese and crackers. I liked him." When I wrote him I received a cordial reply and a pleasant reception when I called at his midtown New York apartment. His wife was a beautiful English-woman, some years younger than he. We had a good hour of conversation, and Young invited me to join them for lunch. He was a good raconteur, his stories made more droll by his accent and hesitant delivery. He described a party at Smith's house in Free Acres to celebrate a royalty check for *Topper Takes a Trip* that made the family solvent again. The other guests included H. L. Mencken and Mae West. A memento was left in the Smiths' *Book of Common Prayer*, in which Mencken had scribbled, "Compliments of the author."

Smith's life ended at forty-two, just when he seemed on the threshold of substantial commercial success. I was sorry that there was not more to tell, especially when I read Ogden Nash's reply to me: "He was very quiet, almost neurotically shy. A little faded wisp of a man with pale gold hair, usually dressed in brown, who reminded me of an autumn scene; always carried a stout cane as if to avoid being blown away. Sweet, but you felt an other-world, changeling quality."

So I finished my first chapter and turned to the French exam. When I sat down to it, I saw at once that the passage was written in a style that seemed familiar, though I didn't recognize the old man obsessively devoted to two un-grateful daughters. But I had been reading Balzac as well as Zola, and though I felt shaky on some of the grammar, I thought I had rendered pretty well the meaning of this passage from *Le Père Goriot*. A postcard informing me that I had passed arrived a week later.

As I began to divide my days between reviewing for the comprehensive and researching the sales of Smith's novels, I felt a growing sense of unease. The back pay from my time in Germany and my long leave was just about gone. The GI Bill would soon end for me, and I didn't think we could squeak along on Yvonne's salary. I would get a job and then do my reviewing and re-search at night. When I passed my Saturday-morning seminar class, I could discard my commuter's ticket with relief. One day when I returned home I reached for my pen, part of a matched Eversharp set Yvonne had given me. When I couldn't find it in my pockets or my briefcase, I realized that it must be somewhere on the floor of a Pennsylvania Railroad car or perhaps lodged in one of the dull green seats. This loss seemed to me symbolic.

Reading the Help Wanted columns immersed me in a cold bath of reality. I had a B.A. and an M.A., but what could I do? There were no factories or radio stations nearby, but I hoped that I might qualify for the advertising industry. So I took the train into New York and made the rounds—to Young and Rubicam, to Kenyon and Eckhart, to Batten, Barton, Durstine and Osborn. The first interview was a preview of the rest. After I made my way through the glass and stone and shining metal of the lobby, I waited for a half-hour before an attractive but brusque secretary sent me to the personnel office. The kindly middle-aged brunette seemed to accept my fiction of advertising experience. "Did you bring any of your tear sheets?" she asked me. I didn't know what a tear sheet was, but I said I would be glad to send some. If I had felt before like Jude Fawley, I now felt like George Hurstwood in *Sister Carrie,* supported by his young mistress. I was one of the unemployed, and after a week of fruitless looking, I sat there at home while Yvonne was out working at AIPO. I felt my self-esteem dropping further than the balance in our savings account.

Yvonne had mentioned my job search to a friend at AIPO, who told her, "Joe should check out Benson and Benson. I heard they got a new client, and they may be hiring." Glad of a lead of any kind, I walked down Witherspoon Street to the old Branch Building and made my way up a staircase walled with dull brown wainscoting. If this were New York, I thought, this place would be a sweatshop.

My visit here was another act in a chain of events that would not play out to their climax for nearly forty years. The large room could indeed have been a garment-district loft if the half-dozen desks had borne sewing machines instead of typewriters and strange-looking devices called, as I learned later, Comptometers. A secretary named Dora led me down a narrow aisle to the middle one of the three offices, where a harried-looking man sat behind a desk littered with papers. "I'm Van Zandt," he said and extended his hand. He looked to be in his forties, thin-faced and balding with tired-looking brown eyes. "You came in at a good time," he told me. "Market research is a pretty steady business, but every once in a while we get a new job that needs more people than our regular staff. Our new account is the W. R. Grace Company. They're interested in making cellophane, and we've got to try to find out whether there will be enough of a market to justify the investment." The salary was little more than my pitiful wages at Penn, but I was ready to accept almost anything.

When I arrived Monday at 8:30 A.M., Dora introduced me. "This is Jerry Bramwell," she said. He was a tall, wiry man in shirtsleeves, vaguely untidy, who clenched my hand in a tight grip.

"Glad to have you with us," he said. His tone was cordial, but I thought there was something of the wary Yankee about him. Dora led me into Van's office, where three men about my age stood together. "These fellows will be working with you on the Grace job," Van said and introduced them. He cleared a space on his desk and handed me a form. "This is the interview," he said. "It's a series of questions about products and packaging." He handed me a list of corporate names and phone numbers. "What I want you to do is call and try to set up interviews." I couldn't help wondering why he would shunt this job off to a new employee and concluded that the account executives had all they could do with other projects. I had already begun to sense that this was a no-frills business with the overhead kept as low as possible.

The day in New York turned out about as I expected. I managed to fit in three separate interviews and felt that I had garnered more information than I had expected about the plans of three food manufacturers. Returning home, I found that I was exhausted. Even worse was the accumulated sense of extracting exceedingly boring information about an enterprise I cared nothing about.

One week and two trips later, Van was satisfied. I was shifted to another job. Miracle Clean was about to go into production on a detergent called Surf, and the ad agency was doing jingles for radio commercials. The goal of this research was to determine which jingle of three would be most appealing. Our research tools consisted of a portable phonograph, a thin plastic disk in a paper sleeve, and pads of tabulation forms. On Van's desk was a map labeled "Trenton and Environs," with lines marking off four districts. "We've rented cars," Van said, "and here are the streets you're each responsible for. With any luck, you should be able to do your interviews in a day."

In my Ford economy rental I headed west on U.S. 1. An hour and two wrong turns later I saw the first block of low clapboard structures with peeling paint that told me I had found the Projects. I walked down the block to a unit where three small girls in pigtails were playing hopscotch. "Is this your house?" I asked the tallest one. She nodded wordlessly, but when I knocked on the door, there was no answer. I knocked again, and the door opened at last. A large and very dark woman in her forties tugged briefly at her housedress and looked at me. "Good afternoon, ma'am," I said. By the window was a four-burner electric stove, its porcelain randomly pocked and dented. A massive black cast-iron skillet dominated all. Standing in the doorway, I went into my spiel. She looked at me doubtfully, and so I repeated my recital with what felt like an idiotic grin. "It'll just take a few minutes for you to listen to these recordings, and I have a little gift from Miracle Clean for you to show our appreciation. May I come in?"

"Aw right," she said and stepped back. I set the phonograph turntable spinning while the three small members of this test group watched attentively. "I'll play three short songs and ask you to tell me how you like them," I told the mother. I put the needle in the groove, and there upon the air of the small kitchen, redolent of fried pork, floated tinny female voices. They were joyous about the virtues of Surf. I picked up my clipboard. "Mrs. Brown," I said, "which one did you like best?" She pursed her lips, and I waited.

"I like the las' one," she said. I was supposed to ask her what she liked about it, but I didn't have the heart. I handed her a small, violently colored box that showed something like a tsunami issuing from a washing machine.

"Thank you very much for your help, Mrs. Brown," I said effusively.

"You welcome," she told me.

As I drove around the block I asked myself, Why did I take up that poor woman's time? What good would this do anybody? I completed five more interviews.

I was glad to see Spiller again. I had been looking for patterns in Thorne Smith's novels, and I had found that marital unhappiness and sexual adventures were near constants, reinforced by a comic use of the supernatural. Supporting my case that Smith was more than just a comic novelist, I felt that his heroes did indeed undergo a change in their fundamentally bourgeois values. Whether or not he had cut the social criticism to ensure sales wasn't clear. What was clear was that he had found a formula that worked. His fourteen books were published by more than a dozen houses in America and at least that many abroad. The books totaled over fifty American editions with more than 225 printings, and gross American sales passing thirteen million.

Spiller went over these figures and my arguments for my thesis. He rocked back in his chair and read the two and a half pages I had drafted. Then he smiled that smile I had come to value. "All right," he said. "I think you've proved your case. Now go home and write your book."

The emotional high lasted into my next Benson and Benson assignment: questioning housewives about their families' purchasing preferences. As I set out with my three colleagues, the day threatened rain. It was Trenton again, a neighborhood of one-family houses with small, thinly grassy front yards. Stan Ellis parked, and we sat going over the questionnaires as the windows steamed up. "Christ," Bob Morris said at last. "They want everything but the guy's blood type."

"Let's give it a shot and come back in an hour for lunch," Phil Morse said.

In my first attempt, an unshaven man in a Notre Dame sweatshirt answered the door. He listened to my spiel and seemed to welcome my company. He had been laid off by the Roebling Company two months before. He had filed for unemployment benefits and recently turned to the Help Wanted ads. I liked him, and for a minute I was tempted to stay and commiserate with him, but his genial response to my questions was somehow strangely depressing.

The skies had made good their promise with a light rain. There was no answer at the next house, and the next doorbell I tried was answered by an aproned gray-haired woman who cut off my inquiry before I finished it. I picked up my pace as the rain increased and returned to the car. "Let's eat," Stan said. He drove to an intersection dominated by an Esso station and a White Castle restaurant. Below the crenellated roof the plate-glass windows were plastered with ads for ten-cent hamburgers. We carried our trays to a corner booth.

"How did it go?" Bob asked Stan.

"Two full pages," Stan told him. "I'm a goddam genius at this." The rain continued steadily. We ate in silence, then went back to the car, where Stan started counting through the questionnaires left on his clipboard. "I've got an idea," he said. "I think we've got a pretty good sense of how John Q. Public thinks. Right? OK. Let's just do the rest of the interviews right here in the car."

"You mean just make them up?" Bob asked.

"Would they be worse than what we already have?" Stan asked.

"Wait a minute," Phil said. "I hear they always catch cheater sheets."

"Who would catch them? Van? I'm not sure they even look at them."

A few minutes later I realized that Stan was filling out the top sheet on his clipboard. Bob sighed.

"What the hell," Phil said, and I could feel Bob writing beside me.

It wasn't hard to imagine a name or an occupation that would fit one of the addresses on this street, but filling in the rest of the profile of my imaginary respondent was harder. As I began to construct this persona, I started to feel queasy, as though my White Castle hamburger had turned to grease in my stomach. As I put my pencil down, I could see Bob erasing what he had written.

Stan turned to look at me. "What's wrong?" he asked. "Stuck?"

I crumpled the questionnaire. "Just chicken," I said.

"They'll can you," he said.

"No," I said, "I'll quit." No one spoke. The windshield wipers clattered as Stan headed back toward U.S. 1.

At home I opened a beer and sat at the dining room table watching raindrops slide down the windowpane. A movie theme full of sweet strings and nostalgic sadness kept running through my head. The film had rendered the longings of Toulouse-Lautrec, but the music captured the melancholy I felt. I had worked hard during these years toward a goal that now seemed impossible. My feeling was not so much frustration as depression.

Yvonne would be home soon. She had never complained, working for a manufacturer of mortician's pumps in Evanston or a tabulator of opinions in Princeton. And she had never voiced any doubts about my ability. It was her fate to be born into a generation of young women with talent and imagination who accepted a role that pushed their own ambitions into the background. I put hamburgers in a pan and set the table. When Yvonne came in, I poured her a glass from our jug of Chianti and gave her the day's mail: a couple of bills and a letter from her sister. When she finished it, I was almost ready to serve.

"Was it any better today?" she asked.

"Actually, worse. I better prepare you." I told her about declining to compose cheaters.

"Good," she said. "I would have been surprised if you had."

I headed back to Benson and Benson late the next morning. I had no desk to clean out, and my crew had already left for Trenton, but the person I wanted to see was still there at a desk in the corner entering figures in a Comptometer. The carriage clattered to a halt and he looked up.

"Hi, Charlie," I said. "I'm glad to see you." It had taken me a while to get to know Charlie Allen because he worked only part time. He had been an English major at John Marshall, but after the war he had transferred to Princeton. Studying psychology, he had acquired enough statistics to work on the Benson and Benson ballots and questionnaires. He was a year younger than I, and besides our educational backgrounds we had the Air Corps and other interests in common, such as football and jazz. About my height, he had curly red hair and dark brown eyes that lit up when he smiled. A West Virginian, he had a Southern storyteller's gift with a sophisticated sense of humor. Now I told him what I had done.

"Well," he said, raising his eyebrows, "I'm sorry I won't be seeing you around here, but I wouldn't be here myself if I didn't have to be."

Now I followed an impulse I had felt before. "Can you and your wife come over to our place for a beer and maybe some bridge?" I asked.

"I'll check with Marnie and call you," he said.

Making my last exit from the big room with the ornate false ceiling, I was in a lighter mood as I walked down the dark stairs into the pale sunlight of Witherspoon Street.

The night they came to our house, we discovered that Yvonne and Marnie already knew each other. Marnie was half a year older, and from Township School they had many friends in common. I liked Marnie immediately. She was a little taller than Yvonne, but also green-eyed with pale skin and dark hair. After one rubber of bridge, we stopped and slipped into lively conversation. We learned that our lives had several parallels. Theirs had been a college romance like ours but a longer one. They had fallen in love before Charlie had gone overseas and then married after his return, two months after Yvonne and I. But they had preceded us in one way: Marnie was now in the last month of her first pregnancy, large in her black dress but not ungainly. When we decided we had had enough bridge, I drew her chair from the table, and as she moved back and began to rise slowly, Charlie came over to her side. "Maybe we need a winch," he said. We all laughed, Marnie not the least of us.

Charlie and I compared notes on Benson and Benson and exchanged wry reminiscences. He asked me where I was going to apply for another job, but I had no idea. "Have you thought about RCA Labs?" he asked. I had not, but we had talked about Dietrich Jenny and a few other engineers we knew. "I know Dietrich has to write reports and patent disclosures on his research," Charlie said, "and I know he doesn't much like it. Why don't you go out and see if you can get a job there?"

I had had no previous inkling of any job possibilities out there beyond the familiar traffic circle that led to the large industrial campus with the red RCA logo within the circle of lightning bolts. I had no prospects at all. So why not try, I thought, with no sense that Charlie's suggestion might lead to another definitive act in my life.

The RCA Laboratories Division of the Radio Corporation of America was just off U.S. 1 only a few miles east of Benson and Benson, but it could hardly have been more different. On a flat landscaped sweep of green one long three-story building was adjoined by five smaller ones, housing almost a thousand employees. Sitting in the comfortable foyer, I wondered what in the world I was doing there, going in cold again. Filling out the application form in the personnel office, I constructed another piece of creative writing based on my earlier ones. With long fingers accented by glossy red nail polish, Miss Cunliffe pushed her tortoiseshell glasses back onto the crown of her hair. "I don't see any legal experience here," she said. "Do you have any?"

"No, I'm afraid not," I said.

She tapped her pencil on her teeth. Still looking at the form, she said, "We have a new department that started up this month, and I think I'll check on something. This may be a long shot, but if you don't mind waiting, I shouldn't be long."

How could it not be a long shot, I wondered, when I felt as though I had blundered into a strange country? I opened the *RCA Review* and tried to read an article entitled "The Application of Microwave Spectral Absorption in the Development of High Accuracy Time Standards." When Miss Cunliffe returned and stood at her desk, I rose.

"There's someone I'd like you to meet," she said. "That is, if you can stay for another half-hour."

"Absolutely," I said.

"It's this way," she said, her heels clicking on the polished floor. "Mr. Dyke is on the next floor in the Patent Department."

When we left the elevator she led me down the hall and into a large room where about a half-dozen women sat at typewriters and four men read from manila folders. At the first office in an adjoining corridor, she stopped in the doorway.

"Mr. Dyke," she said, "this is Joseph Blotner."

A smiling man about my height stepped from behind his desk. "I'm Gordon Dyke," he said. "Glad to meet another former member of the armed forces." There on a side table was a photograph of a pleasant-looking woman and two small boys. Another portrait showed a man with navy lieutenant's stripes on his sleeve.

"That's an interesting vita you have," he said.

"I wish it showed more technical background," I said, feeling a blip in my stomach.

"I'll tell you why it interested me and what we're doing here. I guess you know that our main product here at the labs is inventions, but they're only of limited use to the corporation if we don't know exactly what we've got for licensing and sometimes for infringement litigation. What I'm doing here, with my small cadre of engineers and lawyers, is installing a system. It will help us describe and classify everything our scientists think is good enough to patent." He was warming to his subject.

"What we do is look at a patent disclosure and application and analyze the general field of the invention, its particular characteristics, and its potential applications." Looking at me intently, he tapped his fingers on the desk as he spoke. "That's why we're called Patent Research and Planning. You see? This is one of my concerns: to improve the quality of writing in the Patent Department, and in the rest of the division, too. That's why I was interested in your background." I felt another blip in my stomach.

He opened a folder and led me through three mimeographed pages. "This is our patent classification system. With these abbreviations we can describe anything from a twenty-four-foot antenna array to a transistor component the size of a needle and tell you what you need to know about them whether you're an engineer or an attorney."

"It's very impressive," I said.

"Absolutely," he said. "You must have done a whole lot with electronics in the Air Corps."

"We got some in preflight," I said, "and then we had to deal with the equipment in the B-17." I was improvising, trying to make what little I could out of that experience without sounding glib.

"Well," he said after a half-hour, "I've enjoyed talking with you." He leaned back in his chair and brushed his mustache with his forefinger. "I've got some ideas about how you might fit in here. Let's leave it this way: I'll try to give you a call by the end of the week."

I gave him my most cordial smile and my most military handshake, waiting to analyze my feelings until I reached the parking lot, making an effort not to get my hopes up because the idea of me working in a research laboratory with a bunch of lawyers and scientists still seemed preposterous.

While I was waiting for Yvonne to arrive home I read the new *Town Topics* and reread the old *Princeton Packet*. There was nothing in Help Wanted for me. When the pale afternoon sunlight had faded toward darkness, I lit the lights in the living room and just sat. When Yvonne arrived, I tried to give her an absolutely factual report of my excursion to Penn's Neck.

"Don't be too pessimistic," she said. "You can't tell. You got the job at Benson and Benson when you were going around the house singing 'Brother, Can You Spare a Dime.'"

I went back to the dissertation and to Thorne Smith. I didn't laugh aloud, but at least there were stretches when I could forget that I wasn't a breadwinner—or a student, either.

Late one Friday afternoon, the phone rang. Yvonne picked it up and said, "It's for you."

"This is Gordon Dyke," the voice said. "Can you come in Monday morning? And bring your social security number."

As I hung up the phone I hoped that I had been coherent. I called to Yvonne. "Sweetie!" I said. "Turn off those hamburgers, we're going to Lahiere's for dinner. Looks like we'll be living like the middle class again."

When I entered Gordon Dyke's office on Monday morning, he rose and gave me his firm handclasp. "Welcome aboard!" he said.

"Glad to be aboard, sir," I told him. And so I was. It was not just that my salary would be more than I had made as a second lieutenant. It was also that the benefits were wonderful, with medical insurance and a retirement plan and employee discounts on products. In that January of 1949 we would buy an RCA radio-phonograph. My first paycheck gave me the sense of security I had longed for. Once again, if there was laughter offstage, I did not hear it. If I felt any immediate anxiety, it was not over my true career's being on hold but from wondering if I could hang on to this job.

It proved to be a strange experience. I read about concepts and devices more foreign to me than the moons of Jupiter. I had never thought of English grammar as one of my strong points, but it was what saved me now. The stilted, precise language of these patents made it possible to follow the referents and modifiers related to the verbs and objects. I found that I could describe a process even if I couldn't understand it—a weird experience, like wading through syrup.

There was one stratum of the Laboratories I saw very little. The third floor housed the executive offices, but occasionally one of their number might appear briefly in our hallway: Dr. C. B. Jolliffe, a slow-moving, portly man who was vice president and technical director of the Laboratories and the parent corporation. A figure of secular veneration was Dr. Vladimir K. Zworykin, a Russian immigrant, an authentic genius and the principal inventor of the iconoscope and the kinescope, the cathode ray tubes on which the whole burgeoning television industry was founded. He no longer worked in the laboratory, but his word was respected throughout the corporation despite an accent like that of the Mad Russian on Jack Benny's radio program. It gave even me something like a thrill to pass his thick figure in the corridor, seeing that broad Slavic face with the eyes that almost twinkled behind the gold-rimmed spectacles.

But the real presence from Olympus I never saw. He had come to Princeton for the dedication of the labs in 1942 and had probably visited them rarely thereafter. Very likely he had been seen even more rarely in the third-floor suite furnished especially for him, complete with hardwood bookcases on which stood rows of attractively bound books purchased by the yard. David Sarnoff, also a Russian immigrant, was another authentic genius whose achievements had made him the nearly mythical figure RCA public relations celebrated. It was he who, as a youthful wireless operator, had first picked up the distress signals of the *Titanic*. A practical dreamer, he imagined a kind of music box that would play music pulled from the ether. The National Broadcasting Company became one embodiment of his dream. He even had an honorific title. As Dwight D. Eisenhower's wartime advisor on communications, he had been given a brigadier general's commission, and he was forever after referred to in the company as General Sarnoff or the General.

I was now experiencing something I knew from books. Sinclair Lewis had given several of his novels the subtitle "The Romance of Business," and the life of a Philadelphia magnate had provided the basis for Theodore Dreiser's naturalistic novels *The Financier* and *The Titan*. I had joined the union at WAAT, and labor-management disputes had been brought home to me by Dad's experience. When he went to work at Mack Motors he had joined the CIO, and they had soon gone out on strike. "He's been out with the rest of the men," Mother had said, "out there in a signboard and walking in the snow on his varicose legs."

The outside world loomed unforgettably in January of 1949. Each year the annual meeting of the Patent Department brought attorneys from all the divisions to Princeton. This year someone had chosen to show newly released government films of the dropping of the atomic bombs on Hiroshima and Nagasaki. They were completely horrifying—not just in the growth of the mushroom cloud but also in the horrible billowing and roiling of those dark masses that looked as though they could expand until they consumed everything. The narration was quite technical, but the whole was like a preview of Armageddon. This sophisticated audience was stunned into silence broken only occasionally by murmurs of awe and shock. To me it seemed to foreshadow the end of our world as we knew it. Awareness of the Cold War only emphasized my sense that we were on the edge of the abyss.

That fear hung over us as we got on with our lives. I kept to my plan, dealing with patents by day and Thorne Smith by night. Gradually the pages piled up. In chapter 4 I dealt with the perceived obscenity and immorality of his novels. I must have had in mind Judge Woolsey's celebrated opinion admitting Joyce's *Ulysses* to the United States when I wrote a paragraph that would later sound embarrassingly priggish to me: "He never wrote dirt for dirt's sake; he never addressed himself to the market for the scandalous and licentious; and through all of the material to which objection may be made runs a vein of laughter, almost always boisterous and exuberant and almost never sly or snickering." I did better in the next chapter with Smith's satire and social criticism. Although I often fell into a patronizing tone, I still tried to make the case for his merits: "With disillusionment and cynicism he wrote about the crassness of much in American life as he saw it expressed in snobbery, knavery, cruelty, and crime. Finally, he ventured into the broader and deeper subjects which have always concerned serious writers—the generalized behavior of people and human nature itself." Much later I realized that I had failed to convey the pleasure I had found in Smith's work. In applying the critic's tools,

I had lost some of the joy of the novels, and I would not want to return to them. But it was a price I would never regret having paid.

Now that I had only to polish the dissertation and then defend it, I could relax a bit as we slipped further into pleasant domesticity and Princeton residency. Our friends were professionals at various stages of different careers. Charlie and Marnie were the closest of these friends. Charlie was still working part time at Benson and Benson and the Educational Testing Service too, a year away from his Princeton B.A. In one way they were ahead of our cohort. In November, Marnie had given birth to a baby with red-gold hair they named Peter Jackson Allen, after the family's most famous ancestor, the legendary Thomas "Stonewall" Jackson. We saw each other when we could, Marnie busy with her young family and Yvonne still working at AIPO and keeping house. In August, Yvonne learned she was pregnant. By fall she finished at AIPO, and it was left to Charlie and me to hold up the side at the Princeton football games. Like the famed Subway Alumni of New York who cheered for Notre Dame, I rooted for the Princeton Tigers, enjoying vicariously the triumphs of the Dick Kazmaier era. One party that fall, though, had nothing to do with football. We had found a larger apartment at 128 Alexander Street, and one weekend Charlie and Marnie and a dozen other friends helped us put coats of cheap paint on the rooms where there would soon be three of us. We enjoyed ourselves with plenty of beer and music and laughter.

The big change came at the end of March, when we got in the car for the ten-minute drive to Princeton Hospital. We were met there by William E. Pollard, a short, sandy-haired doctor with a slight mustache, beloved of his patients and fabled to have had an earlier career as "Hot Lips" Pollard, a sideman in the band of Ben Pollack. In the corridor I left Yvonne as she was wheeled through the doors into the Labor Room. The next day the telephone rang in our echoing apartment at six in the morning. We had a daughter, Tracy Wright Blotner, tiny and blue-eyed and beautiful. We were nervous new parents. We made her formula and sterilized her bottles with the care of Paul de Kruif's microbe hunters.

The dissertation made it past Spiller and the other members of the committee. I paid the typist for the 214 pages bound in soft gray covers. I made it through the defense by the grace of God and the kindness of the committee. They led me through the genesis and research on the dissertation without any hitches. Soon I was excused, and when I returned from pacing the hall they congratulated me. The ordeal was over. On February 10, 1951, we drove into Philadelphia for the Convocation. There I sat on the stage of crowded Irvine Auditorium with the other degree candidates and heard an indefatigable poli-

tician named Harold Stassen, now the university's president, give the introduction. At last I rose with the others, perspiring in my rented cap and the
gown. Hearing a quiet clicking, I looked and saw that it came from a short
plump nun, her eyes closed as she told the beads of her rosary. As we stood
outside in the chill wind, there was joy amid the popping of the flashbulbs.
Mother's smile had never seemed brighter, her eyes bluer. Back home she telephoned the East Orange relatives. To call me to the phone, she sang out, "Doctor Joe!" My cousin, Father Ed, probably was not there, but I think she felt
that she had made her point. I would later take some consolation that despite
my apostasy and the other grief I had caused her, the events of this day and the
birth of Tracy gave joy to her mother's heart.

Sometimes it seemed we were all going through a series of changes together. By 1952 Charlie and Marnie had two more sons, and they had moved
to Rocky Hill, into a two-hundred-year-old townhouse where Marnie's grand-
parents had lived. Yvonne and I had a second daughter in March of that year,
Pamela Wright Blotner, a chubby, happy, blue-eyed baby who loved corned-
beef hash and blueberry jam. With a thousand-dollar gift from Dad and
Mother we bought a two-bedroom house for $11,800 and moved a mile east
onto the fringes of a new development built on the red Mercer County earth,
moist enough to leave a foot of water in the basement after a day's rain. When
my parents visited, Dad enjoyed sitting in our Lincoln rocker to hold Pamela
and give her a bottle, as he had done with Tracy. I had been touched to learn
that on both births he had passed out cigars at work.

Summer was hot that year, and by early July we were opening the screened
windows every night. Then one morning the phone waked me with the news
that Dad had died in Muhlenberg Hospital. I had not known he had any major problems until one day when I had seen him place a small white pill under his tongue. "It's only a nitroglycerin," Mother had said. I hadn't known
that he had atherosclerotic heart disease. She had never believed in complaining about illness, her own or others'.

I drove to Plainfield for the start of "the viewing." The embalmer had
done a fairly good job. Dad looked like himself without looking like himself. It wasn't just the missing glasses or the gloss of makeup with the hint of
pallor beneath. I think it must have been the look of weariness. Years later
when I first heard the phrase *stanco morto*—not just exhausted but weary unto
death—I would recall that look. I leaned down and kissed his cheek. It did not
feel cold—only like a substance I had never felt before. I wished that I could
cry, but tears did not come. Looking down at him, I said an Our Father and a

Hail Mary and went out to find Mother. Two days later I returned to greet the relatives and friends. Then at last we were riding together in the back of the undertaker's car. Now I felt not just grief but anger too—that he was gone so suddenly after I had begun to come closer to him than I had ever been before.

The world constantly intruded. I had not yet heard what someone would later relate to me as an ancient Chinese curse, "May you live in interesting times." Other adjectives would have been more apt as Charlie and I perceived our times. On June 25, 1950, North Korea had invaded the South, and reservists like Charlie and me were being reevaluated. We were both cautiously reclassified by the air force with a second specialty in intelligence, but I would never feel safe until March 1953, when I would seize the opportunity to decline appointment as a first lieutenant in the Air Force reserve and so finally be free. That December in Stockholm, William Faulkner put our deeper malaise into words: "Our tragedy today is a general and universal physical fear so long sustained by now that we can even bear it. There are no longer problems of the spirit. There is only the question: When will I be blown up?"

It was good that I had been busy at RCA, with writing that helped to achieve my transfer to Research Services under Douglas H. Ewing, a handsome, hard-bitten graduate of the University of California's Radiation Laboratory, who had shrewdly perceived that his career lay in administration rather than research.

I looked around me and reflected. Your professional life could be rewarding if you were a bright young scientist like Dietrich Jenny or an old man full of honors like V. K. Zworykin. I looked at company veterans who worked at their desks—answering the telephone, reading reports, writing reports—until they were eligible for retirement. Could I do that? After three years at RCA I had a family, a home, and a comfortable income of $5,750 a year. I could probably continue to receive a modest salary for the rest of my working life.

One day when Doug Ewing invited "readability expert" Rudolf Flesch to lunch, I went along. Like me, Flesch had a Ph.D. in English. After he left the table, I told Doug I was glad to see another Ph.D. in the humanities there at the Labs among all the holders of doctorates in the sciences. "He's really made good use of it," I said.

Doug smiled. "What's yours good for?" he asked.

Yvonne had taken a Saturday-morning job as a receptionist for Orrin Jack Turner, Princeton's best photographer. His son and daughter-in-law were about our age, and through them we had made other friends. Two were Dick and Marjorie Snyder, the most interesting people we had met in a long while. Dick was a professor of political science at Princeton, and he was especially sympathetic toward me for my career that was going nowhere.

"Last week," he told me one evening, "I met an interesting man in the publishing business. His name is Saxe Commins, and he's a senior editor at Random House. He's William Faulkner's editor, and he lives here in town. Why don't you call him up and ask him if you can come and talk to him about the publishing business?"

Despite his fussy manner on the telephone, Commins invited me to visit him at his home on Elm Road. A stooped man with an expression that reminded me of a bloodhound, he listened as I told him about my hopes to find work in something like my chosen field.

"I'll show you something I think would interest you," he said. I followed him into his book-lined study to a table covered with pages held together with clips and elastic bands. "This is William Faulkner's new novel," he said, and paused for effect. He picked up one of the bundles and held it out for me to see. The pages were clearly the work of a neat but amateur typist, with marginal notes penned in the tiniest script I had ever seen. "It's about the return of Christ during the First World War. I don't know what we're going to call it yet. Either *Who?* or *A Fable*."

"You asked me about getting into publishing," he continued. "There are two principal ways. You either bring an author with you or you invest money in the firm." (I didn't know then that Commins had first been Eugene O'Neill's dentist, and when O'Neill had gone to Random House, Commins had gone with him.) As soon as I worked my way to a polite departure, I thanked him and left.

When I told Dick about the meeting he was sympathetic. "I was hoping for something a little more useful," he said. "But I've been thinking about another possibility. I'm editing a series for Doubleday called Short Studies in Political Science, and I want to get more variety into the series. How would you like to do a book for me about politics in fiction?"

"Sounds like a great idea," I said. My heart sent out a blip again. Spiller had sent my dissertation to the University of Pennsylvania Press, but it had been declined, and I was too tired of it to contemplate revisions. Doing this book for Dick was a much more viable possibility.

"I'll send you a contract before we see you again," Dick said. He was already my good friend. He might also be my academic savior.

The house was quiet, and I sat at my desk in our bedroom that night, as I hadn't done since finishing the dissertation. It was clear now of drafts, just a folder there labeled "Placement." I had activated my file at Penn after writing fifty English departments asking if they had a vacancy. All the responses had been form replies, except for one from Colby College. Colby had simply returned my letter with "No" written in the margin. There were two notices in the folder. One was for an instructorship teaching four sections of composition and technical writing at the Rensselaer Polytechnic Institute. The other was for an instructorship teaching three sections of composition and one of journalism at the University of Idaho. Neither was what I had envisioned in graduate school, but as I looked back on my labors in market research and technical writing, I was beginning to think of them as the Lost Years.

One of the books on my desk was *Complete Poems of Robert Frost.* I riffled through the pages, and they fell open to a familiar poem: "Two roads diverged in a yellow wood. . . . I took the one less traveled by, / And that has made all the difference." My eyes were tired, and I closed the book. In the morning, I would look at the folder again.

ELEVEN

Heading West

I HAD DESCENDED THROUGH THE DIMINISHING BITTER-root Range, traveling west toward the leveling land of Idaho where the legendary first white men were remembered in the names of towns. With the morning sun on the road signs, I thought of the place names Walt Whitman and Stephen Vincent Benét had used. Here on the approaches to Moscow in Latah County they stood out on the map: Potlach and Lapwai, Palouse and Waha.

With Yvonne still in Princeton to sell the house, I slept on a cot in a modest white clapboard on Deakin Place in Moscow. It was set among more than a dozen just like it in the sloping hills a fifteen-minute walk east of the campus. From the back stoop you could look west where the road led toward Washington State College in Pullman. Athwart it, halfway there, were the Two Sisters, massive hills rising from the undulating prairie like the afterthought of a playful glacier. The weather would come from that direction, the snows that could pile up nearly two feet between dusk and dawn. And the following chinook might dissolve the sparkling white billows as if by a prestidigitator's trick.

A downhill walk led to the campus with its modest imitations of collegiate Gothic. Not yet sixty years old, the University of Idaho was a land-grant institution dependent on the state and federal governments, the budget reflecting revenues as well as needs. Boise got the penitentiary, and Moscow got the university. With the influx of veterans under the GI Bill, the enrollment had risen to level off now at thirty-five hundred, and many of the classes in the College of Liberal Arts were still held in the former barracks that had housed wartime programs. The administration building was another of the sentimental neo-Gothic structures. It housed the English department, a "service department" that taught composition to all undergraduates. The highest degree awarded was the M.A. When I learned that the university library was housed in the administration building, my heart fell. No wonder they didn't offer the Ph.D. For research, faculty often had to drive across the state line to the Washington State College library. As yet I had not absorbed the full irony of having left a laboratory staff function to enter a department that served a staff function.

The chairman was C. Norton Coe, a Yale Ph.D. A thin man in his late forties, he had blue eyes and crinkly graying hair. He welcomed me cordially and confirmed that I would be teaching three sections of freshman composition and one of journalism each semester. I walked a few blocks down the hill to the frame building that held the offices of the one-man journalism department and the student newspaper. Wayne Young was a balding man with the face of an aging athlete. When I asked him what I would teach, we settled on feature stories. There would be no textbook. "What I'd do," Wayne said, "I'd talk about different kinds of stories and assign some and then discuss them in class." It sounded like Penn all over again, being assigned a course I had neither taken nor taught.

I was relieved to learn that we would use a widely adopted textbook, for I had been excused from freshman composition at Drew and depended for my knowledge of English grammar on what I had learned in high school. When I inscribed in my grade book the thirty names for each of my sections, I felt a new respect for my colleagues. Some of the early themes assigned might be a page or so, but as the semester proceeded they might grow to five hundred words or more. The students were to correct or rewrite according to the correction symbols and our comments. This process was going to be as much of a learning process for me as for them. We would hold office hours throughout the week, at least two hours each day. In the other hours of the workweek we would grade papers and prepare for classes. Time for any research or writing would have to come out of what was left.

I was learning about my new colleagues—chiefly the younger ones, for we had little in common with the older ones. They had taught composition for many years, and though they did little research and published nothing, they were assigned almost all of the literature courses. The rest of us would meet at midmorning or midafternoon in the coffee lounge of one of the white wartime buildings. We would exchange stories about our classes, the howlers perpetrated in themes, and the difficulties of starting useful discussions. More often we talked about the activities that gave intellectual interest to our lives.

John Haislip was a nattily dressed, ruddy-faced man working on his Ph.D. and an admirer of the poet Theodore Roethke. Haislip was one of a small circle interested in literary criticism. Another was Jim Baker, a slim, handsome young man who had come under the influence of Alan Swallow. With Swallow's encouragement, Jim and his friends were starting a little magazine they called *Twentieth Century Literature*, and Jim urged me to write for it. Over coffee we would talk about new books and articles in magazines and reviews I hardly ever looked at: the *Sewanee*, the *Partisan*, the *Hudson*. Most of us would have called ourselves modernists, but our interests were wide-ranging, from psychoanalytical criticism and myth criticism to linguistic criticism.

You never knew what you might hear. Glenn Pedersen was a short, balding thirty-year-old man with a broad Swedish face who was immersed in the mysticism of William Blake's *Songs of Innocence* and *Songs of Experience*. Glenn never hesitated to share with us. "I had a wonderful experience last night," he said one morning as he stirred his coffee.

"What was it?" asked Lou Leiter, a thin-faced man with black hair receding along both sides of his widow's peak. "Was it Blake?" he asked with a smile. "Was it a dream?"

"It was more of a visitation."

"What did he say to you?"

"Nothing. It wasn't Blake. It was his mother."

Lou's eyebrows shot up and his head fell back. And we all laughed. You couldn't be offended by Lou. Brilliant, witty, and a little fey, he was easy to like. He strengthened my impulse to write criticism, and before long I was well into it—the mythic, Freudian, Jungian, and wholeheartedly symbolic—and sending essays to magazines. As an only child, I had invented games I played against myself. This literary criticism was a new kind of challenge.

As a further hedge against the soul-deadening routine of teaching each class three times and laboring over the themes, the instructors had formed a Thursday-evening discussion group. I had admired Robert Penn Warren's *All the King's Men*, but now I came to know him as a fine poet. We savored poems such as "Bearded Oaks," which combined the elegance of the metaphysical poets with the lush imagery of the Louisiana bayous. We read on to John Crowe Ransom, one of Warren's mentors and a leader of the group who published a little magazine called the *Fugitive*. My introduction to Ransom was a bleak one. I couldn't bear "Bells for John Whiteside's Daughter." This restrained poem about the once lively child now lying "so primly propped" in her coffin was simply too painful. "Danny Boy" seemed to me one of the saddest of songs. I knew that its power came not just from the anticipated final separation of the lovers but also from my growing knowledge of tragic Ireland and her bitter history. I was only half-Irish, but I had absorbed much at family gatherings, and I wondered if some gene could be the cause of the underlying strain of melancholy I began to perceive in myself.

My feature-writing course moved me not to tears but to irritation. I had one good student among the eight who sat around the tables, a plump and agreeable girl named Mary Carmichael who wrote for the *Daily Idahonian*. She could devise a topic such as "The Domestic Science Courses Men Take" and turn in five pages of tolerably interesting copy. I once asked them to write a simple description of an object that could be as small as a pinkie ring. A fresh-faced farm boy named Herbert Mills raised his hand.

"Can it be something as big as a house?" he asked.

"Yes, Herbert, it can," I told him. "You can write about anything. It could be here at the university or something at home."

"Good," he said. His face brightened, and so did that of the big student beside him. Checking my seating chart, I saw that his name was John Baskett. When I collected their themes on the due date, I put his at the bottom because I didn't want to be disheartened at the outset. There were paeans to cars, to dogs, to firearms, and, in a few cases, to fish. When at last I got to John Baskett's theme, I found that it consisted of one short page. It was entitled "I-Tower." I put my red pencil aside and read, "On University of Idaho campus is I-Tower. You can see it from far away. On tower is painted big I. Inside I-Tower is water for University of Idaho." The rest consisted of similarly indisputable statements and then the conclusion, "You can see I-Tower from all over University of Idaho."

At coffee time I showed it to John Haislip, who smiled wearily.

"Let's see that," said Jack Fulton, another veteran instructor. "Ah, yes," he said, "John Baskett. He has taken this course before. He's a full-blooded Nez Perce, and we don't offer 'English as a Foreign Language.' I'll go find Norton and see if there's anything we can do." On Monday, John Baskett was not there, gone whither I didn't know.

I decided to see if the students could do any better with the narrative than the descriptive. "I want you to choose something you remember vividly. It can be anything—your first date, or the time you hit a home run," I told them.

"Could it be about rodeoing?" asked Jim Beasley. He was a short, muscular boy who wore blue work shirts and baggy overalls.

"Sure it can," I said, encouraged. "That would be perfect." I had learned that *rodeo* was a verb the day he asked me if he could miss a Friday class be-cause he had to rodeo at Idaho State in Pocatello.

"Could it be about something on the farm?" Herbert Mills asked.

"Certainly," I told him. "Just try to write it in a clear sequence that your reader will be interested in following."

A few of the narrative themes provided pleasant surprises. Jim Beasley wrote plain unadorned prose on the varieties of competitive riding, from bucking broncos to the dangerous bulls. Then he described his own first try, from the instant of climbing atop the huge white Brahma bull. He also ventured some dialogue. "See that big hump flopping around on that Brahma's neck?" one of the cowboys asked a well-dressed spectator. "If you never seen one before, it looks strange, but if it's on a steer instead of a bull it makes a real good pot roast." Herbert Mills presented a progression signaled in his title, "Driving a Tractor I Had Never Drove Before." I gave a B+ to both.

My problems with composition were put in perspective by a call from Yvonne. Her voice sounded thin and weary. "It's Pam," she told me. "She's got pneumonia. She started running a high fever, and day before yesterday Dr. Moore put her in the hospital, and he said I ought to send for you." Shocked and frightened, I hurried home to call Northwest Orient Airlines. They put the flights together for me from Spokane to Chicago and La Guardia.

There was an hour to wait before boarding the flight. I had brought papers to grade, but I couldn't concentrate on them. There was a movie I couldn't get out of my mind. We had taken Tracy to see a Disney film called *Song of the South.* Based on the *Uncle Remus* stories of Joel Chandler Harris, the film reached an emotional climax when one of the old storyteller's charges, winsomely played by a curly-haired little actor named Bobby Driscoll, fell desperately ill. Uncle Remus pleaded his case directly with the Lord because he was "such a little chile" who "only been here such a very little while." I could think only of Pamela, just twenty months old.

At Princeton Hospital I hurried to Intensive Care, where I saw Yvonne before she saw me. Smiling tearfully, she told me that Pam's fever had broken. We sat close to her, and Yvonne wiped her forehead, moist with the perspiration that had soaked her feathery light hair. Pam tried to raise her arms to me, but only one was free, the other taped to a board holding the tubes, antibiotics, and other fluids. I leaned down to kiss her.

"Are you feeling better now, sweetheart?" I asked. She moved slowly.

"They broke my little arm," she said softly.

In another two days they would discharge her. I wanted to stay, but I had to return to meet my classes. There was time for a brief visit with Gramma and Uncle La in Rocky Hill and a phone call with Dick Snyder about the book on the political novel I would do for him and Doubleday. In what seemed an extraordinarily short time, I was preparing to say goodbye to Yvonne and to leave once more.

We stood and waited on the platform at Princeton Station as the last of the commuters thinned out. Then I saw two men at the end of the platform. They were short and unremarkable except that one of them was wearing a jaunty green Tyrolean hat and a dark trench coat that seemed too large. Then it hit me. "Look down there at the man in the trench coat," I said to Yvonne. "That's William Faulkner."

Just then the shuttle pulled in, and the two men moved toward it for the short ride to the main line at Princeton Junction. "Let's sit behind them," I said, and when they moved, we followed. I realized that the other man, who had been hovering solicitously about Faulkner, was Saxe Commins, still fresh in my mind from his dismal assessment of my chances of breaking into publishing. Now he saw Faulkner to a seat and handed him his briefcase. After what seemed like admonitory pats on the shoulder, he wrung Faulkner's hand and left the car. We sat in the seat behind him. Faulkner settled himself and gazed out the window as the train moved slowly from the station. From his coat pocket he extracted a box of kitchen matches and a cigarette. He struck a match and blew out a puff of blue smoke.

Yvonne and I settled back, our antennae focused on this celebrity whose presence was more electrifying than that of any movie star. I had been engaged in a struggle between good manners and acquisitiveness. In less than ten minutes we would be at Princeton Junction. The impulse toward good manners lost, I reached into my briefcase and withdrew the copy of *Go Down, Moses* I had brought with me from Idaho. I unscrewed my fountain pen and handed it to Yvonne with the book. "Ask him to sign it," I whispered. She looked at me uncertainly. "Go ahead," I said. "Ask him to sign it."

She did it gracefully, edging into his range of vision and making the request with a smile. As he turned, there was that famous face with the crooked aquiline nose, the epicanthic eyelids drawn down at the outer edge of brown eyes so dark they looked almost black. He took the book, looked at the title page and riffled through the pages with his thumb. Stamped on them, I saw with a twinge of embarrassment, was "University of Idaho Library." I couldn't interpret his expression, but I watched him take the book and the pen. That was what I had been hoping for, that he would do something for a pretty girl he might have refused to do for me. The rattling of the train and the pen point on the coarse paper made for a slow and scratchy signature, but there it was,

"William Faulkner," in tiny vertical strokes. Yvonne thanked him and we sat back, I with the feeling of having extracted a treasure from a vault. We didn't speak as the shuttle slowed and stopped at the main line. There we boarded the same car Faulkner chose, several rows behind him. In our last glimpse we followed the small erect man in the green hat moving slowly into the bustle of Penn Station.

One other chance meeting of that day was emblematic of the way our generation's lives were in flux, as we moved from one job to the next and one house to another raising our children. In the crowded station, I almost collided with one of the hurrying figures. It was Marnie Allen, on her way to meet Charlie in New York. There was time only for a quick grasp of both hands before we were swept along on our different routes. As I had escaped from RCA, so Charlie had evaded a plan for him to join the family business.

Nothing seemed to have changed at the university or in Moscow. There had been a long spell of unseasonably wet weather, but now the fields stretching out beyond the Two Sisters were a light tan, the grasses left by the mowers rippling in the wind. The overarching western sky seemed wider than before after the comfortable suburban enclaves of Princeton. I checked the weather forecast each day as December came in, and each night I stood on the back stoop, sniffing the tangy air and checking the moon for rings.

On December 10 I drove north and stood behind the hurricane fence while the huge propellers droned to a stop. At last I saw Yvonne emerging from the line of descending passengers, carrying Pamela and holding Tracy's hand. Then the two in their matching snowsuits toddled toward me. The baggage took a long time, but at last I was driving them to their new home. Yvonne and I caught up on the news. I talked about the department and the countryside.

"The rain almost ruined the pea crop," I told her. She laughed.

"Joe," she said, "I think you've been here too long."

Our Thursday-night meetings were our aesthetic and emotional salvation. We read our own work, and I continued to learn from Lou Leiter. In an explication of *Death in Venice*, he followed Thomas Mann's gradual revelation of Gustave von Aschenbach's homosexuality and mined the whole story for the meaning and coherence of its mythological references. I had been reading increasingly in the work of Joyce's contemporaries. As I immersed myself in *To the Lighthouse*, it seemed clear to me that the figures of Mrs. Ramsay and her foster daughter, Lily Briscoe, were best understood through myth and Jungian psychology. Virginia Woolf was enlarging the education I had received in graduate school.

I was also blocking out material for my book on the political novel, learning more about literary history and the relation of novels to their times. I was setting the pattern for my life in this new world: preparing the material I was teaching and dealing with classes and other departmental responsibilities. Although there was some satisfaction in the improvement in my students' writing, the best part came from teaching short stories and trying to lead discussions so that the work revealed its richness. This was why I loved Joyce and Mann and Woolf. There were usually a few students I could rely on for discussion, though often I felt as if I were carrying all thirty on my back.

The approach of the end of classes brought a nagging problem closer. Spread over nine months, the salary was just enough to make ends meet, and I would need to find work for the other three months. We concluded that this would be a good time for Yvonne and the girls to make a brief return to Princeton. It was a lonesome errand, putting them on the airplane and returning to the empty house on Deakin Place.

With my four sets of exams finished, I went job-hunting, and in two days I found one, working for H. D. Powell, Plumbing Contractor, as a laborer. A bluff and gruff self-made man, he hired me as a helper for Ben Johnson, a steamfitter and plumber. A handsome, easygoing man in his forties, Johnson smilingly asked me, "Do you know what Powell's initials stand for? Hard Dome. That's what I call him, Hard Dome Powell."

When I told Lou Leiter about Ben, he said, "Have you ever asked him if he had trouble writing *Volpone?*"

The truth was that there was never much time for conversation apart from our thirty-minute lunch break. We were updating a fraternity-house heating system in Moscow, and I was outside digging the pit for the new fuel tank. At another fraternity house just across the line in Pullman the strain was on my hands rather than my back. To install new urinals, the old ones had to be freed from the white tile floor. Whereas we removed wooden flooring with the aid of drills that wrenched themselves violently from your grasp if you hit a knot, my tools for the tiles were a chisel and mallet. I didn't feel their full effects until night, when I lay on my back with hands tingling until at last sleep overcame them.

Home before sunset, I would stand under the hot shower while some of the weariness drained out of my arms and back. I would put a simple supper on the stove and enjoy my biggest indulgence, a can of Ballantine, while I read the *Daily Idahonian* and listened to "Golden Oldies" on the radio. I was ravenous, but I wouldn't linger over supper. I would walk down Deakin Place past the stately stone Latter Day Saints church to my office in the journalism department. There I kept my notes and books for the essay I was writing on *To the Lighthouse*. But now I was also accumulating material for what would be *The Political Novel*.

First I had to deal with definition. What made a political novel? Was *Uncle Tom's Cabin* one? What about John Steinbeck's *In Dubious Battle*, about organizers who manipulate a strike to serve the purposes of the Communist party? Remembering von Clausewitz's dictum that war is a political instrument, I concluded that I should deal with political activity at many levels. I finally wound up with eighty-one novels, half of them American and the rest drawn from six other national literatures. I decided to try to make this material manageable by treating the novel as a mirror of national character and the novelist as an analyst of group and individual political behavior. Dealing with the artist's intention by indirection, I would study the murderous violence of nihilist revolutionaries and perverts in Fyodor Dostoevsky's *The Possessed*, and revulsion at Stalinist methods in Arthur Koestler's *Darkness at Noon*. This reading and writing led me to classics I had missed, such as Stendhal's *The Charterhouse of Parma* and Henry Adams's *Democracy*. Others such as Ralph Ellison's *Invisible Man* nourished my growing interest in the literature of the American South.

My postgraduate education in modern literature continued for the rest of that summer. Its counterpart, manual labor for H. D. Powell, continued in the houses of Moscow and Pullman. My hands calloused, I was glad after the three months to put aside the tools. By the time I met my family again, I had typed out drafts of three chapters.

This year I would have for my fourth class an upper-level English course. It went to my head, and I elected to teach "The Stream-of-Consciousness Technique in the Modern Novel." I chose *The Sound and the Fury, To the Lighthouse*, and *A Portrait of the Artist as a Young Man* plus parts of *Ulysses*. The wonder was not so much that I was allowed to teach it as that anyone signed up for it. One was a short, plump graduate student in education named Sarah Primrose. She must have been in her late forties, her eyes wide behind the large lenses of her glasses and her attitude one of scrupulous attention. Happily for me, Mary Carmichael elected the course and contributed faithfully to class discussion.

The third student was the joker in this small deck. Sally Jo LeMonnier made it clear that her core identity was that of a painter, and she immediately proclaimed an affinity with the rebellious Stephen Dedalus. She quickly roughed out a large canvas of a nude, flat-chested woman on horseback and called it "I Shall Not Serve." A thin, dark-haired woman in her mid-twenties, she too was in revolt against a range of enemies, from convention to her mother and her own femaleness. "I wear blue jeans and tight sweaters because they make good work clothes and minimize my hips and boobs," she told me. In class I welcomed her linking of modernists in painting and literature. One afternoon she compared Joyce's use of everyday objects with that of Marcel Duchamp. She described his famous sculpture *Fountain*, featuring a urinal. Sarah Primrose's eyes opened wide. "You know," Sally Jo said, "when urinals were first being attached to the walls of men's toilets, they were installed in ladies' rooms, too." I thought I saw Sarah Primrose's eyes roll toward the back of her head. "Women were supposed to squat over them," Sally Jo continued, "but somehow they never caught on." I quickly shifted to Joyce.

If such unlikely collisions with the avant-garde in Moscow were rare, encounters with the earthy were not. Our daughters had returned west in time for the first rodeo of the season. At the rodeo grounds we took seats close to the wire barrier. The girls were fascinated by the plunging broncos rocketing out of the wooden chutes, cowboys clinging to their saddles with one hand and waving the other wildly. Over the explosive and furious motion came the announcer's voice counting off the seconds before the riders were unseated. The girls screamed as they watched the ropers fling themselves from the horses onto the steers, wrestle them to the ground, and whip a rope around their feet.

The attention shifted to the rodeo clowns as the announcer's voice blared, "Let's have a nice hand for Bingo and Sam and Wrangler!" They were traditional clowns with their buttonhole daisies that spouted water, their baggy pants and painted faces under battered hats, tripping clumsily but spurting with sudden speed to avoid the lethal hooves of the broncos and Brahma bulls, diverting the animal and giving the rider time to scramble and vault over the railing of this dangerous corral. Between events, the clowns would stroll languidly, replying to the announcers' banter or telling barnyard jokes. As we listened, Bingo slowly walked toward our part of the arena. He stood there in his orange fright wig and bulbous red nose, hands on hips. The girls watched him, fascinated. He came closer and stared intently at us. "HELL-O, Mr. Blotner!" he shouted. Tracy and Pam looked at him and at me. In a second I perceived beneath the circus makeup the honest face of Jim Beasley. A charging bronco called him away as I tried to explain.

My interest in myth criticism continued to grow, and it dawned on me that *To the Lighthouse* would make a perfect demonstration piece. Virginia Woolf was an early feminist, and I sketched out the argument that her concept of woman's role in life was crystallized in the protagonist, Mrs. Ramsay, whose attributes I saw as those of major female figures in Greek myth, especially the Primordial Goddess threefold in relation to Zeus: mother (Rhea), wife (Demeter), and daughter (Persephone). Mrs. Ramsay is a fostering mother and an ardent matchmaker. Her counterpoise is her authoritarian husband. Caught between the two is their young son, James, in what seemed to me a clear paradigm of Freud's Oedipal conflict. I took a break from *The Political Novel* and explored the idea in a twenty-page essay. When I read it to our group, they liked it, and Lou said I should send it to *Publications of the Modern Language Association of America*. Even though *PMLA* seemed to me a long shot, I thought, Why not? And I decided to go to the annual meeting of the Modern Language Association in Chicago.

By late October I was seeing results. One of the editors of *PMLA* wrote that they liked my essay and enclosed parts of a letter from one of the referees. Carlos Baker was a Princeton professor, an authority on the romantic period who was also doing modernist criticism. I followed his suggestions for sharpening my argument, and after I sent back a careful revision, the editor replied that he was taking the essay. At about the same time, Dick Snyder told me that he would send me comments on the last chapters of *The Political Novel*, and if I could do revisions without delay, I might have galley proofs before the end of the year. I was elated.

My new job-application list was much shorter than my earlier one. I labored over the letter, but the first responses were disappointing. No, there were no vacancies at these schools where enrollments had not yet rebounded from the Korean War. Then one noon the phone rang in my office. "You've got a bite at the University of Virginia!" Yvonne said, "and they want to set up an interview."

My heart started racing. I cut short my office hours and hurried home early to pore over the letter. The name alone, Archibald B. Shepperson, evoked white columns and ivied walls. The position, he wrote, carried two sections of freshman composition and two of sophomore literature. The salary would be $4,400 for the year, and the rank was assistant professor. They were sending for my dossier from Penn.

"Don't get your hopes up too high," Yvonne cautioned me.

"I won't," I said. "It's only the Time of Possibility, but at least it's that."

With the materials for the MLA annual meeting in Chicago had come nametags listing our university or address, and it became an acquired mannerism to glance at them swiftly, especially in the elevators. Standing before a display promoting a critical study of Henry James, I exchanged a few words with a balding, blue-eyed man a few years older than I. His tag read, "EDWARD STONE University of Virginia."

"I have an interview for a job there tomorrow afternoon," I told him.

"Well, I wish you luck," he said, with an enigmatic smile. We turned and walked toward the corridor where large meeting rooms were rapidly filling. Stopping before a placard on an easel advertising a major address, Ed exchanged a few words with a wavy-haired older man who stood there, hands behind his back, seemingly scanning the faces of those entering. "That's Arlin Turner," Ed told me, "one of the pillars of American literature. I had his courses at Duke. He's looking for former students."

"Is Clarence Godes at Duke?" I asked. I tried to seem familiar with the lore and makeup of the major departments of English.

"Oh, yes. The terror of graduate students and junior faculty. That's part of the game," Ed went on. "Most departments have their great men, and they tend to be intimidating. Some aren't as fearsome as they appear, but Godes is."

"Are there any intimidating great men at Virginia?"

"You might meet one. Let's get together after your interview."

There was no one waiting in the corridor, and I was afraid I was late, but then the door opened, and a tall, white-haired man welcomed me. He spoke rapidly in a deep voice I found hard to understand. His nametag identified him as Archibald B. Shepperson. Sitting there were four others, all at least twenty years older than I. As Shepperson introduced them I tried to read the nametags without craning. "Here's Mr. Stovall, and Mr. Hench, and Mr. Hubbell, and Mr. Bowers," he said. His accent couldn't be anything but Southern, though it was not one familiar to me. Words such as *out* and *about* came out as *oot* and *aboot*. Ed Stone had prepared me for his introducing his colleagues as Mister rather than Professor, for titles in general were eschewed at Mr. Jefferson's University.

He took the top dossier from the pile. "Well," he said, "since we both specialize in the novel, I'll take the privilege of beginning. I'm much more comfortable, though, with Fielding and Sterne than with your Hemingway and Anderson." This preference seemed appropriate, for this smiling, red-faced man with his harrumphing delivery looked like a well-upholstered character from an eighteenth-century drawing room. This interview was beginning to seem more like a conversation among gentlemen than an interrogation.

"If you were to teach a course in the novel, before you got to Faulkner and Lawrence and the others, what would you begin with?" Feeling at ease with him, I took a minute to ponder.

"I think I'd start with *Tom Jones,* and I think I'd include *Tristram Shandy.*"

He smiled and nodded vigorously. I had struck a rich vein. My other choices led us into a discussion of mutual favorites.

"Yes," he said, "yes." He added, shaking his head, "I declare, I don't know what I'd do to make a living if I couldn't teach English." He began to laugh at the thought but then stopped to suppress a fit of coughing. "I'm enjoying this, but I think I better give somebody else a chance."

I was at ease now, but I wondered how long this would go on. Two others in corner armchairs hadn't spoken. The one behind Shepperson was a tall, slim old man with a shock of white hair. The other, in the opposite corner, was the youngest, a robust, balding man, ruddy-faced with lively brown eyes and a half-smile that made me think of a Buddha.

"Our honored colleague here," Shepperson said, nodding toward the first, "you probably know, Jay B. Hubbell. He's with us for just this year, but we try to get all the work out of him we can."

If I needed putting at ease, Hubbell's slow drawl would have done it. He had been the great man of his department, I would learn, without terrifying people, buoying them up instead through the long haul of the dissertation. "Mr. Blotner," he said, "I see that you did American literature at Northwestern with Leon Howard. What did you study?"

This was a gift. I told him how Leon had taken us through Twain and into Melville, and instead of a question-and-answer session, it became a discussion of what we had learned from that wonderful Alabamian. I had just gotten into Leon's tour of the major novels when Floyd Stovall, who was chairman-to-be at Virginia, spoke up.

"Please excuse me, gentlemen," he said, "but I've got to break in. Was Leon working on his Melville biography then?"

"Yes," I said, delightedly, and we launched into a three-way discussion of what we had learned about *Moby-Dick* and the other major novels from Leon. It reminded me that he himself was a great man who was warm and nurturing. There weren't many of them.

Stovall was a distinguished Americanist, a short, solid Texan who had a slight squint, as if from looking too long on sunny landscapes. He recalled work that he and others such as Spiller had done. "We were working on Melville and Poe and Whitman in those years. Poe and Whitman absorbed me. There I was, a Texas boy, a pillar of the Baptist Church, and I was spending my days and nights on an alcoholic and a homosexual." The laughter was neither forced nor embarrassed. When he asked me about my current research, I took the ball and ran with it.

At last Shepperson said, "I'm afraid I've let this run on too long, and Professor Bowers, I haven't asked you to take over." He looked back toward the large figure sitting with his hand over his eyes. He straightened up as if he had been attending to every sentence. "Perfectly all right," he said, "perfectly all right."

"Fredson," Shepperson continued, "would you like to ask Mr. Blotner some questions?"

Bowers waved his hand in dismissal and smiled. "Oh, no, oh, no," he said. "I've heard enough." He spoke rapidly with an accent that was neither Southern nor British.

"Well, then," said Shepperson, "I thank all of you, and especially you, Mr. Blotner." After this unexpectedly warm hour, I felt that I had some hope.

An hour later in the coffee shop Ed Stone gave me his full attention. "Who grilled you?" he asked. He nodded as I mentioned each name. "Pretty good. What did you think of them?"

"I liked them, Hubbell and Stovall especially."

"None better," Ed said.

"Shepperson was nice to me and Hench was agreeable, but Bowers didn't really take part, and I wondered if he was asleep part of the time."

Ed gave a short laugh. "He doesn't miss much. But then you're not in any of his specialties: Shakespeare and Renaissance drama, and textual bibliography. He's got more energy than any of the others." He smiled. "And more irons in the fire."

"Are you happy there?"

"It's not what I'd call a happy department, yet I can teach Henry James there as well as another place."

"It's not a happy department. What did you mean by that especially?"

"It's just the whole picture. Too many ghosts, for one thing."

"You mean Thomas Jefferson?"

Ed laughed. "No. If you get the job, I'll tell you some stories."

By mid-February I thought I saw signs of a premature spring, but then one morning we woke to a gray sky that had piled a foot of snow on the back stoop. I put on my boots and my old trench coat and plodded my way down past the LDS church to the campus and the journalism building. I met my classes and held office hours, but no one came. The next day we woke to glorious sun glinting on the sparkling mounds of white, and by the time I was bundled up for the trek to school, a chinook was magically molding the masses piled against the walls and windows. Most of my students were there for classes, when I would gladly have given all of them cuts.

When my office phone rang, it was Yvonne. "Joey," she said. "You better come home. There's a letter here from Virginia."

"Open it," I said.

"No, I'm too nervous."

Striding through the snow, I was home in record time. As I opened the door, Yvonne handed me a four-by-nine envelope rather than one of those ominous small ones. It held a full page, dated February 21, 1955, and signed by Archibald B. Shepperson.

"Listen to this," I said, and began to read. The University of Virginia was offering me a three-year contract for an assistant professorship with a starting assignment of two sections of freshman composition and two of sophomore literature, at $5,200, with the possibility of summer teaching. I seized Yvonne and waltzed her around the room in the brilliant afternoon sunlight streaming through the still frosted windows.

TWELVE

The University and Mr. Faulkner

THAT SUMMER OF 1955 WE WERE GLAD TO BE GOING to Charlottesville by way of Princeton. Gramma, now "Mammer" to the children, was doing better after heart trouble, but our reentry into the world of the east coast was still shadowed. We knew that Mother had been ill, though her letters supplied only a general description of abdominal problems that might require surgery. When I telephoned my cousin, Mary Krug, she told me that they had taken her to Cranford Hall to recuperate.

Mother's joy at our visit was the only positive note. Her blue eyes seemed enormous in her thin pale face under the white hair pulled back from her brow. She leaned forward to kiss Tracy and Pam and then moved back against her pillows as if wearied by the effort. When a nurse brought two capsules, Mother took them and then gestured to me. "This is my son," she said. There was such poignancy in her tone that for the moment I could not speak. The sallow, middle-aged doctor down the hall was matter-of-fact. The overhead light glinted on his large spectacles as he leafed through the folder on his desk. "The cancer seems to have started as an ovarian cyst," he said. "I couldn't tell her that it was probably too late even before the operation." There seemed little to ask, but we asked the futile questions anyway.

There was a lot to do as the countryside began to flower. Each summer, units in "The Project" on Harrison Street were freed by the departure of graduating students. We had visited Charlie and Marnie when they lived in these remodeled clapboard barracks before buying their house in Rocky Hill, and so it was as if we were repeating the past when we sublet a unit and moved in. We repeated the past in another way when I decided I had nothing to lose by knocking on RCA's door again. I had written to Doug Ewing, proposing that I return to Research Services for the summer at a modest figure that was still larger than my Idaho salary. I could work as an editor with the engineers, give lectures on writing to them and the lawyers, and then publish the series under the RCA imprint. To my surprise, he accepted.

When we returned to Cranford Hall a week later on a warm day in early July, I was shocked by the change. Mother's skin was the color of the sheets where her thin hands rested. Her plain gold wedding ring looked much too large, and those fingers I remembered from childhood—holding the sewing basket or slicing apples—seemed not just bony but paler than they had ever been. I told her about the girls' activities and my work at RCA, and she listened attentively. I sat by her bedside searching for things to interest her. Then she broke the silence. "How old are you now, Son?" she asked.

"I'm thirty-two, Mother," I replied.

She shook her head slightly, and a faint smile moved her pale lips, but she didn't speak. What, I wondered, was she thinking. Yeats's question came unbidden to my mind:

> What youthful mother . . .
> Would think her son, did she but see that shape
> With sixty or more winters on his head,
> A compensation for the pang of his birth,
> Or the uncertainty of his setting forth?

A few days later when the phone shrilled in the paling dawn it took me a minute to divine where I was. "Your mother expired at five o'clock this morning," said the voice. Rising through the mists of sleep, I saw that it was six o'clock. A few days later I set out in the incongruously sunny morning already resonant with birdcalls.

Cranford Hall was busy with the routine of medication trays and vacuum cleaners. The manager and I went through the lugubrious business of documents and forms while my mother's body was being transferred to the Scotch Plains funeral home my cousin Mary had selected. As I filled in the date, I realized that Mother had died on the twelfth, the same day of the same month as Dad's departure. No symbolic significance to that, I thought, with all that was earthly of him in Holy Redeemer in South Plainfield, the closest one to Scotch Plains, but thanks to my thoughtlessness in a plot for one grave, and herself a county away in Mount Olivet in a plot marked by a dark weathered monolith bearing the carven word SLATTERY. She would lie among her people while he would be as far from his as he had been in life.

The dwindling number of Slatterys and Sullivans, Carrolls and Connollys, sat with Yvonne and me in the front pew of the Church of Saint Bartholomew the Apostle. Father Nelligan was a short, plump man whose face was flushed redder than usual above his elaborate white vestments. He swung the clinking censer with practiced assurance. The acrid smoke rose in shadowy clouds past the dark polished coffin and vanished against the windows of the chancel where the saint held out supplicating hands.

We drove through the dense suburbs to Newark where the hills swelled with their variegated crop of stones and statues. At last we stood on the arsenical green artificial turf above the mahogany box while the undertaker fumbled in his pocket for his black missal. I tried to concentrate in the hum of traffic, then gave up and said silently an Our Father and a Hail Mary and then the remembered phrase, "May her soul and the souls of all the faithful departed through the mercy of God rest in peace."

During our six-hour drive south on a hot late-August day, it was as though we were moving through zones from present time into the past. Down highways and parkways, over bridges and through tunnels, past the blue waters of the Chesapeake Bay, we moved through the arteries of the metropolitan areas and on toward white-fenced paddocks and farmlands on the approaches to the Blue Ridge Mountains. When we arrived on the outskirts of Charlottesville, we had only a fragmentary sense of the town. The streets seemed narrower than those we knew in Princeton, and many of the brick two-story homes and businesses reminded me of pictorial Civil War histories.

It was not until the next day that we began to get some sense of the town and its centerpiece. Driving along University Avenue, we slowed to look at Thomas Jefferson's tall statue there before the Rotunda dominating the Grounds, the central part of his "academical village." We climbed the stone steps to gaze at Jefferson's majestic form and then gazed down the Lawn, where Old Cabell Hall closed the long, downward sloping rectangle and blocked most of the distant Ragged Mountains. Serpentine walls of single courses of brick and formal gardens with still-blooming bushes and flowers set off the scene. We felt surrounded by Jefferson's neoclassical vision of symmetry and grace.

At Penn I had heard the name of Benjamin Franklin invoked with reverence. Now I began to be immersed in accounts of Jefferson the patriot, statesman, and visionary. "Mother of Presidents" Virginia had been, but the Old Dominion had also been the most influential part of the Confederacy, and it had paid as fearful a price as any of those other eleven states, and more than most. Despite its prestige, the university currently enrolled fewer than five thousand students—by law, white males except for a few women in the Nursing School who were enrolled in undergraduate courses.

One symbol of Virginia's proud traditions flashed dramatically across the green turf of Scott Stadium on Saturday afternoons: a magnificent stallion under a rider who waved his saber grandly to the roaring crowd. The Virginia cavalier evoked the aura of aristocracy, the plantation tradition—in a phrase, the Old South. Coats and ties were *de rigueur*. Professors were addressed as Mister, and so were students. The university had produced more than its share of brilliant and distinguished alumni, but over time it had also experienced some decline. The Southern universities most likely to be mentioned for the breadth and excellence of their graduate and professional schools by consensus now included Duke, the University of North Carolina at Chapel Hill, and Texas. The University of Virginia had some excellent schools and departments, but at best it was regarded as a good regional university. At worst, its undergraduate college was regarded as a party school, an institution where for some the gentleman's C was still the norm. Its decline was vividly exemplified in a character in William Faulkner's most notorious novel, *Sanctuary*, in which the dissipated Gowan Stevens boasts, "I went to school at Virginia. Teach you how to drink there."

The reality of the University of Virginia for me, however, was very different from this stereotype. The students were generally good as well as mannerly, and some were excellent. The junior faculty was a good and energetic one. Most of them came from east-coast graduate schools, a majority with Ivy League Ph.D.'s, and Southerners were in the minority. They knew that publication was the name of the game, and promotion and tenure were far from the rule. By and large I liked my colleagues and felt comfortable with them. As chairman, Floyd Stovall headed a small Executive Committee. The most distinguished of the elders, long retired but still an august presence, was James Southall Wilson, a short man with silver hair and shining spectacles. His speech revealed not only his cultivated Virginia background but also a hint of English accent and intonation.

Mr. Wilson made a lasting impression on me at one luncheon when he said to the five of us at the table, "I know that you are interested in American literature. So I'm going to tell you my one, almost firsthand, story about a great figure in American literature, Edgar Allan Poe." He had our attention immediately, if only because of Poe's local status as minor literary deity. The room he had occupied briefly as an unsuccessful undergraduate at the university was still there on East Lawn, its desk, fireplace, bed, and discreetly placed chamber pot easily observed through an open barred door, as if his somber shade with its melancholy visage still hovered close by.

"I must warn you," Mr. Wilson said, "that these are an octogenarian's memories of the memories of another octogenarian. This is what he said." We waited expectantly. "'It was my privilege to be invited to a small dinner where Mr. Poe was the honored guest. The setting was perfect, the silver and china and crystal all elegant. All was *comme il faut* in the candlelight. The butler carefully poured the wine. Mr. Poe took a sip. Then he took another, and almost immediately his face began to flush. Very shortly he seemed on the verge of collapse. He rose and left the table, and he did not return. Ever since that evening, I have never believed the stories of Edgar Allan Poe as a hopeless drunkard. I think he simply suffered from an intolerance for alcohol.'" Mr. Wilson did not elaborate on this opinion. It was an introduction to the intriguing way the past was likely to enliven the present in Charlottesville.

All the full professors ranked equally, though the chairman made administrative decisions and could influence policy in subtle ways. The hearty, red-faced Archibald B. Shepperson clearly was not cut out to be a chairman, and it was equally clear that he had been delighted to relinquish that responsibility to Atcheson K. Hench, no better suited to the chairmanship than himself. A classically trained philologist, Hench could make precise judgments on words, but he found it difficult to take a firm stand on policy, and some years later I would see him steel himself to declare vehemently, "I've never been more on the fence in my life!"

The other two full professors, Arthur Kyle Davis, Jr., and Fredson T. Bowers, seemed to have only one sentiment in common: Anglophilia. (Gossip was even more relished at Virginia than at the other schools I had known, and a recurrent bit had it that Davis and Bowers had shared a competitive ardor for Nancy Hale, a talented fictionist and a beautiful woman who ultimately became Bowers's wife.) Possessed of a rich Virginia accent further enhanced by his years as a Rhodes scholar, Davis had been a college pole-vaulter, though his porcine appearance belied it. He directed his share of theses and dissertations in the romantic period, and he had once carried an early tape recorder into Virginia mountains searching for Elizabethan ballads. Bowers was bald and burly and had a florid complexion. Far more energetic than Davis, he was a textual bibliographer who specialized in editing Renaissance dramas, striving to come as close as possible to their authors' original versions. It was common knowledge that he cherished ambitions for the department and the chairmanship for himself.

If Bowers gave augury of change, Shepperson was, like James Southall Wilson, a representative of the *ancien régime*. One Sunday afternoon Shep and his wife were agents of the general culture shock we were encountering in addition to the academic variety. Our earliest shock had occurred in our first domicile, a briefly occupied rental that introduced us to a reality of Southern living. When Yvonne tugged on a reluctant kitchen drawer, it flew out of her grasp and landed upside down. Instantly the whole floor began to move. "Cockroaches!" she screamed. We had to call the Orkin Man. "Don't be surprised that you have these visitors," he told us. "We visit Jefferson's home at Monticello regularly."

The culture shock conveyed by the Sheppersons could not have been more different or genteel. Old Farm Road, where we had by now bought a house, was quiet most of the time, and it was particularly quiet on this Sunday afternoon at the children's naptime and our own as we sought to recoup after more settling in. Yvonne was asleep in the bedroom, and I was dozing tieless in the living room when I heard the polite knocking. When I opened the front door, there to my shock and dismay were Archibald and Philippa Shepperson, she a stately, deep-bosomed woman wearing white gloves. Her dark dress was adorned with a tasteful brooch and a scattering of cigarette ashes. Dazed but coherent, with sense enough not to rouse my sleeping wife, I invited them into the living room. When I offered them tea, they declined with the greatest politeness.

"We can't stay but a minute," Shep said. "But let me leave these with you before I forget." He handed me his wife's card and two of his own, one private, the other professional. This was protocol for a ritual Sunday-afternoon call, and our turn as new faculty had come round without our realizing that it was imminent. They made polite conversation and soon verbal preparations for departure. I felt that I had been totally inadequate.

But the Sheppersons had certainly contributed to our education about this complex, highly nuanced society. Like them, many of the senior members of departments came from old Virginia families, and it was almost expected, as at some Ivy League schools, that faculty might have private means. Virginia was one of the universities regarded as trading in "psychic salary": elements such as beauty, tradition, and amenities of life that might compensate for a less than comfortable income at the various ranks.

Now, however, there were the beginnings of gradual change. Money was not yet available for recruitment to compete with major institutions, but the appointment in these years of three young Harvard-educated associate professors was a favorable sign. A tall handsome Americanist named Frederick L. Gwynn was hired from Penn State. Sears Jayne, a Renaissance scholar, came from California. The one with the greatest visibility was Edgar F. Shannon, Jr., back from a distinguished career in the U.S. Navy, who had returned temporarily to Harvard after earning his Ph.D. as a Rhodes scholar. These were moves that would counteract another aspect of Virginia's reputation. The department had been known as an unhappy one, riven by rivalry and marked by the departure of a few of its most distinguished senior members. And there were cases of misfortune Ed Stone and others had heard about: a suicide and a professor's departure to join a major department with the ensuing discovery of irregularity in his credentials.

The new appointments were only a beginning. Floyd Stovall had built his career at the University of Texas and the University of North Carolina at Chapel Hill. He was a leading Americanist when he came to Virginia as chairman. But even though he was a chaired professor, he found that his duties prevented him from doing the research he had planned. Shannon and Jayne looked to him for leadership in the ambitions for the department they shared with Bowers, but they were disappointed. Shannon would remember Stovall's response: "Don't knock yourself out. We are a second-rate department, and we just are not going to be able to attract the best talent."

It was possible to put together much from the received lore and the coffee-time gossip. And the fact that there were factions ensured partisan gossip. We knew who the protégés of Fred Bowers were. A. K. Davis had had a few, but one was gone and the other would soon be gone. But in spite of the negatives in its history, I was glad to be at Virginia. I knew the name of the game, and I would play it. I had written myself out of Idaho, and I would write myself out of Virginia if I had to.

I enjoyed writing and scholarship, but I had to be selective. One of Herman Melville's most memorable phrases for me came not from *Moby-Dick* but from a letter to Nathaniel Hawthorne. "I am damned by dollars," he told him. I had felt damned by dollars in Idaho, and here I could afford, just barely, to spread my annual salary over twelve months. I had done better at the RCA Labs. And there were still times when I would drive into the nearby Gulf station and say, "A dollar's worth of the regular, please." Then Ed Stone put me in touch with Dayton Kohler at the Virginia Polytechnic Institute in Blacksburg, who edited *Masterplots Annual* and the *Cyclopedia of World Authors*. I began writing pieces for him. Each one brought in a welcome fifty dollars, and I hoped that the term *essay-reviews* would take the curse off their being academic hackwork.

In the first term I had become well aware of the active undergraduate social life climaxing in "Openings" and "Easters," a spring bacchanalia that saw much of central Rugby Road virtually impassable with crowds from the fraternities and social clubs. The heavy drinking was one part of the Virginia mystique, seen in one of its grossest forms in the football fans who staggered, bottles in hand, behind the stadium seats, many of them carted away later by friends or police. The parts of the mystique most revered by the enthusiasts of all ages were loyalty and honor. To the tune of "Auld Lang Syne" they would sing, "The good old song of Wa-hoo-wah, we'll sing it o'er and o'er," vociferously to its ending: "So let's join hands and give a cheer for the good old UVA." The nickname for the Virginia teams was the Wahoos. The dictionary defined this entity as a large, warm-water mackerel, but no one seemed to know its relevance to Virginia culture.

Honor was a totally different matter. One of the handbooks informed first-year men that upon graduation they could say, "I have won the honors of honor: I have graduated from the University of Virginia." All incoming students were rigorously indoctrinated in the Honor Code. A student might take a test without supervision so long as he signed it, "I declare on my honor that I have neither given nor received assistance on this test." He was to be always on his honor, and if he or a faculty member observed an infraction by him or another student, he was obliged to report it immediately. It was then to be reported to three students from the same class, who would determine if there was cause for an honor trial. If the student judiciary found the student guilty, he had forty-eight hours to leave the university.

This draconian system periodically aroused controversy. As we were all obliged to do, I reviewed the system for one of my sophomore literature sections, carefully explaining that a student had to treat borrowed material as direct quotations with full attribution. I read from Brooks and Warren's *Understanding Poetry* as an example of how to explicate a poem. When the papers came in, I found to my dismay that one student had quoted two paragraphs verbatim from the same essay. I was bound by the code, and I put the machinery in motion. Forty-eight hours later I received a telephone appeal from the student's devastated father, but there was nothing I could do, and shortly after the boy's appeal, he was gone. I regretted my part in this matter ever after.

I was not alone in my sentiments about this cornerstone of the University of Virginia's official value system. Within a few years Sears Jayne would present to the college faculty a full formal indictment of the code and the mentality it represented. He pointed out that an underage student could walk a few blocks from the Grounds to an Alcoholic Beverage Commission store and falsely sign a statement that he was old enough to buy liquor legally. But because this declaration was not made on the Grounds or under the Honor Code, he would not be liable for violation. "What are the watchwords of other great universities?" Sears asked in ringing tones. "*Lux!*" he intoned, "*Veritas!*

What is it at Virginia? Honor!" Before long, Sears was gone too—to Brown University.

I had a feeling of optimism in December when I was offered the contemporary literature course in the summer session. But my strongest emotions came from a different quarter as the end of 1955 approached. Yvonne and I were awaiting the arrival of our third child. When Nancy Wright Blotner arrived on January 8, another petite and beautiful blue-eyed brunette, our family was now genuinely, if only in part, Southern. It was fortunate that we had bought the house on Old Farm Road. It wasn't as elegant as Bobby Gooch's across the street, but it provided enough room for us and, when the leaves fell, it afforded a glimpse of the foothills of the Blue Ridge Mountains.

My professional life remained challenging, with the course in the novel scheduled for the fall, but my teaching load would be cut by one course the next semester. Not long afterward Floyd Stovall asked me to serve as assistant chairman. I was under no illusions about this job, but it would enlarge my service record. In a relatively small department such as ours, the professional often went hand in hand with the social. Once a month the members lunched together and gave research papers drawn from their research. The speaker one Thursday was Walter Harding, a leading expert on Henry David Thoreau. His wife, Marjorie, was a Princeton girl Yvonne had known. I also learned that among the Hardings' friends were Paul D. Summers, Jr., and his wife, Jill, a twenty-three-year-old matron awaiting their first child. Jill also happened to be William Faulkner's only child. When Walt and Marjorie had Yvonne and me to dinner, the other guests were Jill and Paul, and we liked them immediately. Our circle of friends was growing.

As Americanists, Walt and Fred Gwynn and I had gravitated together at the luncheon, and Fred and I learned about an enthusiasm we shared for a brilliant writer not far from our own ages. Jerome David Salinger had started publishing uniquely original stories in 1940, gradually attracting an audience that had expanded dramatically in 1951 with the publication of *The Catcher in the Rye*, a short novel that would make Holden Caulfield the subject of more commentary and criticism than any fictional American youth since Huckleberry Finn. Our enthusiastic conversation took us from "A Perfect Day for Bananafish" to "The Laughing Man" and back to *The Catcher in the Rye*. We decided that we would explicate more of these stories. Fred was editor of *College English*, and he asked me to be book-review editor. It would not be research, but it would certainly be service. Before long, my department service would produce unexpected consequences.

When the will of the journalist Emily Clark Balch was probated, it became known that she had left a substantial sum to the university for "the encouragement and production of American literature." Half the income went to the *Virginia Quarterly Review* and half to the English department, which set aside most of its share for a writer-in-residence program. The committee chairman for the program was Floyd Stovall—not just a logical choice but a good one, too. A genial man, he had enjoyed his duties at Chapel Hill with visitors such as Robert Frost. There would be a good deal of incidental work, and so he appointed Fred Gwynn and me as the other two members of the committee.

The first thing we had to do was find the writer, and so Fred and I made up a list of names. That was the easy part. William Carlos Williams disqualified himself because of illness, and Salinger said that kind of thing was not for him. We received a printed postcard that began, "Mr. Edmund Wilson Does Not." The last of the several activities listed, "Serve as Writer-in-Residence," was checked. Fred regarded William Faulkner as the greatest living American writer, but he had a reputation for generally avoiding public appearances, and we did not think it worth inviting him. The matter was becoming discouraging when one day Jill Summers said quite casually, "I think Pappy might be interested in that." Her mother, Estelle, had already made several Charlottesville visits in anticipation of their first grandchild, and her husband would do the same. Fred wrote a careful letter and sent it off to Oxford, Mississippi, and we waited.

It was just as well that our memories of Charlottesville did not stretch back more than a few years. We did not know of a signal event in its cultural life twenty years before. Ellen Glasgow, a Virginia novelist and literary *grande dame*, felt that Southern writers in New York were kept from seeing each other by their isolation in the bustle of metropolitan life. She proposed a gathering of a score of leading writers in some pleasant place where they could talk. The president of the university endorsed the idea, and the committee invited thirty-four, including Thomas Wolfe, James Branch Cabell, and William Faulkner. Against his inclination and better judgment, Faulkner made one of the number on October 23, 1931, eagerly awaited because of the publicity that had greeted his sensational novel *Sanctuary*.

Genuinely shy, and convivial mainly with a few friends and then intermittently, Faulkner attended only a few of the sessions. His old friend and sometime mentor, Sherwood Anderson, later wrote, "Bill Faulkner arrived and got drunk. From time to time he appeared, got drunk again immediately, & disappeared. He kept asking everyone for drinks. If they didn't give him any, he drank his own." When it was time for departure, Faulkner was glad to accept the dramatist Paul Green's offer of a ride to New York. This was the beginning of a circuitous journey back to Mississippi that would add to the lore of Faulkner's drinking exploits. Memories of these events were still green in Charlottesville in 1956. One of the journalists who had covered the Southern Writers' Conference was Emily Clark, and now it was her bequest that would provide for the return of its most spectacular participant.

When Faulkner replied to Fred Gwynn's letter, he indicated his interest and supplied a short list of his needs, including "a place to live and a servant to clean it." When Fred and Floyd Stovall drove out to see him in April at Fox Haven Farm, where Jill and Paul Summers were living, Stovall said with embarrassment that he doubted if they could raise even $2,000 for a stipend. "Don't worry about money," Faulkner replied. "All I need is enough to buy a little whiskey and tobacco." He agreed to come in the late winter and early spring. The three of us on the Balch Committee were delighted, and Floyd moved quickly. He urged the appointment to President Colgate W. Darden, a tall, spare aristocrat, former state governor and a member of the Dupont family by marriage. "It would add prestige to the university," Floyd said in summing up.

"The University of Virginia," replied Darden, "has sufficient prestige without William Faulkner."

Floyd deduced that Darden had heard about Faulkner's last appearance at the university. "I feel sure nothing like that will happen again," he said reassuringly, and the president agreed to recommend his appointment as writer-in-residence for the second semester of 1956–57.

Preoccupied as we were in that fall of 1956 with the imminent arrival of our first writer-in-residence, I held my other concerns in abeyance, but we were on the threshold of a half-decade of emotionally charged years. Clearly Faulkner's presence would matter to me professionally, but I could not foresee the emotional crisis Yvonne would undergo or the uncertainty of my prospects for promotion.

In January I glimpsed Faulkner from the end of the long, dimly lit corridor when he made a brief visit to the fifth floor of New Cabell Hall. A small man, severely erect, he moved slowly, turning into Fred's office and out of my sight. On February 15 he strolled the Lawn in a tweed suit and overcoat and the familiar Tyrolean hat, casually trim and elegant. After a press conference in Cabell Hall with the journalists and photographers who had trailed him, he met with students and visitors in Fred Gwynn's graduate course in American fiction.

The session began with questions about *The Sound and the Fury.* He answered slowly and carefully in his light, soft tenor. Then he would look down at the desk, idly turning over a matchbox housed in a metal holder decorated with RAF wings. His calm belied his feelings. "I'm terrified at first," he would say later, "because I'm afraid it won't move." But it did, and the hour passed quickly. When a reporter asked why he had accepted the invitation, he answered, "It was because I like your country. I like Virginia and I like Virginians. Because Virginians are all snobs, and I like snobs. A snob has to spend so much time being a snob that he has little left to meddle with you, and so it's very pleasant here."

Fred and I formed a silent cheering section. Now that he had accepted the gambit, we were eager that he should succeed. We soon learned that he was articulate but not voluble, and he could tolerate silence as few people could. He had undergone many interviews and developed a number of formulaic answers, often wry and funny or lit with the flash and brilliance of epigrams. But he also had a spontaneous phrase-making gift. Though he looked attentively at questioners, I had a sense of distance imposed between himself and the rest of us. This appearance had been an unparalleled experience for Fred and me. When I returned to my office after meeting another class, Fred stuck his head in my door. "I'll go get Mr. Faulkner and we'll have coffee in my office," he said. Before I could compose myself, Mr. Faulkner joined us.

He had an extraordinary presence. As I thought about it later, I realized that he radiated power. It was the kind of effect attributed to great tenors and bullfighters. This effect sprang from a number of things: from knowing I was with the creator of so many works of art, a man blessed with such a profusion of gifts, and from knowing, despite his aura of calm and silence, how withdrawn and sometimes irascible he was said to be. When Fred introduced me and he extended his hand, it was not a handshake but a handclasp, the hard, firm grip of a man used to training horses and using hand tools. He spoke softly and casually. "Morning, Gin'ral," he said.

He appeared perfectly relaxed in Fred's large cream-colored office, waiting quietly while the steaming Nescafé cooled, lighting a pipeful of his strong, rich-smelling tobacco, a blend so distinctive that you could enter a room and know that he had been there. As we sipped he answered questions slowly and politely, but he obviously felt no need to initiate conversation. He had been cordial, but when he left, walking slowly down the hall, head up, eyes straight ahead, Fred and I sat down as we would have after strenuous exercise. Then Fred apologetically explained Faulkner's odd greeting. Remembering that Faulkner had served in the Canadian RAF during World War I and trying to make interesting conversation, Fred had told him that he and I had both flown during World War II. After Faulkner's expression of polite interest, Fred had said, out of a mixture of nervousness and attempted humor, "I'll go get General Blotner and we'll have some coffee." So his strange greeting had been an attempt to be congenial. He did not use it again, and soon he was calling us by our first names. We had enjoyed being with him, but it would be some time before we were at ease in his presence.

Relatively few students took advantage of his office hours. "I sat there," he said later, "and answered questions that could have been answered by a veterinarian or a priest." Our colleagues kept up a steady stream of requests for him to appear in their classes. As the junior member of the committee, I helped Fred in setting up his schedule and escorting him to class. When Floyd Stovall had written him, he had offered the department as a shield against outside engagements, and Faulkner had gratefully accepted. It fell to Fred and me to do most of the shielding. We did it gladly, with the sense of intimacy it gradually helped to produce.

It occurred to us that we had an obligation to others besides the writer-in-residence. There were the students and teachers who would come after us without the chance to ask the author of *The Sound and the Fury* and *Absalom, Absalom!* about his work. One day Fred and I resolved that after time spent with him we would record what he said. But when we compared our recollections, we realized that this wouldn't work. We couldn't be his friends, recording secretly what he said when he had thought he was talking casually. Only a few of his remarks at universities had been recorded, and others had been misquoted or quoted out of context, causing misunderstanding and hurt feelings. There was one thing we could do. Fred suggested recording all the sessions. Faulkner readily agreed, and so one of us would carry a bulky tape-recorder to class. The sight of two average-sized men in raincoats flanking a smaller one and carrying a large object reminded some of sinister characters in movies. When one observer mentioned it to him, he replied, "They're doing pretty well. Next month I'm going to teach them to fetch and carry."

There was no telling when or how that sharp wit would flash out, though now it was good-natured rather than acerbic, as in the years when envious locals had called him "Count No 'Count." One of my students was a talented caricaturist. Al Carlson sketched him as long-nosed and spindly, cuffs over his knuckles, a book under his arm, and one hand resting on a broken column as he looked smiling ahead. When Al handed him his copy of the *Virginia Spectator,* I watched the subject, himself a talented caricaturist, take it and slowly inspect the cover. His face flushed with soundless laughter that grew until he was overcome with the paroxysms of coughing of the inveterate pipe-smoker.

Because of Fred's duties with *College English,* he had less of Faulkner's society than I did. Some mornings he might stop in at my office to sit there and check his morning mail. Occasionally he would surprise me with a comment. He had told Atcheson Hench that the mail seemed initially to come mostly from old ladies criticizing his remarks about Virginians being snobs. He could never tell what subject they might broach. One morning he opened a letter, read it slowly, and then refolded it. "This woman says how she likes my work and then tells me what a hard time she's having," he said. "That means she'll let me give her some money." He deposited the letter in the wastebasket. He unfolded his *Times* and settled his dark-horn-rimmed glasses more firmly on his nose. I turned back to my preparations for class.

His sessions and occasional readings were interrupted in March by a two-week visit to Greece for the State Department. His busy schedule was crowned by his being awarded the Silver Medal of the Athens Academy, but this triumph came at a cost. The combination of fatigue, celebration, and his pattern of retreat from crowds precipitated a debilitating cycle of drinking. Before long, however, he had recuperated enough to resume riding and jumping lessons for fox hunting with the Keswick and Farmington Hunts, where Grover Vandevender, the Huntsman, became a good friend.

This was not something I had the skill or time to share, but fortunately there was another activity I could share. I had been helping to judge track meets for the recompense of two football season tickets. Faulkner joined me at the finish line of the 440-yard race. Our job was to pursue the first three finishers to get their names accurately. Most of the athletes appeared not to recognize this official in the khaki pants, linen jacket, and old Panama hat who conscientiously walked after them asking, "Young man, young man, what's your name?" One contestant, however, was different. The mile relay had just been won with a brilliant sprint by the visitors' anchorman. A moment later he walked up to us, his face flushed and his chest heaving. "Sir," he gasped, "in our class"—he struggled for breath—"we've just been reading your book." He held out a copy of *Light in August*. "Would you please autograph it for me?" Faulkner smiled and signed it.

One of the other officials had observed our officiating. "Well, Mr. Faulkner," he said, "I see they've put you to work."

"Yes," he replied. "Blotner and I are workin' for our letter. When we get it, we're goin' to put it on a sweater. I get to wear it on Saturdays."

The ambience at his various appearances was unpredictable and sometimes anticlimactic. On Friday, April 12, John Dos Passos arrived to address the Jefferson Society. A large man, smiling and diffident, he talked at a reception with undergraduates clustering around him. Then the circle broke as some of the boys made way for another guest come to congratulate the speaker. When they saw it was Faulkner, they fell silent to hear the exchange between the two novelists who—according to Faulkner—were among the five best contemporaries in their craft. Faulkner extended his hand, and Dos Passos, a good head and a half taller, grasped it. "Hello, Dos," said Faulkner.

"Hello, Bill," said Dos Passos.

They exchanged casual pleasantries as the circle reformed at a respectful distance and a photographer recorded the meeting. Dos Passos did not give the impression of shyness Faulkner did, but neither was he voluble, and so the two frequently fell silent as they sipped their drinks. After a short but polite interval, Faulkner offered his hand again.

"Well, good night, Dos," he said.

"Good night, Bill," his old acquaintance responded genially. As the ring closed once more, Faulkner set off for home.

For his scheduled public appearances, he usually rose to the occasion, anxious to give what he considered full value for his appointment, and he remained wary of drifting into a formulaic routine. Near the end of April it was time, he suggested, to "put the show on the road." Students and faculty at other Virginia institutions were eager to hear him, and so we set off in my car one sunny afternoon for Mary Washington College in Fredericksburg, an hour away. Well turned out, his hair white from the morning's shower, he was in good form. Reading rapidly as usual from his story "Spotted Horses," he held the attention of the young ladies of Mary Washington, listening in a hush. As if put on his mettle by their presence, he was witty and responsive.

Leaving Mary Washington, we walked through the somber brick-walled cemetery where Confederate soldiers lay beneath dark weathered stones with fading letters. We stopped by a meadow and uncorked the bottle of Jack Daniel's he had brought along. Talking casually, we looked out over the country. We had a second drink. When it was finished, Faulkner said, "Let's have another one."

"Why don't we go on," Fred Gwynn countered, "and find a restaurant where we can have one while we're waiting for dinner."

"I don't see why we can't finish the bottle here," said Mr. Faulkner, with what sounded to me like the slightest edge to his voice.

Fred and I exchanged fleeting wary glances. The American ambassador to Sweden had recalled that after Faulkner discharged his last Nobel Prize obligation, he helped himself liberally from the drinks tray as if to say, "School's out."

I said, "Let's have one more here and then go." Fred poured the drinks, and we enjoyed them without further discussion. We found a restaurant that served moderately good steaks, and at last we returned home in the fragrant evening.

There were further occasions for relaxation that spring. Each of us on the Balch Committee found occasions to invite the Faulkners for drinks. If William Faulkner tended to be withdrawn, Estelle Faulkner had always been outgoing and popular—so much so that Faulkner's college friend and first literary agent, Ben Wasson, would recall her as "the Butterfly of the Delta." Slim now almost to the point of emaciation, she dressed elegantly. She had long since mastered the traditional arts of the Southern belle. Graceful and animated, never at a loss for conversation, she charmed, effortlessly. "Call me Stelle," she said and made us feel perfectly natural when we did.

The Town made its appearance early in 1957, the second volume of the projected trilogy describing Faulkner's fictional Snopes family, and he gave us our inscribed copies. In the warm sunlight of late May, he and Estelle entertained the whole English department, the French doors of their graceful Georgian home on Rugby Road thrown open to the spacious flagstone terrace. By mid-June, with the last of his university obligations discharged, we were free to go on the first of several planned expeditions. One bright morning at 5:30 his gray Plymouth station wagon arrived, and I went out to join him, Paul Summers, and Estelle's son, Malcolm Franklin, for a tour of the Seven Days' battlefield. We took turns driving and then, as the day wore on, made our way from Malvern Hill to Petersburg and Amelia Courthouse. We stopped frequently to orient ourselves, and it became obvious that Faulkner knew the battles in considerable detail, far better than any of the rest of us.

That evening, the Faulkners gave a "squadron dinner" on the terrace at Rugby Road. We had started referring to ourselves as a hangar-flying squadron, with Faulkner being the Chief. We were even acquiring our own memorabilia, though we had thus far obtained only the model RAF Sopwith Camel aircraft for the Chief and not yet the TBF bomber for Fred or the Flying Fortress for me. We savored Estelle's giant-shrimp curry, ate quail eggs, and drank champagne. After dessert we had coffee and brandy in the candlelight.

In a momentary pause, the Chief spoke. "Lieutenants Gwynn and Blotner, front and center," he said in an abrupt, clipped voice.

Fred and I rose, stepped forward together, and came to attention. He made a short rapid speech about our work in the writer-in-residence program. The surprise still lingering, we said, "Thank you, sir," saluted, and performed an uncoordinated about-face. Fred was then forty-one, six years my senior, but I think he must have felt a glow as I did.

By late June Faulkner was gone, back home in Mississippi attending to Rowan Oak and the needs of his Greenfield Farm out in the country. It would be five months before he and Estelle could return to Charlottesville.

If my emotional barometer was high, Yvonne's was often low. A talented actress, she had begun appearing with a local theatrical group, the Virginia Players, and the warm response she received had partly compensated for the love and emotional support she had lost when her father died young. While his body lay in the parlor downstairs, three of his army comrades (who must have been drunk) had decided that he should be buried properly. They had lifted him from the coffin, clothed him in his uniform, stood him in the corner, and stepped back to survey their handiwork—just at the moment when Yvonne had slipped from her bed to kneel at the top of the stairs, to see her dead father standing at attention. This shock had been compounded by the dispute between her mother and grandmother over custody of herself and Nancy, climaxing in a traumatic court-custody case. One of the lasting effects was a hypersensitivity to criticism and susceptibility to depression. Yvonne's Virginia Players notices were generally good, but a single negative comment could devastate her.

These effects were compounded by the social milieu of Charlottesville and Albemarle County. Yvonne charmed people with her outgoing personality and flair for drama, but she was not fully aware of the nuances of the world in which Charlottesville's other young matrons moved. For most of them the inner circle was represented by the Junior League. Admission could be gained by family, the connections of friendship, and good works. Membership provided an affirmation of status and an entree into broader social spheres. Yvonne's calendar was filled with activities of the Virginia Players. She was not aware that this tipped the balance in the wrong direction.

One afternoon I walked home after my last class to an almost silent house. Because the blinds were drawn, it took me a minute to see that Yvonne was lying there on the sofa opposite the fireplace. She was staring at the wall.

"Sweetie," I said, "something's wrong. What is it?"

"Nothing," she said.

"Tell me," I insisted.

At last she did. The invitations for membership in the Junior League had gone out, and she had not received one. It was the kind of wound her psyche could not bear. Depression descended upon her, and it persisted. At last I went to the Department of Psychiatry, and it was arranged for her to be seen once a week by a young resident for a fee we could manage. But Charlottesville had been poisoned for her, and only desperate measures could help. I promised her that I would go to Wisconsin for the annual meeting of the Modern Language Association in September to look for a job at another place. I was deeply troubled at the thought of leaving this tenure-track job and the friendship of a great writer, but her situation seemed acute, and I could take my chances again in the world of academia.

Ed Stone and I drove to Wisconsin in my blue Buick, and there in Madison I experienced the chaos of MLA again. I did not find a new job but told Yvonne I would keep trying. Then I had an inspiration. I would apply for a Fulbright lectureship to teach American literature abroad for a year. This plan was only a holding action, but it seemed to mitigate the effects of the news I had brought home from MLA.

The Faulkners returned, bringing with them paintings by his mother, Maud Faulkner—now increasingly well known for her realistic "American Primitive" style—one for the Gwynns and one for us. Although the Chief rode and hunted and sailed his sloop at home, he found more diversion in Virginia. Having gone to track meets and Little League baseball games with me in the spring, now in November he was ready to sample University of Virginia football. "I like this," he told me. "This is real amateur sport. At home they got a tame millionaire and he buys a team for them." Before half-time began the radio producer asked me if I could persuade Faulkner to talk with "Bullet Bill" Dudley, a Virginia "football immortal" doing the "color" for the game. When he agreed and followed me up the crowded aisle into the broadcast booth, the effluvium of his farm trench coat was nearly overpowering. From the producer's note, Bullet Bill read, "It's a real pleasure to have with us today Mr. William Faulkner, winner of the Mobile Prize for literature."

The laureate was a unique and increasingly visible presence in Charlottesville, and he had begun talking about moving here permanently. He broached the subject one day in my office: "I was thinking that it might be good to have some connection with the university after I'm through being writer-in-residence—if they can still use me, that is." Floyd Stovall and Fred and I determined that we would bring the matter up with the administration again.

It was not as if Faulkner did not have work of his own to do. He was now well into *The Mansion*, the volume that would complete the Snopes trilogy begun so long ago with *The Hamlet* (1940). In January he remained faithful to a schedule of office hours that saw him seated at his Cabell Hall desk from ten-thirty until noon five days a week. When he had no callers, he would read his

New York Times and then take from his trench coat a thick roll of white copy paper. Soon anyone passing could hear his slow tapping on Floyd Stovall's portable typewriter.

Faulkner had given us leave to ask him anything during the class sessions, and he obviously made an effort to answer conscientiously. Our unspoken part of the bargain was to respect his personal and professional privacy. When we talked as friends in the Squadron Room, as we had come to call Fred's office, we did not ask the kinds of literary questions he had been hearing for years. One result was an unexpected volunteering of information virtually fresh from his worktable. Greeting him one morning, I asked how he was feeling. Not only was he fine, he said, but "I even got back to work on my novel."

Another morning in mid-February found him even more ready to talk. "Get any work done this morning?" Fred asked.

"Yes," he replied, stirring his coffee. "I haven't worked for so long that it's fun again. I got back to that Memphis whorehouse in *Sanctuary*, Miss Reba's. That's where I am right now. Senator Snopes is in Memphis, and the nephew is going to barber college, and they're trying to preserve his innocence." This was the kind of storytelling he had done as a young aspirant in Greenwich Village, sitting shoeless on the floor among friends, his imagination still busy with his creations.

When Fred asked if Eula Varner's daughter had reappeared, he surprised us. "No," he said, "that's the third-act curtain to the whole thing," and he went on to describe the murder on which the end of the plot turned.

In February he wrote out a talk he had been invited to deliver. The political atmosphere in Virginia provided a special element of drama. The governor had promulgated a doctrine of "massive resistance" to federal pressure for integration. It would have been politic for Faulkner to avoid the subject, but when he brought his text to Fred's office at coffee time and asked us both to read it, we saw that he had instead met the issue head on. "A Word to Virginians" was an appeal to lead the whole South in educating the Negro. The other Southern states still looked to Virginia as a mother. They had ignored her counsel once before, to their grief, but now, he wrote, "Show us the way and lead us in it. I believe we will follow you."

"How's that?" he asked us. We had both read quickly.

"Good," I said, thrilled more, I believe, by his request that we read his work than by the carefully worded appeal itself.

As spring came in, we had a sense both of the end and the beginning of things. The Fulbright Commission offered me an appointment at the University of

Copenhagen. Yvonne and I thought that sounded attractive. Though the stipend was generous, I would have to borrow the money for our voyage because the University of Virginia did not provide travel grants. It would take years to pay it off, but the trip provided the psychological lift for Yvonne that I sought, and we repeated the familiar parental rationalization: "It will be a wonderful experience for the children."

On the fifth floor of Cabell Hall we still gathered for coffee each morning, the Chief sitting in the low camp chair Fred had stenciled "Balch Chair of American Literature." Katherine Anne Porter had been chosen as the next writer-in-residence. "I guess we ought to get a pipe," I said, "and have it engraved 'Emily Clark Balch Pipe of American Literature.' That would still be yours." Faulkner chuckled soundlessly.

If we needed evidence that some did not share our regret at his vacating the position, I heard it a few days earlier from a new member of the Balch Committee, Fredson Bowers, who seemed likely to succeed Floyd Stovall as department chairman. "Did Pappy get over the idea that he was going to be the permanent writer-in-residence?" he asked, with what seemed to me a malicious grin. I said he had never seriously entertained that idea, and more than once he had asked me to tell him if he stopped being effective in the job.

Sometimes now Faulkner's remarks would take on a valedictory tone, and we began a round of squadron dinners, for in late May the Faulkners would return to Mississippi for the summer. Not long after that the Gwynns would be leaving, as Fred had been appointed chairman of the English department at Trinity College in Connecticut. Then, in August, Yvonne and I would be departing for Copenhagen. But these dinners were gay occasions. Knowing Faulkner's taste for French cuisine, Yvonne served beef bourguignon, with *babas au rhum* for dessert. As he put down his spoon he asked, "What time's breakfast, Miss Yvonne?"

He fulfilled his last public obligations and continued work at home on *The Mansion*, which would appear in the fall of 1959. Earlier he had told Fred and me that he wanted us to see his new book. Because I had thought this just a polite remark, I was totally surprised when he arrived at our door one afternoon and handed me a manila portfolio.

"Here," he said brusquely, "you can read this." A glance inside showed me that it was a typescript, not just a carbon copy. It was the first third of his new novel, he said.

"You have another copy at home, don't you?" I asked anxiously.

"No," he said abruptly.

After he had left, I showed Yvonne what he had given me. She was aghast.

"You don't mean you intend to keep that overnight in a house with three little girls with crayons?" I read it that night, put it on top of our highest bookcase, and returned it to him the next day at cocktail time.

Even though the time was short, Floyd Stovall decided on one more try and walked up the Lawn to the president's pavilion. "Mr. Darden," he said, "I'd like to propose, with the concurrence of the English department, that Mr. Faulkner be made an honorary lecturer in American literature to keep up his connection with the university."

"There are no honorary positions at the University of Virginia," was the reply. Colgate W. Darden continued to bat zero.

There were, however, some tangible mementos. One night as the Faulkners sat in their Rugby Road living room, there was a knock on the door. He opened it and found no one there, but on the steps was a large package containing a silver tray from the Seven Society, an anonymous group of the university's most distinguished sons. It was engraved to him in tribute to his contribution to the life of the university.

Our Fulbright year of 1958–59 passed rapidly with my teaching at the University of Copenhagen, lecturing elsewhere as well, and traveling strenuously in the summer through the Alps and as far as Rome before our return to Charlottesville in August. The Faulkners were back as the gold of October gave way to November. Back in time for the Blessing of the Hounds, he was togged out in derby, stock, and shining boots. He had finished *The Mansion*, and it was published on November 13, 1959.

Reading something he had written recently, I never knew when I would experience the shock of recognition. When I read chapter 13 of *The Mansion*, I sat straight up in my chair. "I enjoyed that part about Chick's experience in Germany," I told the author later.

"I used your story about being bombed in POW camp," he said with a smile. "I lifted that right from what you told me." Sitting in Fred Gwynn's office during those coffee and hangar-flying sessions, we had told war stories. Fred had said little about flying a TBF off a carrier in the Pacific, but I had told about the end of my brief career as a bombardier when we were shot down over Cologne, and about watching helplessly as green target flares drifted right over Stalag XIII-D when the RAF came over to bomb one of Germany's largest marshaling yards.

There were other items that drew on our experiences. Fred and I had edited the Chief's class conferences, and thirty-six of them would be published that year as *Faulkner in the University*. Saxe Commins at Random House had feared it would be thought to be Faulkner's last word on his work, but then it was agreed that the University Press of Virginia would publish it, with the royalties to be split evenly among the three of us. We also made the joint resolve that they would always be spent on Jack Daniels.

When I had talked with Floyd Stovall about my prospects for promotion, he offered to raise the question with the tenured staff. Then one day over drinks I mentioned my concern to Faulkner—casually, with no ulterior motive of seeking assistance. He said, "Why don't you go see Shannon"—Edgar Shannon, my departmental colleague who had during the last year been elected president of the university—"and tell him, 'If Blotner goes, maybe Faulkner will go, too.'" He thought for a moment and then added, "I've got only two friends in Charlottesville, Blotner and Vandevender, and if Blotner goes, Faulkner will spend all his time out at Farmington." I knew that this was the hyperbole of friendship. When he urged it again later, I said I would do it, even though I knew how ineffectual it would be, and that I would not do it in any case.

After two weeks the senior staff held its meeting. I was in my second three-year term as an assistant professor, and my future would not normally have been considered until the following year. The decision, Stovall told me, was to do nothing now. The next afternoon the Chief stopped in at my office. He stayed for a while, and finally I told him what I had learned. He scraped the large bowl of his pipe, then loaded and lit it. After a moment he spoke. "Let the word get around," he said. "If you go, you'll take Faulkner with you. There's no problem for me, I can go two or three places. I just haven't figured out where yet."

He was nonetheless an acute assessor of the academic profession. In the semester after we returned from Denmark, the dean of the college had asked me if I would serve as Fulbright advisor in the capacity of an assistant dean. I liked Bill Duren but finally decided to turn his offer down. When I told the Chief, he said, "Good, you should stick to teachin'. Five hundred dollars ain't that important. There's plenty of five hundred dollars, there ain't but one Blotner's career. If you need five hundred dollars I can lend it to you. You can give me a note for it." He paused and smiled. "I can make you a loan out of my athletic and scholarship fund. You can get some burnt cork and put it on your face and put on some black gloves and say, 'Yes, suh, I'll pay you back Satiddy night.'"

During the months that followed, Yvonne and I continued to think about leaving, but no new job possibilities appeared, and meanwhile our ties in Charlottesville grew stronger. The Faulkners followed their traditional Christmas ritual of inviting friends in for sangaree. When we arrived at about ten-thirty that morning, the Chief met us at the door. Before we could present our plum pudding he said, "Here's your Santy Claus" and handed me a package containing a bottle of Jack Daniels.

I continued with my teaching and writing as usual. My book on the political novel had appeared along with the short paperback study of J. D. Salinger that Fred Gwynn and I had done. The matter of promotion was still in abeyance, though it was never far from my thoughts, even in social situations. During the cocktail hour at one dinner party, departmental affairs came up. I praised a proposal Fred Bowers had made about revising the English major. Floyd Stovall and Atch Hench looked at each other. Thinking I hadn't made myself clear, I elaborated on my comment. Floyd and Atch said nothing. Then Floyd said, "He's no friend of yours, Joe." Taken aback, I said nothing. I was certainly not one of his protégés, but this statement and its implications had surprised me.

"That's right, Joe," Atch said. "He's no friend of yours."

After this unexpected information and warning, it was an enormous relief to receive the letter telling me that I had been recommended for promotion to associate professor with tenure. When I went to Floyd to thank him for his support, I had to accept a less encouraging reality.

"Congratulations," he said, "I'm glad you made it, but it wasn't clear-cut." I looked at him and waited. "Fred Bowers opposed it. Finally I said to him, 'Who's going to do the work of the department?'"

This was another blow. I knew perfectly well that the senior professors did much committee work, but it hurt my feelings and my pride to think that Floyd had felt he had to argue for my promotion on the basis of my sharing the administrative load.

I was under no illusions about Bowers's attitude toward junior staff members. His conversation on the subject made me think of a *New Yorker* feature called "Dr. Arbuthnot, the Cliché Expert." For a candidate to be considered for promotion, he had to "show the color of his money." To be retained, he had to produce, because "no tickee, no shirtee." And if he was not kept on, it was no great loss, for he was "cannon fodder." I wasn't sure what I had expected from Bowers for myself—at least no adverse prejudice, I hoped—but now I thought back to my MLA hiring interview, to the kindness of old Jay B. Hubbell in the front row, and Fredson T. Bowers in the back, with his strange, almost Oriental smile, his nearly closed eyes, and his silence. The incoming chairman's view of my value to the department was no reassuring augury for the future.

THIRTEEN

Moving between Worlds

ALTHOUGH I WAS INVOLVED IN WILLIAM FAULKNER'S life only from time to time, that involvement was a central part of my own. Our original unspoken agreement still held: I was free to use the things he said about his work, but I would not be a secret Boswell. I never knew when he would draw from his past life, sometimes something personal or trivial. Before walking home from Cabell Hall one day we stopped in the fourth-floor men's room. "That's what they used to tell us," he said. "Empty your bladder before you start on a cross country." It was certainly a prosaic comment, but it made me think of his RAF stories, "Ad Astra," "All the Dead Pilots," and the others. I was fascinated by this continuous surfacing of the past. I would learn that he had flown little if at all in the RAF, but it was interesting to see how real some probably imaginary experiences were.

Faulkner did not seem to be one who would readily reveal intimate feelings, but I was wrong. One time, not long after Faulkner had succumbed to a drinking episode, his stepson Malcolm did, too. As he and I walked down Rugby Road toward home, his annoyance escaped into words. "Now I've got to take care of him," he said, "and he ain't even my son."

He and his stepson, Malcolm Argyle Franklin, had a sometimes troubled relationship. Faulkner had been very close to Malcolm and his sister, Victoria (called Cho-Cho), since before he married their mother. He had played with them and had tried to be a father to them. But he presented a dangerous example, at times a severe disciplinarian and at other times indulgent, and Malcolm shared his admired stepfather's problems with alcohol. Although Faulkner had insisted on going his own way, attending high school only briefly and seeking little further formal education, he had encouraged Malcolm to pursue a career as a naturalist and a herpetologist, but he had not progressed beyond laboratory assistant.

I felt I had to make some response. "I guess it's not easy to be close to somebody who wins the Nobel Prize," I said, feeling awkward. "It could make you look down on your own efforts." Faulkner was silent for several paces.

"Yeah," he said, "but it ain't even his racket." I had no rejoinder.

As the end of the year came on, we went to the Vanderbilt football game, his progress through the crowd slowed by the greetings of friends from the track field, the hunting field, and the English department. Once he had turned aside a literary question from Atch Hench with the brusque dismissal, "I'm off duty now." There was no doubt that we were both off duty now, I from a second book on political novels and the Chief from one he had long been meditating. He was calling it *The Horse Stealers: A Reminiscence*. Returning the early chapters, I told him how mellow and funny I found them. He gave me the third and fourth, and I looked forward to the next installment.

The winter proved to be a bad one for him, however. He came down with pneumonia in Charlottesville and suffered a recurrence in Oxford. His childhood schoolmate, Dr. Felix Linder, gave him penicillin, which Faulkner supplemented with his own course of bourbon therapy. Before long, his brother John drove into the yard at Rowan Oak, in an ambulance. As Faulkner recalled it, John said, "I'm going to save you." They made the trip together to Wright's Sanitarium, a small hospital fifty miles away in Byhalia. Gradually weaned off the whiskey in a convalescence enlivened with poker games, he was able to continue his recovery at Rowan Oak. He recovered enough to accept an assignment from the State Department, and in April of 1961 he spent two weeks in Venezuela meeting groups and accepting awards and honors.

Back in Charlottesville, he wrote and rode. By August he had completed his novel, now called *The Reivers* (1962). With the manuscript in New York, he was free to follow his fancy. A sixty-four-year-old man who had just completed his nineteenth novel had a right to be in the saddle as much as he wanted, especially in the pink coat of the Farmington Hunt.

But November proved to be another difficult month. Estelle came down with bronchitis that became pneumonia. When Faulkner took me to visit her in Martha Jefferson Hospital, she looked pale and drawn. After several days she was able to go home, only to return in early December. By mid-December it was her husband's turn. He caught a cold that developed into an acute respiratory infection. His habitual dislike of the hospital environment grew so strong that he finally succeeded in arguing for his discharge, with the warning that he would have to follow orders if he wanted to be home for Christmas.

When Estelle and I went to pick him up, we found him in an armchair in a state of quiet exhaustion. The books he had asked me to bring were there on his bedside table, his habitual hospital reading: Taylor's *Holy Living* and *Holy Dying* and Boccaccio's *Decameron*. I tried without success to get some coffee for us while we waited. A cleaning woman came in, and he mistook her for an attendant. "I'm sorry I gave you so much trouble last night," he said.

Estelle and I helped him dress. When she left to get the car, I collected his medication. When the cleaning woman reappeared, she indicated me and asked Faulkner, "Is he your son?" He was suffering from exhaustion and a medication hangover, and it was a long moment before he answered, his voice slow and tired. "He's more or less my son," he told her. "He's my spiritual son. He loves me better than he does his father."

Finally Estelle and I helped him out of the building and into the car. I was distressed to see how debilitated he looked there in the back seat with his trench coat collar pulled up around him, his eyes sunken and darkened by deep circles. I stood there by his open window. "Come out soon, Joe," he said. "I need you."

Driving home I thought about these words, more than a polite invitation. For a long time now our relationship had been easy and informal, and I had tried not to impose on it. At one point, more than a week elapsed between my walks over to Rugby Road. When he opened the door I saw Estelle seated on one of the living room sofas, and there were glasses on the grog tray. "Come in," he said. "We were just talking about you. Where the hell have you been?" He made drinks—club soda for Estelle, bourbon for himself and me—and we discussed events of the intervening days. It was a pleasant and lively time. After I declined a second drink, he saw me to the door. As I left he said, "Come in any time. When we're not here, just make yourself a drink." I said I would, and so I had done over the past five years.

I was unexpectedly reassured that this was not a one-way street one night when I responded to a knock on our door and it was he. I poured two glasses of port. From a copy of the *Manchester Guardian* he read me an account of the tributes paid in Parliament to Ernest Bevin, one from Winston Churchill. Then he mused on Churchill's greatness. "I wrote him once during the war," he told me. "I said that his speeches would be studied by schoolboys when Hitler was forgotten." Then he turned to a photograph of a party scene with two women in the foreground. One was Eleanor Roosevelt, smilingly talking to the other, Marilyn Monroe. "She's something of the new age," he said, "wiggling even while she's standing still."

I had never encountered in anyone else his capacity for silence, and I had learned to accommodate to it. Inner-directed and often withdrawn, he had no small talk, and he knew that he needed none with me. With others from the county he could talk about fox hunting and the world of the outdoors. Our conversation was casual, and though it touched on books—portions of his work I had chosen for his public readings or favorites such as Victor Yeates's World War I novel *Winged Victory*—it was never self-consciously literary. When Fred Gwynn left for Trinity, there was left only one other department member who shared our particular bond of military aviation. Jim Colvert, a decorated B-26 pilot, was a congenial companion, but our old squadron had been disbanded.

When I told the Chief that I had been awarded the Fulbright lectureship in Denmark, he said, "Good for you," and gripped my hand hard. If there was anything I regretted about the lectureship, it was that it meant the loss of a year in our friendship. He was into his sixties now, and his lifestyle—risking his bones in the saddle and his constitution in protracted bouts of drinking—had probably diminished his resilience. I kept in mind the benefits to Yvonne of a change of scene, but I felt a twinge when we said goodbye.

I felt another when we entered our cabin on the *Bergensfjord* and opened the small envelope attached to the bouquet of flowers flanked by two bottles of Peiper-Heidseck. The card was signed, "Bon Voyage, Bill and Estelle." Years later I would see a letter Faulkner had written to Don Klopfer at Random House. "A family named Blotner, pair and three little girls, English teacher at Va. now on an exchange fellowship to Denmark, sail Aug 13, 11.30 am. on the Bergensfjord (Norwegian-Am line) Pier 42. They are nice young people; this will be their first trip abroad (except one in '42–46 most of which Blotner spent as a shot-down bomb aimer in B 17s, in hun prison camp) and Estelle and I want to send to the ship flowers and a bottle or two of champagne. Will you be kind enough to ask Mary or whoever is handy, Jimmy maybe, to be kind enough to attend to it, and charge it to me at R. House."

Later still, when a young colleague asked me about my relationship with Faulkner, I told him about our time together at UVA. "I think there's more to it than that," he said. "Have you read the first poem in *A Green Bough* lately?"

Faulkner had written that volume as an aspiring poet, but it had not been published until after his early novels had made him famous. The protagonist of the first one, *Soldiers' Pay,* was a moribund aviator. His voice and that of the pilot in *A Green Bough* were almost identical:

We had been
Raiding over Mannheim. You've seen
The place? Then you know
How one hangs just beneath the stars and sees
The quiet darkness burst and shatter against them.

My friend smiled. "You must see," he said. "Even though you weren't wounded or killed, you had lived out his dream. And you were an aspiring writer even if you weren't a poet."

His doctors had assessed their patient all too well, and on the morning of Christmas Eve they decided that he belonged in the Tucker Neurological and Psychiatric Hospital in Richmond. Paul Summers drove up to our house in the Faulkners' red Rambler, and I got in the front seat and talked with the Chief, semireclining in the back. He appeared not so much sick as severely debilitated from an exhausting illness that deprived him of dignity as well as strength.

His voice hardly seemed his. "Paul," he said, "don't let's go to Richmond."

Paul silently concentrated on the driving while I searched for subjects to distract our passenger. I told him that I had just read an article about the great American ace Captain Eddie Rickenbacker. There was a long moment. Then, with an almost physical effort, he mustered his spirits and picked up on the subject, speaking coherently but very slowly. We talked about the men and planes of the First World War, and the hour passed slowly until at last we drove up to a large stone gate. It was a slow process walking him to his first-floor room. He sat there, wordless in the overstuffed chair, looking small and wan while a nurse and an attendant bustled about.

"Well, I guess we can go now," Paul said.

I leaned over the chair to say goodbye.

"Will they give me a drink now?" he asked.

I said I thought so, not knowing that Tucker excluded both alcohol and paraldehyde. Then we departed, leaving him to enter the twilit world of the treatment he detested. His recuperation was complicated by an old back injury, and the whole cycle of recovery was delayed. When finally he would be well enough to be discharged, it would be to return to Mississippi rather than the planned holiday activities he had looked forward to in Albemarle County.

When the Faulkners did return there in early April, the Chief's appearance testified to his recovery. He lost no time in resuming his riding, and even on an unavoidable literary occasion in New York, he had what Malcolm Cowley called "a country look, his face bronzed under the white hair and apparently glowing with health." He and Estelle enjoyed their return to Virginia, in a cottage at Knole Farm, Jill and Paul's new home out in the country. When I saw him there, fresh from the shower after an afternoon ride, I asked him if he had recovered completely from the mishaps of January, including the falls from horseback that had required dental work.

He said he had recovered completely. "I decided if I ever got some store teeth they were really going to look like false teeth, just like china," he said.

"Do they?" I asked.

"Yes," he replied, turning his face slightly and lifting his upper lip with his forefinger. "See?" There beneath the sweeping mustache, bright against his tanned skin, gleamed a row of pearly teeth.

"They look great," I said, and he smiled with pleasure at his private joke.

Shortly after his return from a ceremonial visit to the United States Military Academy, he stopped in at my office, and we talked casually. Finally he brought up another subject. "I have to swot up a speech for that Gold Medal," he said. It was the Gold Medal for Fiction of the National Institute of Arts and Letters, to be presented on May 24. I waited, but he did not elaborate. Then, looking out the window toward the Ragged Mountains, he said, "I wish somebody would write one for me." I waited, but he said no more.

"Do you mean that?" I asked.

"Sure."

"Well," I said hesitantly, "I'll be glad to see if I can come up with a couple of pages of something. Will next week be all right?"

"Fine."

This would be a challenge, especially after teaching his work in the classroom and hearing the cadences of his speech and his own prose. The next day, I settled down to this assignment using language and images that I believed would appeal to him. I began by trying to invoke the aura of the past through the names of World's Fairs that appeared with the gold shields on the labels of vintage wines along with the appointments of purveyors to the royal names.

When he stopped in at my office on a bright May morning, I gave him two pages. "Here's some bogus Faulkner," I said. "Maybe you can make something out of it." He thanked me and pocketed it. Four days later he handed me my draft and a carbon of his version. "Here's your copy," he said. "Maybe you can make some money out of it sometime."

When I read it I saw that he had transformed the counterfeit into the true sovereign metal: "This award evokes the faded airs and dimming rotogravures which record that vanished splendor still inherent in the names of Saint Louis and Leipzig, the quality which they celebrated and signified recorded still to-day in the labels of wine bottles and ointment jars." I was thrilled to recognize behind his prose the shadows of my own. "I think that those gold medals, royal and unique above the myriad spawn of their progeny which were the shining ribbons fluttering and flashing among the booths and stalls of forgot-ten county fairs . . . affirmed the premise that there are no degrees of best; that one man's best is the equal of any other best . . . and should be honored as such." There was a kind of closure for me in Malcolm Cowley's reaction. The acceptance speech, he said, had "a tone of retrospection, of lament for the dig-nity and freedom of the past, that was not exactly new for him, but that seemed to have a new resonance."

These days almost anything Faulkner said might make the newspaper. One morning I met the head of the university information service in the hall. "Joe," he said, "I've just had a call from *Newsweek*. They want to know if Mr. Faulkner will say why he turned down President Kennedy's invitation to the White House. Do you think he'll say anything?"

I said I didn't think so, but I relayed the question to him. "You don't want to say anything, do you?" I asked.

"No," he said. Then as I turned to go he stopped me. "Tell them," he said, speaking rapidly, "I'm too old at my age to travel that far to eat with strang-ers." *Newsweek* quoted the remark, and so did several of the wire services.

We saw him only briefly as May drew to a close. He stopped at our house for a drink, bringing with him our inscribed copy of *The Reivers*. We sat on the terrace enjoying the fragrance of the new buds and leaves. Yvonne excused herself, and he and I sat silently in the twilight. Then he slowly rose, straight-ened his back, and said he had better be getting along. In the kitchen, he paused to say goodbye to Yvonne. Then she and I walked him down the front path. There he bent down to talk to Nancy, our youngest. "I had a little girl like you once," he said softly, "but she grew up on me." We saw him on his way and went back inside.

"Did you hear what Mr. Faulkner said to me in the kitchen?" Yvonne asked. "He said, 'Come and see me in Mississippi, Miss Yvonne.'"

"That was nice," I said.

"When he said it there were tears in his eyes," she said.

Whenever he had made an appearance as writer-in-residence, it had fallen to me to introduce him. Now I remembered the last such appearance, three years before in 1960. In my introduction I had recalled the beginning of the program, an auspicious beginning, I said, "through its good fortune in securing as the first incumbent the greatest of living novelists." I went on to mention the turn-of the-century announcements of concert artists' appearances—"positively for the last time this year." Unfortunately, I said, that was the case this night. After the resounding applause he stood at the lectern, donning his black horn-rimmed spectacles, his white hair gleaming.

"Yes," he said, "we have finally come to the end of this interminable valedictory." He paused. "Sometimes when I hear Mr. Blotner making one of these introductions, I wonder who he's talking about." In his high soft voice he read from "The Old People," his story of a boy's initiation into the big woods, climaxed by the quasi-mystical appearance of a great buck hailed by the last surviving Chickasaw: "'Oleh, Chief,' he said. 'Grandfather.'" The applause resounded again, celebrating this triumph of art and dispelling something of the valedictory aura of the reading.

On their last evening, he and Estelle went to a picnic up in the hills at Grover Vandevender's place, where they sat by the campfire listening to the music of the hounds. This was the kind of thing he enjoyed. Others were welcome to White House dinners. The next morning they got in the red Rambler while we stood there waiting to wave. He opened the window. "Get you a ride on a Freedom Bus and come down and see me," he said. "We'll go to Shiloh to the battlefield." Then they drove away, down the long road and out of sight.

We did not know that there would be more than summer weather for them to contend with at Rowan Oak. The trouble began in June. Early on Sunday morning, the seventeenth, Faulkner walked to the stable and saddled Stonewall, a big tough-mouthed stallion inclined to be fractious in the hunting field and on the roads near Rowan Oak. Through Bailey's Woods he was skittish, and his rider had to work with reins and crop to control him. Near the Old Taylor Road, Faulkner turned him and headed home. Then the animal arched and threw his rider against an earthen bank. His back, already painful from old injuries to several vertebrae, took the full impact. A few moments later, from the kitchen where she was making biscuits, Crissie Price saw a riderless horse heading for the stable. He was followed by his rider, limping angrily toward home. With the help of Andrew Price, his yardman, Faulkner remounted Stonewall and rode him around the paddock and over the jumps.

When he went in pain to his old friend Dr. Felix Linder, Linder told him, "You were a fool to do that. You could have killed yourself."

Faulkner bristled. "You don't think I'd let that damned horse conquer me, do you?" he said. "I had to conquer him."

For the next few days he tried to carry on normally, but the pain persisted. On July 3 he took Estelle to dinner at the Mansion and ordered filet mignon, as usual. When the owner, Aubrey Seay, asked him how it was, he said things hadn't tasted right. "The meat and bread taste alike."

Later that night Jimmy Faulkner stopped by and found that his uncle had begun drinking. The next morning when Jimmy telephoned, he was still in bed and still drinking. He was also dosing himself with prescription pain-killers. When Jimmy and Estelle asked Faulkner's doctor, Chester McLarty, if it was not time for him to go to Byhalia, Chester agreed that it was. Jimmy drove, and Estelle sat with her husband. He was admitted to Wright's Sanitarium at sundown on July 5, 1962. The big clock in the hall ticked past midnight, and July 6 came in with no promise of a letup in the oppressive heat. A few minutes after half past one, Faulkner stirred and then sat up on the side of the bed. Before the nurse could reach him, he groaned and fell over. Within minutes Dr. Wright was there, but he could not detect a pulse or heartbeat. Forty-five minutes of external heart massage were of no avail.

At Rowan Oak the ringing of the bedside telephone woke Estelle at two in the morning. She was stunned, devastated by the brief call. Still half unbelieving, she called Jimmy and asked him to call Jill and me in Virginia. Soon the rituals began, and the reverberations quickly resonated from Oxford to the world beyond. John Faulkner sat on the steps of the Douglass Funeral Home waiting for the ambulance to return, bringing his brother back to Oxford for the last time. Next occurred a series of events that might have amused the author of the bizarre burial sequence of *As I Lay Dying*. Now, in Oxford, it took two trips with different coffins across Oxford before the Douglass Funeral Home wheeled the bier and final coffin of William Faulkner into the parlor at Rowan Oak.

Yvonne and I had been waked that Friday morning at five minutes after seven. It was Paul Summers's friend and lawyer, Leigh Middleditch, with the request that I go with Jill to Mississippi to represent the University of Virginia. In a hastily arranged flight we flew first to Louisville, where Paul was on temporary reserve duty. When our white Piper Aztec finally set down at the Oxford airport, we could see heat waves shimmering. It seemed incongruous that the Square could look so ordinary when we passed through it. In a few moments we drove down Garfield Avenue and past the row of pines toward the house. A policeman waved us up the long rutted drive between the dark overhanging cedars to Rowan Oak.

There were mourners on the broad front gallery of the old plantation-style home. We first ascended the wide staircase to Estelle's bedroom, where she sat looking out the back window toward the lawn and the meadow. "I just can't believe he's gone," Estelle said, her handkerchief clutched tightly in her thin hand.

By suppertime the clan had gathered, the kin by blood and marriage. We did what we could: answered the telephone, accepted the neighbors' cakes, signed for the telegrams and bouquets. All day the press had been arriving. Tall, sad-faced Jack Falkner, now the oldest brother, arrived from Mobile. "We understand your mission," he told the newsmen, "but we can't permit any interviews or photographs here at his residence. Until he's buried, he belongs to the family. After that he belongs to the world."

By noon the next day the house was full of family and friends. Duncan Gray, Estelle's minister, had been with her earlier. At two o'clock, clad in white surplice, Book of Common Prayer in hand, he moved into the parlor. He intoned the Order for the Burial of the Dead, his voice steady above the hum of the fans in the fierce midday heat. Finally we said the Lord's Prayer, and the service ended.

The cortege of sixteen cars moved slowly down between the cedars and on toward the Square and to the outskirts of town. The sun beat down as we stopped on the sandy roadside at the edge of the new part of St. Peter's Cemetery. On the hill above arched the shady cedars, beneath them the carpet-smooth old turf and weathered stones of the Faulkners. Up there stood the boxwood and magnolias. Here, in the new section of the cemetery, a canopy provided shade at the graveside, and soon Estelle was sitting there, her hand held tightly in her son's. At the hearse, we waited. The men from the funeral home carefully slid the coffin out. The last of the six pallbearers, I took hold of the silver handle. As we walked, I realized that my hand would be the last to set him down. Our brief task and last gesture performed beneath the canopy, we stood for Duncan's final prayers, and then it was over.

Back at Rowan Oak, where the great oak table was spread with dishes and plates as for a holiday dinner, the murmur of conversation signaled the transition from the observance of death to the resumption of life. By afternoon, departures had thinned the ranks of the mourners. A day later, it was mainly the family: the Faulkner men, Jack and John, Jimmy and Chooky and their wives, the in-laws and stepchildren from Estelle's first marriage, Victoria and Malcolm. By the next day, the atmosphere had become more like that of a long-delayed gathering of a lively family. Estelle had begun to rally, supported by Jill and Victoria and Malcolm. Victoria and her husband, Bill Fielden, had come from Caracas. Slim and petite like her mother, vivacious and flirtatious, she was still known within the family by the name given her in childhood by her amah in Shanghai: Cho-Cho (Butterfly).

It was pleasant to be at Rowan Oak in the midst of Southern storytellers and women schooled in the art of charming conversation. This gathering had evoked family stories, and the stress of bereavement had rekindled varying emotions as well as memories. I had found myself sitting, drink in hand, with family members from taciturn Jack Falkner to "little Vicki" Fielden, Cho-Cho's daughter, who had inherited the sensuous charm of her mother and grandmother. Late one afternoon as she and I sat together on the top step of the front gallery of Rowan Oak, Cho-Cho rounded the corner. When she saw us she stopped. "Joe," she said, "isn't it time for my session now?"

I had no idea then how these social conversations would prove to be more than just a temporary enjoyment to me.

At home again, I continued to stop in once or twice a week as usual for the cocktail hour at Rugby Road on my way home from school. One day in early March of 1963, as I sat there with Estelle and Jill and Paul, I told them about the books coming out on William Faulkner. They seemed a bit appalled at the amount of material and uncertain about the nature of some of it. It was Paul, finally, who said, "Joe, you knew him. Why don't you write a book about him as he really was?"

I sat, taken by surprise, while Jill and her mother looked at me with what I took to be polite interest. "I don't know what to say," I finally replied, "but let me think about it and tell you the next time I see you." Walking home slowly, I pondered.

When I told Yvonne, she replied immediately. "Of course you want to write Mr. Faulkner's biography."

Not long afterward I brought with me to Rugby Road brief written requests that people provide such help as they could in my work. Estelle signed hers quickly. So did Jill. "We think it's wonderful that you want to do it," she said as she handed it back to me, "but I'm sorry for you with that kind of a job." I could not guess how much of a job it would be. But these significant acts—theirs, and mine—would shape the rest of my life.

I was immersed in school again, busier this summer than ever in chairing the writer-in-residence committee. We had sounded out John Dos Passos about a term's appointment, and he had invited Jim Colvert and me to his home in Westmoreland County in the northern neck of Virginia. As our tires crunched on the fine white stone, he strode from the broad porch, looking very much the lord of the manor. But there was nothing pretentious in his warm greeting as he led us inside to the broad front hall. The day was warm, and as he answered our questions about his land and the region, he carefully filled tall frosted glasses with gin, tonic, club soda, lime juice, and other ingredients identified in the recipe he gave me later. The good host, he asked Jim and me about our work. Our business discussion consisted of describing the program we had evolved with Faulkner, and he agreed affably that it would be fine for him.

When we left I had a feeling of double satisfaction. Dos Passos's acceptance as writer-in-residence was definitely set, and the day itself had been a splendid one. Driving back to Charlottesville with the late-afternoon sunlight bathing the pastures in many shades of green, I thought of the crucial acts and strokes of luck that had shaped my life. The weary months in factories and boring days in business offices, the long hours of English composition in Idaho, the anxieties of MLA meetings—these were now just sequences of memories, and the uncertainties of Charlottesville were no longer the threat they had once been. I had gratefully accepted good health as I had the luck that had gotten me through the war. I felt good about the work ahead, and I was anxious to begin to grapple with its marvelous challenge.

First, however, would come the grind of summer school, made more involved by my having accepted Fred Gwynn's offer to teach at Trinity College in West Hartford. He had made it clear that there would be possibilities beyond just a higher salary. The thought of seeing more of New England also appealed to Yvonne and me, and we thought it would be good to broaden the children's sense of their country. It was rewarding to explore the house where proper Olivia Langdon had completed the taming of her wild western Sam Clemens. This ornate specimen of Steamboat Gothic testified to his newfound eastern social prestige and precarious prosperity. Never again would I teach *Huckleberry Finn* without visualizing the rooms where he had labored long and intermittently, designing scenes from his Missouri childhood. In Mystic we saw recreated the streets and shops of a whaling port at the height of America's domination of that perilous enterprise. We looked into the shockingly narrow whaleboats, still holding the harpoons and lances their doughty seamen had wielded against the leviathan. Never again would I teach *Moby-Dick* without imagining Captain Ahab walking these decks again.

I had to put aside preparation for the fall term. John Wyllie, head of the university library, was an extraordinary librarian with a capacity for seizing opportunities. At Faulkner's death, John had speculated about the library at Rowan Oak with Linton Massey. A short, energetic, ruddy-faced man, Linton was an astute investor and an avid bibliophile who had delighted in entertaining the Faulkners and in showing them the volumes that lined his walls. Linton and John agreed that Faulkner's library should be catalogued before it was disturbed. They suggested that I should do it, and Estelle and Jill gave their approval.

On September 26, Jill and I flew to Oxford. Estelle was already there at Rowan Oak, putting things in order. As we drove through the Square I felt a growing familiarity with this town that had provided material for Faulkner's Jefferson, the seat of his Yoknapatawpha County. From the rutted road between the cedars I could see Andrew Price leading a chestnut in the paddock. Entering the foyer I could hear Crissie Price's soulful voice from the kitchen. As I brought the suitcases in, Estelle was there, delighted to have her daughter with her in this lonely house.

"We'll put you upstairs, Joe," she said. Jill led me up the broad staircase to the bedroom on the right that once had been hers and that later, when she was off at school, became the one that Renzi, the man of all work, called "Mr. Bill's drunk bed." Through the front window I could see above the small second-story balcony railing the brick walk running out to the front gate beyond.

"This was Judith's room?" I asked.

"That's right," Jill said with a smile. This was a special item of Yoknapatawpha apocrypha Estelle had heard many years before from Ellen Bailey, the former owner of the house. Colonel Shegog's beautiful daughter Judith had fallen in love with a handsome young Yankee lieutenant. When it came time for the regiment to leave, the officer silently made his way into the shadow of Judith's porch. He quickly tossed a rope ladder over the railing. Moving carefully in her voluminous skirts on the swaying rungs, she suddenly lost her balance and pitched backward. She struck her head on the brick walk and lay there before the horrified eyes of her lover, her slim neck broken. Now, on some nights, Miss Ellen said, she could hear the faint steps and feel the sad presence of the dead girl.

Estelle remembered hearing unexplained soft music in the summer darkness, notes from her own piano like a piece a child might play. In October, when Jill's friends came to her Halloween party, Pappy would sit at the top of the stairs and tell them the story. After asking who would like to go out with him to see the lovers' graves, he would walk slowly down the steps, hands raised before him. He would lead them out across the lawn where from within the grove came the sound of chains, and from the forest a fluttering glimpse of white under the magnolias. Later he would say that Estelle's piano made those faint sounds because it had been damaged by seawater. "Every old house should have a ghost," he said, "and so I invented one."

I neither saw Judith nor heard her music. My powers of observation were devoted to the shelves of books in the library, the living room, and the room where Faulkner had worked. Hour after hour I read onto waxy discs the data for each book together with their new notations. The twelve hundred volumes were highly eclectic, ranging from Honoré de Balzac's *La comédie humaine* to E. T. Baker's *The Home Veterinarian's Handbook: A Guide for Handling Emergencies in Farm Animals and Poultry.*

I looked around the office before we were to go and realized that I hadn't checked the adjoining closet. On its floor were worn boots, not the carefully shined pair in his Farmington Hunt Club portrait. There were patched jackets. Then one sturdy leather object caught my eye, resembling a belt but more than a belt. Then I realized what it must be: an orthopedic brace or truss. At that moment I felt that I was intruding upon the privacy of this most private of men. I knew most of the ills he had suffered, and the pain suggested by this device made me think about the will that had driven him to the work he achieved. Henry James had written about the "envenomed curiosity" that would drive the researches of future biographers. My curiosity had been tuned to a higher pitch than ever before, and all I could hope was that it would add to my understanding of this remarkable artist and his extraordinary work.

As the time approached for us to leave, I thought of my previous departure from Oxford when crowds were gathering to protest the registration of James H. Meredith as the first black student at the University of Mississippi. Jill had an errand in town, and she asked me if I would like to ride with her. "But," she said, "don't open your mouth." I realized that with riots in the offing and National Guard troops arriving, this was not an auspicious time or place for my Yankee accent to be heard. As we entered a small side-street grocery, I stood quietly as Jill named her purchases to Mr. Fudge, the proprietor. He looked somehow familiar to me, a squat man with a thin mouth, beaklike nose, and grayish complexion. It was only as we drove away that I recognized the resemblance: it was to Flem Snopes, the archvillain of Faulkner's Yoknapatawpha saga. Several of the Snopeses were as dangerous as predatory animals, and so, it proved, were members of the mob that gathered the next day, massed before the Lyceum Building and hurling invective and missiles to disrupt the proceedings. Late that day one of the victims, a handsome National Guard lieutenant, suffered a broken arm. He was Chooky Faulkner, a pleasant nephew of William Faulkner and an ardent segregationist.

The fall semester was busier than usual, but what I wanted most to do was to work my way carefully through the large Faulkner *oeuvre*. I had determined that I would have to write a biography of the works as well as the man, to discuss their growth as an integral part of the life. I would have to start by reading preliminary material such as notes and sketches. Then there were the holograph manuscripts. Faulkner had mentioned one reader who said his writing looked as if a caterpillar had fallen into an inkpot and then walked across a page. He had to type it out as soon as he could, Faulkner said, because even he found it too difficult to read if he waited too long. Then came the typescript, revised and corrected versions, galley proof, and page proof. These were the primary materials, but Linton Massey had gone even farther afield, collecting revealing letters that Faulkner had written to agents, editors, and publishers. That wasn't all. I would also have to trace the way the published work changed. Parts of some of the novels such as *Absalom, Absalom!* were difficult enough without going back to earlier editions to see how the work had developed. I worked every night from seven o'clock until about nine. This meant less time with my wife and daughters, but it was a part of the overall bargain I had struck.

I had plenty of obligations to distract me from the convulsions of the outside world. One was running the writer-in-residence program, welcoming these short-term guests and arranging for their lectures and entertainment. They were a mixed lot that semester. The first was tall, lanky Erskine Caldwell, a Georgian famous chiefly for novels such as *Tobacco Road* peopled with sharecroppers and other unfortunates whose bawdy humor obscured the tragedies of their lives. Suave Glenway Wescott, an influential novelist, followed him. Then came the one I liked best, novelist Peter DeVries, author of comic masterpieces such as *The Tunnel of Love*. Like S. J. Perelman, DeVries usually wore a deadpan expression. As we stood at the base of the marble steps leading to Jefferson's statue in solitary grandeur before the Rotunda, I risked telling him the story of a long-ago visitor who questioned a university employee about the use of this classic structure. After a brief pause, the mocha-colored silver-haired man, reputed to be an unacknowledged son of Jefferson, answered, "Well, we uses it mostly foh a Rotunda." DeVries gave a short but seemingly genuine laugh.

In February I learned that I had been awarded a second Fulbright at Copenhagen for 1963–64. Yvonne was happy, and I was reassured to know that there would be much more time for research and writing there than at home. The salary would be better, but the bottom line would again be a loss. The Alumni Association had granted me a $3,000 interest-free loan for the first trip. It was almost paid up, but I would need help again.

I perceived an even bigger catch. I wanted to get on with the research and writing, but now I would be spending the better part of a year away from my base of operations. I was thinking not just of Charlottesville but also of the whole state of Mississippi. I told myself that I would simply find the time, somehow, to go to the places that had been important in William Faulkner's life—New Orleans, Hollywood, the Mississippi coast, and the big woods of the Delta. And I would have to use lecturing opportunities to visit other necessary places: Italy, France, and England, where he had traveled in his *Wan-*

derjahr after World War I; Stockholm, where he had reached the pinnacle of his fame; Greece and the other countries he had visited as cultural ambassador. I had a friend who could help. Joe Vaughn, the provost, had an entree to the Old Dominion Foundation, financed by money from Andrew Mellon. I applied for a grant and waited.

It seemed that now there were always decisions to make. One morning in mid-March, Professor Charles Jelavich at Indiana University invited me to attend a seminar on literature and political science at Zadar on Yugoslavia's Dalmatian coast in June. This would be my first international conference, a chance I couldn't decline. Half the American participants were social scientists, but among the distinguished humanists was Mark Schorer, a literary critic and biographer of Sinclair Lewis. The Old Dominion Foundation had come through with a $3,000 grant for Denmark that I would not have to repay. I could fly to Belgrade by way of Copenhagen to find housing for the Fulbright year. Complicating my life as never before, I telephoned Charles Jelavich and accepted. From now on, conferences would become a major part of my life.

War-damaged Belgrade, with the walls of the mighty Kalamegadan Fortress on the height above the Danube and the Seva, presented strong culture shock. With street signs in Cyrillic, I felt lost even in the central openness of Trg Republike, Republic Square. I waited for Charles Jelavich in the lobby of our hotel, the dark and ornate Metropol, where a few elderly men sat idly in worn leather chairs. They were stocky men just past middle age wearing baggy suits. When Jelavich appeared—tall, thin, and dark—he was cordial and knowledgeable. He took me out for a passable meal with Elaine and Seymour Gross, a substantial dark-haired man with gold-rimmed glasses, a Fulbright lecturer assigned to Macedonia. "*Zhee veelee*," Charles said, raising a small pale glass. "You might as well begin your initiation now." Sy knocked his back with a grimace. "Slivovitz. Plum brandy at 100 proof," he said. "Some call it Sleep-in-Ditch."

An hour later we were in the countryside. Traveling north through Bosnia and Croatia amid rapidly changing landscapes, we passed Orthodox churches with onion-shaped domes and mosques with slim towers. In hilly country we saw cairns of whitish rock. "Charles," I asked finally, "what are they marking?" He looked out at them meditatively.

"Only the people under them," he said grimly. "Mikhailovich's Serbian guerillas or Tito's Croatian partisans. You'll see them all over this region. The Germans and Italians took their dead with them when they could escape from the ambushes." What we saw were reminders of the more than million and a half who had perished.

We passed sparse pine forests and then undulating fields. The scenes reminded me of Russian novels with woodcuts of stout women in babushkas laboring with sickles amid the grain. Here the men were chiefly pipe-smoking drivers with whips sitting above the oxen. I felt transported back centuries. I was glad when the farms gave way to clusters of clapboard houses and an occasional factory, signaling the long journey's end. Soon we were in the city, and it was the kind of European city I knew.

The Hotel Esplanade was distinctly a step up from the Metropol, its lounges fusty but roomy, like a stout dowager dressed in her best showing quality in spite of age and wear. Sy and I went out into the city for lunch with Mark and Ruth Schorer. Cyril Black, a Princeton historian, led us to a good restaurant. Cy was a large man with a broad face and blonde hair, and he made another good leader. I didn't realize then that his first name was that of two of the great saints of the Middle East. His accent was straight Ivy League, but he had taught at the American University of Beirut, and I had the impression that his fluency in Slavic languages was derived from his mother. After lunch we wandered through nearby shops. That afternoon the University of Zagreb's faculty offered us hospitality, proffering the ritual Slivovitz before my lecture. I managed to repress a shudder and say *"Hovoyeh yako dobra,"* as if I really thought it was very good, and got through my lecture.

Once the capital of Dalmatian Croatia, Zadar now owed its growing eminence to the tourist trade. Entering the city through one of the gates that made me think of Rome, I saw in the massive wall the brick and mortar representation of the lion of Saint Mark, a memento of Zadar's allegiance to Venice in her prime. Zadar was a good point of entry, as our activities would shift from conference sessions to the Hotel Zagreb and the beach. All we had to do was give our papers.

Our social scientists talked about the states and the federal government, and the humanists dealt with contemporary literature. At each place was a headset and a dial to be set to English or Croatian for simultaneous translation. This soon proved unsatisfactory, and the sole responsibility was turned over to a slim man in a colorful sport shirt. He was Dragi Tudorovic. He stood at the end of the platform with his hands behind his back and waited for Alpheus Mason to begin his lecture, "Constitution Making in America." A full minute must have passed before Alph stopped. Then, in precise and only slightly accented speech, Dragi translated the English into Serbo-Croatian. He stood motionless, his eyes fixed in a gaze like that of a nursing infant. I had never seen such a feat of memory. Alph resumed his lecture, and then Dragi continued.

The only Yugoslav I had talked with was Aleksandar V. Stefanovic, a youngish, dark-haired, heavyset man. He was a Belgrade journalist who had run a small magazine until the government shut it down. We knew that Tito's presumptive successor, Milovan Djilas, had been removed for proposing greater democracy and then jailed for supporting the Hungarian revolution and divulging official secrets. So Stefanovic's presence here made me wonder about his status. He was listed as an "Observer." When I asked Cy Black what this meant, he said, "Maybe they're giving him a chance to rehabilitate himself."

The lecturer I had looked forward to most was Mark Schorer, a graceful essayist who wrote well about the way the novelist's style was determined by his subject. With dark wavy hair and a resonant baritone, he had the best delivery of all of our people, and if the Yugoslavs were hoping for high seriousness, they got it from him in "Philosophical Concepts of Man in Contemporary American Literature." We had a longer than usual cocktail period that evening, and I said to Sy Gross, "I have been trying, but I haven't been able to keep up with Mark."

"He gets a pretty good start at lunch," Sy said.

"He deserves it when he can perform like that," I said.

The conference was winding down, and I was glad. At dinner that night Cy Black tapped on his glass. "I think you know," he said, "that our conference party is tomorrow, but we couldn't let this day pass unobserved. Today is Joe's fortieth birthday, and here's a toast to it." Taken by surprise, I managed a sentence of thanks. At the end came a birthday cake, and I was surprised at how touched I felt.

I felt the same warmth the next day when we boarded a large boat for a quarter-hour ride out to one of the string of small islands that looked like a necklace separating the coastline from the Adriatic. Hotel employees were setting up a barbecue pit, and behind a rough table stood galvanized tubs icing beer and wine. Soon one group was singing. After a half-hour in the water we moved to the table for drinks, savory broiled fish, rough-cut cole slaw, and crusty bread. Because it was Sunday, our last night, a three-piece orchestra played, and as coffee was served they did "Carry Me Back to Old Virginia."

Mark was sitting beside me. "Before I forget," he said, "do you have an agent?" I was flattered. "For your Faulkner book you really should have one," he told me. He wrote on his napkin and handed it to me. "Mrs. Carol Brandt, Brandt & Brandt, 101 Park Avenue," I read. "Of course I have no personal in-

190

AN UNEXPECTED LIFE

terest in this," Mark said, "but I've been with her for twenty-three years, and if you'd like, I'll write to her."

The next afternoon we took a coastal boat to Split. It was dusk when we slowly docked, and the floodlit wharves made me think of nighttime transport in the war. There was just enough time before the bus arrived for a short walk to glimpse the Emperor Domitian's Palace. *"Do vijenya,"* Cy Black said in farewell, and we began moving from the fourth century back to the twentieth to catch our Air France flight to Paris.

On the PanAm flight to Idlewild, I had a hard time staying awake long enough to reset my watch, even with an engine roaring just outside my window. I tried to bring some coherence to my memories of the last three weeks, but they were kaleidoscopic, blending the European and the Middle Eastern, the ancient and modern, let alone the Yugoslavs' complex construct of countries and cultures. I wondered doubtfully, Had our whole enterprise achieved any good?

FOURTEEN

In Pursuit of Faulkner

As I walked up park avenue, the city pulsed with a special excitement for me. The hurtling traffic, even the cacophony of horns and brakes, seemed part of something new in my life. I was headed for my appointment with Carol Brandt, one of New York's leading literary agents. After Barnard she had eloped to Budapest with an aspiring writer. His novel did not move, and she decided she would write one herself. She finished it in sixty days and called it *Wild*. In Paris she went to work as secretary to the novelist J. P. Marquand and gradually moved further into the world of authors and agents. Back in New York, she went to work for Carl Brandt's literary agency. After Brandt was divorced, she married him. She was talented and ambitious, combining literary taste and business acumen. In time she took six of the firm's writers and started her own agency. When she returned to her husband's agency, it was renamed Brandt and Brandt.

Her relationship with Mark Schorer revealed her talent and her capacity for becoming friend as well as agent to her clients. She arranged a lucrative contract for him to write Sinclair Lewis's biography. Mark had thought he would develop an affinity for his subject, but he was a sophisticated novelist and critic himself, and he discovered that Lewis, with his often broad and heavy style, was antithetical to his own taste and temperament. With Carol's encouragement, however, Mark went on to write the standard biography.

When the trim secretary ushered me into the inner office, Carol, a handsome woman with dark hair and blue eyes, rose to greet me. It was obvious that Random House, Faulkner's publisher since 1936, should be at the top of the list. Carol smiled. "I've known Bennett Cerf for years," she said. "In 1945 Mr. Mayer hired me as east-coast story editor of Metro-Goldwyn-Mayer.

191

Three years later Faulkner published *Intruder in the Dust.* It became his first big popular success since *Sanctuary,* and I knew it was prime picture material." So did Bennett Cerf, the cofounder with Donald Klopfer of Random House. Cerf was a witty and ebullient man, intensely competitive and a celebrity in his own right. At that point Albert Erskine, later to be Faulkner's editor, did Carol a favor. With the permission of another Random House partner, Robert Haas, he showed Carol a copy of the manuscript of the novel. When galley proofs went out for motion-picture company bids, she immediately phoned Cerf. "I'll offer you $50,000 for the new Faulkner," she told him. Cerf did not know how she could have read the galleys so quickly, but he accepted without waiting for counteroffers. It was not until Erskine returned from Europe that Cerf finally understood how she could have made such a speedy decision.

"That," Carol said with a chuckle, "was one of my best triumphs, screwing Bennett Cerf."

I had already written Erskine, asking to interview him and to see the Faulkner files at Random House. "Because of all the correspondence in the files," I told Carol, "it's absolutely essential that I do this book with Random House."

She sat in silence for a moment. "I understand," she said, "but I *implore* you not to let *them* know that."

I felt again the combination of excitement and nervousness as I walked up Madison Avenue and turned into the courtyard at 457. There, across the street from St. Patrick's Cathedral, stood a brownstone palazzo designed by Stanford White. Handsome yet gracefully symmetrical, its etched likeness provided the distinctive logo for Random House books.

I walked through the massive doors and up the marble stairs to the second floor. There Albert Erskine was waiting for me, a slim, brown-eyed man in his middle fifties, well over six feet tall and handsome in a way that reminded me of Gary Cooper. He led me into his wood-paneled office. Erskine was one of the firm's senior editors, numbering not only William Faulkner among his writers but also John O'Hara, James Michener, Robert Penn Warren and several promising younger ones such as William Styron and Cormac McCarthy. He spoke with a soft Southern accent and immediately put me at ease. We talked casually about Faulkner until we were joined by Bennett Cerf and Donald Klopfer. Cerf showed the same warmth and ebullience that had made him a favorite on a popular television quiz show. I saw why Faulkner had once said of him, "Bennett suffers from a case of eupepsia." Donald Klopfer was officially the publisher of the firm. Quiet but cordial, he had supplied most of the financial expertise since his first partnership with Cerf after their student days at Columbia University. He was as tall as Erskine and, like him and Cerf, an inveterate pipe-smoker. Soon the office was redolent with clouds that colored the shafts of light from the tall windows.

I told them stories about my time with Faulkner, and they reminisced about theirs. I found myself genuinely liking these three men who moved in the real world of big-time publishing. After a half-hour Cerf rose to say he had to get back to his desk. I was feeling relieved and pleased. I felt fortunate again that Carol Brandt was representing me, because I knew little about commercial publishing. I was so anxious to go with Random House that I probably would have agreed to any terms, but I didn't want to appear like a hick in this sophisticated world. "Well," Bennett said as he turned to leave, "I hope we'll be working with you."

I returned to New York two weeks later to plunge again into the gathering phase of my work there. Ivan von Auw, Faulkner's current literary agent, allowed me to borrow correspondence between Faulkner and Harold Ober. I read letters in which he confided to Ober the circumstances that left him wondering in the 1940s how long he could continue paying his bills. Other letters contained overtures to Knopf and Viking toward a change of publishers he would have preferred to avoid. Thanks to von Auw's trusting generosity, I made a start on this rich material and left with a full briefcase. In these days before the ready availability of commercial copiers, I turned to an old source: I drove out to RCA Laboratories in Princeton and found Tom Cook, who had illustrated manuals I had written. Soon I had sheaves of photostatic copies. In Charlottesville, Linton Massey gave me carte blanche for copying materials he had deposited in the University of Virginia library.

I had managed to cram in other visits while in New York. I had paid a call on Gordon Ray, head of the Guggenheim Foundation, a silver-haired man so massive it was hard to believe he had once been handball champion of the University of Illinois. A celebrated biographer of Thackeray, he showed me some of his recently acquired treasures from other major novelists. I was glad of the chance to tell him about evidence I knew would interest him, documents such as Faulkner's enlistment papers in the RAF–Canada, bearing facts he had invented. Ray's good opinion would be essential, for I was competing with at least one other aspiring Faulkner biographer. Carvel Collins already had a lead on me, having taught in 1948 what he said was the first course devoted solely to Faulkner in an American university. He was a handsome Harvard Ph.D., charming and witty, who had been assiduously collecting Faulkneriana and cultivating the friendship of wealthy collectors. Possessively obsessed with Faulkner, he had already published editions of Faulkner's early minor works. He supplied tantalizing notes and introductions, alluding to previously unknown aspects of Faulkner's life without, however, revealing enough to supply leads for other scholars.

There were disappointments. Harrison Smith had befriended Faulkner early and published four of his greatest novels. When Faulkner invoked Smith's help and New York hospitality for Joan Williams, his protégé and lover, Faulkner had told her, "Smith is a good man for you to have seen. He will do a great deal for me that doesn't cost actual cash money." By now, however, Smith was said to have grown increasingly eccentric. He had not responded to my letter, and so I decided to chance it and simply knock on his door. It finally opened to reveal a short, gray, neatly dressed man who appeared to be in his late seventies.

When I told him my errand, he eyed me carefully without speaking, and so I showed him Estelle Faulkner's request for assistance for me. He did not take it but simply continued to stare as I looked back at his watery eyes and cheeks marked by small broken red veins. Then he stunned me. "It's the money, isn't it," he said and closed the door. I turned and had begun to descend the stairs when I suddenly resolved not to admit defeat. I walked back and knocked again. In a few moments the door opened slowly, and I was fixed not with a basilisk stare but with an emotionless gaze.

"I'd be grateful if I could just ask you a few things about your experiences with Faulkner," I managed to say.

After another long moment he spoke. "It's the wife, isn't it?" he said. Baffled, I strove to offer some reassurance, but the door closed again. It was a strangely discomfiting defeat. Years later I learned that Harrison Smith had already been diagnosed with Alzheimer's disease.

I walked up Fifth Avenue to stop in for a drink at Carol Brandt's large and handsome apartment overlooking Central Park. She was sympathetic and understanding, and shortly she took me to lunch at the Baroque, where we sat at her regular table. I spent part of the afternoon at Random House with Albert Erskine and Donald Klopfer, who talked as if our future association was pretty well set. In a less perturbed frame of mind, I headed for home.

On the morning of August 24 our family of five boarded the Swedish America Line's sleekly modern *Gripsholm* for Copenhagen. After enduring a rough five-day North Atlantic crossing, we finally sailed up the Skagerrak and down the Kattegat to dock in Copenhagen by the mustard yellow houses the Danish government provided for retired mariners. Karin Fennow, a friend from our last stay in Denmark, was there to meet us.

We couldn't expect to find another pleasant coastal town like Rungsted, where we had lived five years before, and certainly no neighbors like Karen

Blixen, the author of *Seven Gothic Tales* and *Out of Africa,* which she published under the name Isak Dinesen. Invited to her house for tea through the good offices of a friend, we had detected something gothic about her. Thin and wraithlike in a white dress and hood, she was hospitable but unpredictable. The poet Birte Arnbaek, another friend, later told how the fabled recluse loved brave children and tested them. She had taken the hand of Birte's five-year-old Ole and gradually brought the tip of a sharp knife closer until it touched his tender palm. When he gritted his teeth without flinching, Blixen said he was a fine brave boy.

That same week we were pleased to rent a floor from a kind landlady in Hellerup, six kilometers away from Raadhudspladsen in the center of the city. When our daughters gained admission to the French School, run by an order of Belgian nuns, we were relieved, as were the girls when none of their new schoolmates attempted to stuff them into garbage cans as their classmates at the Kommunalskole in Rungsted had done because they didn't like the smell of their peanut-butter sandwiches.

It was an autumn filled with new activities for all of us. Yvonne was invited to join the American Women's Club. The husbands were often involved in club activities, and so it was that we met members of the American Embassy. Several were my age, including Ken Hull, a quiet Ivy League graduate with an innocuous-sounding job title in the Economic Section that one woman said was a cover for his CIA duties. The Hulls introduced us to members of their set. We ate lunch at the embassy and were invited one night to a theater to see a rented first-run movie with a dinner party afterward. William McCormick Blair might have been an ambassador from Central Casting. Not only a Democrat, McCormick was also a friend of John F. Kennedy. Karin Fennow was glad we had made these amusing friends but pleased that we lived in Hellerup instead of what she called the Red, White, and Blue Ghetto.

My university work involved no administration, only the classroom, but there was one ceremonial duty. Each year in the Royal Theater the Universitets Arsfest celebrated the university's founding in 1479. As chairman of the English department, Carl Adolph Bodelsen had unofficial minor cabinet rank and was expected to attend this event. "Joe," he said, "would you be interested in standing in for me? The king will be there in his box. He's a rather hearty former sailor, and he enjoys singing along to 'Gaudeamus Igitur.'" And so one night in late November, after a formal dinner, I stood in borrowed formal dress and listened to a medieval ceremony conducted in Danish and Latin.

A day later we were sitting at home when Tracy received a call from a classmate who was the daughter of the American press attaché. John F.

Kennedy had been shot in Dallas. We sat up into the night waiting for more reports as an era ended.

Now that we were living abroad again, we anticipated the mail more eagerly than usual, and not just for news from home. I was an angler who had lines out for several awards and grants. From my study I could see the red-jacketed postman wheel up to our gate on his plain black bicycle. If I missed in the morning, there was another chance in the afternoon. An unusual-looking envelope arrived in the morning mail a week before Christmas, and it brought the joy of an unexpected gift. It was a cable from Carol Brandt. Random House was offering a $15,000 advance on a contract for William Faulkner's biography. Now I knew where some of the money was coming from for my research trips. A month later I would sign the contract for a total of 150,000 words in five installments, the last to coincide with the delivery of "the work" on the first day of September 1968.

A different kind of information brought me up short three days before Christmas. A front-page *New York Times* article was captioned, "Sofia says U.S. Paid a Bulgarian at U.N. $200,000 for Spying." A former member of the Bulgarian mission said he had made contact with the CIA and was subsequently met by an agent who identified himself by the name Anderson but later revealed "that his real name was Kiril Black, son of Floyd Black, former director of the American College in Sofia." At one contact in Paris in 1960, the account continued, "Kiril Black and another American communications expert gave him cipher equipment, [and] a special radio to monitor secret messages from a station in Greece."

Could this be my Cy Black? I thought back to our time together at Zadar, and there had been nothing about him that seemed remotely to suggest the CIA. The agency had declined to comment, but a short piece attached to the lead story reported that "the spy charges were dismissed tonight as 'complete nonsense' by Cyril Black, professor of History at Princeton University. 'The entire story is a fabrication,' Professor Black said." I vacillated, one moment rejecting the idea of Cy Black as an agent, the next moment telling myself not to be naive. Finally I decided that when I got home I would try to find out more from Cy himself.

The Danish winter was settling in when our door's metal slot banged one January morning to admit a fat letter. It was a request from the Guggenheim Foundation for a budget, should my application be funded with a fellowship. So I began preparations for following Faulkner's trail, accumulating maps, sketching research routes, and writing to prospective informants. Early in the month I fled the gray skies of Copenhagen for Paris.

At the offices of Gallimard, Faulkner's French publisher, I met an editor whose admiration had helped advance Faulkner's reputation and popularity. Michel Mohrt was an urbane prizewinner with the moustaches of a guards-man and the panache of a boulevardier. He took me to lunch at an elegant res-taurant and told me stories of his meetings with Faulkner. He introduced me to Monique Lange, another Gallimard employee. She and her husband had helped make a foursome with Faulkner and a Swedish admirer he had first met at the time of the Nobel ceremony in Stockholm. Else Jonsson recalled for me something of that august occasion, and I looked forward to getting to know her well enough to ask more after some of her reticence vanished.

I walked the streets of the Latin Quarter until I found the building on the rue Servandoni where Faulkner had rented a room on his first trip to Paris. On the city's Right Bank in the elegant George VI, I met Harry Kurnitz, who told me about doing screenwriting for Howard Hawks in Egypt when Faulkner had put himself *hors de combat* as an antidote to the boring job and melancholy over the sad ending of a romance. This research beat scribbling in library stacks and manuscript rooms.

A week later I flew to England for lectures in London, Manchester, and then the coastal city of Hull, where, lying under several comforters with a hot-water bottle at my feet, I watched liquid damp slowly trickling down the bed-room wall. I walked through Piccadilly again, looking up at the statue of Eros in the center flanked by the big Bovril sign. It felt as though much more than twenty years had passed since I had strolled there through the blackout with those who had survived the blitz. I visited the dark Dickensian offices of Chatto and Windus. Norah Smallwood was a partner, and she tried to find in-teresting materials about Faulkner's career with the firm, but most of the Brit-ish reading public had not cared very much for the novels of Yoknapatawpha or any of the others. This was one of literature's ironies, for their Anglophile creator had thought the Kentish countryside beautiful, "the quietest most restful country under the sun," and had stayed at Brown's Hotel in town, the favorite of retired officers of the Indian service. But there was little Faulkner-ian material for me at Chatto and Windus.

Home again in Hellerup, I studied foreign words and phrases—Greek for a trip to trace one of Faulkner's cultural trips for the State Department, and Serbo-Croatian for lectures I had promised in Zadar. I gave the first one in Novi Sad, fifty miles northwest of Belgrade and sixty miles west of the Ro-manian border. My berth in the rattling sleeper was both cold and narrow, and the sight of Zagreb the next day was even more welcome than it had been before.

The next morning I overslept and discovered too late that my train would make the three-hour return to Belgrade without food aboard. I looked about for a vendor, descending and then running the length of the car until I saw a pushcart. The train was just beginning to jerk into motion when I pulled myself back aboard. I sat down on the hard green felt seat to consume my repast, two salami sandwiches and a bottle of Yugopop.

My lecture went well, and there was an unexpected pleasure in seeing a familiar face in the audience. It was Aleks Stefanovic, his hair still hanging down darkly over his forehead. I asked him to have dinner with me, and he picked a small restaurant that served a surprisingly good goulash. I ordered a bottle of Cerno, and it proved to be the most full-bodied red I had tasted since my first dinner in Zagreb. When I asked Aleks about his status, he told me that he had not yet received government permission to reopen his magazine.

"Did you see the pieces in the newspapers about Cy Black and the Bulgarians?" I asked him.

"Yes," he said and broke a piece of bread to sop up the last of the savory dark brown gravy.

I poured the rest of the bottle into our glasses. When he raised his dark eyes to mine, I asked him the question. "Do you believe Cy Black was running agents in Bulgaria?" He broke off another piece of bread.

"I'll tell you something, Joe," he said in his deep rumble. "Before the conference started, they told us that one of your people was CIA."

"Did you believe it?"

"He never said anything suspicious to me, but why not?"

I dropped the subject, telling myself that I would have to try to find out what I could in Princeton. But as it turned out, that would take much longer than I expected. When I telephoned the next time I was in Princeton, he was out of the country. And when I tried again a few years later, I learned that he had died. So I did what I could have done earlier and turned to reference works. In his distinguished career Cy had served in Eastern Europe during World War II as a political advisor and officer in the U.S. State Department. He might well have served in the CIA, too. I would never have known. It was a reaffirmation of something I had already learned as a biographer: there are some things you just can't know. In any case, I was richer for having met him, and he had lent something exotic to my work in literary research.

I was glad to board the well-worn United Arab Airlines plane. With a little effort the swarthy stewardess could have made herself truly rude rather than just surly, and the pilot landed the aircraft as if he were testing the landing gear. This trip provided more cultural than scholarly benefits. Faulkner had gone to Athens in March of 1957 to receive the Silver Medal of the Athens Academy and to attend a Greek production of his play *Requiem for a Nun*. What he had enjoyed most had been cruising among the islands and the company of Voula Zoumboulaki, the statuesque black-haired actress who had played the protagonist, Temple Drake. As the visit wore on and the whiskey ran out, he became thankful for the availability of the pale anise-flavored ouzo. I interviewed the academy's presiding officer, Athanasiades Novas, even though my French was worse than his English. I finished my interviews with a day to spare and spent it walking in the city. Then, after returning to Hellerup long enough to greet my family and consolidate my gains, I prepared to set out for Stockholm.

I had written to Ambassador W. Walton Butterworth, and he had replied with his recollections of the 1950 Nobel Prize occasion and Faulkner's celebrated acceptance speech. He included the Stockholm address of his former press attaché and suggested that I might want to try a former butler at the embassy, an Englishman named Geoffrey Button. Button had been assigned to Faulkner as a sort of batman, and Faulkner had formed an attachment to him. He might not still be there, for Butterworth had heard that Button had come upon hard times, and had fallen or thrown himself into one of the canals, but I wrote to him along with the others.

Geoffrey Button responded, arriving at my hotel one afternoon, a tall, thin, stooped man with a fiery complexion. I ordered coffee, and he seemed to be trying to dredge up what he could remember. As I refilled our cups, he drew a sheaf of papers from an inner pocket and said, "You might be interested in these, sir." He went on to tell me that one of his duties had been to check Mr. Faulkner's wastebasket because he seemed to be depositing all his mail there, including an invitation from King Gustaf to one of the several receptions. I assumed that the papers were probably a mimeographed schedule, and I waited until there was a lull in Button's quiet recital. Looking down, I found that I was holding a sheaf of seven pages and immediately recognized William Faulkner's tiny crabbed hand. Then I realized that they constituted early drafts, in pencil and pen, of his now famous Nobel Prize acceptance speech. I read through them again.

"Mr. Button," I said, "would you like me to act for you in disposing of these? I think they would bring a respectable price." I could already see reproductions that would enliven my chapter on the Nobel Prize.

"Whatever you think, sir," he said diffidently. I packed the pages carefully in the folder I would carry aboard my SAS flight back to Copenhagen and wrote Linton Massey and Jill Faulkner Summers about my find.

The other high point of my trip to Stockholm was meeting Else Jonsson. Her husband, Thorsten, had been an influential journalist and literary critic who had traveled to Oxford in 1947 to interview Faulkner. A widow with a small daughter, Else went to work for Bonniers, Faulkner's Swedish publisher, and Kaj Bonnier asked her to help whenever they entertained the new laureate. Still grieving over her husband's death, she responded to Faulkner's intuitive kindness, and they formed an immediate rapport that soon led to brief but deep intimacy. It was resumed on his subsequent European trips. When she invited me to her home in Stockholm's Old Town, I could see how Faulkner would have been attracted to her thirteen years before. She was a tall woman, graceful and chic. Her hair was a glossy red, her eyes a violet blue-gray, her finely shaped features set off by clear skin. I asked her to go to dinner with me the next night, and before I left Stockholm I felt that we had formed a friendship. We agreed to correspond, and over time the genuine affection I felt for her would lead, in spite of an innate shyness, to her sharing with me letters and photographs that provided an insight into Faulkner's life I could have gained in no other way.

As the spring came on, I worked at my desk in Hellerup to organize the material I had gathered. I flew to Jutland to lecture at the University of Arhus, and when I returned we went, all five of us, to Tivoli Gardens, a magical amusement park there in the middle of Copenhagen. In early May I made a quick trip to Milan to interview the few members of the firm of Mondadori who remembered Faulkner's well-publicized visits. Relaxing in the warm sun and hospitality after his taxing trip for the United States Information Service, he had felt a special affinity for Italy and declared that he would return. My own bonus on this trip was twofold: to contemplate *The Last Supper* and, like one of Faulkner's characters, to stand in blazing sunlight on the Piazza Maggiore at the Duomo.

A month later I rented a car, and in it the five of us boarded a ferry to Germany, where we traveled south into the Alps. The beauty of Geneva and its lake had not prepared us for the snows and spires of Chamonix and Mont Blanc, and the girls were almost surfeited with scenery by the time the spectacular curves of the Simplon Pass led us down into Italy. The logistics of getting a family of five around Venice reminded us that seeing lagoons and canals had its price. Surviving the dangers of the Autostrada's manic drivers, we found a family hotel on the beach at Cesenatico, where, after three days, Yvonne and I concluded that we simply could not consume five collations of northern Italian cuisine daily, no matter how delicious. The beauty of hilly Perugia and Ravenna's mosaics swiftly palled on the children, and soon their parents too were almost ready for the madness of Roman traffic and the trials of the Colosseum with its persistent salesmen and cats. Then, despite luxurious days on the beach at Aiguebelle on the Riviera, the wonders of Fontainebleau, the Louvre, and the Eiffel Tower produced cultural overload. Someday the children will really appreciate this, we told ourselves, and carried on. One more visit to the offices of Gallimard provided psychological reassurance that I *did* need to follow my author's trail, and soon enough we would be back home in America leading our ordinary lives.

Leaving Denmark was a time of mixed emotions. As we stood on the deck, the ship's superstructure gay with the fluttering flags and banners, the band on the stern struck up "There Is a Lovely Land," the Danish anthem. With the ship's movement swelling perceptibly now, the familiar lilting strains of "Wonderful, Wonderful Copenhagen" helped carry us toward the open water. The girls held tightly to their versions of *Dannebrog*, the Danish flag, balancing against the swelling seaward motion.

Yvonne was holding a handkerchief to her face. A stout Danish matron put a comforting hand on her arm. "There, there, dear," she murmured. "You'll like America."

Plunging again into the continuing cycle of interviews in New York, I telephoned Ruth Ford, whom Faulkner had first known as a girlfriend of his brother Dean at Ole Miss. A striking, dark-haired, pale-skinned actress, she starred with her husband, Zachary Scott, in the stage version of *Requiem for a Nun*. We met for a drink at the St. Regis's King Cole Bar and then went on to their apartment in the prestigious Dakota building. I had written Jean Stein Van den Heuvel, a talented young writer-to-be who had entertained Faulkner among others at her Paris salon. When I telephoned her, she accepted my invitation to dinner. Slim and graceful, she was striking in a low-cut black dress at Charles à la Pomme Soufflé. In the flush of Faulkner's Nobel fame, friends had seen Jean fling her arms around him, exclaiming, "My king!" I hoped that she would provide insights, but I was grateful for just names and places.

In Princeton I found generous friends. Carlos Baker had won my admiration for his thoroughgoing biography of Ernest Hemingway, and now he had practical tips for me. One of his colleagues had followed an even longer trail. Robert Frost had made Lawrence Thompson his official biographer. These two veterans provided comradely support. In a reply to problems I described, Carlos wrote, "You're getting your reward now." As Mark Schorer had helped me to plot my way carefully, so Richard Ellmann provided reassurance against the waste of psychic energy. After showing him some of my treasures, I told him about the ample resources of my chief rival. "Don't worry, Joe," he said, "Carvel will never finish his book."

I left Princeton, as always, with mixed feelings. I sat with Charlie and Marnie Allen on the screened-in porch of their farmhouse. We talked about their three sons and our three daughters and the paths our lives had taken since we had first met in our impoverished student days nearly twenty years before. I had felt a kind of twinge, however, walking down Professors' Row on Prospect, the feeling of an outsider in this academic community. But I thought again about Mark Twain's Mysterious Stranger, who told Theodore Fischer that if a man should skip one act in the chain that made up his life, his career "would change utterly, from that moment; thence to the grave it would be wholly different."

It was early August when I returned to Charlottesville, and a week later I flew to Memphis to take the Greyhound bus for the hot, bumpy two-hour ride to Oxford. The University Press of Virginia had sent me the galley proofs of my edition of *William Faulkner's Library: A Catalogue*, and now I would check them against the books themselves at Rowan Oak when I was not doing interviews with friends and acquaintances of William Faulkner from childhood to adulthood.

I had learned a great deal from Shelby Foote's three-volume history of the Civil War, but knowing also that he thought of Faulkner and Marcel Proust as his great mentors, I was determined to ask him about his fellow Mississippian. He not only offered to meet me but also suggested that we visit Shiloh. A vivid raconteur, he told me about strolling there with Faulkner. Faulkner had a close knowledge of the battle, and Shelby described to him his own efforts to imagine it. "On this one rise here," he told Faulkner, "I wanted to know how it must have felt to charge the enemy. I looked around and spotted a tree limb. When I hefted it, I thought it must weigh something like a musket those Confederate troops were carrying. I asked him if he thought that was a good idea." Shelby smiled as he recalled the drawled response.

"Yes," he said. "That was a good idea. Just the way to do it."

Any careful student of Faulkner could not forget his assertion, "There is no such thing as was. The past *is*." And so I was trying to get some sense of life in north Mississippi during the years when his family rose to prominence there. In the antebellum Oxford courthouse I studied wills, checked records, and began to read issues of the *Oxford Eagle* from 1885 to 1962, deeply thankful that it was a weekly newspaper.

When I was invited to dinner, I knew sometimes that the host and host-

ess as well as some of the guests had served as models for Faulkner's characters. Dr. Ashford Little was a short, trim man who had been the model for
Dr. Alford in *Sartoris*, Faulkner's third novel. The dinner fare at the Littles' was
always good and often unpredictable. As Minnie Ruth Little served the entree
from a large painted china tureen that had been her great-grandmother's, Ashford passed a platter of steaming cornbread. The aroma from the dark gravy,
which revealed morsels of meat and corn kernels, was spicy and appetizing.

"Joe," he said, "have you ever had Brunswick stew?"

"No, sir," I said.

"It's got everything in it that beef stew does," said Chester McLarty, "and
a few things beef stew usually doesn't—some rabbit and squirrel, and some
strong New Orleans spices." Minnie Ruth looked at me expectantly.

"I think I'll ask for seconds right now," I said. The dish was at once savory
and piquant, and the whole meal was seasoned with genial laughter and droll
stories from north Mississippi.

Soon it would be time to start a new sequence of discovery. Far to the
south were New Orleans and Pascagoula, sources of realistic and exotic material for early poems, stories, and novels. To the west was the seductive Delta,
the Big Woods, with their mystique and initiation into hunting. To the north
lay the gambling dens and whorehouses of Clarksdale, places of initiation that
Faulkner had encountered under the sponsorship of his early mentor, the attorney Phil Stone. Farther north was Memphis, the metropolis of the whole
region, where veteran newspapermen would escort him into purlieus that
would provide the vivid details for *Sanctuary*, the novel that would shock reviewers as a revelation of Dostoevsky in the Deep South.

By November I was back in the North, bringing with me memories of
people and events. One inhabitant of both these worlds was Joan Williams, a
young Tennessean whom Faulkner had met in 1950 when she was an aspiring writer and student at Bard College. She was a slim, quiet girl with green
eyes, reddish hair, and freckles and an engaging quality of innocence. At odds
with her family and depressed with her lack of progress, she had gone to see
him at Rowan Oak in the hope of finding answers to her frustration. They began to see each other, in the South and in New York. Soon this developed into
an increasingly troubled relationship, with both of them at cross-purposes.
She wanted him to be her teacher and guide. He wanted her to be his lover.
Over the next dozen years they continued intermittently, surviving distance,
separation, and renewal until she married a talented young sports writer
named Ezra Bowen. Faulkner told her to remember, "I will always be to you
the best friend you ever had." He retained hope for more than just friendship,

though, as his scores of letters—passionate, plaintive, and sometimes angry—revealed.

Joan and her husband and their two sons lived in Westport, Connecticut. I had planned to visit Albert Erskine there, and so I wrote to ask if I could visit her, too. She had received requests from other writers, but her innate shyness had made her decline. When she received my letter, she asked the advice of a veteran editor who had helped her. When he told her he thought she could trust me, she wrote me to come ahead. We had met briefly in Oxford, and now we got on as easily as we had then. There were few people she could talk to about Faulkner, but I knew both their stories, and she found it easy to return to the past with me.

Joan proved no less generous than the friends who had helped me in Stockholm and Oxford. Toward the end of the first day, she asked if I would care to see Faulkner's letters. She left the room, and when she returned she carried a box full of them. They were evenly divided between his amateur typing on his old typewriter and the familiar tiny script. Instead of asking to borrow them, I asked if I could read them into my micro-cassette recorder. I was mortgaging hours of work with the painstaking transcription I would have to perform, but I didn't want to take the risk of asking for too much. So I made the request, and Joan granted it. There were just over a hundred letters extending over an important six-year period. Once more I had encountered both luck and generosity.

It was not far along the hilly, stone-lined country roads to the Erskines' home where Albert did as much of his editorial work as he could and tended his vegetables and flowers. A cordon-bleu chef with files full of delectable Italian recipes, Marisa Bisi Erskine used Albert's garden produce for casual lunches as well as elegant dinner parties. I had found not only a paragon of a hostess and friend in Marisa but also my ideal editor in Albert. I went over my recent work with him and made plans for the next steps.

This was an evening when the Erskines were giving one of their celebrated parties. The guests would usually include sophisticated suburbanites, some of them easily recognizable. David Wayne was naturally cordial, with nothing of the movie actor about him. After Albert introduced me to Richard Rodgers, I remembered seeing his photograph with articles about Rodgers and Hart or Hammerstein. One year Whitney Darrow had presented Albert with a birthday card, now framed, done in the style I recognized from his *New Yorker* cartoons. There was lively talk and laughter in the large living room. As Albert and Peter DeVries and I stood for a moment in an adjoining study, a news program showed a massive demonstration by radical students. Deeply conservative, Albert viewed the scene with a scornful smile. "Marx said that every revolution needs a certain number of necessary idiots," he remarked. Peter turned slightly toward his wife.

"Katinka," he called to her, "Albert has just called our son a necessary idiot." Over time Albert's friends learned to appreciate, or at least tolerate, his acerbic humor.

After dinner we sat in the living room over liqueurs. Earlier I had noticed a woman I thought I recognized. She was wearing a slinky black dress that emphasized her thinness. Her long black hair fell about her shoulders, and her expression seemed to me somber. To Marisa I whispered, "I recognize that woman, but I can't recall her name. Who is she?" Marisa smiled.

"You saw her in the *New Yorker*. She was married to Charles Addams, and he used to put her in his cartoons."

Stopping in New York, I met more kindness from attractive women. The wise and witty Dorothy Parker told me stories about Faulkner in the company of her friends among the celebrated wits who shared the Round Table at the Algonquin. Anita Loos recalled the pleasure of his company in New Orleans years earlier when he expressed his admiration for *Gentlemen Prefer Blondes*. She had the same star quality as that of a woman decades younger. Lauren Bacall made time to see me one afternoon while she was having a quick lunch in her dressing room before the matinee performance of *Cactus Flower*. I enjoyed her stories of events during her time as a Hollywood starlet when Humphrey Bogart brought her and Faulkner together with friends such as Hoagy Carmichael, whose wit was different from that at the Algonquin but no less engaging. She told me how much Faulkner enjoyed it. "Women ain't like us," Carmichael told him, looking at the passing starlets, their hips swaying as they hurried to the commissary for lunch. "They're one-dog people."

In January of 1965 I was making a swing through warm-weather country again. Staying in the comfortable Forty Acres Club of the University of Texas, I spent three days studying manuscripts of early Faulkner poems and prose in the Harry Ransom Humanities Research Center. Through William Faulkner's niece, Dean Mallard, and Emily Stone, Phil's widow, Carvel Collins had learned about materials in Faulkner's mother's attic and helped to negotiate their purchase by the university. Some were restricted to his use and were denied to me specifically by name. I became aware of an intriguing irony twenty years later when the remaining materials were made available to me at last through administrative action of the director of the center. As we looked through the folders, we found that they comprised photographs of places where Faulkner had lived in California, mimeographed handouts, and newspaper clippings. I couldn't help thinking of E. M. Forster's remark about Joseph Conrad's much-praised style, which he likened to a casket said to contain a wondrous precious gem, only to be found, upon opening, to be empty.

I returned home by way of New Orleans and Pascagoula, interviewing people who had known Faulkner as an aspiring writer and lovelorn artist in the late 1920s and early 1930s. In Pascagoula I strolled the beach where he had walked disconsolately. One of my trips back to Virginia took me out into Albemarle County to Red Acres, where Jill and Paul were converting one of their rooms for Estelle. She said that the Rugby Road house was too big for her, and the traffic made it unsafe for her grandchildren. "It doesn't make any sense for me to be in that big house alone, so I think I'm going to put it on the market."

"What about you?" Paul said to me encouragingly. "It's just three blocks from where you live now."

I said I thought we would be interested. The more Yvonne and I thought about the handsome two-story four-bedroom Georgian-style red brick house, the more attractive it seemed. My salary was $11,500, not counting the summer-school earnings and income from writing essay-reviews for the *Masterplots Annual.* In late February Paul told me that the Faulkner house had been appraised at $42,500. I had learned that my book, *The Modern American Political Novel,* would be published by the University of Texas Press, but it would be a long time before it earned any royalties. We decided to stop wrestling with the decision and go ahead.

I was still traveling—a week in New York, then three in the West. In the East I was spending time with literary journalists like Harvey Breit, who had interviewed Faulkner often. I had profited from Malcolm Cowley's *Portable Faulkner,* which had done so much in the 1940s to help bring Faulkner's work to a wider audience. He told me of his plan to publish a book to be called *The Faulkner-Cowley File: Letters and Memories, 1944–1962.* Cowley had invited me to visit him at his home in Sherman, Connecticut, where I could see this unpublished material. In return he asked if I would use my good offices with Jill to help him gain permission to publish what Faulkner had written him. I would long remember the thrill of sitting at the desk in Cowley's small upstairs study and reading through these revealing answers to the questions of this admirable literary critic and historian.

In California, I worked my way through filing cabinets of motion picture scripts. Each noon I would go to lunch in the studio commissary, where actors in top hats and actresses in hoop skirts ate their hamburgers carefully so as not to smear the makeup that made them look like animated waxworks figures. Most of my labor involved checking screenplays with Faulkner's name on them and reading correspondence that supplied his assignments and salary scale. By now the actors he had liked were dead or departed for other places: Humphrey Bogart, Clark Gable, and Ronald Colman, Estelle's special favorite. But there were still writers and directors who had worked with him. John Fante had felt something like hero-worship for his collaborator.

"Bill gave me some advice," he told me. He said, "John, you've got some talent. You ought to get out of this town and write." He said it with a melancholy smile. "Bill left Hollywood for good after he finally got some financial security. I never did. I should have tried to follow his example."

Other screenwriters had begun with hero-worship and then developed personal bonds with Faulkner. During World War II, when affordable housing was scarce in Hollywood, A. I. "Buzz" Bezzerides invited him into his car pool and then into his home. Even Dorothy Parker, celebrated for her caustic wit, had responded to him immediately. "He seemed so vulnerable, so helpless," she said. "You just wanted to protect him." When an emotional crisis led to what Faulkner would call a "collapse," friends such as Bezzerides became intimate participants in the process. They might go to his room to check on his condition when he hadn't shown up for work. They might then seek medical attention, which led to his spending time recovering in a facility in the Valley.

I had as much good luck with producers as I did with screenwriters. One of my biggest breaks came first. A professional racecar driver in his teens, Howard Hawks had drawn on his adventurous life for classic films such as *Dawn Patrol.* Easy and cordial, with nothing of the celebrity about him, Hawks told me about his collaboration with Faulkner as well as their dove hunts. I gradually became aware of Faulkner's involvement with a secretary for Hawks named Meta Carpenter Rebner. A divorcee from Mississippi, she later lived with Faulkner from time to time, hoping that he would marry her. Estelle's reluctance to give him a divorce, and his fear of losing Jill and all that he valued in Mississippi, ultimately doomed their affair. I had written to her, but she declined to help me in any way. This was another lesson to be learned, that there would be some things you just couldn't know, and that you simply had to do the best you could to discover and construct your story.

Late December of 1965 found me in Washington, where I interviewed State Department professionals who had accompanied Faulkner on trips to Europe and Japan. At home, we were well settled in our new house and decided to celebrate. We were making up for lost parties with our friends on the last day of the year when Yvonne motioned to me from the hall, holding out the telephone. The caller apologized and explained that she had been asked to tell me that Fred Gwynn had died that day. He had taken his son, Andy, and a friend skiing in Vermont. Fred had climbed with them to the top of the ski run and collapsed. He was only forty-nine years old, with no apparent illness. There was a bruise on his face from his fall, Anne Gwynn later told me, but that was all. What Japanese antiaircraft fire had failed to do, a Vermont mountain had done. Fred had been a fine scholar and teacher, and one of the best friends I would ever have. I went to the funeral in West Hartford, feeling not only grief but also an increased sense of my own vulnerability and the need to make haste. Eight months later we went to Mammer's funeral in Princeton. My time sense was changing, and I felt strong intimations of mortality.

Fred had considered Henry James the greatest American novelist. Others might have chosen Herman Melville or Nathaniel Hawthorne, but to me it was William Faulkner. My work afforded the greatest opportunity I could have to contribute to the study of American literature, and I approached it like a zealot, with the feeling that *anything* he had written might be useful to me. Resonating in my mind was Ulysses S. Grant's dispatch to Washington before Spotsylvania Court House in May 1864: "I propose to fight it out on this line, if it takes all summer."

I thought too of the novel that had brought Buzz Bezzerides to Hollywood, a story of long-distance truck drivers. Made into a motion picture, it was called *They Drive by Night*. I liked its original title better: *The Long Haul*. That was what I was in this job for, and I meant to complete it.

FIFTEEN

Professional Joy and Private Woe

I WAS FORTUNATE TO BE IMMERSED IN MY PROJECT. It kept me from dwelling on departmental matters, and it brought opportunities in its train. Albert Erskine had suggested that I interview Robert Penn Warren, a longtime admirer of William Faulkner. Warren and his wife, Eleanor Clark, were known for their hospitality, and in his reply to my request Warren had invited me to his home in Fairfield, Connecticut. It proved to be a good trip, both for the information I gleaned about the Warrens' friendship with Faulkner and for the links they provided with other Faulkner friends.

In Charlottesville both the university and the English department had been undergoing changes. Edgar Shannon had proved to be an energetic president intent on improving the university and increasing its distinction. Fredson Bowers had similar aims for the department. New money was now available for programs and the recruitment of promising graduate students and prominent professors. The new colleague who made the greatest difference for my friends and me was George Garrett, a prizewinning poet, novelist, and essayist. An artist of dazzling imagination and a humorist of genius, he taught overflowing classes and revitalized the creative writing courses. It was an exciting time, but also a troubled one.

Returning to the classroom was a necessary interruption to my writing, and I had my usual duties attending to visiting writers. Had I been less absorbed in the writing, I might have done a better job in at least one instance. One of our visitors was Howard Nemerov, a distinguished poet and a good friend of Nancy Hale, the chairman's wife and his official hostess. I sent out the usual notices for Nemerov's public reading, but it had simply not occurred to me that I should recruit enough students to guarantee a full house. As a re-

sult, Nemerov gave a fine reading to a scanty audience and a scattering of polite applause. Nancy lavished attention on him while Bowers briefly directed
his remarks to me. His fury gave his ruddy countenance a deeper hue. "You've
got to be *sure* that our visitors have a good audience!" he hissed at me.

While I was in Denmark, George Garrett had showed how to do it. When
he had persuaded Shelby Foote to come for a week as writer-in-residence,
Bowers's reaction had been to tell George he had made a mistake and wasted
$400, because no one would come to hear Foote. "You see," Bowers said, "it's
a matter of visibility, publicity." He did not know that George had written a
film for Sam Goldwyn, Jr., and helped to promote it, Hollywood style. For
Foote's appearance, George circulated photographs and news releases that
made front pages all over Virginia. He offered the football players in his survey course a guaranteed B if they would recruit and usher in an audience for
Foote's lecture. He hired a student trumpeter and his band. When a cold February rain descended, a sympathetic librarian invited the musicians inside. In
single file they led a raucous Dixieland parade through the library stacks and
into the crowded Macgregor Room. There the football players shut the doors
behind them. Foote gave his lecture to a standing ovation. One of the reverberations came from an emeritus professor in the *Cavalier Daily* denouncing
"barbarians and Visigoths." When George stopped in at the department offices later, Bowers simply tossed him a copy of the *Cavalier Daily* carrying
complaints from several other distinguished scholars.

"I thought you wanted visibility, sir," George said, but he received no
reply.

One of the times of increased tension came early in the year when departmental recommendations for promotion went to the deans of the colleges.
As an associate professor I had tenure, but under Bowers I could imagine staying at that rank. I felt no anxiety about my publication record of five books, a
good number of articles, fellowships and lectureships, and much of my
Faulkner manuscript already written. The suspense was ended on March 11,
when I learned that two of the younger men had been promoted but I had not.
Next year, three more would be put up for promotion.

I found that I simply could not wait until next year for some further inkling of my fate. When I entered the chairman's office, he tilted his chair back
and looked at me expectantly. He was wearing neither a poker face nor the
fixed smile that always made me think of Sax Rohmer's "insidious Dr. Fu
Manchu."

"Fred," I said, "can you tell me when I'll be put up for promotion again?"

"No," he replied, his face simply expressionless.

"Not even an approximate idea?"

"No," he repeated.

In my few dealings with him I had liked and trusted Robert Harris, the dean of the College of Arts and Sciences, but there was nothing he could do now except to counsel patience. When I went to Floyd Stovall for advice, he said what he had said before: "Joe, Fredson is no friend of yours."

I thought I knew why. I had not come into the department under his auspices, and now I held a tenured position that might have gone to one he thought better fitted for the department he was building. Working for him one summer as department executive secretary when he was away much of the time, I had done what I thought was a creditable job, and we had a civil relationship. One of the outstanding textual bibliographers in his field, he also had credentials as a newspaper music critic, Irish wolfhound judge, and bridge expert. Nancy Hale was one of the most visible writers in Albemarle County. When William Faulkner came to reside on the scene part-time, he overshadowed all other resident celebrities. Nancy had seemed to like and admire him, but her husband, I thought, did not. He seemed glad, though, to try to make use of Faulkner's prestige. As writer-in-residence, Faulkner had the use of one of the department's prized single-occupant offices. When his term was through, the chairman told me one day to try to find him a different one.

Some distance away in a busy corridor was a large room that housed spare furniture, including a massive table occasionally used for oral examinations and seminars. "Let's put his name on the door of that one," Bowers said.

My response was almost involuntary. "Why don't we just put his name on the door of the Men's Room?" I asked and walked out without waiting for a response. This was rude and impolitic but deeply satisfying.

I found myself glad to be busy as spring came in. Research, teaching, and business helped to keep me from brooding about my professional situation. I corrected proofs of my new book on the modern American political novel and returned them to the University of Texas Press. I organized the brief appearance of William Styron, then enjoying the success of his new novel, *The Confessions of Nat Turner* (1966). There were, however, vibrations in the air from resignations and anticipated departures of staff, both untenured and tenured, three of them leading to prestigious appointments elsewhere. Jim Colvert adapted the familiar phrase about the Old Dominion and the nation's presidents to coin a new one. "Virginia, mother of chairmen," he observed.

It was early May when I received a call from Frank Hereford, a distinguished physicist, now provost of the university. He echoed the appeal Bob Harris had made. "Be patient," he said. "Bowers can't block your promotion forever." Then he made me an unexpected offer: "Would you consider becoming assistant provost?" I declined with thanks and no regrets. By January of 1967 I was tired of this game of patience, and when I received the chairman's notification that I had again not been promoted, I told a few close friends that I was going to look around.

My mental landscape was brightening. In the fall I had traveled south again to Memphis, eager to learn more from Shelby Foote and from two veteran newspapermen who knew the old Memphis. They drove me down Gayoso Street in the heart of what had been the red-light district fifty years before and told me about that demimondaine culture that had helped make Faulkner's *Sanctuary* the sensational novel it was. In the files of the *Commercial Appeal* and the *Press-Scimitar* I read up on the gangsters and gamblers whose world Faulkner had known. And now a letter from the Guggenheim Foundation arrived, requesting a budget estimate for a renewal of my fellowship.

One of those I had told about my plans to look around was George Garrett. He had immediately called friends, and by the middle of January I had an invitation to visit the University of North Carolina at Chapel Hill. I knew Chapel Hill well by reputation, and now I looked forward to meeting the faculty, which included eminent students of Southern literature, well-known scholars such as Hugh Holman and Louis Rubin. The genial chairman, Carroll Hollis, provided warm hospitality. The University of North Carolina seemed larger than the University of Virginia in every way. Nearly as old, it had the kind of climate and architecture that inspired one writer to call it "the Southern Part of Heaven."

Then, on one day in mid-February, I had two long-distance calls. The first was from Carroll Hollis. During my visit I had told him about my situation at the University of Virginia, where my associate professor's salary was $11,500. "Joe," he said, "we're offering you a full professorship, of course. You'll teach the minimum load. The salary will be $17,800," he said and paused. "That's what I get as chairman," he added. The second call that day was from Russell Fraser, a prolific Renaissance scholar and department chairman at Vanderbilt University in Nashville. He invited me to visit Vanderbilt.

My feelings were clear and largely unmixed. Yvonne agreed that we should take the North Carolina job. After all that had gone before, it would be unthinkable not to. The future now seemed secure, with my pride and my self-confidence restored. But the move would be much more emotional for her than for me. She loved our handsome house on Rugby Road. We had lived in that beautiful part of Virginia for a dozen years, where Nancy, our third child had been born. But for the present, the positive factors were exhilarating.

It was a time of telephoning. My conversation with Carroll Hollis was a happy one. The conversation with Russ Fraser also laid the basis for a warm friendship. I was in no hurry to visit my dean or my chairman, though I looked forward to both. When I went to Bob Harris, who knew Vanderbilt and North Carolina well, his congratulations were warm and his regrets sincere.

When I entered Bowers's office, he swung around in his chair. "Fred," I said, "I've received a nice offer, and I'm going to take it."

"Oh, congratulations," he replied and gave me that familiar smile.

I paused for a beat and then told him the name of the university, the rank, salary, and the minimal course load. He paled and went silent. He had perhaps thought I would receive an offer from one of the schools that hired cannon fodder. Going down the hall, my step was light.

Matthew Bruccoli, an energetic graduate student clearly headed for a university career, said to me, "Wow! That American literature faculty will give Carolina the greatest lineup since the 1927 Yankees." Another friend told me he had been present at the coffee bar in the basement of Old Cabell Hall when my new job was mentioned. It was well known that the University of North Carolina had been involved in prolonged budget negotiations with the legislature. The matter naturally attracted attention in other schools also dependent on their state governments for support. "They'll never be able to pay him," Fredson Bowers declared.

I had decided to call my first group of chapters "The Ancestors." By July 27, 1967, I had gotten my hero born. It had taken me 122 pages, but I did not let that bother me. I felt that I had too many responsibilities for that—to the scholar, the critic, the general reader, and William Faulkner himself. In mid-November I traveled to Oxford again. When I met Howard Duvall—a literary-minded Oxford merchant and fellow tennis enthusiast—on the Square in the shadow of the Confederate soldier, he seized my hand with his usual vigor and exclaimed, "Welcome home!" When Sallie Murry Williams invited me for drinks and showed me pictures of herself and her cousin William on the front lawn of her childhood home, her affectionate welcome helped give me the sense of reentry reconfirmed by interviews with old and new friends.

At home in Charlottesville we were doing preliminary packing. We had forgotten how laborious such a move was, and we were making notes against forgetting special items in the attic. One was a large, meticulously made dollhouse that had stood in the window of Thorngren's, the famous toy store on Stroget in Copenhagen. Tracy had saved a long time for it. It was January now, and eight months of Guggenheim time lay ahead of me. My pages of manuscript kept piling up. On May 9 as the sound of the carillon chimes striking five floated through the soft spring twilight, I took page 1,000 out of the typewriter. Yvonne began to deal with a local realtor and made a preliminary trip to look at Chapel Hill housing. I decided to approach Vincent Shea about our plans. A handsome, thin-faced man with silver hair, he was the comptroller of the university. I inquired if the university would be interested in acquiring our house. No, he replied promptly, but "if, however, you should wish to give it to the university, we would be very happy to accept it."

On August 21, in the blue 1958 MGA convertible bought from my Random House advance, I drove for the last time from Charlottesville to Chapel Hill. The white house with the red door at 306 Glendale Drive was a two-story symmetrical clapboard with a circular drive backed against the forest. I liked my colleagues in the English department and my courses, and Yvonne and I were better off professionally and financially than we had ever been. The golden Indian summer seemed auspicious. When we filled out our change-of-address postcards, it struck me that our street number was the same as that of the air force group that I had left so unceremoniously. But I was not going to be superstitious. If the number was unlucky, we would find out.

It was the fall term of 1968, and I was a new member of an English department for the first time in thirteen years. I had met most of the English faculty during my exploratory visit. One was a thin-faced man with a pinched face and neatly parted gray hair. His speech was very Southern with something of a fastidious upper-class English accent. His whole manner was courtesy itself, but his first question took me off guard.

"How does it happen, Mr. Blotner," he asked, "that a Yankee like yourself is writing William Faulkner's biography?"

The best response, I thought, was the direct one. I tried to explain the circumstances briefly, and then I said, "I realize, sir, that most Southerners are born knowing some things in their bones that a Northerner can't acquire, but I'm doing the best I can."

Dougald Macmillan gave me a wintry smile and said, "Yes, yes. I understand." I regarded him somewhat warily when we met again two weeks later. "I've just finished reading this," he said, and handed me a copy of Philip Roth's *Portnoy's Complaint.* "I think it might amuse you." Later I told him he had been right and thanked him again, realizing that, like so many with a taste for eighteenth-century fiction, he enjoyed the bawdy as well as the proper.

Some of my colleagues I knew and liked from past acquaintance. I had met Louis Rubin at Penn through Robert Spiller. He and I were of an age, and like me he had used the GI Bill to study for his Ph.D. in American studies at

Johns Hopkins. He was a burly, bespectacled man with closely cut hair. He kept his office door open, and I would see him hammering away at his massive typewriter and puffing a pipe or cigar. Later I learned that he might very well be composing rather than simply typing, for he had an easy facility at writing and a great deal of energy. A founding editor of the *Southern Literary Journal*, he managed to produce a steady flow of scholarship and journalism.

Others I came to like immediately. Lewis Leary was a tall, wiry New Englander who had chaired the large English department at Columbia University for decades. He was an able administrator with a wry sense of humor who managed stars such as Lionel Trilling and William York Tindall as adeptly as he did his hard-worked junior faculty. He was a fine raconteur with highly developed social skills and savoir-faire. During the war he had gotten on well with his colleagues in British intelligence. When I asked about his success, he said he attributed it to the strength and quantity of the martinis served and his own capacity to tolerate them while they loosened the tongues of others. On one occasion he had particularly valued their potency. When his arm was injured in a brush with another motorist, he not only remained alert under the sedative and local anesthetic but also discussed *Ulysses* with the surgeon who made the repairs.

I had known Hugh Holman long before I met him at the annual meetings of the MLA. He had made a living outside academia. Like many Southern writers, he had taken a stab at surviving in New York. He worked in radio, writing scripts for soap operas, but he found the pace tiring and the work unsatisfying. So he finally decided to return home. An even-tempered, congenial man, he was a natural teacher proficient in a wide range of subjects but found his deepest satisfaction in such writers as Thomas Wolfe and Faulkner. I had been teaching Faulkner's work for years when the *Sewanee Review* brought me "*Absalom, Absalom!* The Historian as Detective." Thereafter I reread Hugh's penetrating analysis every time I taught the novel.

At a small party just before we left Charlottesville, Atch Hench had risen and said, "We want to congratulate you on your move to North Carolina. You are leaving for a valley of humility between two mountains of conceit." I would conceive an increasing admiration for the Old North State and those virtues persisting from Revolutionary days that paradoxically made it a bastion of liberalism to some and a hotbed of radicalism to others. I was enjoying my classes, for I found the best of my Carolina undergraduates the equal of the best at Virginia, although a larger number at the latter had been better prepared. Carroll Hollis saw to it that I had graduate seminars each semester, and one of them was the best class I ever taught anywhere. There did not seem to be the kind of separation between junior and senior faculty that I had known at Virginia. We were welcomed with parties, especially a familiar kind of cocktail party. There· would be two or three dozen couples mingling in the amiable hubbub, fueled in the dining room by a large brimming bowl. It was Chapel Hill punch, composed solely of bourbon and soda with ice cubes. As soon as we were well settled, Yvonne began entertaining in her usual style, with cocktails and canapés followed by a five-course candle-lit dinner served with her best crystal, silver, and china.

On the day after St. Patrick's Day in that year of 1968, I finished my draft of chapter 25. I was one-third of the way through. But sooner than I might have thought, events occurred that a superstitious man might have taken for signs and portents. Before I had arrived from Charlottesville, Yvonne had bought a dog, a cross between his golden retriever dam and his Irish setter sire. Sean had her beauty and his mindless love of speed. Though the girls loved him and pampered him, he ran away twice. We cruised through the whole neighborhood, Nancy leaning out the window, at intervals calling out in a tear-choked voice, "Sea-a-n! Sea-a-n!" A woman telephoned, and we found him on her hearth gnawing on a large bone. He declined to recognize his name or us. Soon he had made friends as heedless as himself. One noon-time in mid-February they dashed en masse across Rosemary Street. They made it, but Sean didn't.

Though we had more income than ever before, Yvonne went to work again to help with the expenses of Tracy's new school. Her secretarial skills were modest, but she worked carefully. I came home from school one fall afternoon and found her sitting on one of the kitchen counter stools, her head buried in her folded arms.

"What's the matter, sweetie?" I asked in alarm.

She answered without raising her head. "It's my leg."

"What did you do to it?"

"I didn't do anything to it. I think it must be my chair at work." She had realized belatedly that the seat cut into the backs of her legs where she crossed them for extended periods of typing. In the last few days this had produced a deep ache in one calf. Our young doctor said he thought it might be a blood clot. He prescribed Indocin for inflammation and Darvon for pain and ordered her to bed. After ten days she was allowed to return to work, but it was too soon. Confined to bed with hot towels, she lay there waiting for her leg to get better. The pain got worse. On some nights sleep was impossible, and our troubles multiplied.

I had caught a cold that moved into my chest. One Friday I began running an elevated temperature and experienced a pain that was new to me, as if a nail were being driven into the top of my head. Our doctor offered to meet me at his office, but I felt too bad to go. After I received antibiotics and felt able to dress and move about, Yvonne drove me to the doctor's office. I learned that I had probably been felled by one of a group of organisms called mycoplasma, which soon produced pneumonia. The congestion in the upper lobe of my right lung proceeded at its own pace, and I slept in a semireclining position. One of my therapies required a device we had used only for the children: a vaporizer. Yvonne would drape a towel over my head and I would sit at her vanity table, looking like some strange sheikh, to inhale the vapor. Then she would pound on my back with the heels of both fists until I began to cough.

The holidays of 1969 came and went quietly. Two areas of our lives preoccupied me: Yvonne's health and my work. Fortunately Pamela and Nancy were in their teens and could do much for themselves. Yvonne could do little for them until she reached the point of wearing elastic stockings, when she could do mild exercise. She was fitted with Jobsts, heavy brown elasticized stockings eventually to be replaced by thin white Teds and, finally, support hose that looked almost like ordinary stockings. But these last were well in the future. There were tests, some at the University of North Carolina Hospital, others in nearby Durham at the prestigious Duke University Hospital.

We sought out new doctors, for the whole process of recovery seemed puzzling and prolonged. Yvonne's thrombophlebitis had been diagnosed as superficial, and we knew of patients with deep clots who had been treated successfully with Heparin and then Coumadin, an anticoagulant so powerful that it was used for rat poison, causing them to bleed to death. Our medicine chest and bedside tables now contained an increasing variety of painkillers and muscle relaxants. One was Valium, the drug of choice for lockjaw but also a tranquilizer capable of side effects such as depression and lassitude. And there was the age-old drug of choice: alcohol in various forms. Bourbon whisky was one I had known even before my study of William Faulkner.

The psychological dimension of Yvonne's illness was just as torturous as the physical. Her crises were intermittent. In their acute form after the first onset, I was instructed to arrange a bed so that her legs were constantly elevated. I should have rented a hospital bed, but instead I stacked the twenty-four volumes of our *Britannica* to form an inclined plane on the daybed in our bedroom. I bought a sheet of plywood to put on it to support the mattress. In this awkward state with her legs pointed upward she got little restful sleep, and I was sure I would have gone mad on this inclined plane of pain. I was both anguished and horrified when, one night in the spring of 1970, she asked me to help her find a way to commit suicide. For some time there had been sleeping pills beside her glass of water, but now their presence carried a mute threat.

There were blessed intervals of relief from the pain. When the warm Carolina spring came, we went sometimes to the faculty swimming pool, Yvonne in her heavy Jobsts. Then in dance class, she pulled muscles in her leg. Her doctor told her to stay off her feet for ten days, and once more she talked of suicide. A month later she turned forty-five.

I had been making my way through my folders. In mid-January of 1969 I had completed chapter 50, to reach the two-thirds point. The astronauts had reached the moon on July 21, and two days later I had reached chapter 64 and William Faulkner's fifty-sixth year. The fall came, and on November 18, with Yvonne in bed and myself two steps away from bed with pneumonia, I had finished my manuscript, now grown to three thousand pages. I had thought it would be an easy transition to move into revision, but the process seemed to go on and on. So it was not until May Day of 1970 had passed that I was able finally to walk into Albert Erskine's office carrying an antiquated suitcase that made me look like a television gangster. I turned it over to Albert, then working on manuscripts from John O'Hara, Robert Penn Warren, and James Michener. Mine went into the traffic pattern on the shelves of Albert's bookcases. Much to my gratitude and admiration, he telephoned in early October and said that he had finished reading it and found the end—Faulkner's death and burial—quite moving.

In late November Yvonne was back to the regimen of bed rest and hot towels, but by early December she felt well enough, she said, to go to the MLA convention. This was a chance for her to get back into life again and for me to go over the manuscript with Albert. At MLA I indulged myself by spending less time hearing lectures and more time seeing friends such as Russell Fraser, now chairman of English at the University of Michigan. I found him as congenial as he had been in Tennessee, a man who would be a long-term friend.

Returning to Chapel Hill, we were back on the emotional roller coaster. Four days into the new year Yvonne suffered such agony with her back that I took her to the Emergency Room, where an orthopedist provided a prescription for the pain. With the aid of scotch, she was able to sleep. Ten days later we drove to Charlottesville to the University of Virginia Hospital. There a sympathetic young internist raised the possibility that she might never have had phlebitis at all, and Yvonne plunged into her worst depression yet. One of Gerard Manley Hopkins's "terrible sonnets" kept running through my mind:

> No worst, there is none. Pitched past pitch of grief,
> More pangs will, schooled at forepangs, wilder wring.
> Comforter, where, where is your comforting?

Four days later she was discharged, with a favorable report and a vial of meprobamate muscle relaxant pills. As we drove south again she told me, "I hate Chapel Hill."

On March 15 Russ Fraser invited us to visit the University of Michigan Department of English. In graduate school I had come to think of Michigan as one of the great public universities, a leader in the sciences and home to visitors such as Robert Frost. In Ann Arbor we were lodged in Inglis House, a mansion built by an automobile entrepreneur that struck me as the kind of establishment Jay Gatsby would have created if he had possessed good taste. The university seemed to me a kind of apotheosis of the style of other schools I had known in the East.

The day before we were to leave, Bill Haber and I sat in the graduate school dean's comfortable office and reminisced about the conference at Zadar. I did not learn until years later what Russ had been doing behind the scenes. Because the departmental budget did not then have the money for the appointment he wanted to make, he had gone to a friend. Philip Power was one of the university's great benefactors. Russ told him how this appointment would fit into his plans for the department and asked for help. Power agreed to supply it. Back in the office in Haven Hall, Russ now made the offer and asked me to tell him if there was any condition I wanted to make. I said there was none and agreed to make my decision as soon as I could.

At home again, not quite halfway through my career, I took time to reflect on it. The survey courses I taught had taken me from *Beowulf* to Virginia Woolf. The feeling I had entertained for Tennyson and Browning that inclined me toward the Victorian period had gradually given way before Gerard Manley Hopkins and his breathtaking lyricism and shocking compression, and the challenge of his sprung rhythm with its Anglo-Saxon echoes. Ezra Pound was a challenge too, but he did not move me. William Butler Yeats stirred my Irish sympathies, and I was drawn further into the complexity of the modern by the poems of Dylan Thomas. Reading Thomas's "Poem in October," I felt something of the thrill of Hopkins's "The Windhover." I was becoming a modernist, finding my way with the help of a book that saved me in the classroom. It was *Understanding Poetry* written by two geniuses I would thank in my writing as well as my teaching, Cleanth Brooks and Robert Penn Warren.

The banner of Joyce was one I still followed, and at first it had been almost as if *Ulysses* was my Bible. It was the fiction of my own country, however, that now drew me most. From the heavy power of Dreiser I moved to the tale-telling of Sherwood Anderson and the tragic dramas of Hemingway. I was drawn to the subtleties of Scott Fitzgerald and the complexities of William Faulkner. By the time I was teaching senior seminars, I would put together semester-long threesomes, drawing in combinations on their work, sometimes linked by a theme. This was pure good fortune, to be able to continue my education while being paid for it.

My undergraduate courses were always filled, and so I felt I was doing something for departmental enrollment statistics as well as for the students. I didn't mind lecturing to 125 students in a fifty-minute class, since one or two graders went with the assignment, and as I lectured I would walk the aisles. But the almost one-on-one feeling of the senior seminar brought out the best, I thought, in me as well as in them. I devised a form that I hoped made the large classes more appealing. One I called "Novels of Adolescence." I tried for a mix of the classic and the popular, and so, by stretching the definition and boundaries a little, I might include among the required eight both *A Portrait of the Artist as a Young Man* and *The Catcher in the Rye*. "Novels of Espionage" sounded as though it was meant to have a high entertainment quotient, and it did, but alongside Eric Ambler, with *A Coffin for Demetrios*, or John Le Carré, with *The Spy Who Came in from the Cold*, I could include Joseph Conrad's *The Secret Agent* or Graham Greene's *The Human Factor*. This way I slipped in the popular with the potentially permanent.

My first Chapel Hill graduate seminar had been devoted to Faulkner. We studied six of the great novels, and I drew heavily on my research. Looking down the table that first day, I saw the cream of the graduate crop. One was a sandy-haired young man in a turtleneck and khaki windbreaker named Patrick Samway. We were two weeks into the course before I noted the abbreviation S.J. after his name. He was not only a Jesuit but also an experienced teacher and promising scholar. His compatriots were distinguished, too. From then and beyond, into the last stages of my work, I had profited from their scholarly skills, their comments and scrupulous corrections to my text. There were students from other seminars who had helped educate me with their dissertations on other novelists and other areas.

So there were ways in which I could only regret leaving Chapel Hill as I

moved ahead into a larger department. And there might be one psychic dis-
advantage: I was leaving the South. I was that typical American phenomenon,
an assimilator and a polyglot. But no matter where I lived, I would remain a
Faulknerian, a resident of Yoknapatawpha County in the heart.

I went ahead to the next step. I had told Carroll Hollis about our trip to
Michigan, and now I had to tell him about the result. It was difficult because
I liked him sincerely and was grateful for everything he had done for me. I told
him simply and directly. He nodded, and his face flushed red, which dis-
comfited me more than a reproach would have done.

"Well, Joe," he said, "I won't try to talk you out of it, but I can say this. If
you stay, the next Kenan Professorship the department gets will be yours."

I thanked him for this further instance of the generosity of the University of North Carolina at Chapel Hill. There was no point in my saying what I
later came to understand more clearly: that on purely professional grounds I
could have had a happy and satisfying career there. Nor could I bring myself
to tell him how Yvonne's ill health loomed so large that it had colored our lives
there. We would leave in time for me to start teaching in Michigan in January
of 1972.

My manuscript at Random House was in the hands of Lynn Strong, an experienced young copy editor. She said she was enjoying the Faulkner material,
though not as much, I feared, as she had enjoyed editing a book allegedly written by Muhammad Ali. The book was not moving along at the rate I had anticipated because of the intermittent claims on her and Albert Erskine by the
work of O'Hara, Michener, Warren, and Welty. Nor would I be free to devote
myself to polishing my prose, for I had reckoned without the unexpected, in
the form of caches of new material that were beginning to surface.

I had hoped that our decision to move to Ann Arbor would relieve some
of the pain and tension Yvonne felt, but instead they grew worse. On Saturday
night, June 5, I went to our bedroom to ask her if she wanted to go downstairs
with me. I tried to open the door quietly, but it wouldn't open. When I asked
Nancy if she knew why the door should be locked from the inside, she knew
of no reason. I tried it again, but it still would not open. Nancy and I stood
there, baffled and alarmed. I knocked and waited, but there was no response.
I pounded, and the result was silence again. So I raised my leg and smashed
my heel against the plate that held the knob.

The lights were on, and the night table drawer was open. Yvonne lay on
the bed inert. She did not respond to my voice or my attempt to raise her
up. Twenty-five years before, I had carried her across the threshold as a bride.

She weighed less now than then, but I hadn't realized how heavy a totally inert person could be. "Nancy," I said, "we've got to get her to the Emergency Room." At nine-forty she was admitted to the hospital and wheeled away. To the stocky young crew-cut doctor I handed the plastic vials from the night table that had held Valium and Nembutal. He scribbled on the clipboard chart and turned to me. "She's pretty well under," he said. "You might just as well go home. We'll be working on her, and you can call me in the morning."

Nancy and I sat at the kitchen table and drank coffee. I felt that there was something I should be doing but could not think what, but for some reason a phrase was running through my head. It was "telling the bees," and I thought I knew its source in folklore: when the wife died, the farmer had to go out to the hives and tell the bees so they wouldn't fly away. Nancy and I went to our rooms to try to sleep.

When I telephoned the next morning, a different doctor spoke to me. "She's still in a coma," he said. The next day Yvonne was conscious. Then, on her fourth day, she was transferred to E wing—for psychiatric patients. Even though her life was no longer in danger and her chief physical problem was a throat painful from the tubes inserted while she was unconscious, she could not come home. There was a state law, he told me, that any patient who had attempted suicide had to remain in the hospital for a minimum of two weeks. For now, the most we could do was to go to the E wing and wave to her through the small window of thick wire-reinforced glass in the door. I thought of the required reading for one of my courses at Drew: *The Inmate of Ward 8.*

On the fifteenth we began receiving anguished letters. She wanted to come home. The staff did not want patients to stay in their rooms alone, she told us. Instead they were meant to be in the Day Room, where more than one radio at a time might be loudly playing. One of the patients sat before the television set but objected to watching channel 6 because, she said, one of the announcers was looking at her and monitoring her actions. Yvonne had already learned, she told us, that the rule for good treatment was "Ingratiate yourself with the staff." But the attendants were a varied lot, and like other female patients, she dreaded being bathed by any of them or being made to bathe under their supervision. She had been wheeled about at first, even though she could walk, and one male attendant had managed to grope her body under her thin gown and robe each time he put her in a chair. By the twenty-first, she had visiting privileges, and Nancy and I were able to see her in the room she shared. She looked as we had expected: wan and worn. At first she had thought she was fortunate in her doctor, a short, blond man whose approach was heralded by the clacking of his high-heeled tooled-leather boots. He turned out, however, to be a tyrant, and she was glad when other doctors participated in her treatment, such as it was. "They're convinced that I'm not really suicidal," she told us. On the twenty-sixth she was allowed to come home overnight, and on the last day of the month she was discharged.

By August she was seeing a Chapel Hill psychiatrist she liked. She had gone from one physician to another and from one treatment to another through these intermittent roller coaster rides of pain and the pinched, narrow life of the semi-invalid. One day in late September she told me, "I'm worse off than before," but by early October she was able to fly with me to Michigan for house hunting. There Jack and Mary Jane Atkinson provided our base of operations, and their friendship and hospitality saw us through two days of disappointing inspections of homes, none of them right except the last one, where we persuaded the reluctant owners to consider an offer.

On the last day of October the first batch of galley proofs arrived, with more promised soon. But at almost the same time Albert Erskine called to tell me that Lynn Strong was ill and couldn't resume her copy editing for at least a week. In my current state of mind, I was able to toss that off. I thought of the prisoner's voice I had heard in my cell in Oberursel: "Time! That's all I've got plenty of—time!" Now life seemed a process of continuing to put one foot in front of another and maintaining equilibrium. All I could do was hope that time would speed up and swiftly take us to Ann Arbor, where I hoped our troubles would abate.

The moving vans arrived, and the sweating laborers loaded the cardboard containers onto them. We drove up steep Glendale Drive for the last time onto Franklin and out of Chapel Hill. This would be nowhere near as long a drive as the one I had made almost twenty years before to begin my full-time teaching career, but by the second day our departure from the South seemed a long one indeed. At last we left I–90 for U.S. 23 and by night entered the state of Michigan. Snow flurries were turning into tiny dots of sleet that bounced across the road in the headlights' beams. At last there was Berkshire Road and our two-story clapboard house, looking every bit as welcoming as when we first saw it.

We took our suitcases and sleeping bags into the warm house. A half-hour later there was a knock on our door. I opened it to admit a tall, lanky, bespectacled man with a smiling woman beside him. He was Alan Smith, the dean of the law school, with his wife, Aline, from across the street. They offered generous hospitality, but we had eaten on the road and needed nothing now. We were anxious to end the day and prepare for the next one.

The huge yellow van was there as promised in the sunny morning, and we began the process of replanting our roots. The unloading seemed to go fast, and almost everything appeared to have traveled well. But left behind some-how in the attic and now irrecoverable was the dollhouse from Copenhagen. Nancy regretted it without grieving over it, looking ahead like us to beginning a new part of our lives.

SIXTEEN

Have Lecture, Will Travel

MY OFFICE IN THE HEART OF CENTRAL CAMPUS IN Ann Arbor was just a twenty-five-minute walk from home. I had a chance to test my resolve on the first day of classes, January 13, 1972, and so I laced on my new suede waffle-stompers and walked to Haven Hall in the snow. Back in the classroom again, I found that the students were good.

With the first batch of galley proof there was a lift in seeing my imperfect typescript transformed into the narrow two-foot-long sheets bearing the magical authority of print. I returned to correcting the printer's errors and my own and responding to Albert Erskine's and Lynn Strong's queries. The mail brought four hundred new sheets of galley proof. The rest arrived in late January, and I was encouraged by Albert's news that we had received some enthusiastic readings at the Book-of-the-Month Club.

But I had reckoned without the unexpected. One day I learned that the New York Public Library had acquired a hitherto unknown first typescript of *Soldier's Pay*, Faulkner's first novel, plus early poems, an essay, and three short stories—all unpublished. But I was familiar with such surprises. Not long before I had learned that another archive had turned up. When I had attended Faulkner's funeral in July 1962, I had stayed on for a few days at Rowan Oak to help Jill and Paul put his literary papers in some kind of order. Manuscripts and typescripts were scattered all over the house: in drawers downstairs in his workroom, in a richly decorated Korean chest in the hall, in big cardboard cartons in the attic. It was a hot afternoon when our task was done, and close to the cocktail hour. We had gone through the Korean chest and examined every likely storage place upstairs.

Descending the big staircase again, I noticed what seemed to be a small door near the base of the wall. "What's that?" I asked.

"Oh, that's just a kind of broom closet," Jill told me. But then one day in the summer of 1971, as part of his curatorial functions at Rowan Oak, the chairman of the English department had made an inspection prior to a termite treatment. He opened the little door, peered into the aperture, and withdrew a cardboard carton that proved to contain two thousand typed pages. Eventually I saw photocopies of all of them, including material new to me: the missing manuscript of one novel, unknown short stories, an autobiographical fragment, and a story that was clearly an early version of *Absalom, Absalom!*, to many his greatest novel. So I had to rewrite more of my galley proof.

By June I had finished and mailed the galleys back to New York. I felt that I was far enough ahead to take advantage of the good tennis weather. One breezy day in mid-July I wasn't doing badly when I felt a tearing pain below my right calf and collapsed. The next day the orthopedist told me I had ruptured not just my gastrocnemius but also the soleus behind it. "They'll both heal back," he said reassuringly. "Meanwhile you'll need bed rest and hot towels and elevation."

I would now know what Yvonne had been enduring. She did her best to shut out her pain, but the Valium and its side effects created a downer that was worsened by the doctor's telling us that it was thrombophlebitis again and she should go back to the hospital for tests. The Chapel Hill doctor who had said she would just have to live with it had apparently been right. We took the roller coaster ride with us wherever we went, or so it seemed.

Fortunately Carol Brandt sent me wonderful letters of encouragement about the book and magazine sales and foreign rights. On September 10, Yvonne's birthday, Albert telephoned with the news that the biography would be a Book-of-the-Month Club Alternate Selection. The progress toward publication was slowing down in early 1973, and I had started to construct the index. Ten years earlier, when Larry Thompson was working on Robert Frost's biography and an edition of his letters, he advised me to try to get approval for a volume of Faulkner letters. I knew that Faulkner would not have wanted such a volume, for he had written Malcolm Cowley, "I'm old-fashioned and probably a little mad too. I don't like having my private life and affairs available to just any and everyone who has the price of the vehicle it's printed in, or a friend who bought it and will lend it to him." Now, however, Albert and Linton Massey thought that this was a propitious time to start work on a volume of letters to follow the biography. Jill and Estelle Faulkner had permitted me to quote liberally from his writings, and now I wrote to them, explaining that the "main purpose of this collection is to provide a deeper understanding of the artist, to reveal as much as possible what one can see in the letters about his art—its sources, intentions and process of creation." When they consented to publication of the correspondence, I was delighted.

The timing was right, too. On January 4 there was a call from Leon Picon, whom I had interviewed about Faulkner's work for the State Department. He had been Faulkner's closest associate on his extraordinarily successful trip to Japan in 1955 as a kind of cultural ambassador. The biography now had a firm publication date in March, and Leon wanted me to come to Washington to do several videotapes as preparation for my tour of several European countries talking about Faulkner and his work.

The Random House publicity department was busy promoting the two-volume book. I had not intended to write a two-thousand-page biography, but I had determined at the outset that I was writing the biography of a great artist, and it should also be a story of the works interwoven with that of his life. I was grateful for all the space Albert Erskine had allowed me, and one afternoon when I arrived home I saw there on the coffee table the two boxed volumes bound in royal purple. *William Faulkner: A Biography* was a handsome specimen of the book designer's art.

I had not realized how much this book would change our lives. In early March, Yvonne and Nancy and I flew to New York for a publicity trip. We registered at the Hotel Algonquin, where the rooms were nothing unusual but the large lobby was like a comfortable living room in a private home where celebrities always seemed to be staying. The interviews were a distinct pleasure, with Random House picking up the luncheon tabs. It was a festive time. Carol Brandt took me to lunch at the chastely elegant Four Seasons. Someone had written that Donald Klopfer looked like a Venetian nobleman, and so he did as he presided genially over lunch at the luxurious Brussels.

The next day before sunrise we walked a block to hail a taxi to take us to the NBC television studios for my interview on the "Today" show. Waiting in the small greenroom, we helped ourselves to coffee and Danish *wienerbrod*. I had not looked to see who was sitting next to me, but I heard the familiar voice clearly. "Wait till we get this guy Blotner on camera. I'm gonna crucify him." I swiveled around to see the laughing face of the show's book critic, Gene Shalit, wearing his customary high-combed pompadour like a fright wig and his bandit's black bushy mustache. When we moved to the stage and sat on our tall stools, he put me at ease. Holding up the boxed set to the camera, he said, "I haven't read all of this book, but I can tell you that it weighs eight and a half pounds." He led me skillfully through the book's origins and then asked what Faulkner had been like in an informal situation.

"One day when he stopped in for a visit," I told him, "my wife and I led him out onto the terrace. As he sat down she pointed to a wet stain on the floor. 'I'm sorry about that, Mr. Faulkner, Nancy had a little accident,' she said. Then she immediately added, 'She spilled her juice.' 'I'm glad,' Mr. Faulkner said. 'I was afraid it was bourbon.' "

The publicity would continue well into the next year and beyond. The stream of visitors to Oxford and Ole Miss had grown so large that a weeklong conference was planned offering lectures, films, slide presentations, panel discussions, guided tours, and dramatizations. Evans Harrington, a novelist and popular English professor, was the principal organizer. Malcolm Cowley and I each gave two lectures, and Jimmy and Chooky Faulkner appeared on a panel with me. The attendance was so large that the program was repeated for a second week. Called "Faulkner and Yoknapatawpha," it would become an annual event.

Conferences were becoming an integral part of my professional life. I flew to Jackson for a Mississippi tour, where some book signings gave me a special pleasure. As I sat at the table at McCrae's Bookstore I looked up to see a lady with a familiar face. "I came to pay my respects," she said. It was Eudora Welty. By now I knew that this kind of friendship and kindness was characteristic of her. And there was more. I had a reward in a week's stopover in Oxford. There I did more book signing at the university bookstore and an outdoor event in the Square. Howard Duvall was nothing if not enterprising. He obtained a consignment from Random House and set up a card table in front of his clothing store a block from the statue of the Confederate soldier. For tennis he enlisted Jimmy Faulkner and Tommy Avent, a classmate and a successful entrepreneur. He was the grandson of a man said to be one of Faulkner's models for the tribe of Snopeses. On the court, he shook my hand and said, smiling, "I'm glad you didn't say in your book that my granddaddy stole the bank from Colonel Faulkner." The two beat Jimmy and me handily.

By late August sheaves of reviews had come in. Louis Rubin had warned me that most reviewers hated long books. One review was captioned "Everything you wanted to know about the man, not the author." A number wanted to find in the book a revelation of the most intimate dynamics of Faulkner's private life as well as the essence of his genius, all briefly stated. Some had an additional grievance: they hated the difficulty of much of Faulkner's work. Randall Jarrell had once railed against readers who wanted poetry "that even cats and dogs can read." I had the bad luck to encounter a number of reviews by such readers, but the worst was a hostile review in *Time*. What shocked me was that it had been written by one of my Virginia graduate students who had been let go after a brief Ivy League teaching career. I wracked my brain without recalling any offense I might have given him. He had subjected Carlos Baker to the same kind of attack, and one friend suggested that he might have had a grievance against the academic world that had rejected him. Whether or not there was any truth in this, I was in good company with Carlos.

Reviews in the literary magazines appeared later, and I took pleasure in most of them, especially those written by people who had gone through the fire themselves. These were friends but also widely respected scholar-critics such as Lawrance Thompson and Carlos Baker himself. His review of *Faulkner: A Biography* was captioned "From Genesis to Revelation." Random House and Carol Brandt were pleased, and there was joy among my family and friends.

Through the end of the year and on into 1975 I taught my courses and traveled. I lectured on Faulkner and Southern literature in Alabama and Arkansas and at Emory and Appalachian State. The first two engagements were joint appearances with Jimmy Faulkner. He would talk about his uncle as he had known him, and I would use this as a springboard to show how Faulkner used his world in his fiction. The latter event was a Robert Penn Warren week. I had agreed to give two lectures, one of them on *All the King's Men*. I had not known that he would be there, and so, to my discomfiture, I found myself discoursing on the virtues of this classic novel with its author seated in the last row. Only later did I learn that Red Warren would usually occupy himself on such occasions by mentally writing a poem.

The most relaxing time came in southern Mississippi's fragrant April at the Greenwood Arts Festival in the heart of the cotton land of the Delta. The festival featured a wonderfully eclectic mix of events. Roger Miller's small group performed on banjos and guitars as he sang "You Can't Roller Skate in a Buffalo Herd" and other hit recordings. I lectured and was glad of the company of a few others including Cleanth Brooks. Howard Duvall was there, too. He set up his card table near the registration desk and did a brisk business selling *Faulkner: A Biography*. Promoters of the festival included Bill Worthington, brother of one of the Delta's wealthiest men and also head of the Cotton Planters' Association. They had entertained Cleanth and me at their home in one of the mansions that lined beautiful Main Street. Noticing Howard's thriving enterprise, Bill turned to me with a wry grin and said, "Well, I see Swifty Duvall made it."

I wondered if Bill might think of me as a carpetbagger. I didn't care, warm in the feeling that though I wasn't a native-born Southerner, I probably had more friends here in the poorest state in the union than I had anywhere else.

Like them I felt the paradox of the mansions juxtaposed with the pitiful tenant shacks, both on the periphery of the fields of white gold sprung from the rich black earth.

In the high hazy distance the white marble columns seemed almost to glow. The golden April afternoon was soft, and the sun felt warm in the mild breeze. Sitting in our underwear on our hotel room balcony, tall beaded bottles of Nastro Azzuro beside us, Yvonne and I thanked William Faulkner and the United States Information Service for this moment. Contemplating the Parthenon's exquisite symmetry dominating the rocky Athenian landscape, we saw history all around us. When Richard Arndt, a Princeton Ph.D. in French and an amateur classical pianist, had given us copies of our revised schedule in his cultural attaché's office in Rome, a glance told us how busy we would be. It had been arranged by his wife, Lois, a petite dark-haired woman who was an experienced officer. She would keep us busy every day, scheduling us on one day to visit three different cities. Before returning home four weeks later, we would be making brief stopovers in Denmark, Sweden, and Germany. There would be more in another swing that would take us to France and Italy.

There was more potential for excitement than we realized. Almost ten years before, a junta of "the Colonels" had seized power and sent young King Constantine into exile. Bitterly hated for their harsh repression, they generated hostility to U.S. policies as well as their own. After my first lecture to the usual mix of students and faculty, one of them told me, "I'm glad it went so well. You're the first American who has lectured here in the last three years. The last one left by a rear window." I didn't worry about negative responses. For one thing, Faulkner's triumphant USIS visit to Greece in 1957, when he received the Silver Medal of the Athens Academy, had left behind an enormous reservoir of good will. Many homes displayed only two portraits: one of the king and one of William Faulkner.

Yvonne and I separated briefly when I flew to rugged Salonika where Thessaloniki perched above the Aegean. I returned in the late afternoon, and we exchanged accounts of our days. My student audiences were polite and attentive, but no matter which of my topics the sponsors had chosen, I usually wound up simplifying it and interpolating brief synopses of Faulkner works. Afterward my hosts drove carefully up hilly, sharply curved roads to take me to see an ancient monastery, now a Greek Orthodox church. The air was heavy from acrid incense swung in smoking censers by bearded priests. On the walls were smoke-darkened paintings of saints, and on the altars, icons in the same flat-faced rendering of martyrs. The next afternoon I climbed up the boulder-strewn side of the Acropolis to make my pilgrimage to the Parthenon and gaze at the statuesque caryatides defaced by time and pollution. At a small restaurant Yvonne and I declined the resinous retsina wine, but we ate green salads decorated with feta cheese and dined on succulent roast lamb. We ended the day with a nightcap as we gazed out over the wine dark sea.

We responded again to the perennial charm of Paris and the comfortable pleasures of Copenhagen. We were too short a time in spectacular Stockholm, where my lecture was enlivened by a drunken student who broke into my discourse. In Bonn we ascended the narrow staircase to the small apartment of Mozart's infancy and mused over the small piano with only a few octaves and an ear trumpet that looked like a torture instrument. In Frankfurt we ate sauerbraten, savory in its dark gravy. I tried to think back to my first time there, but the scenes outside our train window were those of a travel folder rather than a grainy Pathé Newsreel. Our seminar for German teachers was held at the Akademie Eichholz in a modest remodeled *Schloss*. I had never stayed in a German castle before, especially one with unisex toilets.

Some of our meetings were informal discussions with a dozen of us around a table after dinner. One participant was a short middle-aged woman who had arrived late from Berlin. Things were not easily arranged, she said, partly because the university was run by a troika of representatives from the faculty, the student body, and the custodial staff. She asked me if I had ever been in this part of Germany. I said, "Yes, but that was a long time ago."

A man at the other end of the table smiled. He was short and pleasant-looking in spite of a distinct resemblance to Peter Lorre and Joseph Goebbels. The professor from Berlin mentioned a conference she had recently attended at Passau on the German-Austrian border. My Lorre-Goebbels lookalike nodded as she spoke. She turned to him and said, "You have been there?"

He nodded and then added, with a smile toward my end of the table, "Yes, but that was a long time ago."

Another participant, a dark-haired hawk-faced man, lodged himself in my memory by his height and commanding presence and the echoes set off by his name. It was von Stauffenberg. Later it came to me: his father was the German who had lost his life after his botched assassination attempt on Adolf Hitler.

We returned home to the kind of spring that compensated for the gray days of the long Ann Arbor winters. I regretted having to break into it with a September trip to Mississippi for a broad-scale film documentary on William Faulkner. Cleanth Brooks and Shelby Foote had agreed to serve as advisors, and I was glad to join them. My biography would be a major source for the script to be written by Buzz Bezzerides, who had known William Faulkner in wartime Hollywood. The director would be Bob Squier, a talented man who would later run one of Jimmy Carter's election campaigns. The narrator would be the deep-voiced Raymond Burr, long famous as a television lawyer. This meeting was intended to begin the process of producing the documentary.

The advisory group in Jackson would eventually number ten, including such distinguished scholars as Lewis Simpson and Louis Rubin. But one problem surfaced at the outset. Buzz Bezzerides, a burly, vociferous man, had been born in Turkey to a Greek father and an Armenian mother. Raised in Fresno and trained as an engineer at Berkeley, he found his true métier in writing. He empathized much with Faulkner, seeing in his own difficulties in getting started a reflection of Faulkner's youth in Mississippi, an identification that skewed Bezzerides's characterization. So the collaboration would often become a battle.

In Ann Arbor, cultural events came right to us. The Unitarian Church at the end of our street held an annual benefit "Jazz Bash." It was a performance by virtuosos for aficionados. To me the stars were three from the music faculty. Bill Albright gave renditions of James P. Johnson's stride piano stomps that shook the sanctuary and the crowded loft above it. Jim Dapogny, with a touch light and inventive, was the leading interpreter and scholar of the large repertoire of Jelly Roll Morton. Bill Bolcom, composer of symphonies and operas, ranged from pieces by Darius Milhaud to exotic South American rhythms. And sometimes he appeared with his companion, Joan Morris, a sumptuous mezzo-soprano, a gorgeously costumed mistress of turn-of-the-century ballads whose performance of "I'm Just Wild about Harry" and "My Handy Man Ain't Handy No More" gave special delight. One of their triumphs was a Columbia LP recording called *Wild about Eubie*. A ragtime composer-pianist, Eubie Blake had grown up in Baltimore in the 1890s playing in bawdyhouses and saloons, and he had gone on to make history with Noble Sissle and as co-author of the epoch-making show *Shuffle Along*. Now ninety-three, tall, thin Eubie Blake was a friend and fellow performer. On November 28, I walked down to the Unitarian Church to see Joan and Bill married. One of his students, a Catholic priest, performed the simple ceremony. A splendid climax came with the recessional as frail old Eubie Blake played "Here Comes the Bride" in ragtime. I had never heard more joyous strains at any wedding.

Jimmy Faulkner and I had lectured jointly in what one Oxford colleague derisively called "The Jimmy and Joe Show." In Canyon, at West Texas A&M,

and at Wichita Falls' Midwestern University we met students as enthusiastic as any we had encountered. At Midwestern we saw a whole corral constructed indoors with painstaking accuracy. I looked for Jimmy and saw him leaning against a railing apparently deep in conversation with a cowboy. I waited and then walked over to join them. The tanned, gray-eyed ranch hand was gazing off into the distance. "Ready to go?" I asked Jimmy.

"Yes," he said as if awakening. "I've just been waiting for him to say something." Clothed in dungarees, furry chaps, and checked shirt, Jimmy's suntanned motionless companion, a manikin, could have stood with figures in Madame Toussaud's wax museum.

At home I found a cable from Dick Arndt telling me that the planned USIS seminar on American literature had been scheduled for mid-April in Rome. Just the thought of living in Italy again, however briefly, gave a new charge to Yvonne's psyche. She planned to study Italian at Michigan, she said. I told her I was determined to study Italian too, for we seemed to be getting into a rhythm that would take us often to that country we were coming to love. I would have my hands full with classes and the coming seminar and *Selected Letters of William Faulkner*.

April in Rome was warm and lovely, but for much of the days we sat beneath an ornate frescoed ceiling in a palazzo Henry James had described, where I tried to tune my ear to lectures in Italian. When I had time, I went to my draft of the introduction to the *Letters*. Faulkner was not a prolific correspondent like James, but by the time we put the text together, we had nearly five hundred pages, some deeply personal. One acknowledged his inability to know from "what god or gods" his gifts had come. Another revealed his frustration at the financial burdens that took so much time from his best work.

It was moving, going through the emotions these letters revealed that had marked his complex life. When I regarded him as his biographer, I tried to be objective, but he had first been my friend, and as I remembered certain episodes, my feelings were deeply personal. I recalled arriving at his house one sunny day to go to a Little League baseball game. "Stelle," he called up the stairs from the hall in his high voice, "Blotner and I are going to the game now." On a day in gray February we drove to the Martha Jefferson Hospital where she was recovering from bronchial pneumonia. We walked into her room, and he said, "I brought Blotner to see you." Then he bent and kissed her on the cheek. It was a tender gesture, but I thought of the pangs of unrequited love he had often suffered—as a young man, as a traveler passing through the middle of life's road, and as an old man, too.

Meanwhile, other projects were maturing. When I asked Albert Erskine if I could say on the flap copy that *Uncollected Stories of William Faulkner* would be my next book, he replied, "Yes, and I already have a contract with Jill Summers for it." On December 13, 1976, the first copy of *Selected Letters of William Faulkner* arrived. For the next book I was tracking down stories that had not appeared in his other volumes. As usual, I was drafting the headnotes for each story, reading new criticism, and compiling a bibliography. Once again I had to pack up my working pages, for we were heading to Ole Miss where I would serve as William Faulkner Lecturer in the spring term. We worked on the documentary, now entitled *William Faulkner: A Life on Paper,* as Bob Squier appeared with a camera crew.

It was easy to become distracted from work at hand, though some distractions I welcomed. I had received a call from Tom Moore, president of Tomorrow Entertainment, Incorporated. By the time we met for lunch at the Côte Basque, I had learned that he had produced documentaries such as one on the racially inflammatory case of the Scottsboro Boys. What he wanted to discuss with me was a television documentary on William Faulkner. "We'll go over to ABC, and I'll introduce you to Tommy Thomopolous," he said. "They call him the Golden Greek. He's young, but he's the head of ABC programming. Bring along a copy of your biography and inscribe it to him."

A week later I did, having paid $35 for a boxed set. In a large office I met the slim, deeply tanned Golden Greek. He was charming, and it was satisfying to sit there looking over the roofs of Manhattan as we talked about how we could use my biography. Afterward we went to the St. Regis for a drink and had a comfortable conversation. Tom thought it had gone well. I would hear about the project, he said, as soon as he did. This glimpse into television's upper echelons had been tantalizing.

I heard nothing more about it, but there was another project in the works. Tom had assembled a group of consultants to vet a script based on the book *Simple Justice,* a story of the way Thurgood Marshall and others had worked to overturn *Brown v. Board of Education* and abolish school segregation. The eleven consultants included lawyers, historians, and other writers, and I learned something about the law and movie making. We wrangled about script writing and cinematography. I learned to cut and paste scenes, to use the language as they did, to say of a new paragraph, "Yes, but will it track?"

Tom wanted to make a movie of *Light in August,* a project at which several had already failed. I did a synopsis and chronology of the action and suggested treatments for dealing with the principal characters and themes. He was also interested in doing something with the long segment of *Go Down Moses* called "The Bear," and I had written annotated genealogies of the McCaslin and

Carothers families central to it. On my next visit I was ready to talk about both scripts at length. Before I got started, he handed me an envelope. Trying to be smooth, I simply thanked him and put it in my pocket. Before I launched into the material, he indicated the envelope said simply, "It's a thousand." I liked doing this kind of business.

Nothing more would come of these two projects, but Tom had already explained the negative ratio of things that flew to things that didn't fly in the entertainment business. And I had my mind on other matters. Among the French Faulknerians was Roger Asselineau, the best-known American literature scholar and professor at the Sorbonne. He had asked if I was interested in spending a year there as a visiting professor. I had said yes, and in early March he wrote that I would shortly receive the formal invitation. The feelings I had experienced as a graduate student reading about the Paris of Hemingway and Fitzgerald and the American expatriates of the twenties flooded back, but soon reality intervened. Nineteen seventy-eight had not so far been a good year for Yvonne, with bed rest and then a hospitalization in January, with new drugs and a new doctor and no clearer idea of the root cause of her illnesses. And she worried about the children and their marriages. After a wrenching decision, I wrote Roger Asselineau with thanks and regrets. I would not be teaching at the Sorbonne, and we would not be living in Paris.

But we were not through with decisions. Russ Fraser had urged me to try for one of the scholar's rewards he had already enjoyed, a month at the Rockefeller Foundation's Study and Conference Center at Bellagio on Lake Como. Friends such as Gordon Ray wrote for me again, and in July 1978 I was invited to spend a four-week residency there at the Villa Serbelloni. What were we to do? I had declined a year's teaching in Paris. Should I now decline a month's research and writing on Lake Como? We decided to accept and then ask for a postponement later if we had to. There was a tentative invitation in January from the International Communication Agency for another European trip like the one I had done for the USIS. For the present Yvonne was sentenced to hot soaks and then another spell in the heavy Jobst elastic stockings. In March we went to another internist, who gave her a good report, and to a cardiovascular surgeon who said we ought to consider any trip very carefully before risking it. I sent back to New York the last corrected proofs for *Uncollected Stories* just as the first batch for *Selected Letters* arrived. When we returned to the surgeon, he told us he thought it would be all right for us to go to Italy.

Pamela came home for a brief visit. She had fulfilled the promise she showed when she won her *foraggiere* as first in her class in Copenhagen and had gone on to graduate with a B.F.A., winning the Pan-Institute Art Award at the Cleveland Institute of Art. I had given the commencement address at the University of Tulsa in a teeming thunderstorm, but I performed that function again at her commencement, one of my proudest moments. Now she was working for her M.F.A. at Syracuse University.

Yvonne and I were fretting over the trip to Italy. I could see that she wanted to go, longing to return to the country where she had been happy. I did not want to be the one to say no, but it was not easy to say yes. I put it to Pamela. "What do you think we should do, sweetie?"

"Go for it, Dad," she said. I was glad but cautious as I made reservations.

The shiny black Ferrari was waiting when we emerged from the main lobby at Malpensa. The gray-capped chauffeur handled the car effortlessly through the Milan traffic and north to the fertile fields of Lombardy. The terrain rose as we made our way past fields green with thriving vines and gold with waves of grain. We were in the province of Como, and now Lake Lecco appeared on our right. We followed it until we reached the promontory where it merged with Lake Como, where Bellagio, called for centuries "the point that divides the wind," looked out onto its blue waters.

Conte Carlo Sfondrati left much of his estate to Conte Alessandro Serbelloni, who spent nearly two million lire to restore the large villa dominating the eastern half of the promontory. Visitors had included Leonardo da Vinci, Alessandro Manzoni, and Gustave Flaubert, who wrote, "One could live and die here. The outlook seems designed as a balm to the eyes—large trees run the length of the precipice . . . and the horizon is outlined with snow." The villa's history read like a chapter in a James novel. In 1928 Ella Walker, heiress to the Hiram Walker fortune, had bought it for her private residence. Upon her marriage she became Her Serene Highness, Ella, Principessa della Torre e Tasso. She died there thirty years later, a childless widow in her palatial Villa Serbelloni. Now the site of conferences, it was also temporary home to individual practitioners of literature, science, and the arts for staggered four-week periods.

The driver stopped at last before the three-story U-shaped villa with its varicolored tile roof. There at the main entrance, under a large, graceful wrought-iron marquee, stood a trim, youngish-looking man with three members of his staff. He was Roberto Celli, who managed the villa with the assistance of his wife Gianna, a slim, attractive engraver and etcher. He led us up the wide marble staircase to a room flooded with light from a broad window. We looked out over the terraces with their trimmed trees and bushes to see in the near distance Lake Lecco on the left and Lake Como on the right.

I placed on the desk the materials for *Faulkner: A Biography,* one volume, revised, updated, and condensed. The four years since the publication of the two-volume biography had brought new books on Faulkner and a torrent of articles exceeded only by those on Shakespeare, Joyce, Melville, and James. But I had winnowed out a good deal. As Cleanth Brooks had written, it was clear "that much of this vast outpouring of scholarship and criticism is . . . positively wrong-headed and perverse, but that a considerable amount is essential reading."

The numerous books were prime material. Malcolm Franklin provided one with an introduction by his mother, Estelle Faulkner. He called it *Bitterweeds: Life at Rowan Oak with William Faulkner.* The title came, he said, from a plant that his stepfather would attack with a hoe when he was trying to recover from a hangover. Other memoirs were more revealing. Joan Williams published an article that provided additional insights into their love affair. I had early become aware of the special relationship that existed between Faulkner and Meta Carpenter Rebner, who had worked for Howard Hawks. She had twice declined my request for an interview. Now, belatedly, I had the benefit of the book she finally published, *A Loving Gentleman: The Love Story of William Faulkner and Meta Carpenter.* She gave me permission to quote at length and recount episodes such as his strewing flower petals on their bed.

There were a half-dozen of his early works being published for the first time, and important Faulkner letters had been deposited in libraries. And there were new interviews. At the Greenwood Arts Festival a young woman told me that her parents had known William Faulkner. When he had returned from Canada wearing his RAF uniform and wings, he had approached her father and said, "Everybody thinks I can fly, but I can't. Will you give me lessons?" So Albert Erskine and I had decided that there was enough new material to justify another, shorter Faulkner biography.

As I finished sorting and arranging the materials, Yvonne told me it was cocktail time. We walked through the large main-floor salon and the wide French doors that gave out onto the railed terrace. There were not only the azure waters of the lake stretching away, with oaks and cypress and slim, tapered pines for borders, but also, for ultimate horizon, the majestic and whitely gleaming Italian Alps. At one side, standing before a large table bearing gleaming bottles and glasses, was a smiling man in an immaculate dinner jacket. He was Franco, the maitre d' and factotum of the Villa Serbelloni. It took him less than a moment to mix Yvonne's bourbon-and-water and my very dry vodka martini. Thereafter he never forgot.

With the fading sun tinting the mountains, we moved inside to two long tables where we would choose one of two entrees. On special occasions there would be place cards, but normally there was a feeling of informality at dinner. There would be a measure of formality in two weeks when the villa would host our first conference. It was to be on the tsetse fly, reflecting the varied benefactions of the foundation. We were "the family," Gianna Celli told us, and were expected to help entertain.

After dinner we dispersed to the overstuffed armchairs and large sofas of the salon. Franco appeared with liqueurs, and we relaxed into casual conversations. A tall, tan young man named Amos Ammons sat down at the grand piano near the French doors and began playing almost atonal music. After a while he switched to the contemporary. A few of us sang along, and when he segued into dance music, one of the other residents reached down to the woman at his side and led her to the cleared space before the wide fireplace. He reminded me of the film veteran Ramon Navarro. He was Gerard Mangone, an expert on the straits of the world. He twirled Alicia, his shapely Egyptian wife, and when Amos changed the tempo, he shouted, "The Tarantella!" and led her stamping through the convulsive dance. But we were tired, and so we hiked up the long staircase to our room. Our sheets were turned back, huge as a sailboat's mainsail, to cover the two beds moved together to form a *letto matrimoniale*. We went to the window and looked out at the circle of lights on the road that encircled the promontory like a necklace, and I thought to myself, Lecco on the left, Como on the right. Enchanting in the moonlight, it was all ours to explore in the days ahead.

We quickly slipped into a comfortable schedule. After breakfast we would return to our room where I would start work, picking up after the first four chapters I had written at home. I went ahead, emphasizing the narrative line more strongly than before and cutting detail about individual works. This time I got my hero born on the first page. Each morning, except for Sundays, I wrote until noon. Then we went downstairs again to the dining room, where I took time to find out who would be congenial and who would be bores.

With some we found a natural affinity. Robert Barnard, a bachelor, had taught at Princeton until illness cost him a lung. I admired his versatility when I learned that he had published a murder mystery entitled *Deadly Meeting*, set at the annual convention of the Modern Language Association and driven by the murder of a hated departmental head. Now he lived in England, alternating seasonally between a London apartment and the country home loaned to him by one of his subjects. There was also Walter Meserve, who was writing a three-volume history of American drama.

The scientists seemed more various than the humanists. Our one physician was an epidemiologist who specialized in problems of world health. Tall, slim, and very self-contained, he seemed like a stage Englishman until the conversation turned to a favorite subject. For him, I learned, the great villains were the large companies such as Nestlé, which he accused of damaging the health of whole populations for profit. "These African women produce perfectly adequate milk for their babies," he said, "and they are propagandized to stop nursing in favor of mixing the formula with water from streams containing God-only-knows-what!"

I continued to take out and put in, most of the time changing, if only slightly, what I kept. The new pages began to pile up. Each day after lunch Yvonne and I would set up two beach chairs at a place called the *spiaggia*. She would read what I had written that morning, and I would plan what I would write the next day. There was no sand on that beach or any beach, but behind the stone parapet we could bask in the bright June sunlight and look out at the blue Como waters. I was delighted that Yvonne was able to walk, sometimes for more than an hour, descending toward the lake through the gardens at the rear of the villa. On one side of the path was a profusion of roses with an exhilarating perfume. We would hear the scurrying of the tiny chameleons with their flickering tongues, like miniature dragons, which changed color as you watched and whisked away into the bushes as you approached.

We walked into Bellagio and down the Via Garibaldi past the shop windows displaying rings and bracelets set with deep red garnet stones, and segmented Pinocchios of all sizes carved from olive wood and dangling from their strings. I bought a bottle of a regional *vino bianco* in a small *alimentari,* and very soon we were in the country. We found a smooth place near the bushes emerging from a lake-fed stream. We spread the lunch on a towel and ate with keen appetite. Then we heard a rustling from a spot where the rushes met the water. Suddenly I saw the source: a plump gray rat. We quickly moved up to the grove behind us.

There were also other instances of the unexpected. One Saturday afternoon we walked from the villa to the Dock House. Standing there watching the rippled waves from the strong breeze were Jane and Walter Meserve. He greeted us happily. "I've been trying to talk Jane into a ride on the lake," he said. "What about you two?"

I looked at Yvonne, and she said, "Why not?"

Walter walked off, rubbing his hands together. When he returned, towing a good-sized skiff, he assigned us to our places, the ladies in the stern. "I'll take the first shot, Joe," he told me.

With a shove from the boatman we were off toward midstream, toward Como, invisible in the distance. After a quarter-hour the wind at our backs had risen, and Walter protested when I stood up carefully to take his place. I had not rowed since our honeymoon on Lake Winnipesaukee. I was glad when Walter said it was probably time for us to head back. It was his turn to row, and I carefully made my way forward to give him plenty of room. At last we reached the dock. I reached out and made a show of steadying the boat as Walter shipped the oars and helped Yvonne and Jane out. Now I could banish from my imagination the newspaper headline "American Scholars and Their Wives Lost on Como."

When we descended the staircase from our room, we walked directly through the salon to the patio. Franco presented Yvonne's drink. Then he turned to me. "A very dry martini for you, sir," he said with a smile. I thanked him and lifted my frosted glass like a sacramental cup.

The conference came to an end at the concluding dinner. The room was filled and loudly murmurous with conversation until dessert was served, heralded by a procession of waiters with Franco at the front bearing a cake topped by fluttering candles. When they halted at the middle of the main table, Roberto Celli stepped to Franco's side. "This is a special occasion," he said, "not just because of the ending of the conference but also because it is a special day for one of our residents. It is the fifty-sixth birthday of one of our residents, Professor Joseph Blotner." Then he led the tsetse-fly experts and epidemiologists in a chorus of "Happy Birthday."

There were other special occasions during our last week. Gianna Celli introduced us to a friend making her annual visit to the villa. She was Germanna Rinaldi, a hearty graying woman who was secretary and librarian at the Johns Hopkins University in Bologna. Gregarious and warmly emotional, she had brought with her a lively younger friend, Maria Angela Bernardi. We occasionally made a foursome on these warm days when we walked down to the *spiaggia*. Like many of the Italian women we had met, Germanna was an enthusiastic smoker who often interrupted her storytelling to light up. But she was also a good listener who gave you the total attention of her dark brown eyes. Both women were pleased that we were studying Italian and helped us patiently. Germanna would sit there on the bench or one of the large rocks, listening intently whenever Yvonne or I made a conversational attempt. Yvonne's command was much better than mine. She had brought her heavily annotated textbook and was clearly gaining fluency and accuracy. Grammar had never been my strong point, but I loved the sound of that beautiful flowing language, and I was enlarging my vocabulary while I still avoided tenses I hadn't memorized. Germanna would sit there on the rock, encouraging my attempts, elbows on her knees, gesturing with her fingers like a baseball catcher signaling an uncertain pitcher. If I hesitated, she would say, *"Diga me! Diga me!"* and I would try again.

They became our best friends at Bellagio and revealed themselves freely to Yvonne, woman-to-woman. There was no man in Germanna's life as far as we could tell. She had many friends, chiefly women, although she liked men, too. She reminded me of Chaucer's Wife of Bath, with her worldly wit and outspoken humor, though she seemed also to be still the good Catholic girl she must once have been, attending mass regularly, as did Mari'angela. Our relationship with these women deepened swiftly. One sunny afternoon looking out over the breeze-ruffled lake waters, she turned abruptly to Yvonne. "My dear," she said, "we will see you next year, and I must tell you my plan. I am going to lose twenty kilos, change my hair to blonde and my eyes to blue, and take Joe away from you." The four of us roared our laughter, while Germanna lit a cigarette and blew a blue plume into the sunlight.

As it turned out, Germanna was not simply fantasizing about seeing us again. She lived with her mother, but she owned a small apartment that she rented to students. "If I have no one in the summer," she said, "you must come back and stay there. It will be wonderful for your Italian, and there are nice people at Johns Hopkins." I knew that it was a very small apartment, though I didn't say so, and I wanted to be at home next summer to finish the one-volume biography. *"Allora,"* Germanna said, turning to Yvonne. "You must come by yourself, and we three women will enjoy Bologna without him."

We were back in Ann Arbor on June 26. I had with me the nine chapters I had written at the big antique desk overlooking the broad waters of the Lago di Como. We were delighted to be home, but it soon proved to be a mixed homecoming. On July 2 Albert Erskine telephoned with the news that the Franklin Mint was doing a special collectors' edition of *Uncollected Stories of William Faulkner* and the Book-of-the-Month Club would make it an Alternate Selection. But then, two weeks later, there was a call from Princeton. Charlie Allen had died unexpectedly of an eleven-second heart attack. There would be a memorial service on the twenty-first, and Marnie hoped I would be there.

I read very little on the airplane, thinking back instead to our first meeting in Benson and Benson's genteel sweatshop on Witherspoon Street a quarter-century ago. We had kept in touch with the Allens as the children came along and we got on with our careers. When Charlie formed a partnership and they moved to Puerto Rico, Marnie kept us up to date with richly descriptive letters about their plan to get away from the stress of New York and guard against the hereditary Allen heart disease. The last time I had seen them, they said they would arrange a lecture for me at the University of Puerto Rico for a long-postponed reunion.

At the Cortelyou home on Jefferson Avenue, Marnie's mother sat on a wide screened porch greeting callers. A moment later Marnie appeared, gallantly serene in her grief. Her dark hair was now streaked with gray, but she seemed to me as beautiful as I remembered her as a young mother. The next day the Princeton University chapel was almost filled. Marnie's sister Priscilla sang, and the organ's sonorous chords reverberated to the tall vaulted ceiling. One after another, mourners spoke their memories and grief. I tried to keep mine short. I told about our friendship and borrowed from a meditation of John Donne. I quoted too from "The Boys," Oliver Wendell Holmes's loving memento of lifetime friendships with its elegiac last line, "Dear Father, take care of Thy children, The Boys."

A group of us crossed Washington Street and followed the strains of "Ballin' the Jack" to the large room on the first floor of the Woodrow Wilson Fellowship Foundation. The familiar music was coming from a New Orleans jazz band. I saw several old friends, dancing, talking, and drinking real punch. I made my way to Marnie and embraced her. I thanked her for inviting me. "I'm so glad you had this kind of reception," I told her. "Charlie would have approved."

She smiled. "It's what he wanted," she said.

I left to catch a bus to the airport in Newark, for I had classes to meet the next day. On the bus I sifted through memories. On the plane I thought of Holmes again, and his departed boys. Then I thought of my own losses. There were the fathers: my own, gallant old Carl Adolph Bodelsen—my chairman at the University of Copenhagen, who had offered to be my advocate for Danish citizenship and who, with his wife, Merete, had become a dear friend—and William Faulkner. There were others too, my comrades: Fred Gwynn, in the earth of New Hampshire, and now Charlie Allen, his ashes in the New Jersey land that he and Marnie had bought for their future.

A week later I departed for Mississippi and the annual Faulkner and Yoknapatawpha Conference, leaving behind me with Yvonne the first copy of *Uncollected Stories of William Faulkner*. I was glad there was more work ahead to do.

SEVENTEEN

Magic Carpet

TEACHING AMERICAN LITERATURE AT THE UNIVER-
sity of Michigan was a fine way to make a living. I had good courses and good
students, and I enjoyed helping the best of them to write dissertations and theses. As for the classroom, I found that I could still feel a high teaching a poem
or story or book I loved, and the students and I fed off one another and caught
fire. But it happened less often now, except in the best small seminars. I had
to admit that what I liked best was writing books and traveling to give lectures
and attend conferences.

When Dick Arndt was planning a seminar in Rome, he suggested that it
would be a good time for a brief holiday, too. "Have you ever been to Capri?"
he asked me. "If you haven't, it's time for you to go."

The two-hour trip on the Express to Naples went fast, but when Yvonne
and I hurried from the station, we found ourselves in traffic the likes of which
we had never seen, not even in Rome's Piazza Venezia. With one hand for each
other and one hand for our suitcases, we scurried across the street to the pier.
We hadn't forgotten movies about the Mafia and the Camorra. We must have
looked, I thought, like Hansel and Gretel hurrying through the forest. Our
forty-minute *aliscafo* ride, with the spray from the powerful boat cleaving the
waters of the Bay of Naples, was exciting but not nearly so exciting as the
shape of Capri emerging in the shadowy distance. Nothing had prepared us
for the spectacular island—the *funicolare* rising at a sharp angle up the leafy
mountain, the profusion of terraced vineyards, and then the masses of flowers. Then each turn, as the porter drove his electric cart through the narrow
streets, created an exotic visual experience. The hotel was larger than we had
expected and the room smaller, but from the little balcony we saw the clifflike
terraced descents and the paths through the glowing gardens.

244

AN UNEXPECTED LIFE

We didn't unpack but walked abroad instead to examine prospects that changed every few feet. We wondered at the Faraglioni, rocky spires rising spectacularly like teeth flung up from the depths of Neptune's kingdom, and delighted in the Arco Naturale, an enormous toy made by some fanciful child of the gods. We browsed in the tiny Piazzetta at the Center, with its small church and outdoor cafes. The drink in the cool bar helped us come down from the high of the montage we had absorbed, and the antipasto and salad and veal in the large dining room were splendid. The dark sky and glimmering lights on the water made a dramatic backdrop for a nightcap on the balcony, but we did not sleep soundly. We were roused from the first sleep of the night by a clamor of racketing shutters and overturning deck chairs. Before we slept again I thought I felt the earth move, and the susurrus of the wind increased before it quieted. In the morning we saw the evidence of its source. On the tile by the swimming pool was a fine brown powder brought from Africa by the *scirocco*. At the end of our few days, it was hard to leave.

The major events in our lives were increasingly highlighted by travel, and they were freighted with the emotions of memory. We had planned for a visit with Marnie and Charlie Allen in San Juan, and they promised they would arrange lectures for me there. And so they did. But now Charlie would not be there, and after the protracted probating of his will, Marnie had returned to Princeton. She urged me, though, to follow through with the plan. But when the time came to escape February in Michigan, Yvonne didn't feel well enough to make the trip. So the first week of the month was a sunny one for me, but a perfect illustration of what we told our classes about John Ruskin's pathetic fallacy. I had never credited nature with the emotions of human beings or felt that her moods reflected mine. There was no way I could perform that feat of pseudo-empathy and feel joyful now. The warm Caribbean breeze fluttered the flags above the ramparts, but I was walking the crowded streets of Old San Juan alone and standing solitary on El Morro where the Spaniards had bombarded the American fleet.

The English department gave a party, and the chairman and his wife presented me with a pale gold pleated guayabera. I wore the thin shirt the next day when they took me to Rincón at the southwestern tip of the island. I looked south and saw nothing but the sparkling Caribbean between me and the Antilles four hundred miles away. Swiveling through a 180-degree arc, I saw no human form on the surface of that wide sea. Having gone this far, I waded on into the clear water. Were there any other creatures there, I wondered, to see me swim for a dozen strokes in that warmth? I stayed in no longer than self-respect demanded, feeling lonelier than I had at thirty thousand feet with only Plexiglas between me and infinity. I felt another kind of loneliness the last night as I walked back to my room among the shadowy boughs. I heard a small voice, high and soft in the darkness. "Co-qui, Co-qui," it called, a tree frog the size of my thumbnail that lived only in Puerto Rico. I tried to imitate its call, and it ceased. Flying home the next day, I felt that I had celebrated a private requiem for Charlie.

A month later, almost to the day, I was landing in Paris. Soon I was sitting in the elegant Salles des Commission at the Sorbonne. Patrick Samway, my Jesuit student from North Carolina, and Michel Gresset, professor of the Institut d'Anglais V of the University of Paris VII, had enlisted eight French scholars, five Americans, and two Germans for "Faulkner and Idealism," the First International Colloquium on Faulkner. Gresset described it as "a chance to pose a theoretical problem and then look for variables that might be part of the understanding of the nature of the problem." As the keynote speaker, I led off with an attempt at definition, and André Bleikasten followed with the uses of ideological criticism. The heady intellectual ambience of French criticism could be daunting, and my own mental boundaries were being extended.

Thanks to Pat Samway, there was more. He was staying in the Jesuit residence, and he had arranged for me to have one of the comfortable rooms. Sometimes Pat and his colleagues wore clerical garb and sometimes mufti. One of the lay brothers in the breakfast line asked me, "Cream with your coffee, Father?" When he repeated this salutation and query on the next two mornings, I felt an antic impulse to say, "Cream, my son," but restrained myself. For dinner Pat steered us to the Marais, an old quarter of the city on the right bank of the Seine, where a Jewish restaurant enlarged my sense of the culinary possibilities of Paris.

A month after Paris I was in Tulsa to give the university's commencement address. It was a memorable visit where green residential areas corrected my expectation of signs of the oil industry. This looked no more like Midland, Texas, than Scotch Plains did. There were, however, memorable elements of Americana. As my host, a rising young Faulknerian named James Watson, drove through the center of town, I caught sight of a solidly built man in a broadly cut chocolate-colored suit going into a bank. His name suddenly came to me. He was Oral Roberts, an evangelist with a large television ministry. When I identified him, Jim Watson smiled. "Would you like to see his base?" he asked and drove onto a beautifully kept campus. "This is Oral Roberts University," he told me. I was taken by the appearance of the students as well. Unlike most on the Michigan campus, these young men and women looked as if they had just left church.

"I didn't realize that the atmosphere would be so sanctified," I told Jim.

"Just wait," he said. As we turned past a large lawn, I saw a huge shape that looked like a piece of modernistic sculpture. Only when we drew closer could I discern what it was. A burnished metal statue stretched perhaps twenty feet high: two hands clasped in prayer. Jim saw my expression and laughed. "Praying Hands," he said, "without acknowledgment to Albrecht Dürer."

I was already impressed that a minister could have achieved what Oral Roberts had done. So I was not surprised several years later to hear about another effort of his. The current fund drive was lagging badly, and he launched a desperate radio-television appeal. If the drive was not successful, he told his flock, "the Lord will call me home." There was no subsequent announcement that the Lord had, in fact, given that call. How Sinclair Lewis would have loved it, I thought. Elmer Gantry would have seemed the merest of evangelistic pikers.

In June it was Yvonne's turn to travel. With Nancy I drove to Detroit Metro, and we put her on the plane to Rome. In a day she would be there, a few hours from Bologna and the apartment Germanna Rinaldi rented to students. I was happy for her, for Italy had become her passion. I wouldn't mind doing for myself, and the work on the one-volume Faulkner biography would keep me busy. It should be a quiet summer, I thought. Three days later she telephoned to say everything was fine. She loved the tiny apartment, and she had met the neighborhood merchants and modestly stocked her shelves. On Sunday she was going to mass with Germanna and Mari'angela.

Then on August 2 one of our neighbors called to tell me that a bomb had exploded at the Bologna railroad station. The preliminary account placed the dead at sixty and the injured at two hundred. I called Yvonne's number, but the circuits were busy. When at last her phone rang, there was no answer. At two in the morning our closest neighbor saw my light burning and asked if he could help. I thanked him and decided to try for some sleep. I thought of Eliot's lines, "Teach us to care and not to care. Teach us to sit still." Easy for him to say, I thought.

My mother had been a worrier, and I may have inherited some of those same Celtic genes. What could I do? I could pray. When the phone finally rang the next day and I heard the hum on the line, I held my breath. It was Germanna. Bologna is located in a bowl among the hills, and when a heat wave became unbearable, people had begun to leave the city. Yvonne had gone to Verona to escape. Two days later, when the phone rang at four in the morning, she was safely back in Bologna. She would be home in two weeks. Her Italian had improved a lot, she said, and she was proud in her sense of being able to fend for herself. She called the experience her Magic Carpet Trip.

I was not surprised when she asked if she could return the next year. Besides her pleasure in the language, the whole milieu was right for her. For our friends in Bologna she had a kind of glamor, the *Americana* who loved their country. She had a gift for people, and with her outgoing, emotional nature, she felt close to them. I often thought that in some ways she was more Italian than they. She drank coffee with them and shopped with them and went to mass with them. We could find the money for this trip. The children were accounted for. Tracy was seeing a graduate student who was everything her first husband had not been. Specializing in the Hebrew Bible and the Akkadian language, Bruce Willoughby was also editor of *The Biblical Archaeologist*. After her divorce, Nancy was making a new life, too, headed for graduate school in English. Pamela was a prizewinner at Syracuse University, and her love was sculpture. So September saw me alone again on Berkshire Road as the four female members of my family pursued their destinies elsewhere. On the afternoon of September 16, 1981, I came to the end of my manuscript. It was over twelve hundred typed pages. Obviously there was only one thing to do: start at the beginning and cut. By October I had finished.

When Yvonne returned, it was time to think about packing our bags again. Two years earlier I had heard from John Hollowell, who had done his dissertation with me. Now he was teaching at the University of Arizona, where the English department was looking for an Americanist. John had put my name on the list, and I had been invited to Tucson to give a lecture. It had been a good visit, and Ed Dryden, the amiable chairman, had offered me the job. By late 1981 it appeared that the economy was becoming shaky, and so I asked Ed if I could come for a semester's tryout. He welcomed the idea, and so we arrived in Tucson on January 12, 1982.

I thought back to my army days in Albuquerque, to the stucco and tile houses with their small front yards. Not far away, the desert stretched out toward the mountains. It was the same warm climate and huge, overarching sky. Tucson was a big city. We rented an apartment in a small complex of adobe-like structures off a highway that led to the foothills to the north. The four-lane arteries, with names like Broadway and Speedway, were crowded with vehicles of all kinds. We drove beside roaring four-wheel trucks on huge tires whose cabs were pushed high with sheaves of springs and surmounted by banks of floodlights. They were favored by young drivers who enjoyed racing on the nearby stretches of desert. At night we would sometimes see beams crisscrossing the darkness and hear sounds like gunfire.

The faculty were as congenial as I remembered them. In an office near mine was Scott Momaday, a large, impassive Native American whose first novel, *House Made of Dawn*, had scored a signal success. One of my other colleagues told me that Momaday considered himself a citizen not of Arizona but rather of a vast tribal expanse of the Southwest. Another important meeting was one I initiated. I thought the best columnist in the *Detroit Free Press* was Andrew M. Greeley, a Catholic priest and professor of sociology at both Arizona and the University of Chicago. I had admired him for his clear, fluent, and forceful style. More than that, I admired him for his courage and honesty, especially where the powerful were concerned. This was true of Democratic politics but most conspicuously of the Catholic Church and its hierarchy. Clearly he was not a man to fear taboos or authority.

"I'd like to meet him," I told Yvonne.

"Go ahead and ask him here for a drink," she said, "and if we like him we'll ask him to stay for supper."

His bright blue eyes and fair complexion testified to one of his proudest attributes: he was Irish, eloquent and voluble with a fondness for slipping into a stage Irishman's dialect. His scholarly output was enormous, and he wrote poetry and prose for pleasure as well as devotional purposes. Fascinated with Joyce, he was not troubled by his rejection of the church and was intensely interested in his use of Irish culture and history.

With his extraordinary capacity for work, he was now making his way through all seven parts of Marcel Proust's *Remembrance of Things Past*. "How's it going, Andy?" I asked him.

He smiled. "He do go on," he answered.

Besides his voracious reading, he kept up a heavy correspondence, and he was not one to shirk responsibilities. Although he had made a powerful enemy in Cardinal Cody in Chicago, he still said mass when he could in his old Chicago parish. In Tucson he did the same regularly. He was now writing a novel, and he would like to show it to me, he said. He invited us to come and hear him preach. When he left we said we'd get together soon. Our first new friend, he would prove to be our best there.

I had been wrong in thinking that Yvonne alone would suffer from culture shock. It was a new world for me, too. On one pristine day we drove west out to where the saguaro cactus began to dominate the landscape. We did not see any forty-footers, but we knew that they could live to be two hundred years old. Their blossom was the state flower, and they were protected by law and by their own considerable defenses, as we learned from a newspaper account of a vandal who had tried to hack one down and died impaled on its spines and crushed by its weight. We strolled through the Arizona–Sonora Desert Museum, scrutinizing at close range mountain lions, Gila monsters, prairie dogs, and even one reclusive tarantula. We saved for another day the Old Tucson Studios, a replica of the town as it was in the 1860s erected by Columbia Studios and made the setting of hundreds of films. We weren't in time for the advertised live gunfight, but we admired the replicas of corrals, trading places, and saloons.

I had plenty of time to revise my manuscript of the biography and send batches to Albert Erskine. I had reckoned without one element, however, that was almost like a force of nature: James Michener. Chapters of his new book, *Poland*, were beginning to land on Albert's desk. There was of course no question which manuscript would take precedence. On what would I spend this luxury of time? I would have to call my own bluff. Years before, I had begun a novel only to abandon it. Now it was time to resume it or start another. I set up my old Smith-Corona on the dining room table and bought a ream of copy paper. I began to sketch out a plot and soon remembered that this was fun.

There was time for other kinds of fun, too. We joined the inexpensive country club a short walk away. There we swam in the Olympic-size outdoor pool, and I played tennis every week. The afternoon sun of late February made the weather fine for doubles until one day, midway through the second set, I chased a lob to the backcourt and when I stopped, I fell down. When I tried to localize the pain, I knew why. Just above my right heel, where I should have felt a tough tendon, there was only a gap, like a slack in a rope. I managed to limp home, where Yvonne called out from the bathroom. "I hurt myself," she said and showed me a huge swelling bruise where she had hit her shin on the bathtub. The Coumadin constituted a hazard as well as a safeguard.

"I hurt myself, too," I said. She helped me to the car and drove.

The resident in the Emergency Room made the diagnosis instantly. "You've ruptured your Achilles tendon," he told me.

"They'll want to operate," I said.

He nodded. "In the morning."

I lay on the gurney in a shadowy alcove, slightly drowsy from the medication, waiting for my room to be ready. I looked at the ceiling and meditated. It was undoubtedly time to hang up the old Adidases. I hated to quit at fifty-nine, but what a fool I would feel were I to find myself looking up from another gurney at another hospital ceiling.

I was glad that I felt no pain, but I hoped never again to need a saddle-block anesthesia. To receive no feeling from half of my body was just too weird. I lay on my stomach, my time sense distorted, drifting in and out of consciousness. When I woke, I was keenly conscious of the hip-length cast partly covering the wire threaded into my calf and on out my heel. There would be three more casts, I learned, and I would still be on crutches when we left for home in May.

My first visitor after Yvonne was Andy Greeley. He did not suggest that we pray. Instead he said with eloquent commiseration, "This shouldn't have happened."

When I no longer timed the shots against the sharpest pain I had ever known, I knew I was slowly returning to something like normal. A week after I came home Andy brought us a hot dinner. A month later he took us to a Mexican-American restaurant where his status was something between family member and demigod.

I gimped to classes on the crutches, my books and papers in my first backpack. I practiced on the crutches in the circle that separated the apartments. At the center were various desert plants from a small saguaro to a barrel cactus. You had to be careful, for if you brushed against it, you would retain spiny needles as souvenirs. People said that the blooms were exquisite and that the desert in bloom was gorgeous. To me it was inimical to human life.

We loved the glorious Arizona sunsets that were like nothing we had ever seen before, the whole wide sky crossed with banners of gold and orange and sometimes blue shading toward purple. At times the sky was huge with marvelous cloud formations like something out of childhood books illustrated by Newell C. Wyeth and Maxfield Parrish, and if you looked away for a few moments the whole panorama changed. I thought how kind the climate was in the winter, the feeling of freedom it gave when you could walk around in a polo shirt on a January day. Then I thought of a new term we had learned, *swamp cooler*—a device that poured water on your roof on the July days when the temperature would soar to over a hundred degrees. I could see that my attitude toward Tucson was being colored by my accident just as Yvonne's toward Chapel Hill had been colored by her bad health.

By the end of April she was packing and shipping cartons home in spite of a renewed siege of pain from her legs. In a warm farewell talk, Ed Dryden renewed the generous offer he had made earlier. A native easterner himself, he understood our reasons for returning home. We missed the profusion of green we had known in Michigan and Virginia. But we would not regret the decision that had so enlarged our lives. In early May we got into our car, with barely room for our suitcases and my crutches. Andy Greeley waved as we left. "See you in Grand Beach in the summer!" he called. We didn't feel we were back in the green world again until we reached eastern Oklahoma.

When I met my first classes in Michigan's summer half-term of 1982, I was still on crutches, but before long I was able to play nine-hole par-three golf.

Yvonne and I took advantage of Andy Greeley's invitation and drove across Michigan. Even before we pulled into his driveway in Grand Beach we felt the Irish-American ambience in the tricolors flying before many of the houses, some bearing Irish legends. In spite of losses suffered in 1929, Andy's father had been able to hold on to their sturdy beach house on Lake Michigan. When *The Cardinal Sins* and succeeding novels became bestsellers, Andy remodeled it and installed an Olympic-size heated lap-pool. His tightly plotted stories of Irish-American families earned him a large following. His prolific imagination and prodigious energy produced linked series of novels based on the ecclesiastical calendar, and his strong narrative gift carried over into a mystery series featuring an adventurous priest. Andy's charitable gifts absorbed a larger part of his royalties than anything else.

We enjoyed our annual visits because of his generous hospitality and congenial guests, usually his family. There was always a good-sized congregation for Sunday-morning mass. On fair days Andy celebrated it in his garden overlooking Lake Michigan. Occasionally you could identify some of the communicants. There was a bald, sturdy blue-eyed man I faintly recognized. I knew there were several Daley brothers, but I didn't know which one he was. When I asked, Andy said, "That's Mike Daley. The family calls him 'the smart one.'" The joke lay in the family's feeling for their legendary patriarch, "Da Mare," Richard J. Daley, former mayor of Chicago, and his whole family of achievers.

With the help of nieces and friends, Andy served his guests himself, ladling out helpings of his own rich sweet fruit salad. He took special pains with Yvonne, who had only now taken off the Teds to dangle her legs in the pool. The bright sun and warm water seemed to help a little. In the early winter Andy would come to us for a weekend in Ann Arbor, but apart from the annual Jazz Bash at the Unitarian Church, there were few such celebrations for us until the holidays.

Yvonne did not go with me to Mississippi in July for "Faulkner: International Perspectives." Participants came from both hemispheres and three continents. There was the pleasure of seeing friends and arranging to see them again. One special friend was Agostino Lombardo, director of the Institute of English and American Literature at the University of Rome. One of the leading Italian Shakespeareans, he was also the university's leading Americanist. A heavy-set genial man, he was referred to as the godfather of American studies in Italy. When he asked if I would be interested in the possibility of lecturing at the university, Yvonne greeted the idea with joy.

In early 1983 she experienced another unexpected pleasure when Michigan staged a multidisciplinary conference celebrating George Orwell's *1984*. One of the speakers was former senator Eugene J. McCarthy, who moved easily between literature and politics. At the program's end, Yvonne invited him to our house. I told him about Yvonne and Nancy's passionate participation in his presidential campaign. Yvonne and I sat with him at our living room coffee table, but then the two of them took over with passionate reminiscences. Yvonne brought out Eugene McCarthy bumper stickers, straw hats, and other souvenirs. They pored over them with nostalgia. I found it touching to hear them, especially when the senator said, "Only two thousand more votes, and we would have taken the state!"

My work on the one-volume Faulkner biography was now just a matter of sending materials to New York—photographs, permissions to quote, and answers to queries. Bertha Krantz, our copy editor, handled most of these. She was a stout, energetic little woman who after years at Crown had started at Random House as a gofer and became one of the firm's most meticulous line editors. She was invaluable in helping Albert deal with as many major authors as he did—authors such as James Michener, who demanded extensive editing and correspondence. But now there was a setback: the arrival of more manuscripts from some of the firm's big moneymakers, and when Albert told me that my book would not be published until 1984, there was nothing to do but accept the disappointing news.

Perhaps, I thought, I could return to the novel I had begun in Tucson with my plaster cast balanced on a chair and my typewriter on my lap. I had brought back twelve chapters. The protagonist was based loosely on a writer-teacher like George Garrett but was essentially a highly fallible version of myself. I placed him in Copenhagen and then Yugoslavia, where the tale began to draw on aspects of my Novels of Espionage course. Later, when John Le Carré published *The Russia House,* it pleased me that I had been working with the same basic situation as his, getting classified material out of the Soviet Union. Immobilized there in Tucson, I had enjoyed working on the novel, but now that I was home, I found that I wanted to return to business as usual. So I put the chapters and my notes away. I had once taken comfort in the fact that Joseph Conrad had been thirty-nine before he published his first novel, and that maybe it was not too late for me. But now I had to consider the possibility that I was simply not a novelist, otherwise I would have produced a novel by now. William Faulkner had often said that the writer was demon-driven. My demon, it seemed, was not demonic enough.

In teaching my novel course I had often described a pattern of two movements working against each other. One of the best examples is *Sister Carrie,* shaped so that Carrie's rise is played off against Hurstwood's decline, with the lines of action crossing as the characters move in opposite directions. Now I recognized a similar paradigm in my own life. Opportunities for the broadening of our experience arose just when Yvonne's health problems were increasing. In mid-July of 1983 we went to Rome for a month, but the benefits were not proof against a new illness with a fearsome-sounding name. In chondromalaccia, deposits on the inside of the kneecaps could make stairs an agony. And surgery was impossible because of the anticoagulant Yvonne took to prevent blood clots. Even the cortisone shots administered by the orthopedist who treated the Michigan football team provided only temporary relief. I thought of the remedy described years before by a Princeton doctor treating bursitis in my shoulder: "tincture of time," he said. I didn't think that was funny or clever. Now it appeared that it might be Yvonne's only remedy.

In the first days of the spring of 1984, the one-volume Faulkner biography appeared, in both Random House hardcover and Quality Paperback Book Club editions. It was not widely reviewed, because many editors thought of it as only a condensation, whereas I thought of it as essentially a new and different book. I could not complain, however, and eleven years later, at an international Faulkner conference, one of the scholars I respected most, Patrick Samway, would call it the best Faulkner biography in print. By then there were several.

Agostino Lombardo's plan had materialized, and on April 13 we left for Italy so that I could begin my month's teaching of Faulkner and other modern American novelists at the Institute of English and American Literature at the University of Rome. We had sublet an apartment by long distance rather than face the uncertainty of searching for a short-term rental on our arrival, and now we paid for our impatience and insecurity. It was a large, expensive fourth-floor apartment with no elevator, but it was in the heart of the city not far from the Piazza Navona. Our street was the Via del Governo Vecchio, and when we climbed to the small rooftop gallery we looked down on the neighboring Chiesa Nuova, half circled by a bend of the Tiber. On the corner I caught the bus that took me out to the parklike estate of the institute.

Our special feeling for Italy was growing as these frequent visits formed a kind of irregular rhythm in our lives. And now we had new friends in Rome. A former UVA student of mine, Michael Mewshaw, and his beautiful wife, Linda, were living there with their two sons. Mike had become a successful novelist in the years since he was a student working on an M.A. thesis on William Styron. He and Linda had a wide circle of friends, primarily writers and other artists. Some were novelists just making their way, while others were established, with big bestsellers ahead of them. Pat Conroy was one of the second group.

Most prominent of all was an expatriate American, Gore Vidal, one of the most versatile and productive artists of his generation. A strikingly handsome man, he had the manners of a sophisticated cosmopolitan. An acerbic critic of academia, he had more erudition than all but the most brilliant of them, and he gave them no quarter. Mike Mewshaw would smilingly call him "the Divine Gore." Through Mike we got to know him and the style of hospitality he offered in his exquisitely furnished penthouse in the history-rich Torre di Largo Argentina close to the Vittorio Emmanuele monument in Rome's heart. At his parties you never knew whom you might meet—a film star, an opera singer, another novelist. He welcomed Yvonne and me. When he learned that I would give a series of lectures that would take us from Bologna to Bari, he had a piece of advice. "It's not well known," he said, "but six kilometers north of Bari is one of the finest restaurants in Italy." I took out a pen and a piece of paper, but he shook his head. "Just tell the taxi driver, and he'll know. And when you get there, don't ask the waiter for a menu. Just tell him, 'un po' di tutto.' A little of everything is all you could want there." That was one of the pleasures of living in Italy. Two weeks before, we had taken friends from Mississippi to Ristorante Passetto in Rome, which Albert Erskine called his favorite. We were spoiled with the epicurean riches of Italy.

Mid-June was a time of transition. Yvonne and I were preparing to send things home from Via del Governo Vecchio by airfreight and were packing our suitcases for our nearly simultaneous departures. The Faulkner conference in Oxford two years earlier, "International Perspectives," had borne fruit in several ways. Two young Soviet scholars, Sergei Chakovsky and Alexandre Vaschenko, research fellows at the A. M. Gorky Institute of World Literature in Moscow, had returned the next summer for the tenth Faulkner and Yoknapatawpha Conference. With them was Pyotyr V. Palievsky, deputy director of the institute. Once again the Soviets charmed their Mississippi hosts, who had responded with their traditional hospitality. "Sacha" Vashchenko asked me if I would be interested in a Faulkner conference in the Soviet Union. I responded by quoting Nikita Khrushchev: "Life is short, see all you can, do all you can, live all you can."

Later Evans Harrington received a message from them. "You showed us the American South," they said, "and now we want to show you the Russian South." I told Evans that I'd be glad to participate, though I really didn't think it would ever come off. But he never lost confidence, nor did Bill Ferris, director of the Center for the Study of Southern Culture at Ole Miss. And finally, thanks to multiple sponsorship, it was on: a three-day symposium on Faulkner and the South at the Institute in Moscow. But that wasn't all. After

Moscow we would fly northwest to St. Petersburg for two days. Our next move would take us fifteen hundred miles southeast to Tbilisi in Georgia, almost a midpoint between the Black Sea and the Caspian. There would be twenty-one Americans, including observers paying their way at standard Intourist rates. At the Moscow conference there would be double that number from many different parts of the Soviet Union. Just to read the itinerary gave another dimension to these international Faulkner conferences we had been staging for ten years on the campus of Ole Miss in Oxford, Mississippi.

It had been nearly thirty years since our writer-in-residence had suggested in Charlottesville that it was time for us to put the show on the road. Now we would do it again, without him but with a group of Faulknerians from around the globe.

EIGHTEEN

The USSR, Rome, Home

YVONNE AND I HAD REGRETFULLY DECIDED THAT Russia was not a trip for her. We could have scheduled her blood tests around the trip, but we feared problems in obtaining drugs in the USSR. So it was that we parted at Leonardo Da Vinci airport on my birthday. When my plane touched down at the Vienna Airport I was prepared to feel some sort of reaction, for I had been told many years before that Dad had been born nearby at a place called Neudorf, or perhaps it was Wiener Neustadt, but I felt no ancestral intimations of any kind. When I showed my passport and ticket I was tempted to imitate the *Gruss Gott* salutations I heard around me, but I was afraid I would botch it. After a surprisingly short time, Austrian Airlines called my flight. As we climbed to cruising altitude we were in the sunlight above the overcast, and it was only as we approached Moscow that I glimpsed the earth, a different and darker landscape than the one we had left behind.

Shortly after the tires screeched, we were taxiing past the huge sign that proclaimed моcквa. Again I felt alone in the stream of travelers. I was usually with a group on these trips, but this time the others had departed from Rome when I was leaving from Milan. My line was herded into a cavernous structure cacophonous with myriad voices. In the Passport Control booth stood two young men, their pale faces impassive under their high-billed caps. They were KGB, State Security. Heads together, they studied my photograph and then looked at me. They spoke to each other and then looked at my passport again. Unless there was something I didn't know, there was no reason for concern. All the same, my stomach told me that I was nervous. At last one of them stamped the passport and slid it back to me. Welcome to the USSR, I thought, and walked rapidly toward the large exit. There stood three yellow buses, their drivers holding signs in Cyrillic letters. Another uniformed man appeared and waved the line impatiently toward the middle bus. I hesitated, and he waved more vigorously. My mimeographed instructions were no help because they were almost all in Cyrillic, too. There seemed nothing to do but to get aboard. The driver slapped the shift into gear, gunned the engine, and drove out past a final guard post.

My stomach told me I couldn't relax yet. The feeling grew as the driver turned from this main road onto a smaller one. The buildings continued to thin out on either side, and I saw nothing that looked like the outskirts of a city. He drove without slowing down, as if he was making a great circle around the airport. The looks of the passengers were not reassuring. They seemed like country people and workmen. Only two were different, clean-shaven uniformed men with Slavic faces whose billed caps bore a winged device and a word that looked like *Aeroflot*. I made my way down the rocking bus and squatted by their seat. I pointed to a phrase in my mimeographed pages: "Akademisk Hotel." With wrinkled brows they read the paragraph and conferred. Now the bus slowed, and with sign language I asked if I should get out. They waved me back and motioned me into my seat.

At the next stop they pointed outside, and I entered another building like the first one, past a few antiquated-looking cars parked in front. I decided that I had to ask for directions. I stopped the first passerby in the large lobbylike room. Receiving only a baffled look, I tried the next one with the same result. About to try a third, I realized that I had been speaking Italian. I looked up and saw a row of offices on a second floor. I climbed the stairs and peered in at each door as I passed. Almost all were empty, and I began to feel as if I had blundered into a Kafka novel or a Bergman movie. In the last office at the end of the corridor sat a man in a swivel chair reading a newspaper. Desperate now, I thrust the mimeographed pages in front of him and pointed to "Akademisk Hotel." He put his paper down and looked at me.

"Mockba?" I asked. "Mockba?" He said nothing but seemed to be pondering. He rose and motioned me to follow. He led me back down the stairs and out the main door where the antiquated cars stood. He began to speak to the driver of the first one, a young man with a girl beside him and a friend in the back seat. Great, I thought. He's negotiating a ride for me with this gypsy cab driver. I dismissed, for the moment, any concern that, just as I had no Russian, so I also had no rubles because we were to receive them at the hotel. But the driver made no sign of bargaining and motioned me into his well-stained vehicle. Before long we were in traffic, and my favorite Russian place name began to appear on signs and markers. What I felt when we pulled up in front of a hotel was more than relief. The driver motioned me to stay there while he stepped out and began talking with a small group of men. He returned with a short, neatly dressed silver-haired man who stretched out his hand to me.

"Professor Blotner?" he asked. He wrung my hand. "Pyotyr Palievsky!"

We found seats in the lobby of the Akademisk Hotel. He smilingly brushed away my apologies. "You want to know what happened?" he asked. "You landed at Sheremetjevo, the international airport, but then you went to Domodedovo, one of the domestic airports." He waved away my attempted apologies again. "Let me tell you something my mother told me," he said. He held me by the shoulders and looked at me intensely. "When you're lost, stay where you are!" And he laughed uproariously. "You must be hungry," he said, leading me toward a room marked PECTOPAH. At that moment I heard voices calling my name. It was Evans Harrington with Bill Ferris and Faulkner textual bibliographer and scholar Noel Polk.

"Tovarich!" Evans called out and then embraced me. "Let's go into this damned Pectopah and have a drink!" They weren't serving dinner yet, but I managed to obtain my first vodka in the USSR.

The hotel provided further learning experiences. Holding the cards presented to me at the reception desk, I took the elevator to the eleventh floor and handed them over to a stout gray woman who might have appeared grandmotherly but for her dour expression. Her desk proved to be the administrative center of the floor. Room keys, messages, and all else were apparently distributed from there. My small room was adequate, with a bathroom, a single bed, and a window looking out on a site being cleared for construction. The brick wall of the adjoining building bore faded slogans below stenciled pictures of Marx and Engels. I turned on a small television set that received one channel, now presenting folk dances from an Asiatic republic. I unpacked and watched more folk dances.

Then the telephone rang, and Evans summoned me downstairs. "Do you think those phones are bugged?" I asked him.

"I imagine so."

"But that's no problem," Noel said. "I heard that they're three months behind in transcribing the tapes." He led the way to the third-floor cafeteria, where we breakfasted on boiled frankfurters, bread, and cheese.

The limousine carried us past blocks of concrete government buildings to a group of elaborately constructed wooden structures that made me think of the film *Dr. Zhivago*. We were led into one of the largest, with heavy peaked roofs and elaborate scrollwork on the windows and eaves. Sacha and Sergei welcomed us to a long table where more than a dozen were already seated. Huge-antlered stags' heads looked down from two walls of the high-vaulted room. Portraits and candelabra decorated the others. Sergei was seated beside me. "I must tell you about this place," he said. "In *War and Peace* this is where Pierre Bezukhov is inducted into the Masonic Order. This building is the headquarters of the Writers' Union."

Sacha turned to helping the bustling waiters. He got our attention with his first question: "How many want vodka?" Pointing with his finger he counted and then told the waiter. The first course was being laid: platters of salads with tomatoes, sliced cucumbers, radishes, and other vegetables on beds of lettuce. Another waiter appeared with mineral water and served a bottle to each guest. The first waiter did the same with 375-milliliter bottles of Stolichnaya. Pyotyr Palievsky, presiding jovially, offered the first toast. A few minutes later, Evans Harrington reciprocated. This was clearly going to be a celebratory evening, and I reminded myself to partake liberally of the mineral water and food. The welcoming dinner went on for three hours.

The next morning found us in what had once been the ornately decorated ballroom of a stately mansion built by a Moscow nobleman in 1820. There were two hundred seats facing the rostrum. To the right, a huge oil painting showed V. I. Lenin and his wife listening to a man at a grand piano. Balancing this on the left was a bouquet of deep red roses arranged below a portrait of William Faulkner. Professor Nikolai Anastasyev, a large, smiling man in an open-necked shirt, gave the first of five major lectures by the Soviet participants, entitled "Faulkner and the Literary Traditions of the American South." Then I led off for the five scheduled talks by Americans with "Re-writing Faulkner's Biography."

Over the next two days of lectures the most avid conference-goer could not have asked for more. We watched the Bolshoi Company dance *Giselle* in an enormous theater within the Palace of Congresses inside the Kremlin. The next morning, buses took us south through white birch forests and fields where men and women wielded scythes and rakes. After nearly four hours we arrived at Yasna Polyana, "The Clear Glade," Leo Tolstoy's home. We made our pilgrimage to the whitewashed rooms where he had written parts of *War and Peace* and *Anna Karenina*. Then we stood in silence in the leafy glade with the mound of flowers where he was interred. The next morning we strolled through the seventy-acre enclosure within the Kremlin, where the shining gold-topped onion-shaped domes of the Cathedral of St. Michael the Archangel towered above the ancient walls, enclosing enormous leaden tsars' tombs and wall-high rows of icons.

The last formal session brought the conference to a close on Wednesday morning, June 27. But before that there were unexpected vignettes for memory. After Bill Ferris showed documentary films he had made of the lives of blacks in rural Mississippi, a plump middle-aged woman with a café-au-lait complexion raised her hand. Was this an idealized picture of black-white relationships, she asked, instead of a true documentary? After Chakovsky translated the question, she shifted from Russian to idiomatic English. She was a fellow at the African Institute in Moscow. Her Mississippian father had left the state after a Ku Klux Klan beating. A farming student at Tuskegee, he accepted an invitation to visit the Soviet Union and decided to stay.

The other vignette came with an invitation from Dmitri Urnov and his wife, Julia Palievsky, both proven Faulkner scholars. He also had other credentials. He was a noted horseman, and when Nikita Khrushchev wanted to reciprocate the friendship of Cyrus Eaton, he settled on a troika of fine horses. Selected to accompany them on the stormy embarkation from wintry Murmansk, Urnov had delivered them after a voyage full of seasickness for both horses and men. The Urnovs surprised me with an invitation for dinner at a time when shopping in Moscow was still a problem. They served more than I could eat, and I feared they would remember me as a glutton, but I had no trouble accepting the cigar and brandy. And so we talked on until Dmitri walked me back under the pale night of approaching Midsummer Eve to the dark Akademisk Hotel.

Before we moved on from Moscow, we rode buses north to the Trinity Monastery at Zagorsk, one of four such centers of the Russian Orthodox Church. Stepping into the Cathedral of the Assumption, seeing the elderly women crossing themselves and lighting candles, hearing the cassocked choir with the rumbling bassos responding to the liturgy from the altar, was like seeing an old film by Sergei Eisenstein. Outside, a dozen bearded priests stood by an open grave, one swinging a censer, another reading from the liturgy. Inside the monastery museum we studied woodcuts, one depicting a fourteenth-century invasion in which twenty-five hundred Russians successfully held out for sixteen months against a siege by fifteen thousand Poles. This gave an insight not only into history but also into what some called the Russian "siege mentality."

Our hosts had not finished showing us Russia, and they were not contenting themselves with just the South. We were already suffering from sensory overload. Now it would be intensified. Six hundred miles to the north in St. Petersburg we were installed in a Grand Hotel that suggested an MGM period film. The city's very location, where the sun shone brightly enough to read a newspaper at two in the morning, emphasized its strange grandeur. The rooms offered comforts beyond those of the Akademisk Hotel, and so it was a surprise to learn that we were not to drink the water from the bathroom faucets, and indeed not even to use it for brushing our teeth.

With the monuments of the city's history all around us, we remembered scenes from Tolstoy, Dostoevsky, Turgenev, and Pushkin. On Peter the Great's orders the French and Italian architects had imbued the city with a classical beauty in the squares and boulevards, the waterways running through parks, the profusion of statues and gilded forms. The Fortress of Kronstadt for defense and the Fortress of Saints Peter and Paul for imprisonment gave us a sense of this capital of the tsars, revealing both the wonderful and the terrible. We explored the Hermitage Museum's vast rooms of paintings and tapestries with ornate ceilings supported by huge marble columns of diverse colors and ornamentation. The display cases of brooches and rings and miniatures testified to the acquisitiveness of these monarchs with the luxurious tastes of Oriental potentates.

In these stunning scenes we were seeing a recreation of what had been destroyed in the bitter two-year German siege. The buildings themselves had been reconstructed to scale from the surviving plans and drawings. Embedded in the earth outside Moscow we had seen the twisted steel rails and tank traps that marked the high point of the panzer advance in 1941. Once that tide of Russian and German blood had ebbed, Hitler had given the orders that led to this other vast carnage. The rebirth of the Hermitage was another dramatic example of the Russian will to survival against storm and siege.

Dinner on the last night in St. Petersburg was another montage for memory as we sat in couples at the small tables with their pink lights and fluted shades while the orchestra played for dancing. Boarding the airplane at the end of these few days of splendor was culture shock again. It was a long Tupolev transport, so stretched out that I thought I could see the fuselage bending in segments as we taxied and took off on our fourteen-hundred-mile trip to Georgia in the heart of the Caucasus.

It was totally different from Moscow, from St. Petersburg, from everything we had seen so far. This land could have been a part of the American Southwest in the desert expanses between the mountains. The people combined Armenian, Georgian, and Russian strains. And though the most famous Georgian of them, Iosif Vissarionovich Dzhugashvili, would become Joseph Stalin, these people looked more like those I had seen in the Caribbean and the American Southwest: tanned, brown-eyed, and curly-haired. Their hospitality beggared what had been showered on us already. Wine, paintings, books, and carved platters piled up in our arms and then in our rooms. We had started with an afternoon of conferences that became a day of visits—to a block-square farmers' market that could challenge San Jose, to the homes of painters and the studios of sculptors—a day that included five full meals continuing after midnight.

262

AN UNEXPECTED LIFE   .

The last night was the best. We traveled in buses northward, ascending winding starlit roads to a massive stone inn with balconies. We were led to a table set for dinner for thirty. At the head of the table with Evans was Ivan, a stout man about my age with an air of authority who had fought in the Great Patriotic War. At my side was Shota Rostaveli, a teacher at the University of Georgia, with a small eight-year-old son who was the image of him. Shota pointed toward the still rising mountains. "Out there," he told me, "thirty miles, they say, is the rock where they tied Prometheus after he stole fire from the gods. And every day an eagle would come and tear out his liver, and then it grew back in the night." An avid Faulknerian, he retold the tale well.

Meanwhile the platters kept coming, heaped with meat and bread and salad, and the chilled vodka and the good Georgian wine. Evans and Bill and Noel were enjoying it as much as I—as much too, I thought, as our Georgian and Russian Faulknerian comrades. By now it was well after midnight, and we were singing as the toasts went round. We avoided national and patriotic songs, instead singing familiar favorites, with the Russian Faulknerians joining in on "I've Been Working on the Railroad." The chilly air was by now suffused with camaraderie as well as song. There were embraces with the toasts. Apparently Ivan and I, as the oldest, were the only ones who had fought in that war, and at that moment it felt natural after an especially rousing chorus to find ourselves in a comradely bear hug. We were all singing as our bus sped down the winding road. Falling silent momentarily after "Someone's in the kitchen with Dinah," we heard, far and faint, the sound of a train whistle. Evans leaned close. "Pardon me, boy," he sang, "is that the Chattanooga choo-choo?"

"Track twenty-nine," I replied, "and you can give me a shine!" And then the others, most of whom had been children when the song was new, joined in as Glenn Miller took us down the mountain.

We had been given so much during our visit that packing was our hardest task, and devising a way to leave gifts behind without leaving hurt feelings was a part of it. Not long after we queued up for our departure, the line came to a halt. A moment later, the burly figure of Ivan appeared at the head of the line. There was a brief conversation, and I saw him extract a red card from his pocket and display it to the attendant, who waved the line on. Saying goodbye to him was my last farewell in Tbilisi.

While we had been in Moscow, François Mitterrand had been there too, to be followed by Helmut Kohl. Soviet-French and Soviet-German relations had apparently shown no more favorable signs than Soviet-American ones. But we were not politicians. We were readers and writers who had traveled far to meet with other readers and writers who felt, like us, that the work of William Faulkner testifies to the strength and endurance of the human spirit—even more, that the artist's work, whether Faulkner's or Melville's, Dostoevsky's or Pasternak's, could buoy that spirit. At the banquet on the last night, one of the Russians had told me that the fact the symposium had been held at all was "a miracle." We must not forget, he said, that "we are but a small island surrounded by a wild sea full of sharks."

Before we left for home, the conversation turned to rivers: the Mississippi and the Don. Then one of the Russians said, "What about another conference here? We could call it 'Faulkner and Sholokhov.'"

One of our people said, "Why not?"

To return to Ann Arbor was to resume the basic pattern of our ordinary lives. I had my research and writing and teaching. Yvonne had her continuing struggle to live a normal life. She came from a family beset by medical problems to an extent that might well have intensified any tendency toward hypochondria. But now it seemed as though her system, her total organism, was breaking down part by part, though we couldn't quite see this progression. I think we would have been reluctant to admit it if we had seen it, in spite of a continuing sequence of tests and treatments and brief hospitalizations. Her defenses were her life force and her courage, and the prospect of a return to Italy.

A sequence of events combined these aspects of our lives. The topic for the Faulkner conference in the summer of 1985 was "Faulkner and Women." I opened the conference under the title "William Faulkner: Life and Art." Two days before the end I called home. After several rings I was about to hang up when I heard the receiver being lifted. It was so hard to hear that I thought it must be a bad connection. Then I realized it was the faintness of Yvonne's voice.

"What's wrong?" I asked.

"I think I've got botulism," she said slowly. Nancy would tell me later that she had been there briefly but had left when Yvonne had said she didn't want to eat. So she had given her a Bloody Mary, settled her in blankets, and left.

"Go right to bed," I said, "I'm coming home." She protested weakly, but there was no way I could stay in Mississippi after having heard that faint voice.

This proved to be one nerve-racking emergency in which everything would go right. Delta Airlines found a seat for me on a flight leaving Memphis for Detroit in three hours. Chester McLarty drove his big Cadillac well, and

264

AN UNEXPECTED LIFE

the flight to Detroit was on time. I found Yvonne on the living room couch and got her into the car as quickly as I could. When they wheeled her into the Emergency Room at St. Joseph Mercy Hospital, I recognized Alec Baskin. "Back again, doctor," I said. We had been there a month earlier when our dentist had accidentally injected an anesthetic directly into a vein. The Coumadin had done the rest, and two hours later Yvonne's face was so swollen from the hemorrhage that we drove to the Emergency Room. I had never seen such suspicious looks as those on the faces of the three women who rode up in the elevator with us.

Four days after this second such admission to the hospital, now for a bleeding ulcer, her color looked almost normal. Though I couldn't imagine how she had managed it, she had already done all our packing for our upcoming summer trip to Italy, and now she pleaded with Dan Fall, her gastroenterologist, to be released in time for us to use our Alitalia reservations. By August 5 her hemoglobin count was still low, but he said that he wouldn't forbid us to go. Three days later, when the wheelchair rolled out with our baggage on Yvonne's lap, the taxi driver asked us, "Where to?"

Before I could answer, Yvonne said, "Detroit Metro, please."

Back at St. Joe's in early October, she bore the procedure bravely as they threaded the tube down her throat. Dan Fall adjusted his white mask and bent over her face to peer intently through the gastroscope. Then he rose. "Would you like to look?" he asked me.

I bent over, closed one eye, and peered into the reticule. The crosshairs and measurement lines looked like those of a periscope in war movies, but this one showed not a green sea but the pink lining of Yvonne's stomach. "The ulcer's healed," Dan Fall said.

In that year we had been planning beyond a return to our favorite Adriatic seaside resort, Riccione. We had been long enough at Michigan for my first sabbatical leave to be coming due, and I began considering what topic I could propose for this generous award. From childhood Faulkner had shown a talent for sketching. By adolescence, when he was deeply immersed in writing poetry, he found fruitful models in the work of Paul Verlaine that were visual as well as verbal. He followed Verlaine's lead in appropriating characters from the pantomime and the commedia dell'arte, an old Italian dramatic genre in which theatrical companies improvised on traditional plots using stock characters. So he drew Harlequin, an elegant frock coat covering most of his familiar domino costume, his hands grasping Pierrette's as she bends back from him, her pointed clown's hat angled toward a half-kneeling Mezzotino, his lute slung around his neck. Faulkner put them and their companions in plays and many poems, and much of this imagery carried over into his prose as well. There was my sabbatical research topic: "William Faulkner and the Commedia dell'Arte." Where could I best study it? Obviously, at its source, in Italy.

January 1986 found us in Rome in a modest apartment in the Viale di Villa Pamphili, but it proved to be two buses away from any place we wanted to go. "We didn't come to Italy to live in a suburban apartment house," Yvonne said, and she was right. In a shop off the Via Veneto I found Dr. Daniele Surina, a bent, courtly septuagenarian. Educated as a lawyer, he had commanded a submarine during the war until the British sank it. He had escaped miraculously, and now he made his living in various ways. He found us a third-floor jewel box of an apartment on the quiet Via dei Foraggi. It was expensive, but it overlooked the Roman Forum and had a reliable elevator. I was glad to place the lire notes on the desk of the shopkeeper who owned it, and I admired the graceful way Dr. Surina's hand reached out to extract his commission from the stack.

So we moved in and found a few small stores in the neighborhood that met our simple shopping needs. In one of them I met Greg, a middle-aged American who had knocked around Europe after the war and married Nuala, a young Irish woman who gave him twin girls and kept house in an apartment smaller than ours. Greg introduced me to his friend Pepe, who seemed to know everyone. He had been a regular with the Lazio soccer team until a compound fracture of his left leg ended that career. One day at Greg's urging he pulled up his pants leg and showed me the grotesque bump that swelled the middle of his right shin. He had earned enough to buy his own taxicab, and he augmented his income by taking visitors on tours and dealing in jewelry, which often required trips to France. He was a short, bald, genial man with a rudimentary knowledge of English. He overestimated my Italian and spoke rapidly. When he asked if I wanted to buy a television set, we decided we did, and he found one for us at a remarkably low price. Pepe became our friend.

Not long afterward we made another friend. Standing on one of Rome's busiest streets, intent on shopping near the Campo dei Fiori, I unfolded a map the size of a tablecloth. It billowed in the wind, and as I folded it in frustration, I saw a tall, imposing man in a dark overcoat and homburg approaching. In my best Italian I asked if I might ask directions. In a deep, resonant voice he asked, "Do you speak German or English?" In our brief conversation it emerged that we were both academics. He gave me his card and invited us to visit him after our shopping. When I checked the address I saw a small engraved coronet above the name, Vinigi L. Grottanelli. We found that he lived in a massive apartment house in Largo Arenula not far from Gore Vidal. He opened the massive door on the fourth floor and led us into a hall full of pictures and then into an elegantly furnished living room. He introduced us to a tall, handsome, white-haired woman of perhaps seventy-five: his wife, Isabella.

The room was comfortable, and so was the conversation. After he poured our drinks, he picked up a large decanter. "I'm having bourbon," he said. "Sure you wouldn't like to join me?" I declined and said I thought there mustn't be many bourbon-drinkers in Italy.

"I became fond of it in Africa," he explained, "and at home after the war I started drinking it again." He told us a few stories about his work with tribes in northeast Africa. Some were amusing, and all were interesting. His absorption with this particular world showed not only a scientist's immersion but also a personal affection. He inscribed a paperback copy of his *Gerarchie Etniche e Conflitto Culturale* for us, and from the author blurb it became clear that he was one of Italy's leading ethnologists. He and his wife accepted our invitation to visit us, and over the succeeding months this relationship further enriched our time in that apartment overlooking the heart of ancient Rome. In politics he was a monarchist—not surprising, since he was the Conte di Grottanelli and Isabella a *principessa* whose family had produced a pope two centuries earlier.

We were fortunate in our American friends, too. Mike and Linda Mewshaw gave us entree into their circle. We also met Italian writers and actors at Gore Vidal's home, one married to a short, shapely actress who introduced herself with straightforward aplomb. "I'm Susan Sarandon," she said, extending her small hand. One of Gore's charms lay in the wickedly amusing stories he told about subjects as different as Jack Kerouac and Charlton Heston. When a troubled producer had asked him to rewrite a script for Heston based on Lew Wallace's *Ben-Hur*, Gore had hit on a solution to make plausible the relationship between Ben-Hur and his friend Messala. "As boys," he explained, "they had been lovers."

The producer blanched. "Don't tell Chuck," he said. "He'll go to pieces."

After telling this story, Gore gestured toward a large, elegant dinner table made of a sheet of glass supported by gilded lion's legs. "I spotted it in a junk shop one day," he said. "When I recognized it as a prop from the movie, I bought it. I got it for a song."

That table was only one of many conversation pieces in Gore's intriguingly furnished apartment. Others included photographs arranged beside large chairs and on book-laden coffee tables. Framed side by side were his friends Paul Newman and Joanne Woodward. "They stayed here on their honeymoon," he said.

It was a fine place for parties. The parties, served by two Filipino houseboys, were orchestrated by Howard Austen, Gore's companion of many years. He had been in the theater, and this provided a congenial subject for him and Yvonne. She enjoyed this ambience, and I did, too.

Thanks to our friends in the Fulbright office and at the university, there was welcome activity for us. I lectured in Agostino Lombardo's seminar, and Andy Greeley put me in touch with John Navone, a priest at the Pontifical Gregorian University who wrote on Tennessee Williams. Lecturing to his class introduced me to the precincts of "The Greg." The devotional prints on the walls of priestly quarters were not surprising, but the exercise room filled with bicycles and weights seemed strange to me, brought up as I had been to think of priests and nuns as a race apart.

I welcomed these distractions from what I was supposedly doing during this sabbatical. I had reread the Faulkner and commedia dell'arte materials I had brought with me, but my frustration grew as I sought Italian research sources. There were problems at the University of Rome. It enrolled well over a hundred thousand students, though far fewer were actually at work there. The library was badly underfunded, and the books themselves were often inaccessible on a second floor overlooking the huge main reading room. The card catalogue, written with ancient nibs in faded brown ink, was sometimes indecipherable. I began having misgivings about the whole enterprise. I had experienced a flash of hope when I learned about the Biblioteca del Teatro, but there were two problems: one was to find it, and the other was to arrive there when it was open. It was March 7 before I achieved both, and the contents seemed less useful for my purposes than even those of the university library. The next week, after a disappointing second effort, I decided to try the large Mondadori bookstore in the city. There I found a beautiful, expensive, illustrated volume full of the sort of material I needed. I couldn't help reflecting that I probably could have obtained it in Ann Arbor by mail.

My enthusiasm was revived by a proposal from the United States Educational Foundation in Italy for an abbreviated lecture tour beginning in Naples, from where we would take a coastal steamer to Sicily. Germanna Rinaldi had always told us that the real Italy was the Italy of the South, and now we could experience it. We were in the dining room of our Neapolitan hotel where dusk was encroaching on the dark blue water. The sky was full of darting motion, the arabesques of bats. We had grown used to their sunset formations during the month we had spent in Mari'angela's apartment in Bologna, and while living in our fourth-floor Roman apartment we had become used to their daily arrivals and departures, like commuters working in the city. But there was somehow something different about these fluttering clouds of Neapolitan bats.

Yvonne ordered one of the featured pastas. When it appeared, it was topped in a style new to us. It was decorated with a small octopus, its legs draped neatly down over the pyramid of pasta. Yvonne was normally adventurous with food, but she asked the waiter to bring her instead a pasta with sauce. I hoped the first dish wasn't an augury of our visit to Sicily.

After my lecture the next evening, we boarded a boat that reminded me of my departure from the Dalmatian coast, with the same sense of an old hull newly painted, the narrow stairs leading to narrow cabins. But we slept not badly and welcomed the sight of our hotel in the teeming center of Palermo. The sun was warm on our backs as we walked to an excellent small restaurant nearby, but Yvonne paid a price with an aching knee. This led to my first expedition in the city, walking through the strange streets with their richly ornamented buildings, blinking against the dust particles whirled by the wind. I walked through the Piazza Vigliena with its four corners formed by nearly identical four-story buildings facing each other like meticulously cut pieces of some monumental puzzle. Reading the map, finding a *farmacia,* and returning with an ice pack, I felt as if I had achieved a triumph. The city reminded me of Faulkner's description of New Orleans: "a courtesan, not old and yet no longer young." I had to remind myself that when New Orleans was laid out, the city of Palermo had already existed for two and a half millennia.

That afternoon Giovanni Vanni and his slim young wife, Francesca, took me to see something of the city. He was a member of the university faculty, and something more. Our USIS guide, Vincente Manfredi, told us that he was now *the* Vanni of his distinguished family, much reduced since its days of greatness in Sicily. Like more than one profile we had seen, his reminded me of images on ancient coins.

As we walked, history, and even prehistory, stood all around us in this capital where the signs of its origins as a Phoenician colony were overlaid by mementoes of the Greeks and Romans, the invading Goths and Byzantines, Arabs and Normans, and then another millennium of conquerors. The cathedral of nearby Monreale with its great central tomb, its mosaics and statuary, evoked the monumental past. So did an even more haunting sight. Descending flights of stone steps into the cold and damp, we entered the catacombs of the Capuchins. Mummified Franciscan friars now stood there, lining the walls in their dark habits, secured so that they leaned out upright among the laity in their disintegrating finery. The bald skulls were inclined as if in prayer or meditation, with name tags above the bony hands wired together. Near the exit were two glass-topped caskets, within them a rouged and mustachioed officer in his uniform and a blonde, seraphic child, like a doll extraordinarily preserved. It was a relief to both body and psyche to ascend from the chill of the stone into the life-giving sunlight.

By evening Yvonne felt well enough for us to go to dinner as the Vannis' guests at a venerable club. It had a familiar look, though it obviously retained little of the elegance it must have presented a century earlier. Then I realized why the tall windows, flowing curtains, and many-tiered chandeliers seemed familiar. I had seen their likeness in the film version of *The Leopard*, in which Giuseppe Lampedusa had described the effects of Giuseppe Garibaldi's invasion of Sicily, and on some level of my mind I must have associated the prince in the novel with Vinigi Grottanelli. My lecture the next day repeated a familiar experience: the size of the audience was respectable, and my sponsors seemed pleased, but I knew that I was learning more from the experience than my students were.

In Sicily you never knew what you might see. Driving through the dark countryside one night, Vincente suddenly slowed an instant before we reached crossroads where a brilliant glare of light almost blinded us. All four sides of the intersection were walled with hurricane fencing and coils of barbed wire. Dispersed at intervals were armored personnel carriers and light tanks with guns poking forward from the turrets. Vincente reassured us. This was a high-security prison housing *pentiti*, confessed *Mafiosi* who had turned state's evidence and were now awaiting a long-postponed trial. We accelerated into the darkness. Driving eastward across the island, we traversed an increasingly stark landscape where sheets of black lava looked like stretches of a planet or asteroid inimically hostile to man. I had read warnings against driving into the interior, where holdups and worse were possible. But Vincente told us that these reports were exaggerated, and we would stay close to the coast.

At Messina on the northeastern tip of the island we looked across a flat sheet of water toward the toe of the Italian boot. I half expected to see some sort of turmoil here where Homer had described Scylla and Charybdis waiting to destroy unwary mariners. I thought of the young Italian teacher I had met the previous week who had told me she had found her first job at the university in Messina right after the Second World War, when housing was short and government checks delayed. She lived in Scilla on the Italian coast, sub-sisting principally on bread and calamari, the ugly but nutritious squid taken from those waters. The next day we drove southwest and stopped at Taor-mina, a resort described enchantingly by D. H. Lawrence, but we were be-coming blasé, familiar now with stunning views of ocean on one side and, on the other, vegetation-crowned crests with dangerous roads perched on their terraces.

We asked Vincente to continue south for Catania, the third of Sicily's three major cities. One thing they had in common: wreckage and rubble whose causes were modern rather than ancient. In some places whole blocks had not yet been cleared. "Is that bomb damage?" I asked Vincente, regretting the question immediately.

"Yes," he agreed.

"The British or the Americans?" I asked.

"The Americans," he answered with something like a smile, as if in a kind of apology for mentioning our wartime depredations. From time to time I had thought of Catch-22, conscious that Joseph Heller and his protago-nist, Yossarian, had been bombardiers like me. I was proud of having flown in the air corps, but again I was feeling as I had in Cologne. And I thought too of the comic strip "Pogo" and its aphorism, "We have met the enemy, and they are us."

There was a new uncertainty confronting us, thanks to the kind of emer-gency that could arise so unexpectedly in Italy. Once we had been forced to change plans because of a threatened strike by air controllers. Now it was threatened strikes and obstructions by the abusivi, squatters who had built homes on contested land after the war and now faced eviction. Demonstra-tions were planned on major roads that would block our way to Palermo for our return voyage to Naples. With the help of Vincente we were able to ex-change our ship passage for air travel back to Rome.

We were there in time for the April rains. Yvonne's knee was no better, and one day she confessed, "I'm a lot worse off than I let you believe." With the worry I felt, I was getting little writing done and so found myself beset with boredom and depressed by guilt over this waste of time. I had planned a three-day stay on Capri for early May but concluded that what we really needed was time on a sandy beach. And so, two weeks later, we returned to our family hotel on the beach at Cesenatico. Then, at our favorite resort of Riccione we lay on the solid, ingeniously made beach chairs with large awn-ings we could adjust to follow the sun across the sky. When it was approach-ing its zenith, I would wade out until I could swim. I hoped the sun was doing its work on Yvonne's knees and legs. Stairs were now difficult for her, so much so that at home she had increasingly begun to spend time in the small first-floor room that housed the television set. One day, as the time approached for packing to return home, she mused, looking out at the sea, "Soon I'll have to return to my prison."

We had a visit in Riccione from Germanna Rinaldi, who proposed a showing of Pamela's sculpture in Bologna. This would be good for her career, and Yvonne would enjoy accompanying her. Such an idea would have been welcome to Yvonne at any time, but especially so now, to occupy her mind and counter her depression. I wondered what I could do about the quality of life awaiting us at home.

NINETEEN

Endings and Beginnings

BACK IN ANN ARBOR IN EARLY 1987, WE FOUND OUR situation unchanged, the major concerns still Yvonne's health and my work, though the latter now received less attention. We had moved into a new phase of medical tests and treatments that seemed to offer no promise, and life in a two-story house was becoming more difficult for her. I knew I was through with Faulkner and the commedia dell'arte. I could have done a mechanical influence study, but I simply didn't have the heart for it. There would be other Faulkner work for me, but right now I was Faulknered-out, and I would have to wait until a new topic found me.

As it turned out, one had been staring me in the face. Over the years I had regularly taught *All the King's Men*, and I had become Red Warren's friend and occasional guest. The power and variety of his work had made him America's leading man of letters. He had won the major awards in fiction, drama, and criticism. I had the same high regard for the man that I did for the work. And I already knew many of his friends, critics, and scholars who had written on his extensive body of work and others who had collaborated with him.

Closest of all to him, except Cleanth Brooks, was a former student, Albert Erskine, still his editor at Random House. By now Albert was semiretired from the firm, though his workload with writers such as Eudora Welty, John O'Hara, James Michener, and Cormac McCarthy was at times heavy. When I broached the idea of writing Red's biography, Albert was not encouraging. He may have known something I didn't know: that Red had already declined requests from two excellent writers. And Red himself had written recently that his poems constituted a kind of "shadowy autobiography." I waited, but then on my next visit I put it to Albert directly. "Go ahead and ask him," he said simply.

Red replied equivocally that he could not undertake anything that would help me but that he was not trying to discourage me. He closed, however, with the words, "Goodbye, and all good wishes." It was not until I was deep into Warren correspondence that I saw that he often ended letters this way. It was at about that time that Albert wrote me that Howard Kaminsky, the publisher at Random House, had approved the idea of a Warren biography and that I should ask Carl Brandt, who had succeeded his mother, Carol, as my literary agent, to call him. Not long afterward, the contract arrived. My editor would be Robert D. Loomis, a veteran whose authors included William Styron. I was glad again to be with Random House, and we tried to resume our familiar pattern.

After another gastroscopy revealed no active ulcer, Yvonne and I went ahead with the trip to Italy we had planned the previous year. The Alitalia flight was uncomfortable, but that night we were settled in at the Hotel Pensione Coronet. The July heat was oppressive, and few of our friends were in town. Again I had the feeling of wasted time. I watched the dust motes floating in the golden rays of twilight between the dark brown velvet curtains. My morale sagged, and I wrote a title in my datebook: "On being sixty-four, sitting in a Roman pensione on a hot Thursday afternoon waiting for eight o'clock." I was glad that I had made reservations for Capri rather than Riccione. The next day we sat on our balcony at La Pazziella holding hands, the perfumes from the garden floating up to us over the masses of blossoms, and beyond us the foliage on the mountain turning purple. From the distance came the strains of the carillon sounding far and away below us. It was not a hymn but was instead the familiar strains of "Someone to Watch Over Me." Yvonne squeezed my hand, and I swallowed hard.

When we returned home in the fall I stayed busy with teaching and departmental duties. I had concluded that the only way to deal with Yvonne's increasing feeling of confinement and pain upon climbing stairs was to find a one-story house. This involved months of inspecting houses and being patient when the agent often drove us to obviously unsuitable places. When at last we found one, we moved into it with a melancholy feeling of displacement. I remembered a friend's aphorism that "one move is equal to three fires." It was a house with a living room–dining area instead of a proper dining room. So we found a contractor, and Yvonne's spirits rose as she took control of the project to build a dining room.

In the summer of 1988 I heard from Red again. There were files in Fairfield that might be of use, he wrote, and there were some stories that had circulated in his hometown of Guthrie, Kentucky, that he wanted to correct. As I made preparations for my trip, one friend asked if I knew Eleanor Clark Warren. I did not, and it was just as well that I did not have the sense of her that her son would convey years later. "She was like a vast force of nature," he wrote, "tides, glaciers, climate change, continental drift, and yes, sometimes earthquake and volcanism." My impressions of her husband would be reinforced: lively, amusing, dynamic, one of the kindest and most generous of men—his words pouring out so fast in his still unmodified Kentucky accent that it would take me time to tune in again on each subsequent visit. Though they were a loving couple, they struck sparks off each other. As far as I could tell, almost no one was spared the rough side of Eleanor's tongue. Saul Bellow said, "She often growled at me for my shell-back social views and pounced on my mistakes in grammar or usage. But that was because she loved disputes, sharp answers, and social militancy. She was a handsome, brave, big-hearted woman."

Suffering from macular degeneration that limited her to peripheral vision, she still ran her household, cooking by memory and determination. I was appointed to pilot their weatherbeaten Volvo station wagon. On one trip from Fairfield to the home of their friend R. W. B. Lewis, Eleanor guided me from memory, shouting the checkpoints for emphasis when I became flustered. She was challenged in many ways but remained indomitable. Once an avid tennis player, she refused to put away her racquet, and when a young man gave their children lessons, she took to the court to rally with him. Early the next year, I would read to them from the *New York Times* at breakfast. Sometimes we would stop for political discussion. Once her riposte to a comment of mine was "You dumbbell!" But I was not outraged, for this was the same expletive she had launched at her husband earlier, and not long after using it on me, she asked, "Would you like some more tea, darling?" I found her an affectionate but difficult woman.

With generous research grants I sought out essential materials. When I was working on Faulkner's biography, I kept seeking letters and interviews almost to the end. By contrast, Warren was a tireless correspondent. By 1988 there were already two volumes of his letters in print and a total of sixty-eight taped interviews at the University of Kentucky, two-thirds of which I would have to transcribe myself. Acquiring copies of all his major works and the critical and scholarly studies of them was not easy. In October after my Random House contract arrived, I closed the year with visits to the Library of Congress and to New York City, completing my search of the Random House files of Robert Penn Warren.

Research took me farther afield than I could have imagined. To understand the background of *Prime Leaf* of 1931 and *Night Rider* of 1939 I had to locate the counties of "The Black Patch" and read a detailed thesis about the years of "The Tobacco Wars." Red indignantly denied that *Night Rider* was a historical novel. "These events belonged to my early childhood," he said. "I remember the troops coming in when martial law was declared." After immersion in Kentucky and Tennessee history, I shifted to Louisiana. Warren saw and heard Huey Pierce Long but once during the time he taught at Louisiana State University. Years after the novel's publication in 1946 he would write, "When I am asked how much *All the King's Men* owes to the actual politics of Louisiana in the 30's, I can only be sure that if I had never gone to live in Louisiana and if Huey Long had not existed, the novel never would have been written." But, "for better or for worse, Willie Stark was not Huey Long. Willie was only himself, whatever that self turned out to be, a shadowy wraith or a blundering human being." Much observation and many memories came together in this creation, from Warren's awareness of Hitler's frenzied orations and the fulminations of Mussolini he had heard in the Piazza Venezia. On a deeper level were events suggested in the novel's epigraph from Dante's *Inferno*.

Successive excursions into history took him back further. One summer morning in 1945 while he was consultant in poetry at the Library of Congress, Katherine Anne Porter, a close friend, crossed the hall from her office and flung a document down on his desk. It was called "Confession of Jeroboam Beauchamp." "This for you," she told him. "I'm giving you a novel." Warren had done library research for *At Heaven's Gate* (1943), but this time he meant to write "a straight historical novel." To compose *World Enough and Time* (1949), he steeped himself not only in the tragic story of the protagonist, his wife, and his mentor, but also in the aftermath of the disastrous panic of 1819. Warren subtitled it "A Romantic Novel." It was, he explained, "a story about the young idealist who can't find an object for his idealism." There were scenes as grisly as any in a Grand Guignol performance and others recalling the events in the Capulets' tomb. The material for *Band of Angels* (1955) was more familiar because of a link to *All the King's Men,* but there was much here—plantation life, abolitionism, the war and Reconstruction—to increase my admiration for Warren's capacious mind.

Almost alone among modern American poets, Warren was challenged by the long narrative poem. *Brother to Dragons* (1953) derived from a horrendous murder committed in northwestern Kentucky by a nephew of Thomas Jefferson with the help of his brother. What, Warren wondered, was the reaction of the Jefferson who had believed in human perfectibility? Intrigued by the question, he explored the ghastly events and their consequences. In courthouse files he had studied musty rolls of foolscap, and twice he had clambered up the steep bluff through thickets to view what was left of Rocky Hill, the home of Charles Lewis, the murderer's father and Jefferson's brother-in-law.

Since Warren's first stay in Montana in 1935, he had been fascinated with Chief Joseph of the Nez Perce. At last he began to tell his tragic story in verse. Finally, 104 years after the chief's surrender, Warren had eight of his poem's nine sections written and rewritten. But there was one problem. He could not see how, in that terrain, fifteen hundred cavalrymen could have gone undetected until their sudden attack ended the Battle of the Little South Bear Paw Mountains. So he decided to see it for himself. Two of his young friends, Stuart Wright and David Quammen, told me that they found "a sort of declivity, and we completely lost sight of the camp itself. . . . And there was the answer. And that's how the cavalry did it. They were able to slip into that point and actually wait to begin the attack because they could not be seen."

Just as former students and young friends responded whenever I asked for help, so did Red's old friends and colleagues. This research drew me back to Tennessee and Kentucky. At Vanderbilt, writers and teachers such as Walter Sullivan described the ambience of the university from Red's student days until his bitter departure. Edwin Mims, the head of the English department, had reduced his teaching load and subsequently given a tenure-track job not to him but to a new Vanderbilt Ph.D. "They fired me," Red would say, and he would often refer to the author of his blighted hopes as "that old son of a bitch, Mims."

His sister, Mary Cecilia Warren Barber, supplied memories of the childhood and adolescence that made him call Guthrie, his Kentucky birthplace, "a place to be from." In Tennessee such friends as Andrew Lytle could recall their days as rebellious graduate students and, later, as prestigious professors. In New Haven, academic stars such as the historian C. Vann Woodward and the critic R. W. B. Lewis helped to bring me up to date on Warren's increasing visibility in the academy. My most encyclopedic informant was Cleanth Brooks, my host both in his home and "at the tables down at Mory's" where the Whiffenpoofs gathered. I looked forward to these trips.

It was fortunate that I did not need to make additional trips soon, for the fall of 1988 was turning even more into a time of tests, with attention now focusing on Yvonne's left kidney. Our longtime neighbor Bob Fekety was a brilliant internist whom we could turn to for answers. Yvonne was afraid and in pain, and he did his best to reassure her. When I walked beside the gurney to the operating room, she turned her head to the wall and held my hand. "I'll never be the same again," she said. I tried to reach her with words at the same time that I was trying to deny my own fears.

The family waiting room was crowded but quiet. When I was called into the corridor about three hours later, I found Dr. McGuire, gowned and capped. "They're pretty proud of themselves," he said with the ghost of a smile. "Dr. Stanley ran into the unexpected. There were two aneurisms. They didn't have much operating room to work, but they did the repair. Now it's our turn." I would later learn that the spleen had been nicked and so had to be removed. This was not, however, the primary problem. I sat, trying to read while the phone rang from time to time at the nurses' station. Pamela and Nancy were with me, and we tried to reassure one another against the anxiety we felt.

At last I saw a door open as Dr. McGuire emerged into a small room adjoining the lounge. He had removed his cap and mask, and he looked weary. "We had to take the kidney," he said. "The other one is OK, and she can get along on it. We were lucky the aneurisms didn't pop before we got started." He stretched and looked down at the floor. Then I saw Dr. Stanley there, too. "The kidney was as hard as cement," he told me. It was as Yvonne had feared. The cancer had probably started in the ureter leading from the kidney to the bladder. There would still be radiation and chemotherapy. Dr. Stanley put his hand on my arm. "If it were my sister," he said quietly, "I'd urge radiation." Yvonne would be in the recovery room for some time. Having received this news, my daughters went home with me on this, the worst day of my life.

In late January we were back at St. Joseph Mercy Hospital on the other side of town. This was for a bleeding ulcer Yvonne had developed, but on the next trip we were there to schedule the radiation. The doctor was young, slim, and very tall, with a fine profile beneath a balding crown. His badge read "DR. NATALE" in an irony we didn't discuss, for in the Italian we had been studying so assiduously, it could mean Christmas. "You understand," he said distinctly, "that we're not talking about a cure." In these careful words he had pronounced her death sentence. Once in a survey course I had mentioned Oscar Wilde, and now for the first time I had some sense of the weight of his poem *De Profundis*. I felt myself now in the depths, and the desolation of Gerard Manley Hopkins's "terrible sonnets" came back to me.

But Yvonne was not about to decline into a passive patient. With the help of Germanna Rinaldi, the exhibition of Pamela's sculpture had been arranged in Bologna. Even though Pamela had looked forward to this first solo foreign show, she now urged that they cancel it. Yvonne didn't look strong enough to go, but she adamantly refused to agree to its cancellation. I saw that this trip was an affirmation of life to her, and I could not bring myself to overrule her. I took her to Detroit Metro in mid-February, and once again we made the wheelchair journey through the airport. I flew with her from Detroit Metro to JFK, where Pamela met her and they boarded a flight for Rome. Alitalia moved her up to first class, as had happened several times before.

I did what I had to do at school and at home, but my most critical responsibility was to monitor events on the other side of the ocean, making sure that Germanna arranged for Yvonne's blood tests and to stand by in case she needed trips to the doctor. But which doctor? That was just one of many questions I might have to ask. By now I had learned a few answers, such as what Maalox could do for my stomach and Halcion for a night's sleep. There were her letters, of course, a few of them. One read, "I walked to the Colosseum today." It lodged a lump in my throat and an ache in my heart.

Things went smoothly while they were in Rome, but there was trouble in Bologna. Yvonne began coughing and complaining of headaches and stomach pain. Recovering from mononucleosis herself, Pamela went out, map in hand, and walked under the connected *portici* that sheltered the dark streets from the weather until she found the doctor's office, where they gave her medication for Yvonne. Yvonne stayed in bed, and the doctor visited her the next day. Phone calls over the next few days told me that she seemed to be improving, and Pamela left her in the hotel in the care of her friends while she got her sculpture out of customs and set up the exhibition. After a few more days in bed Yvonne's condition improved. So did her spirits, until the last days in Bologna. She had basked in her friends' love and admiration, but now she felt they were drawing away from her, knowing that she was dying of cancer. A day and a half back at the Hotel Coronet helped her to face departure, but Pamela wished that the strains of "Arrivederci Roma" had not filled the cabin as they flew up and away from Leonardo Da Vinci.

I met them at JFK, where Yvonne was one of the first wheelchair passengers off the plane. She looked as though she had been more than halfway around the world and back. Nancy was there to meet us at Detroit Metro. In the tardy spring of March, Yvonne recovered from a pulmonary embolism and began a series of radiation treatments, complete with the side effects we had been warned about. She had bought wigs in anticipation of chemotherapy, but as it turned out, that additional humiliation was not required of her.

The days and nights passed slowly, and just before the fall term began I had a call from Albert Erskine. On September 15, Robert Penn Warren had died in the small bedroom he shared with Eleanor in their Vermont summer home. Rosanna, their daughter, had lain on a mattress between them so that she could hold both their hands in the night. "Pain," she had heard him say, and "Help me." Then at last there was only quiet. We gathered on October 8 in nearby Stratton for a service without a clergyman. After two hymns and friends' brief reminiscences, the last of Cleanth Brooks's reading died away on the still air: "Then shall be brought to pass the saying that is written, Death is swallowed up in victory." I left then and was home in time for the beginning of Yvonne's chemotherapy. The irony of this conjunction of events was overwhelming.

A brief brightening of the Christmas season came for us with the news that Pamela and Eric Stover would marry in the spring. A writer and forensic anthropologist, he was a human-rights advocate whose courage and skills had led him to work with teams investigating the cases of "the Disappeared" in Argentina and Chile and others murdered by death squads. We were lucky in Pamela's choice of a husband, and we knew it. We were lucky in our friends, and we knew that, too. On some afternoons Jack and Mary Jane Atkinson would arrive. He had been putting his files in order, and with Yvonne lying on the living room couch, he read aloud from the letters that Mary Jane had saved from the time when he and I had entered the air corps. They told a story of religious difficulties overcome and of patient fidelity. I watched the motes floating in the afternoon sunlight, thinking back to those years when we were young. I hoped that Yvonne was thinking of them, too.

Our days were marked now by a new schedule: the times when I would go to the refrigerator for a vial of Demerol to load the hypodermic and add another dot to the angry circle of them on her abdomen, making the needle's jab as quickly as I could. She was thinking ahead. One day she told me about asking a question of another surgeon whose name had ironic overtones. "Dr. Belleview," she said, "how long have I got?"

He was a handsome man who maintained his composure well. "I'd say you have several months," he told her.

"Do I have a year, do you think?"

"A year would be pushing it," he said gently.

There were two more operations in late February. In the first, Dr. McGuire returned to the original trouble site. I didn't know he was back from surgery until I felt his hand on my shoulder. "I'm sorry," he said. "There was nothing we could do." The next time there was something they could do: they removed a bowel obstruction. It seemed as though they were fighting a series of holding actions, and I could see how Yvonne was clinging to the hope that we would use the reservations for Italy I had made some months before. One day she said she would like to go for a walk on the lawn with me. "I want to be able to walk when I get there," she said. One of the oncologists, Dr. Stella, wanted to talk about more radiation or chemotherapy. I declined.

Pamela was beautiful in her white gown against the blossoms of late May.

Yvonne didn't have the strength to make it to the church. One of the brides-maids took Yvonne's corsage and, in a well-intentioned gesture with a heart-breaking effect, placed it at the side of the altar.

At home, immediately after the reception, I resumed my role of caregiver. Though there was gradually less to do, I had been doing the housekeep-ing with the aid of a cleaning woman. One day as I carried clean clothes from the dryer, Yvonne said reproachfully, "You mustn't take over all my jobs." I shopped, looking in health food stores for nutritious drinks she could keep down.

On good days she walked briefly on my arm across the lawn. I had the air-line tickets dated June 14. The day before, she was still determined to go. The next day dawned sunny and clear. Our bags were packed. I carried Yvonne to the living room couch. At ten o'clock she said she had to be sure all her med-icine was packed. When she found that she could not rise, she lay back against the cushion and closed her eyes. "Come on, sweetie," I said. "Let's get you back in bed." I carried her back, tried to settle her down, and then called the airline to cancel the reservations. When I returned to the room I couldn't be sure if she was asleep. I sat down in the chair beside her. Suddenly very tired and not entirely coherent, I asked myself silently, Where is God? and tiptoed out of the room.

By August we had entered the Hospice program. The room was re-arranged, with an oxygen machine by the door and a folding chair commode close at one side. A hospital bed had taken the place of our double bed, and I slept across the hall. Her dreadful disease was diminishing one thing after an-other. Privacy and fastidiousness were gone now. So was all interest in books and newspapers, or even television. Yvonne had joined the Hemlock Society and read the instructions for swallowing a large dose of pills and then slipping a plastic bag over her head. But this filled her with a nameless revulsion. One day as I sat at her bedside, she made an appeal to me. "Joe," she said, "get me a gun." Now it was I who felt revulsion. I simply could not do it, for reasons my psyche would not even allow me to contemplate.

Each day she slept more, but one night she turned to me and said, "I love you in spite of everything." By now the Demerol no longer relieved the pain, so I gave her from the dropper the smallest possible dose of the morphine so-lution that had lain there in the drawer for a month now. She seemed not to need another.

She spoke little, expressing herself in the emotions there in her eyes, which seemed to be growing ever larger. Then one afternoon I felt the slight pressure of her outstretched hand and turned to see her looking at me in-tently. "Does Andy know?" she asked.

"Do you want me to call him?" I said, and she nodded. "Do you want to be received into the Church?" She nodded again. When I reached him in Chicago, he said he would be there the next day.

Andy Greeley had always said that his primary identity was that of a priest, and so he was as he entered the room where Tracy and Bruce, Pamela, and Nancy sat with her. Around Yvonne's fingers was the rosary Nancy had brought back for her from Rome. I left briefly to perform this last errand for her, returning with consecrated wafers from the nearby Church of St. Thomas the Apostle. Gently Andy led her through the ritual that he concluded by administering the oils to her and the sacrament to all of us.

That evening Janet Holmes arrived from Hospice so that I could sleep, as she and Peggy Holmgren had been doing for a week. I slept fitfully until Janet woke me at 6:45. "She's gone," she said gently. In the silent room I let down the bed's side bar and took her in my arms. I held her hand, her cheek cooling against mine. It was September 10, her sixty-fifth birthday. We had been married forty-five years.

Three days later Andy returned to conduct at her Service of Resurrection. Nancy read from First Corinthians. Andy and Pat Samway delivered their homilies. Interpolated into the recessional was one strain Yvonne had chosen years before, "When the Saints Go Marching In." I walked down the aisle of the crowded church and out into the light, followed by my three beautiful daughters and my three bearded sons-in-law.

That night I slept without Halcion until I woke at the sound of a voice. "Joey," it said. It was hers. I sat up to hear, but it spoke no more.

For months I had been able to do only a little on Red Warren's biography, and now I found I couldn't work in the study I had made in the basement. So I moved everything into the rear room upstairs looking out on the wide expanse of green, trying to erase the memory of Yvonne's dark observation: she had called it "our Forest Lawn." On the dining table I spread out the books and notes and the maps of Kentucky and Tennessee. On the evening of Friday, March 1, 1991, I began writing again, my memory and my unconscious somehow trying for a synthesis, drawing on both present and past. One night in a dream I was somewhere with three other people. Lou Leiter, my witty Idaho colleague, was there. Yvonne was there too, but she was transparent. Black-haired, green-eyed Marnie Allen was there, looking just as she had when we visited the Allens in Rocky Hill not many years before. Was it, I wondered, some sort of acceptance dream?

Soon I was back up to speed, writing more than I had in many months. And as I was getting used to walking in the world as a single man again, disparate elements were surfacing and linking. There were the friends for continuity, Jack and Mary Jane as always, and colleagues who helped me expand my small circle—Frances McSparran, black-haired and blue-eyed, whose Ulster accent had Andy Greeley imitating it in five minutes, and her husband, the linguistic authority Ernst Pulgram, who told me that in Austria my name could mean "leaf." They went with me to *Don Giovanni,* and my best friend and singing partner, banjo virtuoso Stephen Dunning, went with me to hear The Chieftains, marvels of melody and dexterity, doing "Here's a Health to the Company" to the accompaniment of the fiddle and bodhram and Uilleann pipes. And it was a joy to sit in the living room where Joan Morris sang "I'm Cravin' for that Kind of Love" and Bill Bolcom played songs from his *Casino Paradise.*

That spring in 1991, the past showed many faces. In mid-April I flew to Western Kentucky University for the annual Robert Penn Warren meeting. Hearing experts read their papers was no longer as interesting as it had been earlier. More profitable and intriguing was the kind of research that took me to Guthrie, where I had sat in the neat living room of the tall, angular Mac Linebaugh, who had taught young Red Warren to play tennis. "Well, let's see," he had said three years earlier when we first met. "Red must be eighty-three, because I'm eleven years older than he is and I'm ninety-four."

I was lucky in weaving together my professional concerns and my private life. On May 30 at the Academy of Sciences of the University of Vienna I gave the introductory lecture of the International William Faulkner Symposium. For five days I suffered happily from cultural overload. It came from everywhere—from the ring of massive busts, Freud to Wittgenstein, on the academy's first floor, and from the great boulevards of the Ringstrasse that circled the city with its burgeoning parks and gardens. Somehow Waldemar Zacharasiewicz had managed not only to put the whole scholarly extravaganza together but even to leave windows of opportunity. In one I visited a museum and bought gorgeous gold-lit prints of Gustav Klimt.

This was another time when William Faulkner expanded my world. I had seen the Vienna Opera House in the movies, but now I had a seat there for Mozart's *Così fan Tutte.* Beyond the city were the Wienerwald and the foothills of the Carpathians. We viewed the rich countryside from a bus that took us to the millennium-old Benedictine Abbey of Melk. From one of its wide porches we saw a shining ribbon that was the Danube, making its way through some of the greenest, most dazzling countryside I had ever seen—mountain, meadow, and plain. I had been forced to wait nearly fifty years to behold the Danube as the fabled river of Strauss's waltz rather than the muddy stream I had seen hiking through snow under guard in the spring of 1945.

I would carry back home many photographs but no information about any Blotners who had lived in this part of *Mitteleuropa*. Dietrich Jenny had told me that he knew of a whole village of Blotners in his native Switzerland. But there was no time to check on that. In a gesture of thanks for my lecture, Waldemar Zacharasiewicz had cooperated with USIS to arrange the last leg of an individual tour. I would lecture in Regensburg, Salzburg, and then Innsbruck before flying home from Zurich. I had no repressed guilt feelings in Regensburg, for that was one city I had not bombed. I liked it immediately, as I had Salzburg, where I gazed at the same mountains Mozart had seen. In one of the shops near the ornate town hall whose gold front intensified the sunlight, I bought a costumed Mozart doll. In Innsbruck I walked the bridge across the river. Then I took a tram to a funicular stop where I rode up into the cold air and then strolled there. The next day I saw more spectacular Swiss valleys with farms perched on them like Tyrolean hats. I slept in a sparse economy hotel to be waked the next morning at an unearthly hour to catch my Swiss-Air flight. I had been gone almost exactly a month, and it was time for me to return to America.

One memento of the trip was another invitation. Among the participants in the symposium was Nicole Moulinoux. Petite and blonde, she reminded me of the Frenchwomen Danielle Darrieux and Michele Morgan had portrayed. Nicole wore suits that could have come from the salon of Dior, but she was also an intellectual like her husband, Jacques-Philippe, a university neurosurgeon. One project she pursued energetically was the formation of a French William Faulkner Foundation. She hoped it would be inaugurated at her university, Rennes 2 of Haute Bretagne. Perhaps I could provide a letter for the occasion for the literary magazine *Europe*, and perhaps I could be there when the foundation was inaugurated. I would be happy to do both, I told her.

Over the next four months my time was spent in the classroom, in my office, and in the dining room where pages were at last beginning to accumulate. I left Ann Arbor twice. Arriving in New York to work with Bob Loomis at Random House, I made a sentimental detour into my past. I took a bus to Scotch Plains to attend the fiftieth anniversary of my high-school graduation. I couldn't recognize some of my classmates, and some I had hoped to see weren't there. The trip would have been a total loss if it hadn't been for Floyd Delaney, my assistant editor on the *Sunrise Herald*, and Dot Jackson, still as blonde as her handsome husband Jess, now ten years dead, had been on the day he was an usher at my wedding. I walked around town, looked in the windows of what had been Dad's restaurant, and strolled two more blocks past the house where I grew up. It was in good repair but looked much smaller. The Olde Historic Inn had been refurbished, and I almost resented that. When my train approached I appropriated for myself Red Warren's phrase about Guthrie. For me, Scotch Plains was a place to be from.

I felt more at home in Connecticut with Cleanth Brooks. I learned more about Red Warren from Vann Woodward. And at the MLA meeting in New York I gained much from Pier Marie Pasinetti, who promised letters not just from Red but from Cinina Brescia Warren, too. They turned out to be worth the trip, letters of travail that would reveal much about the demons that had plagued her and ruined their marriage.

Five months later I made another trip filled with echoes of the past, my own past. In the last phase of Yvonne's illness we had tried anything that seemed to offer some measure of comfort. We bought inspirational books and therapeutic recordings. The sufferer could listen to soothing sounds—breezes blowing, lake water lapping, rain gently falling—and try to follow the instructions for meditation and visualization meant to bring peace if not healing. On afternoon visits Nancy would lie beside Yvonne while she thought of places meant to evoke peaceful feelings and memories. Such a place was Capri, and one day Yvonne told Nancy that was where she wanted to be buried. For a year and a half a sealed black container had stood in the closet of the room where she died. Now it was past time to fulfill that wish. So Nancy and I retraced the journey we had made under such different circumstances.

The island seemed as beautiful as ever in the pale May sunlight. The garden was flowering at La Pazziella, and the next morning there seemed to be more wildflowers than ever at the sides of Via Tiberio as we began our long walk up toward the emperor's villa near the northeast tip of the island. At last we stopped on the topmost stone platform and walked to the protective rock wall. Standing there in the shadow of the Blessed Virgin's statue, we looked out toward the Gulfs of Naples and Salerno. I bent down, and for the first time I untied the black container. In it I found not the expected gray ashes but a mass of white fragments looking almost like popped kernels of corn. We waited until the last of the tourists had headed down the path to return, and together Nancy and I held the container over the edge to empty it. The stream of white bounced down over the rocks of the cliff face, drifting into the brush and blowing out toward the bay. We stood there silently. Better this way, I thought, for the remains of the poor tortured mortal vessel to become a part of earth and water than to lie in a box, an embalmed mummy in the darkness.

My next trip was a celebration of life. Yvonne's and my wedding gift had helped to take Pamela and Eric to Ireland. On June 2 I flew to Dublin to join them briefly. We rented a car, and Eric drove it with the skills he had polished on three continents collecting forensic evidence of crimes against humanity.

His map reading and sense of direction took us steadily west, often on poorly marked winding roads crowded by massive herds of sheep. In the towns we saw names that evoked Yeats and Joyce, and entering Galway we passed one street that made us think of Nora Barnacle Joyce. There was no hurry, and so we indulged ourselves with our first four o'clock pause in a dark comfortable pub for pints of Guinness and bags of crisps. We stopped before a store window of Donegal tweeds. "Dad," Pamela said, "you need a jacket, and so does Eric." I gave in reluctantly, and he and I separated to browse, returning with our choices to the cheerful young clerk who saw that we had chosen the same jacket. I was about to return it to the rack when he spoke. "When you get back to the States," he said, "you can have a wee band."

We drove west into Connemara to the head of the bright wide bay where I had a reservation at Cashel House, which boasted that General de Gaulle and his wife had stayed there. In contrast, Pamela and Eric stayed close to the shore where they could take the chill off their cottage with its peat-burning hearth. It was historic as well as picturesque. The owner was the son of Sean MacBride, one of the martyrs Yeats had celebrated in "Easter 1916." Showing that he was no mere deskbound anthropologist, Eric pulled on a pair of Wellingtons one afternoon and waded out, returning a half-hour later with a pail of mussels he had wrenched from the rocks.

During the next two weeks we traveled north until it was time to turn south and make our way through Derry, where helmeted soldiers patrolled the streets in armored vehicles. Eric and Pamela took me to dinner on my birthday, and when the waitress asked me what I wanted after dessert, I said, "The wine of the country." She brought the Jameson's promptly.

I had checked the maps and books in Cashel House, finding only that my mother's people, the Slatterys, came from East Clare and the Sullivans from South Tipperary. But we had stood before the Book of Kells in Dublin at Trinity College, and so I felt not totally delinquent in my pursuit of Irish lore. It made me feel more Irish than my half-Irish credentials really permitted, but in Eric's photos Pamela looked as though she could have posed for the Irish Tourist Board. We managed in our last few days to walk the narrow steps to the windy top of Yeats's Thoor Ballylee and to stand in Drumcliffe churchyard by the massive stone that bore only his name.

The feeling of renewal would be stronger a little over a year later when we met at Shannon to drive into Galway City and on north to a series of abbeys. Eric and I climbed through pastureland to see ruins and more abbeys. We went on to Tipperary, where a friendly couple spoke about their Slattery rivals of Cork. These bed-and-breakfast nights felt colder than any since the war, and I slept in my parka. Compensation for all this was the wonderful Railway Inn of Westport, where I looked out the window into the stream rippling alongside a bronze statue of Sean MacBride. After an Irish breakfast that rendered me nearly immobile, we boarded a small boat for a trip to "gorgeous Achille Island," as Pamela described it, in "an absolutely turquoise ocean lapping up against a little golden crescent beach." We hiked up the steep hill to see the other side of the ocean, but there I dropped out and waved them on to negotiate the "Precipice Walk" of "One Man's Pass" without me.

The next day we saw Croagh Patrick rising against the sky beyond Lewisburgh, but we spotted no pilgrims, barefoot or shod, making their penitential way up the distant steep stony path. As if in compensation for the slogging, we found a magical beach walk at Delphi's Killary Harbor along what Pamela called "the most beautiful sun and seascape I have ever seen." From the fine sand we selected a white oval rock, and then stopped, hearing suddenly from high above a sound of absolute purity. We stood still, listening in this brief moment to the lark ascending. But our time swiftly outraced the retreating tide.

TWENTY

View from Lookout Mountain

AS THE YEAR'S END LOOMED, 1993 PROMISED A TIME of celebrations. We just didn't know how many there would be. All the talents Marnie had employed as project director at the New Jersey Committee for the Humanities would come into play. Widowed for almost fourteen years, she had carried on her part of raising three sons, and she would now bring her life and mine to a culmination at a ceremony in her hometown. The wedding she arranged for 150 guests that wintry January displayed her characteristic style. All the expenses normally borne by the parents of the bride fell to her. She planned the reception dinner there at the Nassau Inn and arranged for the ceremony in the Universalist Unitarian Church. Its protocol called for us to meet the minister who came with the church. An agreeable man in his forties, he checked off the items on his list while his seven-year-old son ran about William Ellery Channing Hall, where the reception would take place. He offered counsel on marriage and seemed disappointed when we did not request any.

Returning to Princeton for the ceremony, we were glad no new snow had fallen, and on January 2 the church was crowded. Marnie's sister Priscilla sang, her lyric soprano fine and true. Marnie was elegant in her long-sleeved winter-white V-necked dress studded at the top with pearls. The celebrants were Marnie's younger brother, Jim, and Andy Greeley. Possessor of a dry sense of humor, Jim noted that we had already proven our ability to fulfill the responsibilities of matrimony. Andy asked the congregation to be seated and then delivered in a rich brogue his American Indian–derived parable of the strawberries. It recounted the discovery by the First Man and the First Woman that the only thing sweeter than the taste of strawberries was the taste of human love. I had never been happier.

In a loud buzz of conversation and laughter, we prolonged our celebration with these 150 friends—some who had known Marnie almost from childhood, the few left from the friends we had loved in the forties, and the large extended Cortelyou and Allen families. As soon as we could get away, we drove across the Delaware to Newtown to our reservations at the Olde Temperance Inn. It was comfortable but most notable for its eight-piece Bear Cat Jazz Band. Marnie had gone there on Sundays with old friends to hear the Dixieland standards that had outlasted swing music. Missy Singleton, more sister than sister-in-law to Marnie, gave our group dinner, and our first day of marriage came to a close in blissful near-exhaustion. I was getting used to the feeling of happiness.

In a spring of travel and change we drove north, across the Straits of Mackinac to the Fort and the hills and beaches of Michigan's Upper Peninsula. Then we headed south down the Mississippi to Memphis and Natchez. I was still collecting Warren and Faulkner material while my retirement went forward. By June it was official, and the seventieth birthday party Marnie gave for me, with invitations hand-made from party-favor blowers, put a seal on it. The joy of it made me think of my seventh birthday, with the rowboats full of laughing, paper-hatted children on Echo Lake.

I was happy too that new work lay ahead. When Literary Classics of the United States had asked me to edit a series of Faulkner novels for the Library of America—a dozen of those he had published between 1930 and 1954—I had agreed with some misgivings. When they sent the first sets of proofs from which the books had been published, which they proposed to use again, I saw that they were so full of errors that scholars and critics would react with cries of horror and execration. I immediately wrote that all of the texts had to be vetted and that the man for the job was Noel Polk, the best textual editor and an exemplary critic of Faulkner. Fortunately they made us coeditors. Noel would do the enormously laborious work of comparing manuscripts, typescripts, proofs, and published books to produce the most nearly correct version possible of the author's last intention. He would also supply detailed notes on the texts with analytical commentary. I would provide an extended chronology of Faulkner's life and work as well as notes on anything in the texts that could not be found in a standard dictionary. By December I had supplied my part of the material for the third volume of the series. Each modest check was welcome, but so was the published evidence that I was still an active scholar.

There were vastly different trips ahead. We had been forced to postpone our honeymoon when Marnie underwent a gall-bladder operation. Now it was as if we were rewarding ourselves when we flew to Mexico City. We rode a careening bus carrying crates of chickens down the dangerous roads to Cuernavaca. We spent Christmas in a guesthouse run by an old friend, the food decent and the weather sunny while Michigan still shivered under gray skies. We had the whole place to ourselves. Every morning we could look out our window and see afar a faintly vaporous Popocatepetl, and our time was pure love and leisure.

Five months later, through the good offices of William Ferris and the University of Mississippi's Center for the Study of Southern Culture, we traveled south again for me to serve as a faculty member. It was an eight-day cruise from Memphis to New Orleans aboard the luxurious *Delta Queen,* a fifty-year-old sternwheel paddleboat combining the great days of river travel with contemporary comforts. I had never before been so richly compensated for talking. I lectured on Faulkner and Southern literature, and Leon Litwack lectured on slavery and the Civil War. We stopped at great plantation houses near state parks bristling with cannon and regimental cenotaphs. We left the *Queen* to stroll between avenues of great trees. We stood on a gallery whose view stretched all the way back to the river, and heard a beautiful African-American student in an antebellum gown describe parties lit by Chinese lanterns. We listened to a Zouave sweltering in a wool uniform as he told us how they served their cannon. The star of our seven-man faculty was Shelby Foote, the novelist and historian made newly famous by his commentary in Ken Burns's PBS documentary film on the Civil War. He stood forward on the top deck as the engines slowed while we approached the bluffs and fortifications of Vicksburg. Bearded and handsome, he described the siege and then the encirclement that finally severed the Confederacy. We listened to him rapt as if he had been there.

There were other rewards for the life and work I had chosen. The annual Faulkner conferences in Mississippi made me feel as if I had a dual identity, reinforced by friends like Howard Duval who would grasp my hand and say, "Welcome home!" The community of Faulkner specialists was now more than ever worldwide. And I was still doing Warren research in what Cleanth Brooks called the Middle-South. The two streams sometimes flowed together. The planning and work of Nicole Moulinoux and her colleagues toward the establishment of the French Faulkner Foundation had borne fruit. The conference to dedicate it would take place in late October at her university on the coast of Brittany.

On October 13 I was relieved to finish the first draft of the Warren biography. Doing the scholarly apparatus would be tedious, but I had always enjoyed polishing my texts. So Marnie and I were able to fly to Paris and check into our economy hotel on the Boulevard St. Michel in plenty of time. Rennes seemed a large and pleasant city, and the hospitality exceeded our expectations. There were many people representing the world of officialdom, the American side led by Ambassador Pamela Harriman and her small retinue. With her blonde hair carefully coiffed, she was elegantly turned out and lived up to her press notices. Tall and self-possessed, she made her short statement in French with a slight Southern accent. I admired her easy movement between politics and literature, and her choice of husbands and lovers. Standing with her in the ceremonies was Nicole Moulinoux, who might have embodied French haute couture. As I looked at the two women I thought that they might have provided a tableau, Feminine Beauty in Youth and Age. Under the lights and mirrors the guests mingled in a hum of French and English. The champagne glasses were continually filled at this official reception.

Marnie and I moved on to the mayor's luncheon on the coast, where we could see across the still water the distant beds where the oysters were seeded and nurtured. In a small cavalcade we drove eastward. I thought of Henry Adams's essays as the granite mass of Mont-Saint-Michel rose ahead. We walked slowly up the circular approach into the thirteenth-century fortress-abbey. I tried to summon up what I had read in my Victorian literature course fifty years earlier about the world of Mont-Saint-Michel and Chartres, but it was hard to maintain a reverential attitude among the arcades dominated by souvenir shops. They evoked the world of the Atlantic City boardwalk rather than Adams's coherent vision of reason and intuition linked symbolically like science and religion.

The three days of lectures and symposia kept Faulkner and the South in both the foreground and the background, but contemporary literature was highlighted by the University of Rennes 2 in its bestowal of honorary doctorates on the much-honored Peruvian novelist Mario Vargas Llosa and the rising young American Richard Ford. We felt at home among the Faulknerians and proud of the generations of Americans represented, most of them younger than I. But there were also very senior people, such as Gallimard's Michel Mohrt, and I began to feel as never before that now I was close to being a very senior Faulkner person myself. I thought of Sinclair Lewis's indifferent novel *The Man Who Knew Coolidge* and hoped the day wouldn't come when I would be invited to conferences only because of longevity.

I had always attended conferences for the pleasure of seeing new places and new people. Now I had another reason too: having Marnie with me. I loved taking her to places and introducing her to old friends. Being in France for almost two weeks seemed too good an opportunity to neglect. So I turned to my longtime sponsor and collaborator, the United States Information Service. Their response was a two-week lecture tour in Italy, Norway, Sweden, and England. We had already logged the transcontinental trip and the flight to Rennes when we flew to Paris and then Milan to begin the Italian leg of the next expedition. The USIS scheduled only one lecture in Milan, but it was fine to be in a first-class hotel in that dynamic city once more.

My second lecture was scheduled for the beautiful but remote medieval town of Bobbio. To reach it we were driven south toward Piacenza with two USIS staffers. The car was small and the roads were rough. When at last after two hours we were able to stretch our legs and walk about, we could see that Bobbio was indeed a city reminiscent of the *"epoca post romantica"* where Irish monks had built one of the region's major libraries and preserved classical Greek and Roman transcriptions by translating them. The monastery and parts of the town were maintained by the John F. Kennedy Trust of County Wexford, Ireland. As we walked the ancient cobbled streets, I asked the project manager the population of Bobbio. "Five hundred and thirty-seven" he replied. A local resident corrected him. "That was yesterday," he said. "One family moved away this morning." A drizzle was falling, and we were glad of the small pizzeria on the curving main street. The next morning I spoke to an auditorium filled with high school students and their teachers. I had the sinking feeling as I plowed through it that the number understanding me must be very low. The ride back to Milan the next morning seemed very long. I realized that I would have to rein in my willingness to lecture in exchange for new experiences.

Our flight to Oslo made me feel as if my time sense had been distorted. It was midafternoon when we arrived, but it felt much later. Before unpacking we just sat in our comfortable Gabelshus Hotel room, and I poured two shots of scotch and added water. I sat back, just beginning to feel relaxed, and Marnie began to peel off her hose. Then I put my glass down and leaned forward to look closely at her left leg. I felt a chill in my stomach when she told me that it felt hot. She had suffered phlebitis once before. I was close to panic as I looked through the phone book's medical listings. Our cultural attaché helped me to find the number for medical emergencies. Oslo's Rigshospitalet looked like the hospitals where I had taken Yvonne in Copenhagen. It was Sunday evening, October 30. After a worrisome wait, Marnie was wheeled down to a room before a large piece of equipment more modern than any I had seen at home. A tall young man in greens who might have been cast as a Nordic skiing instructor studied the outline of veins and arteries on the screen. A red spot glowed in Marnie's left calf.

"Yes," he said, "it's thrombophlebitis." We knew what would come next:

hospitalization with round-the-clock shots of Heparin in the belly. "If you had taken two aspirin before you got on your plane," he told her, "this probably wouldn't have happened."

"That certainly is a well-kept secret," Marnie said after he left.

So it was she who suffered in the line of duty from my zeal to work with the USIS, and I was filled with guilt and remorse. Heavy with anxiety, I took a taxi back to the Gabelshus. I sat at a small table overlooking an empty courtyard. In the neat and quiet Norwegian dining room, I ate the pink salmon and drank the Carlsberg beer, feeling like a character out of a Bergman movie. In her room in the national hospital Marnie had little appetite and could sleep little. Her roommate was a stout countrywoman who had undergone a heart transplant. During the day she knitted endlessly, and during the night she cried.

I gave my two scheduled lectures in Oslo and flew to Uppsala, revisiting that beautiful university after thirty years. At the University of Lund an American expatriate drove me around through the countryside of pastoral Scania as I admired the Swedish landscape I had wanted Marnie to see. By November 4 her prothrombin time was good enough for her to be switched to oral Coumadin and discharged. With the help of the nurse Marnie said goodbye to her roommate, who put down her needles and kissed her goodbye.

I waited in the echoing lobby of Stockholm's Arlanda Airport, where the reunion with Marnie in her wheelchair was joyous. The next morning the embassy limousine was driven by an obliging young man who was distressed that Marnie had seen nothing of the city nor even a glimpse of the archipelago that guidebooks called the Venice of the North. So finally she had two hours of chauffeured sightseeing before we boarded an airplane from which she could glimpse some of the scenery.

Back in London, she was once more the stay-at-home in a small hotel while I went lecturing again to cordial university audiences, first in the city and then in Nottingham and Exeter. Leaving the train in the station with the throng of homebound commuters, I thought back to graduate school and to Philadelphia and Princeton. It was a fifty-year trajectory that had taken me from there to here. After one more blood test, Marnie and I boarded our flight for home.

As we looked toward the New Year, we saw more decisions ahead. I didn't have to wonder what I would do with the time freed by my exit from the classroom. I would be busy correcting galley proof for my biography of Red Warren. And in spite of our bad luck during our last trip, we had already agreed to a conference on Faulkner's short stories in May that would take us back to Oslo. But there was a more basic question: would we stay in Ann Arbor? We liked the university and the town, and there were friends of more than twenty years. But then there was the weather. When I had first come to Ann Arbor, Jack Atkinson had warned me that we must get used to gray skies. The winters were long and cold, and neither Marnie nor I was a winter-sport enthusiast. Two of my daughters were living in Michigan with their husbands, and Marnie's three sons lived in the east. Where would we move? Princeton would be expensive, and I felt no nostalgia for Mississippi or North Carolina. I still nurtured feelings of resentment that I had not been promoted to full professor at Virginia the first time I had been put up for it. But now Marnie was leaning toward Virginia, and when I thought how our new life had begun there in Charlottesville on Lewis Mountain Road and how much of my Faulkner life had been centered there in central Virginia, we decided to drive south and look for a house.

The handsome Georgian brick structure on Rugby Road that Yvonne and I had bought from Estelle Faulkner was on the market again. It was advertised as the residence of three writers (my name was kindly added to those of William Faulkner and Peter Taylor, to whom we had sold it in 1960). The asking price was now over $300,000. Buying it back was out of the question, so we launched into the exhausting business of house-hunting and finally found one a mile out in Albemarle County, in the foothills of the Blue Ridge mountains. At the end of the month the huge yellow truck pulled, grunting and snorting, into our Ann Arbor driveway. The last night we slept in the Atkinsons' house and then set out the next morning for Virginia, forty years after Jack and I had looked ahead in the hope that someday we could lean on the same ivy-covered wall together.

In the spring Marnie was outside establishing her garden while I was in my new study working with my new copy editor on the life of Warren. Publishing was changing. No longer did I go up to Connecticut to work with Albert Erskine or to New York to work with Bertha Krantz. Bob Loomis was a fine editor like Albert, and we used the mails, but Bert was retired now, and the copy editing was farmed out to a freelancer in Vermont. Soon Federal Express was carrying proofs and photographs between us as we tried to wrap up the book. Benjamin Dreyer, the production manager, kept me apprised of the whole process. I was on an increasingly cordial basis with our Federal Express driver, who arrived on the last day of July with a large package under his arm.

"Here's your book!" he exulted. I started in immediately to correct the page proofs, but it was not until early October that I received a call from Benjamin. He didn't need to identify himself. "We have a beautiful book!" he said.

The Faulkner and Warren conferences went on, and soon it was 1997. Our first copy of the book arrived on February 3, and by March most of the major reviews were in, led by *Publishers Weekly* and followed by the daily and Sunday *New York Times*, which would later make it one of their highlighted Hundred Books of the Year. Other reviews kept arriving, and they were favorable. At last we could begin to relax. By June bluebirds were nesting in the house Pamela and Eric had nailed to one of our oaks. As they returned, we were taking time off for trips to Savannah and Charleston, and later I would think at times that we should have stopped while we were ahead.

In early February Nicole Moulinoux had written to invite me to the symposium at Rennes in October. She also asked if I would help to obtain Faulkner materials that could be put online during the symposium. I also agreed to that and to convey their hope that Jill Faulkner Summers would attend, though I knew this was unlikely because she detested this kind of activity as much as her father had. In March, Nicole wrote that she was applying to the minister of culture for a decoration for me.

While I busied myself with these efforts, I also worked with George Core, the *Sewanee Review* editor, and with Gary McDowell, the director of the Institute of United States Studies at the University of London, to organize a conference—"Robert Penn Warren, Cleanth Brooks, and the Southern Literary Tradition"—to coincide with the publication of my Warren biography. We would have an apartment in Mecklenburgh Square along with other friends: Walter and Jane Sullivan, of Vanderbilt, and George and Susan Core. It promised to be a lively four or five days in London. My first misgivings came when my raincoat and suitcase jammed in an airport escalator to the sound of a klaxon, to be unjammed only by an alert fellow passenger.

I thought ahead to Rennes in October. Then a letter from the minister of culture dated May 26 arrived informing me of my appointment to the Legion of Honor as an *Officier dans l'Ordre des Lettres de la République Française*, enclosing the diploma and letters from the French embassy in New York and the consulate in Chicago. They had been sent in July—to Ann Arbor. Nicole wrote that she hoped I could receive the decoration during the centenary. She asked me to talk at the unveiling of a bust of William Faulkner commissioned for the occasion, and I agreed to do it. I wrote my talk and composed a letter for Jill Summers expressing her appreciation of the centenary and her regret that she could not be present.

The *commémoration nationale du centenaire* was carried out *sous le haut-patronage de Monsieur Jacques Chirac Président de la République,* and the last three days of it took place in Paris. We stood for a ceremony on the rue Servandoni before the new plaque noting that William Faulkner had occupied a room in that building in 1925. I had made my first journey to this same place thirty-four years before. And now, as far as I knew, I was the only one in the throng who had known the man we were commemorating.

For the rest of that year and into the next, life continued to open out as Marnie and I drove from Berkeley to Mendocino and from Cape Cod to Seal Harbor. A year later we took the sun on St. Croix, and the year after that we cruised the misty fjords of Alaska's Inland Passage. In mid-May of 1998 I finished recording the last tape of my two biographies of William Faulkner and the one of Robert Penn Warren for Reading for the Blind and Dyslexic, in a solitary return to the private worlds in which I had lived for so long. I was glad to have my diploma from *le Ministre de la Culture* on the wall, but I was at least as proud of two others I received the next year. One was an honorary doctorate from the University of North Carolina at Chapel Hill. The other certified my election to the Fellowship of Southern Writers. Walter Sullivan told me that I was the only Yankee among them. Marnie and I flew to Chattanooga, where I was inducted into the fellowship, deeply proud of the beribboned medallion for my neck and the rosette for my lapel.

I had discarded two ideas for biographies, but I would doubtless find myself writing again, with Marnie as my in-house editor—reading, commenting, correcting. With luck there might be time for another book, and in some form the South would be intrinsic to it. I didn't feel quite as Yeats had, that I would be content to live it all again, but telling part of it might not be a bad way to spend some of what was left. As I gazed at Lookout Mountain, rising majestically to where it viewed five states and the Civil War's historic field of Chickamauga, I began looking inwardly too, over the improbable path that had taken me far from my natal town in the hills of New Jersey to the multiplicity of the South and finally the green country bordering the Blue Ridge. I gazed, in the scenery of the mind, at landscapes and portraits, the rich land for background, and in the foreground the outline of that artist who was the principal author of the good fortune I had enjoyed in my life as a writer and a teacher.